MW00580629

LAURA NADER

LAURA NADER

Letters to and from an Anthropologist

Laura Nader

CORNELL UNIVERSITY PRESS   ITHACA AND LONDON

First published 2020 by Cornell University Press
Printed in the United States of America

Every reasonable effort has been made to identify rights holders of the letters and images included in this column; if there are errors or omissions, please contact Cornell University Press so that corrections can be addressed in any subsequent edition.

Library of Congress Cataloging-in-Publication Data

Names: Nader, Laura, author.
Title: Laura Nader: letters to and from an anthropologist / Laura Nader.
Description: Ithaca [New York] : Cornell University Press, 2020. | Includes
    bibliographical references and index.
Identifiers: LCCN 2020024241 (print) | LCCN 2020024242 (ebook) |
    ISBN 9781501752247 (hardcover) | ISBN 9781501752254 (pdf) |
    ISBN 9781501752261 (epub)
Subjects: LCSH: Nader, Laura—Correspondence. | Anthropology—Philosophy. |
    Anthropologists—United States. | Anthropology—History—20th century. |
    Anthropology—History—21st century. | LCGFT: Personal correspondence.
Classification: LCC GN33. N334 2020 (print) | LCC GN33 (ebook) |
    DDC 301.01—dc23
LC record available at https://lccn.loc.gov/2020024241
LC ebook record available at https://lccn.loc.gov/2020024242

To Nadia, Tarek, Rania, and the memory of Samya Rose Stumo

Contents

Preface

Thomas Jefferson wrote about half a dozen letters a day, communicating widely. That was two hundred years ago, yet it is still an inspiration today. Now modern options exist as alternatives to letter writing—emails, texting, and more—and there are those who lament that the gentle art of letter writing has been sidelined. There are truths in such laments, but I find myself in an office with thousands of letters written by a wide variety of letter writers. My attention was initially focused on file drawers full of hundreds of letters for the most part alphabetized, simply because I needed to sort overloaded office files. In rereading some of the letters, however, I realized there were stories there. Such correspondence, received over half a century since coming to Berkeley in 1960, was making connections between the academy, sometimes described as an Ivory Tower, and the public. Indeed, the university is now seen as inextricably linked to the world outside the university.

In anthropology there are few published books of letters from well-known academics. Margaret Mead's letters, both private and personal, were selected for publication after her death by editors who found the materials in the Library of Congress archives—*To Cherish the Life of the World: Selected Letters of Margaret Mead*.[1] The correspondence between Edward Sapir and A. L. Kroeber covered letters written between 1905 and 1925—a total of 363 letters, many handwritten, some in pencil saved by Kroeber, thrown out by Sapir.[2] Niko Besnier wrote *Literacy, Emotion, and Authority* about the transformation from a nonliterate to a literate society.[3] In addition, there is *The Story of a Marriage: The Letters of Bronislaw Malinowski and Elsie Masson*—letters between Malinowski and his wife, a chronicle of their marriage including letters from the field.[4] Mark Goodale's *Letters to the Contrary: A Curated History of the UNESCO Human Rights Survey* deals with a complex history of the human rights movement.[5]

The letters selected for this volume give a glimpse of academic life mostly unseen by academics and by the public at large. They were sent by academic colleagues (to be expected, perhaps), but they were also sent from lawyers, politicians, citizens, people in prisons or on death row, Peace Corps workers, members of the military, scientists, and more. Letters not included here were the massive correspondences between my students and me, letters of promotion, of praise, invitations, and thank-yous. Personal letters and family letters have also been left out. But what does remain are personal stories of half a century of our country's history from below and above, both from inside and outside the academy—conversations, if you will, between a world full of folks and the anthropologist.

Most collections of letters are letters sent, not letters sent and received. There are probably good reasons, especially those related to legal requirements for permission to publish. For this collection, we sent physical mail to each of the selected authors. This required tenacious detective work, patience, persistence, and of course time.

Interestingly, among hundreds selected we received one negative response from someone who heard me speak on the BBC and strongly disagreed with what I had to say. A second negative was from someone I knew personally who simply did not want her letter published but gave no explicit reason.

An interesting set of observations resulted from the permissions process. Older people enjoyed being reminded of what they were like in their younger days, some children remarked that their parents would be pleased to be remembered, while a few other children felt that bad behavior should preclude their parents from receiving further public attention. Some were surprised that I did not take offense at the criticism received in certain letters. Still other family members of well-known academics had not seen the materials sent to me, and one author found it most useful in the biography he was writing about a well-known sociologist. Some wrote additional letters catching me up on what they were presently doing since sending their original letter. And many said that they would like to read such a book!

The letters that follow appear in their original form, with only minor edits made. Spelling corrections that did not alter meaning were made without brackets. Punctuation was standardized in accordance with the *Chicago Manual of Style*. In a small number of instances, bracketed words were inserted to address any outright typos or dropped words or spell out acronyms.

This collection makes available correspondences that are usually unknown because they are mainly private, in contrast to letters written to the editor of a media outlet. As one of my students noted, "The only letters my generation gets are bank statements, credit card bills, or letters from colleges." Hopefully the letters in this volume will inspire both young and old to experience the privacy and freedom such communication affords, whether they be interested in history, law, science, modes of censorship, the evolution of social action, or just plain curious as to what happens when pen is put to paper, or when pen is put down to ponder.

LAURA NADER

Introduction

We live in a time of worldwide connections made possible by technological innovations. For example, Facebook has over two billion users who communicate with others. It is far from private, as we now know. Data and information on Facebook or Google can be bought and sold and personal data misused to generate profits or exploited for nefarious purposes. Communication via personal letters is one on one. And unless permission is given, letters are private. No one censors letters. In fact, people are generally surprised that the letter writer is the owner of that letter, not the one receiving the correspondence.

Because we have generations of people who "have never seen such letters," this volume has a wider purpose—to help reveal a world of letters to the interested reader as a way of seeing what may not be available in the media or in the classrooms; to know how a man on death row thinks, how scientists feel about their controversial workplaces, how one anthropologist ponders issues of American survival, how this anthropologist became known to publics here and elsewhere by means of her life as a public anthropologist. Letters humanize life in a technologically driven world, and connect academics to life outside the Ivory Tower. Besides, letters are a primary source for historians to document history in a culture where increasingly "history is bunk."

For a young professor, certain institutions serve to connect faculty beyond their own departments. There are conferences both disciplinary and multidisciplinary. There are places such as the Center for Advanced Study in Palo Alto, where I was fortunate enough to have been invited in 1963–64 with at least a half-dozen anthropologists from multiple universities. It was there that I came to know Paul Bohannon, especially important since we both shared an interest in the anthropology of law, warfare, and the wider world. It was also there that I teamed up with faculty from Berkeley's Boalt School of Law to return to Oaxaca, Mexico, to make a film on the Zapotec court—*To Make the Balance.*[1] Arrangements for filming in Oaxaca and ethnographic fieldwork led to encounters with missionaries from the linguistic institutes, who flew me into the Rincon Zapotec because I was three months pregnant at the time. The rest of the team went in by truck—a rough trip. The missionaries Claude Good and Walter Miller helped me with linguistic materials, especially on the Trique language. That same year we held the first Wenner-Gren Conference on the Ethnography of Law, bringing together anthropologists such as Leo Pospisil and E. A. Hoebel, also interested in the study of law. In addition, my year at the center provided introductions that led to co-teaching at Stanford Law School, and later at Yale and Harvard Law Schools as well. Teaching at Yale was where I interacted with Professors David Trubek and Richard Abel, and at Harvard I met with Professor Lon Fuller, among others.

In between such visits, other research opportunities opened up, such as a year at the Woodrow Wilson Center in Washington, DC (1979–80), and the opportunity to deliver the Phi Beta Kappa series of lectures around the country that same year. All expanded the possibilities for reaching audiences beyond the academic. In addition, the fact that many anthropologists came to the Palo Alto Center each year allowed me to meet and correspond with the British anthropologist Sir Edmund Leach. At law conferences I met with foreign scholars whose correspondence I include—especially Pyong Choon Hahm from South Korea, Hendrik Pinxten from Belgium, and Vilhelm Aubert from Norway. The politics of the early 1960s that linked anthropologists and counterinsurgency also meant interaction with the administrator of the American Anthropological Association offices in Washington, DC, Stephen T. Boggs, among others. Some of this history of contact will be spelled out in the five chapters that follow to further contextualize the letters by colleagues who addressed me by my first name.

But what about letters to and from people I had never met personally—the more formal letters? I sent letters to university administrators about the absence of maternity leave, the importance of academics over sports, the importance of CALPIRG (Public Interest Research Groups), and the need for administrators to respect rather than denigrate faculty, to mention a few examples. In addition, letters to people in government dealt with the absence of justice or the need to know all the facts that precede administration of justice, US foreign policy in the Middle East, a Korean scholar's different take on conflict vs. harmony in Korea, or the antilaw movement launched by Chief Justice Warren Burger in the 1970s—a movement to change the civil justice system in response to false arguments about

Americans being "too litigious." Another focus of my letters was in response to criticisms received from scientists relating to my research on energy policies.

Interestingly, the letters written to me were more varied, sometimes linked to my publications, to films I made, and to hundreds of public talks or television appearances but sometimes received out of the blue. A few of the letters from my colleagues were ethnographic: for example, letters from my dearest departmental colleague, Elizabeth Colson. Her letters from Zambia relate daily events there, plus a sharp perspective on the United States from a retired-to-Zambia ethnographer. But the out-of-the blue letters include one from an eighty-five-year-old Californian farmer on the causes of aggression, a man on death row in Maryland, and a third-year African-American law student who writes about the law itself being a problem. Sometimes my writing and public appearances stimulated people to write indicating relief that they were not "crazy" or off the mark. One article published in *Physics Today* and later in *Chem Tech*,[2] from a talk initially delivered at the Mitre Corporation, generated over a hundred letters and phone calls, all of which taught me a good deal about science practice: what happens when a scientist doesn't fit the indicated mold. The letters reminded me that members of previous generations, such as Niels Bohr and Albert Einstein, knew that scientific understanding is only part of reality. These letters also noted how today scientists work in collectives, such as laboratories or universities, where there is a loss of individuality.

A most thoughtful letter by Paul Bohannan after he had heard me deliver a public talk on controlling processes as the dynamic component of power— dealt with more than three single pages of early morning thoughts on what he regarded as antisurvival happenings in the United States. In my own case, I wrote a letter to the chief justice of the US Supreme Court chastising him for supporting the majority opinion on the pregnancy pay benefits case and reminding him of his duty to encourage access to law, the latter being a central concept to much of my work as illustrated in the PBS film *Little Injustices*.[3]

Responses to such letters did not always indicate agreement. Rather, debates were initiated, leading to the rethinking of issues not likely to be brought up at conferences or in other public places. I included letters of validation as well as dissent to give the reader a fuller perspective of the ways in which people think and communicate. A California farmer shared his critical thinking and insight into questions of war and aggression in light of our primate origins. Clearly thought and insight are not limited to people with advanced degrees or specific socioeconomic standings. The same letter writer now sends me copies of letters he has sent to our elected politicians, along with the evidence he uses in advocating against war. By means of letter writing, the powerless as well as the powerful can forge their own channels of communication with otherwise isolated parts of society on issues that matter to them. Somehow, email (which I avoid using) is not up to the task of substantive sustained collegiality, which is often written in a conversational tone missing from email messages.

The letters I received were about workplace science, about empowerment, about teaching, about football and budget proposals, about our country. The letter I wrote to Chancellor Bowker at Berkeley saying that I would no longer serve on university committees until the university had a decent maternity leave policy, resulted in a maternity leave policy of no less than one semester of paid time. Writing to the top worked better than slugging it out in university committees that were arguing over whether maternity leave was sick leave or not. The early letter from my chair Sherwood Washburn, chastising me for being too tough a teacher and grader, taught me that a teacher had to understand her audience—in this case students who often held down several jobs while attending Berkeley. A teacher needs to know who is listening or if they are. Washburn changed my pedagogy full bloom when I realized how the impact of my class on controlling processes could be life changing. Good teachers have to understand their student audiences—they are not empty vessels.

Over these five plus decades, there was faculty concern over the link between the national laboratories and the university. At Berkeley, a group of scientists (including myself) had mobilized concern over university administration of national laboratories such as Berkeley, Livermore, and Los Alamos National Laboratory. I was invited to speak about "Barriers to Thinking New" at Los Alamos. Newspaper reports on faculty activities in this domain encouraged a few scientists at Los Alamos Laboratory and Lawrence Berkeley Laboratory to write to me about the absence of academic freedom in their scientific environment. Some scientists were fired without cause. At Berkeley a group of "ousted scientists" came together to call attention to such firings. These personal stories through letters argued for honesty and transparency. Some, such as John Gofman of the Livermore Laboratory, blew the whistle on questions relating to safe radiation levels and paid for it by being forced out. And today in 2019, there is still lack of job security in US laboratories as compared to laboratories in Europe, for example. Some things don't change.

In energy research, however, we have moved from "solar is just a bunch of mirrors" to an age of appreciation for renewable energy. Early on, I received a letter from a nuclear engineer who equated nuclear accidents to accidents from windmill turbines falling off and injuring people. In further correspondence, the author seemed geared toward complex solutions to the point where he was willing to justify his position with completely illogical comparisons. Although mindsets can be revealed through any form of written communication, the selected letters offer insight into the minds of the authors from across the spectrum.

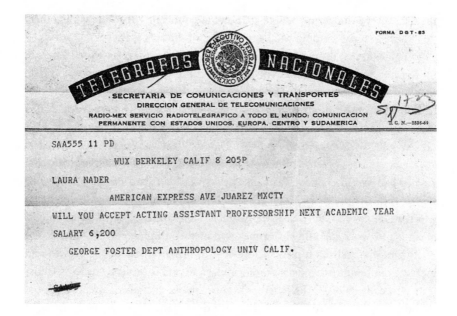

FORMA D G T - 83

TELEGRAFOS NACIONALES

SECRETARIA DE COMUNICACIONES Y TRANSPORTES
DIRECCION GENERAL DE TELECOMUNICACIONES
RADIO-MEX SERVICIO RADIOTELEGRAFICO A TODO EL MUNDO; COMUNICACION
PERMANENTE CON ESTADOS UNIDOS, EUROPA, CENTRO Y SUDAMERICA

G. N.—2536-69

```
SAA555 11 PD
          WUX BERKELEY CALIF 8 205P
LAURA NADER
          AMERICAN EXPRESS AVE JUAREZ MXCTY
WILL YOU ACCEPT ACTING ASSISTANT PROFESSORSHIP NEXT ACADEMIC YEAR
SALARY 6,200
     GEORGE FOSTER DEPT ANTHROPOLOGY UNIV CALIF.
```

FIGURE 1. A telegram I received from the University of California, Berkeley, in the spring of 1960 offering me a position as an assistant professor.

Whereas peer-review may exclude some from finding a voice, letters are a form of communication that only require pen and paper, time, and the cost of a stamp.

"The Public/Academic Disconnect" by David Brown, which bemoans the chasm between academics and the wider citizenry, does not apply to this anthropologist and may not always be as wide as some critics of higher education think.[4] In my case, hundreds of public talks to nonacademic audiences including physical therapists, church groups, world affairs groups, trial court judges, the American Enterprise Institute, the Sun Valley Forum, the Los Alamos Laboratory, the Gordon conference, and a mental health professional association generated correspondence. People will reach out if they think that someone will listen.

In this book, letters are presented chronologically by decade, from 1960 to the present, rather than by theme. I wanted to preserve the excitement of anticipation and not knowing what comes next. Besides, some letters are unique and not so easy to put in one box. Each chapter has a brief introduction to the letters that follow within the decade, providing some context. While the moods embedded in the correspondence may be optimistic or pessimistic, thoughtful or not, self-enhancing or admiring, for me the re-reading and selection of the letters has had a net calming effect. Events may repeat themselves, and each time are found shocking once again. The anxieties of the letters from the Reagan years are comparable to those of George W. Bush, and now Donald Trump. And throughout the decades we find some people are good at connecting the dots while others don't have a clue, including people in and out of the academy.

I might add that the present effort is not the first time that I have used letters in my research. I analyzed hundreds of consumer complaint letters sent to my brother, the consumer activist Ralph Nader throughout the 1960s and 1970s, in the hope that he would do something about their problems. Some of those letters were published in *No Access to Law* and formed the basis for the PBS documentary film *Little Injustices*.[5] While I was working on my book *What the Rest Think of the West: Since 600 AD*, I made use of Zeyneb Hanoum's letters to Grace Ellison, a British journalist that Zeyneb had met in Fontainebleau after Zeyneb and her sister traveled to Europe.[6] Ellison gathered the letters in a book—*A Turkish Woman's European Impressions*, which was reviewed at the time in the *New York Times* and the *Times Literary Supplement*, so rare was a collection by women writing their impressions of the West.[7]

In sum, the collection provides "inside" information about the growth and merging of one anthropologist's professional and public careers. The letters illustrate how collegiality works, whether as constructive critique or supporting possibilities. The letters also reflect change over time in the US academy, a writing of sorts about the changing purpose of higher education, and a sense of what we've lost with corporate and technological fixes. Connected via the internet is not the same as self-reflection and spontaneous or sustained exchange.

1

GETTING STARTED IN THE SIXTIES

Moving from graduate school at Radcliffe College to UC Berkeley at age twenty-nine was a major transition—from young student to young faculty, from being the only female member on the ladder in the Anthropology Department to joining the UCB faculty at large, which included Berkeley's Academic Senate. In addition, the sixties were a decade of concurrent movements: civil rights, Vietnam War protests, Native American and women's movements, consumer movements, and environmental movements, all of which had an impact on anthropology. At the same time, law was central to all these movements: US law, international law, and independence movements worldwide all accompanied by military activities. Thus I went from Harvard and McCarthyism's focus on communism and the red threat to Berkeley and what in hindsight were predictable movements that had been percolating during the years of right-wing US politics.

In this context my work in anthropology, the university, and the wider community got started. The letters that follow reflect much of these politics and more. Teaching was a challenge, and as noted earlier, my chair Sherwood Washburn wrote to me saying I was overdoing it on required courses, all of which made me shake up my pedagogy by having students in my law class keep complaint diaries. They were revelatory. I got to know something about the lives of my students. I was married in 1962 and had my first child in 1964 with no maternity leave, which inspired my interest in women's rights in the United States. Margaret Mead wrote me to point out a slight inaccuracy in my comments about the status of women at Columbia University. Women faculty at UC Berkeley were few in number. We did not get equal pay, something we learned when students wrote the respective salaries on the elevator door! When after some years I was making $27,500, my male colleagues of the same range were making $55,000. Women were unable to cross the Great Hall in the Men's Faculty Club to get to meeting rooms on the other side until the mid-1960s, although we could climb in the window to such meetings. And we did!

In the summer of 1961, with a small grant from UCLA, I worked with Shia Muslims in South Lebanon to learn about dispute settlement in villages and examined whether it was secular or religious. Professor G. E. von Grunebaum had awarded this grant, and so followed an exchange of letters with the distinguished professor. By good fortune, I spent 1963–64 as a fellow at the Center for Advanced Study in Palo Alto, allowing me space to return to Oaxaca and the mountain Zapotec of Mexico, the site of my dissertation fieldwork. There I filmed the Zapotec court, resulting in *To Make the Balance*.[1] Because I was pregnant, the better part of wisdom was to fly into the Sierra rather than travel by truck. Only the missionaries could fly me in, and so began a correspondence with Claude Good and Walter S. Miller, which includes letters regarding Trique linguistics. Translating the Christian Bible into indigenous languages was a central part of their missionizing, and I had spent the summer of 1962 working with the Trique to write an essay for the *Handbook of Middle American Indians*.[2] The Conference on the Ethnography of Law held at the Center for Advanced Study was expanding my network in and out of anthropology. Underneath all this was my concern over promotion and tenure. I reached out for advice, first to Sir Edmund Leach for feedback on my Zapotec law material and kinship, and later Rob Burling of Michigan's Anthropology Department after my first monograph was harshly reviewed by Charles Leslie. Both were enormously supportive and helpful, as indicated in their letters.

My concern over anthropologists as spies and counterinsurgency in Latin America led me to write to the American Anthropological Association (AAA), and to Stephen Boggs, who was administrator of the AAA. It was during the US Army's Project Camelot in Chile, but there was more to it than that. International conferences on law introduced me to my South Korean colleague Pyong Choon Hahm, who was more interested in Korean harmony than disputing (he unfortunately died at a young age in a plane accident), and Vilhelm Aubert, a Norwegian sociologist working on the "Lappish problem," the Lapps being their indigenous population. Law and development movements were in full swing, especially in Ethiopia and Kenya—with new African states appearing after the wars of liberation from Western colonialism and Westerners eager to help new states develop in our own image. Legal development movements inspired lawyers to write me for advice on what it might take to move "law" to development in new states, later a cause of new problems within states between "customary law" and state law. And as my project on comparative law was initiated, my work on Zapotec law interested a broad audience beyond anthropology. Lon Fuller at Harvard

Law wrote about his interest in "primitive" adjudication as it relates to "basic legal processes," and wondered what anthropologists had to say about the subject.

The first letter in this collection from E. R. Leach was very important for me, symbolically and otherwise. He was a model for all anthropologists. He brought the concept of power into the ethnographic picture of highland Burma (relevant to the Kachin people today), he was well aware of tensions between generations, aware of class variants and their impact on the sociology of knowledge, provocative and unpredictable. In the sixties my interest was predominantly in law in other societies. I had yet to turn my interest back home, here in the United States, an interest that would blossom in the seventies with the reinventing of anthropology colleagues. But the letters tell the story.

April 23, 1961

Dear Dr. Nader,

I should have written sooner to thank you for the copy of your "Law" paper which is full of interest. You now ask for my comments—I doubt if they can really be of much value. I take it that part of your thesis is that if close kin (affinal or consanguines) take a case to law the precise subject of dispute is only part of the story—the accusation is simply a symbol for the general state of hostility. The nature of the accusation is defined by the sex and kinship status of the parties rather than by any circumstances to the alleged offense. This seems reasonable.

Roughly the position seems to be how a wife takes her husband to court when his ill-treatment of her is (by local standards) notorious and intolerable and she charges him with quite stereotypical offences. At pg. 13 you express surprise that the plaintiff usually wins; I myself find it surprising how the plaintiff sometimes loses! I should have thought that all cases would be "open and shut" cases and I find it odd that a plaintiff should take a case to court if that were not so. It is the cases where the plaintiff fails to win which seem to me the interesting ones. Have they any common features?

I don't really think the hypothesis at pg. 13 will hold up. Assuming that slander can be equated with witchcraft—which is plausible, though rather dubious—there is quite a lot of data available about sex linkage of such phenomena in different types of society—offhand, I should not have thought that the patrilineal/matrilineal dichotomy has significance (eg. matrilineal Ashanti accuse female matrilineal consanguines of witchcraft, patrilineal Tiv accuse male patrilineal consanguines of witchcraft, matrilineal Doubans accuse male affines of sorcery, female affines of witchcraft. Patrilineal Kachin accuse male affines of witchcraft, male consanguines of slander, etc. etc.). On this point do you know Nadel's paper in *American Anthropologist* around 1950/53 "Witchcraft in Four African Societies?"

With regard to Chapter 2, I am puzzled as to why you have only considered the sex of the defendant. To make a comparison with the statistic of pg. 7, the initial categories of *Chart I*, could we not also have a chart similar to *Chart II* confined to the accusations between kin, and which distinguished in separate columns the accusations. . .

M v M

F v F

M v F

F v M

(e.g. take simply the 15 cases listed as slander, interference, assault, battery, make a total breakdown showing in full the relationship between accuser and accused in each case).

My hypothesis would be that the nature of the accusation is determined (in the main) by the kin relationship existing between accuser and accused, which includes sex of both parties and also the affinal/consanguine distinction.

The general methodology certainly has possibilities. Something of the sort might for example be applied to the English 16/17th Century witchcraft trials where a lot of court records exist which (in form) are not unlike the first page of your paper.

Yours sincerely,

Edmund R. Leach
Center of Advanced Studies in the Behavioral Sciences

In the following letter I responded to a challenge from the Department of Justice.

December 28, 1961
Mr. Lee Loevinger

Assistant Attorney General
Department of Justice

Dear Mr. Loevinger:

Although it has been some time since your interesting letter of November 6, I will not contain my response any longer. The following thoughts occurred to me.

You are perfectly right in saying that anthropologists and other social scientists ought to begin some studies of our own legal social structure, and at present I have some of my students doing field work in Oakland and environs on same . . . but you are dead wrong in saying that a study similar to the one on Zapotec law done in the Municipal Court in San Francisco would be more difficult or "considerably more instructive." The paper I sent you dealt with but one small portion of Zapotec legal institutions. This would be comparable with an analysis of all the cases that go through the Juvenile Courts in San Francisco during one month's time. I won't push the point though, but you ought to try it (primitive law) sometime. It would be particularly instructive, from the point of view of perspective, for American lawyers to get some idea of the diversity of legal systems in the world—for through a comparative outlook one can better see what the implications of certain legal forms are for society. An anthropologist studying the law in a preliterate society is made to deal with and analyze data—which has the advantage of making us build theories from concrete materials rather than just theory building on theory.

Your comment: "Although this kind of thing is not commonly done in a formal manner, I think it represents about the kind of information that most lawyers have with reference to their own local courts." But this is the point. As Edgar Jones has so eloquently put it, "to the degree that law is what courts do ... it is knowable only by the folklore rumor of average practicing lawyer to know which local judges are tough or easy in that particular types of cases ..." Let me analogize: It is one thing to know that things fall to the ground (gravity) and quite another to know why this happens and what the consequences and interrelations are for physics and astronomy ... and so for the law. It is one thing to know that as a person's income increases he will spend a smaller proportion of it on food, anyone "knows" this, but establishing it for certain and deducing from it permitted the idea to go down in history as Engel's Law. But where we are in the study of law, we don't even know the simplest statistics, except by "folklore about 'primitive' law—or complex law." And it's the simplest kind of patterns I want to know about American law at this point.

Well, it's rather fascinating, and I hope in a few years—with the help of some of the younger members of the Boalt Hall faculty—we can begin to write the ethnography of American Law.
Sincerely yours,

Laura Nader
Assistant Professor of Anthropology
University of California, Berkeley

January 24, 1962

Dear Miss Nader:

When we corresponded last year about your projected study "Comparative Village Law Middle East and Mexico," I found your problem as intriguing as it is difficult to handle. I hope you will forgive my curiosity when I ask you how your researches are developing and whether any results of local or general significance have come within your grasp. I trust you understand that I am writing this inquiry because of my personal interest in a little explored but important field which touches significantly on my own.

I should greatly appreciate if you could take ten minutes off and let me know how far you have gotten.

Sincerely yours,

Dr. G. E. von Grunebaum
University of California, Los Angeles

February 10, 1962

Dr. G. E. von Grunebaum
University of California, Los Angeles

Dear Dr. von Grunebaum:

Thank you for your interest in writing me. I will not postpone this letter any longer in the hopes that I will have more time to write you about my field work on law in a Shi'a Moslem Lebanese village.

The summer was a most pressured one. I was so aware of the short time, and there was much I wished to do. I began my work with a survey of several villages in the Bekka Valley, around Zahle. Lebanon was as tight as a drum. On the one hand we had fear of Nasser among Christians reaching a paranoid extreme, and on the other adoration of Nasser combined with hatred for the West—all of which made entry into a Moslem village by a Christian, a bit difficult. I found the best intro into villages was through the local politicians, and this is where family contacts were especially helpful. They helped me locate some villages, and I settled on a Shi'a Moslem village in the southern Bekka Valley, simply because I thought it was a place where I would get the most work done in a relatively short time. There was one important lineage in this town which was greatly indebted to my family because they had once made a wasta (legal remedy) for them.

The village, Libya, was located near Marjayoun and is not to be found on most maps of Lebanon because the road only went in there last winter. The population is about 1,400. There are 8 large families in the town, some 400 houses. It is approximately an hour and a half from Zahle. It had taken approximately 2 weeks after arrival to find this village. My family felt relatively safe about 'allowing' me to sleep there because of the previously mentioned connections.

Much wasted time was spent at the (AUB) [American University of Beirut] during the first part of the summer trying to locate a student. Living in a village doesn't appeal to most Lebanese students, and the pay they asked was far more than I was living on. My alternative plans were to train a village boy to be my assistant, and I had a very good fortune in finding a good, and conscious helper. He helped me map the village, take a census, and was especially helpful with regard to the collection of case materials. I collected mainly cases of wasta (remedy) making, and histories of conflict cases. Some of this I wrote, some he took down in Arabic, and some I recorded on a tape-recorder I had borrowed (of the three, by far the best technique). The tapes are so much richer in contextual information. I collected case-histories of conflict-strife cases in order to get at the process of settling conflicts because I doubted whether I could in the short time get enough actual cases that would constitute a large enough sample for statistical analysis (I have some 40 cases). There was little mention of Moslem law (even in domestic relations cases), and I suspect that villagers don't get as involved in Moslem law as urban folk might. But the really interesting patterns had to do with the number and class of persons that Shi'a Moslem villagers comes in contact with when he is in trouble, and whom he goes to depends in part on the trouble he is in and the man who is to judge him in the civil court. They have a most incredible knowledge of interpersonal relations among the politico-elite of Lebanon, and it's a rather admirable game they play—the defendant and plaintiff—to see who can get to the best connections fastest. When their power is more or less in balance, they often just drop the case by mutual agreement. It was per se irrelevant whether the man or men they went to was one of religion or another—but perhaps this is just peculiar to the Shi'as. I had the feeling though that this way of settling conflicts through the institutions of wasta was common to Lebanese villages, whether they be Maronite, Sunni, Shi'a or something else. It would be interesting to look elsewhere on this. Perhaps the Ayoubs have information. Another interesting pattern I was able to observe was the following: I have a second cousin who is in the legislature there. He has several brothers. All of these men are professionals (meaning that they get paid necessarily) wasta makers, and they are that by virtue of being politicians. It is in fact the duty of a politician, as elsewhere, to settle the conflicts, on almost any level, of his constituents. This work is not accomplished at the office necessarily, but concentrated at their homes. I woke up one morning when I had been visiting in one of these households—to note that from 6:30 that morning, along with the first cup of coffee, in came the villagers, in groups, single, even in busloads. The old pattern of the tribal sheik is still working.

As this letter indicates I have not been able to analyze my materials yet. I am swamped with teaching duties, but hope to have time during this quarter since

I am teaching a course on the Ethnography of the Middle East. I do not yet know for certain my future plans for field work in Lebanon. There is a possibility I may work out something for NIMH [National Institute of Mental Health]. The student I had in mind for this project has found more prestigious work, and there is yet a tradition to build here at Berkeley, in the Ethnography of the Middle East.

I wish to say that I profited tremendously by my experience last summer. I took a short trip to Syria, Jordan, and spent 10 days in Egypt at the end. I spoke with government people and anthropologists about field work possibilities in these areas, and even had a few days of work in a little Egyptian village half-way down the Nile. It should all make my course that much more interesting for having been there.

Early this fall I heard Prof. Coulson speak on Islamic Law here. I should like to know if any of his work has been published. He gave a first-rate talk.

Thank you for your attention.

Sincerely yours,

Laura Nader
Assistant Professor of Anthropology

February 26, 1962

Dear Miss Nader:

In general I do not believe in burdening people's files by sending them "thank you" letters. But what you had to tell me about your work in Lebanon was so interesting that it simply called for an expression of appreciation. I very much hope that you will be able to go on with your studies which promise so many and such interesting results.

Mr. Coulson has not published much. I have read three articles of his, one of them dealing with Pakistani law, the other out with various aspects of the position of law and legists in relation to the executive power in early Islam. They are concise, rich in detail and keep very closely to their appointed scenes. A book length study of his on any aspect of Muslim law would be something to be anticipated with some impatience.

I trust our exchange of letters can be followed up before too long by personal acquaintance.

Sincerely yours,

Dr. G. E. von Grunebaum
University of California, Los Angeles

April 11, 1962

Dear Laura:

Many thanks for the list of lectures for Anthropology 125. My own feeling, relative to the course is that the words "social structure" mean different things to different people, and that this is part of the trouble. It is inadvisable to try to teach all the different things which should be taught under the label "social structure" in a course, and I believe that we would be in a better position if we had a course on kinship and the family, small group and role, and social structure in economics or politics, etc. The main point at the moment is that, since 125 is to be required, it should be taught, at a level which is fair for the undergraduate major who is not a pre-professional. The vast majority of students in the course have no intention of going into graduate anthropology, and I am afraid that 125 as taught this last year was too difficult. You must remember that undergraduate students here take five courses, and many of them are supporting themselves by working on the outside. This means that the average undergraduate cannot pull in many hours of preparation per lecture in the course.

I trust these matters will all be cleared up in the near future.
Sincerely yours,

Sherwood L. Washburn
Chair, Department of Anthropology
University of California, Berkeley

Early on the missionaries came into my orbit.

October 19, 1962

Dear Laura:

I won't take up your time with apologies for not writing. First I want to thank you for the new tapes you sent. I'm afraid the exchange wasn't even remotely fair for you. The two tapes you sent were of much better quality than the one you received. Thank you anyway.

We have been here in the city for seven weeks. The first six I had an informant with me and I learned a few more Trique words. I had planned for him to stay longer but he begged to go home and they tell me that he threatened to kill his buddy that came along with him so I left him go. There are a number of Triques here in the city and I have some contact with them.

Sorry I didn't get any more information for you and also you probably have everything written up by now. It wasn't until several weeks after you left that I discovered that the Triques use the same term for brother-in-law and cousin-in-law. I just didn't have my ears open when we were getting those terms.

Aurelio also told me how the older men feel that the highway was able to come through. The engineer was bringing the road out from Tlaxiaco and when he got to the place where there are high rocks on either side, the devil came out and told him that he would not be able to go through. They then made a bargain that if the devil would permit the road to go through the engineer would give his permission for the devil to do what he wished with the drivers that would use the road. Maybe this has more truth to it than we think!

Soon after we left on our way to Tlaxiaco we met an anthropologist by the name of Bob Ravicz (sp.). He knew you and we had a nice chat. There was also a German ethnologist all ready to do a year's work in Copala, but in trying to get permission from INI [Instituto Nacional Indigenista] in Tlaxiaco to live there they gave him such a run around that he finally gave up and is going to some other place. He stayed in Copala for one week and said that he got a good reception.

Would you by any chance happen to remember either the name or address of this lawyer from Copala? It would be invaluable to me. Also the name of this priest from Oaxaca of which you spoke so highly? Are you acquainted with the new book that deals somewhat with the Triques? It is called *Pinotepa Nacional* and is written by a man by the name of Tibon. It is in Spanish and came out in 1961. Sorry I don't know the publisher. I hope to look it up in the next few days. If you are interested let me know and I will try to give you more information. Bob Longacre tells me that it is a bombshell. It goes into detail about the exploitation of the Triques around Copala. The author says that the Triques have been treated worse than any people in Mexico. In 1845 the Triques fought for 5 years to expel the white man and in the opinion of the author are still in the same mood. The area around Copala is ideal for our type of guerrilla warfare.

We are really anxious to hear from you. Alice would like to know more about your wedding. We sincerely wish you the very best. One thing we are sure that you will not lack are servilletas in which to keep your tortillas. I'm sure that your husband thinks that you make the best tortillas in the world. Sincerely,

Claude Good
Oaxaca, Mexico

Paul Bohannan was always a letter writer from our first acquaintance.

December 19, 1962

Dear Laura:

I am grateful for the comments, and particularly for the one about the fact that we often get a counteraction to see whether or not a norm has indeed been broken. Of course we do. This is important, and it means that the ultimate analysis must be a scheme into which you can break in any place.

You are right that I am working on the same kind of thing that "Goodenough" Hymes and Co. are working on, but I am very reluctant to use their term "cognitive system" because of what it means to philosophers, and also because of the fact that it seems to me to have an inescapably psychic dimension. I am not against psychic dimensions, I only want them recognized, and "cognitive systems" seems to me to underemphasize the social and cultural.

The groundwork for all this—and I feel it is inadequately represented in the American viewpoint—is to be found in Malinowski's appendix to the old "Meaning of Meaning." Indeed, Richards' position throughout is the earliest and best statement of a great deal of what it is that all these people have been working on. Of the lot you name, I think "Goodenough's" paper on "Residence" is the clearest statement of what it is we all have to do. However, everybody is in the swim, and we are all of us working through the same general area. Louis Hielmslev and Marc Bloch are also important figures representing this point of view.

I have just got a note from Ralph saying that Max Gluckman is not able to come to the Center next year, which gives him a slot which he is inviting you to fill. I am delighted. I'll be seeing you again. Again, thanks, and I shall send you some comments on the two manuscripts, which I am very glad to have, toward the end of the Christmas vacation.
Yours ever,

Paul Bohannan
Professor of Anthropology
Northwestern University

June 10, 1963

Dear Professor Nader:

Many thanks for your very helpful letter of May 16th. I am most interested in your suggestion that eventually there be set up in Ethiopia an Institute for

Ethnological Legal Research. If there is any interest in your department—and particularly with respect to yourself—I would be very pleased to receive a more detailed exposition of your ideas, including any ideas you may have with respect to cooperation between your University and our Law School-to-be. In this field we shall have to grapple with that problem of customary law immediately in Ethiopia. It is imperative that we collect and reduce to writing some information however crude our techniques may be. I have been active in the establishment of a Peace Corps. A program to send young Americans—law school graduates—to Africa on a variety of projects calling for use of their legal training and skills. I expect to have several young volunteers attached to our Law School staff, and I expect, if the funds can be found, to develop, as quickly as possible, a project to put these men out in the field to gather as much information as they can about the legal traditions and institutions of the various parts of Ethiopia. I'll take no pretense that this will be a "scientific" undertaking, and it is most regrettable that our people will not be properly trained for this work, but the urgency of learning all we can as fast as we can is obvious.

If there is any way in which you or other anthropologists can help us, particularly by giving me some advice on the proper techniques to use to investigate and reduce to writing information about customary law and its administration in Ethiopia, bearing in mind the limitations under which we must operate, I should most appreciate your help. I do know Tony Allott whom you mentioned in your letter and expect to see him shortly in London and, hopefully, secure some advice from him.

Thanks again for the bibliography and for your expressions of interest. Sincerely,

James C. N. Paul
Professor of Law
University of Pennsylvania

I was writing a piece for the Middle American Handbook on the Trique. Again, missionaries were helpful on linguistic questions.

July 20, 1963

Dear Laura:

Thank you for sending me a copy of the manuscript. I enjoyed reading it and learned quite a bit in the process. You obviously spent more than an afternoon on research. Soon after reviewing it the two girls from Copala came here for a visit and of course wanted to read it. I am enclosing the suggestions that one of them wrote down. She corrects linguistic papers for the institute and she couldn't help writing some things down. After reading the paper she said that she would like to meet you so we gave her your address and she may look you up when she attends a wedding in California in August.

I hope that the suggestions I made are of help. The specific ones I mentioned I am willing to defend. There are others where it was just a matter of disagreement between my informant and your informant and I did not consider it worthwhile to write them down.

There is one more book that I wish you could have used for your research. It is *Oaxaca Recondite* by Wilfredo C. Cruz, 1946. He has a beautiful text from Copala and also one from here on the origin of the sun and the moon. The texts of the two boys killing their father the deer is apparently Mixteco since I have read it along with other Mixteco texts and they being the dominant culture in the area it became a part of Trique cosmogony. The text that Cruz obtained from the Triques has to do with a large snake who pulled the world and was overpowered by two Triques who then carried his two main eyes up to the top of high trees and they became the sun and the moon. Sorry to bother you with all this confusing evidence but I just read it a few weeks ago. I include this for your question mark on p. 21.

In regard to the first paragraph on p. 4 you might be interested to know that during the latter part of June this year, 200 Mexican soldiers came into Copala (Cruz Chiquita) and killed about 20 people. They were guided about by a Trique from Outla who pointed out the "guilty" and upon which the soldiers immediately shot the person and hung him up on a tree. This information was given to us by Barbara Ericsson who also wrote the comments. Sincerely,

Claude Good
Oaxaca, Mexico

January 27, 1964

Dear Laura:

Now I know! Don't know where I got the idea you were from the East Coast. I guess I never did know your last name, that's why it didn't ring a bell. Now it seems that you must have told us you talked to us in Oaxaca just before we came up. My mind was taken up with preparations for our trip and it probably didn't sink in. Just before we left there, the pilots from all the Mexico bases formed their own corporations—I don't know just what their new regulations are. Also, the pilot who flew us out and who had flown into the Yagallo strip for Earls was gone, no one is flying into Yagallo and there is no guarantee the strip is being kept up as it was when Bob was there to see to it.

Previously, the Gov't prohibited our pilots from flying "nacionales" except to bring emergency cases in to the doctors. This would not have prevented flying one not a Mexican. I know the new Asociacíon Civil can still fly our folk, but I can't say whether or not they could fly you. Also it seems to me that Bob generally went out overland to check the strip before flying in the family. So I'm not all sure that the pilot would land there, even if he had permission to fly you. Salubridad had been building something at Yaée but I can't remember whether it was just an oncocercosis center or an airstrip. The Gov't had asked our pilot to fly the doc to Yagallo when their plane was out of order—which he did several times. They might be flying in there to one of the two towns.

I have no way of being able to tell you whether or not you could get in there, though I can sure understand what you mean about the trip out to Ixtlan or Natividad and walking in. I went with the pilot to survey the Yagallo site for fixing the strip. We drove in a power wagon to a site just above Yagallo. What a road! The climb from Yagallo's strip to the trail above the town, leading to Talea, is plenty tough. But it would be far preferable to the other.

I will write to Mitla and see if I can find out from the colleague there that present situation is concerning the pilot and the Yagallo strip. Should I find out anything favorable, I'll let you know. If the answer is that the pilot isn't landing there or couldn't fly you, there's little use in my retelling you that. Sorry I couldn't do more to help.

Sincerely yours,

Walt S. Miller
Tulsa, Oklahoma

March 11, 1964
Walter S. Miller
Tulsa, Oklahoma

Dear Walt:

I just want you to know that I've returned, mission completed, and that I owe great thanks to you and your colleagues in Mitla—John Crawford and Floyd Bishop. Floyd did a beautiful job flying me in and out, and we got the film we went after. Rather incredible too. We were filming law cases the second day after arrival. Years of rapport building paid dividends.

Thank you again for your help.

Sincerely yours,

Laura Nader

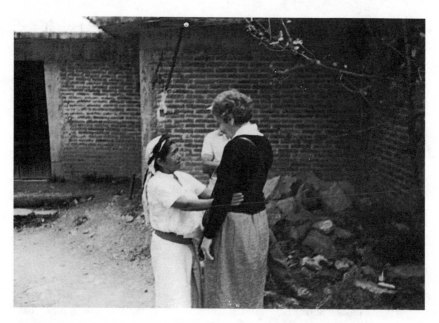

FIGURE 2.   Me and a Zapotec friend from southern Juquila. Photograph provided by author.

March 16, 1964

Dear Laura,

Thanks so much for your letter of March 11th telling of your successful trip. I am delighted: John Crawford wrote that you and your husband had gotten there and that he had enjoyed talking with your husband. He also said Floyd had flown you out to Yagallo, but he must have gone on a survey trip of his own for I have had no answer to my inquiry about arrangements for getting you out again.

It is unfortunate that the exigencies of his own particular work tend to make every investigator, be his own "what-have-you," seem to be less human to his scientific colleagues than he is (or is forced to be) to those of the culture he is investigating! In answering your initial queries, please believe me, my reticence in encouraging your going to Mitla stemmed from what I had seen the former pilot forced to do by the strictures of his Mexican flying permit. When we came out in May of last year, our own preoccupation with packing and getting off to the States with everything we might need for study—that is my only excuse of not thinking to inquire as to the present status of things under the corporation—Alas de Socorro. It is anything but pleasant to have to refuse to help folks when we could do so with no inconvenience to the pilot or our own flying program. Yet, in the past we have been forced to refuse even Gov't men.

I share your amazement at your accomplishment! I know of <u>no one</u> who has been permitted to do such a piece of documentary filming in any of the Oaxaca tribes. A synchronized tape of such case, along with a film, would be enlightening and, at least in Juquila Mixes, amusing at times.

Best wishes for your continued success in carrying your work through to a conclusion.

Sincerely yours,

Walt S. Miller
Tulsa, Oklahoma

March 31, 1965

Dear Professor Laura Nader:

It has passed about two months since we left Berkeley. Here in New York, we are all very well, though we are still in the winter and sometimes enjoying a snowy morning. I hear it is already (or almost) summer in California. If so, we envy you. We still cannot take off the winter coat.

Nevertheless we feel the spring is at the door. We hope we will have a good time in the rest of our stay here.

At the Columbia University, although I am categorized as a visiting scholar to the School of Law, as I was doing at Berkeley, I spend most of the time in the classroom either in sociology or anthropology. Professor Merton's "Social System" and "History of Sociology," Professor Goode's "Systematic Analysis on the Modern Family," those courses I am auditing. In Anthropology, Grandmother Dr. Margaret Mead is teaching a fascinating subject "Culture and Personality," I am spending a wonderful time in her class, even though it is from 8 to 10 in the evening.

I am now writing a small article which is to appear in Japan this autumn. It is dealing with the American studies on judicial process. It will cover from those works done by the lawyers to those by sociologists (including the Berkeley center) and political scientists. I would like to cover those done by the Anthropologists, but my knowledge is not so enough to do so. I hope I will be able to do that in my next article. Anyway, I wish I will be freed from the present paper, since I wish to have more time to access the anthropological studies. I feel that to my study, especially to the study of our society, anthropology is extremely useful. It seems to be able to show us the unknown aspects of our culture and society.

As I discussed last time, I do hope to engage in research work in Africa. At the moment, I am thinking the time available for me, judging the circumstances around me, would be in 1968 or later. Till then, I think I should do my teaching job in my home university. I wish to utilize this interval to make myself more familiarized with anthropology.

My stay here will be till June. If other things should not be changed, we will leave the States at the end of that month. I intend to stay at Berkeley for a short while. I wish I will be able to see you again. Probably, I will be able to talk to you something about my plan with I am going to do immediately after I will be back to Japan. If there is something which I can help you with, please let me know. Cordially yours,

Zensuke Ishimura
Visiting Scholar
Columbia University, New York

April 16, 1965

Dear Laura Nader,

While I was in California someone told me about a lecture you had given some women's group in which you discussed the lack of recognition that Ruth Benedict and I had received, particularly on the question of full professorships. Ruth Benedict was the first woman full professor in the Division at Columbia; to this day she is the only woman whose photograph hangs in the room where PhDs are given. I was offered a full professorship at Columbia ten years ago, but refused it in favor of my present arrangement, as fairer both to Columbia and to the Museum. I don't think that this really alters your point which was, as I understand it, that institutions of higher learning are chary of giving good academic appointments to women. But someone might pull you up on the facts. I am a full curator here at the Museum.

With all good wishes.
Sincerely yours,

Margaret Mead
The American Museum of Natural History

May 14, 1965

F. Clark Howell
Professor of Anthropology
University of California, Berkeley

Dear Clark:

You may recall I promised to get some information to you before the AA (American Anthropology) board meeting in Washington this month. The following is as much as I could piece together.

The problem: the Defense Department in recent years has displayed great interest in developing tools for counter-insurgency in both new weapons and anti-guerrilla force expertise. In recent months, the Department of the Army has shown interest in sponsoring research to determine the conditions that make people in the underdeveloped world ripe for insurgency and to study the factors to counteract these conditions or beat back the insurgency should it get underway.

Involved in this research on insurgency and counter-insurgency is knowledge about peasant people, tribal people, etc., in specific countries and regions which have a high priority. For example, special attention is being paid to Latin America. Great amount of money is being targeted for social science research which will include field work. Example—a three year, $5 million contract to Special Operations Office of American University to make a series of reports and studies. The Army is interested in being able to predict the likelihood of uprisings by a counter-derived assemblage of data and key factors to watch out for. The insurgency studies will be conducted by carefully screened American social scientists; some of the "social systems case studies" will hire some Latin social scientists to do local polling, etc.

It seems to me that the profession of anthropology, as a profession, should be concerned right now when there is time, less anthropologists and other social scientists begin to do field research in underdeveloped areas under the pretext of research for academic purposes (scholarly purposes), when in effect they are mission-directed government agents. Whatever the government wants to do in this area is an issue for citizens; but to anthropologists, masquerading as scholar-anthropologists to collect data that may be used against the people studied is doing research under false pretenses, is exploiting the image of the anthropologist for purposes of military considerations. If such deception is uncovered or suspected by indigenous peoples, hostility and violence are likely to be the result and genuine anthropologists pursuing their field research may find their lives endangered or their presence excluded because they are suspected of being US government people probing into their lives for eventual referral back to the US military. This could wreck anthropological fieldwork.

Perhaps the best way to describe the "new breed" (and note the degree level of subject described) is to give a sample write-up of a Research Associate at Human Sciences Research Inc., in McLean, Virginia (receiver of government contracts). Needless to say there is no reflection on the man implied, only on the kind of function he has or could perform.

1. Terry Rambo
   Research Associate
   B.A. Anthropology, University of Michigan, 1963

Mr. Rambo is an anthropologist with specialized training and experience in the Latin American area. He has studied the problems of culture change and political instability in peasant communities and has made a cross-cultural study of the preconditions of insurgency in underdeveloped countries in Latin America and Southeast Asia.

Mr. Rambo has done extensive field work among several indigenous groups in Central America and has developed considerable fluency in Spanish and Kokechi Maya. While maintaining interest in the Indian cultures of the region, he has shifted his focus to more dynamic Mestizo peasantry who are emerging as a political force in much of Latin America.

Since joining HSR, Mr. Rambo has participated in a study of counter-insurgency in Southeast Asia and has begun preparation of his field data in Central America to provide a basis for further study of economic development and political change in the area (taken from Human Sciences Research, Inc. brochure).

I just hope you will see fit to bring this before the board of the American Anthropological Association. This situation brings to mind an abortive attempt on the part of Dr. Richard Adams to focus anthropological attention on just such problems at the Chicago national meeting a few years ago. You and I both know what the A.M.A [American Medical Association] would do if pre-med students were to be hired in a comparable situation.
Sincerely yours,

Laura Nader

September 14, 1965

Dear Professor Nader,

I have been on the verge of writing you about the outcome of Project Camelot nearly every week for the past month. However it is now clear that it will be quite some time before the problems and implications of military support for anthropological research are thrashed out within the profession and government. The officers of the Association and myself are giving first priority to these matters now and will undoubtedly be required by events to continue to do so up until the time of the annual meeting. At that time we plan to have prepared a factual statement about involvement of anthropologists with the military, in so far as it is known to a number of those involved, and a statement of issues which this involvement raises. We hope that the Council will be prepared to discuss these issues and raise others. Solutions for the issues raised in your letter are not going to be easy to find. But we must start to find them.

I will, of course, include the issues stated in your letter in my suggestions for the Council. If you have any further thoughts before the meeting I would be glad to receive them personally or in writing.
With all best regards,

Stephen T. Boggs
Executive Secretary
American Anthropological Association

September 15, 1965

Dear Professor Nader:

This is an interim reply to your communication to the Board on the subject of the involvement of anthropologists in research on "counter-insurgency." As Clark Howell told you, I hope, he passed on your communication to the Board, where it was vigorously discussed. As it happened I had received a number of expressions of concern about this matter before your memo arrived, and so was glad to see it discussed. Inquiries are now under way at a high level within the administration to determine what role the various agencies involved intended for anthropologists in connection with this research. I can assure you that the President of the Association and I will follow up these inquiries most carefully and let you know as soon as possible about the outcome, and what the course the board intends to follow in any action which may be necessary. There seems to me little doubt that anthropologists on a whole would object to their employment in file research under false pretenses, such as those you describe. I will look forward to writing you again.
Most sincerely,

Stephen T. Boggs
Executive Secretary
American Anthropological Association

November 11, 1965

Dear Laura:

So glad to hear that you have not forgotten the Triques. Your letter came to us by a circuitous route. I am at Hartford, CN taking a year of anthropology under Paul Laser. So sorry to not be down there to help your student. There is another family in the tribe now but at a different location. They live in Laguna which is about three miles beyond our place on the way to Putla.

I think the Triques might have some unique features in the language of conflict. I am referring to the custom of the women (mostly older) publicly excoriating those with whom they are in conflict. I have been told by Triques that the women have very vivid imaginations during these demonstrations. I told one Trique that I wanted to record it sometime but didn't want to embarrass the women. He replied that she wouldn't even know that I was around.

We were so glad to hear about Nadia. We like the name. Bring her to Mexico sometime.

With our best wishes,

Claude Good
Oaxaca, Mexico

November 30, 1965

Dear Laura,

Partially to redeem myself, I am sending you a batch of reprints, some of which you may not have seen. But in particular, I am eagerly looking forward to your reaction to my most recent piece: "The Effect of Dominant Kinship Relationships on Kin and Non-Kin Behavior: A Hypothesis." You said you were going to write me about it after you had a chance to look at it now I am taking you up on it.

In all honesty, I am not anti-feminine-intellectual, but I know words prove much less-than deeds. At any rate, I am glad that I have been able to keep your fury down a bit and hope you will give me further opportunities of improving your image of me.

My symposium occurs in Austria about ten days after yours. I expect to be in Europe a few days before the twentieth of August and hope that in some way, we can meet again.

Best wishes.
Sincerely yours,

Francis L. K. Hsu
Department of Anthropology
Northwestern University

January 4, 1966

Dear Laura,

A good many years ago when I was a graduate student and when I first began to read the *American Anthropologist* and other journals of its like,

I made a silent vow that I would never demean myself by replying to a lousy review in print. Just as a matter of self-respect, it seemed to me that aloof indifference was a more intolerable emotion than injured pride. Now it also strikes me that as a matter of professional strategy the author always seems to come off second best. The reviewer writes a rejoinder and has the last word—and he can always say stronger things than he said the first time. Under these circumstances most reviewers have made most authors look pretty silly.

My own experience with reviewers is that they usually do a pretty crummy job. Rengsanggri had a review in the *American Anthropologist* without a word of evaluation except the word "painstaking" (if that's an evaluation). The review amounted to little more than an abstract of the contents of the book. And the only review that my Garo Grammar had was in *Language*, and the reviewer picked on silly little things, most of which he misunderstood, and then he proceeded to dismiss the whole job. By comparison, one could claim that you got a thoughtful if severe review. Of course Leslie used your book as an excuse to go off on his own tangents, and no doubt he was unfair in spots, but he did not say nice things too, and it was easy to see what sort of a reply he could write to any objections you or anyone else could make: "I repeat what I said in the review . . . valuable addition of having written the perfect book was not achieved. It has the deficiencies which I pointed out in my review."

I know what I would have said in reply to Dell if the first version of my review of his book had been published and if he had written the objection that he threatened. I almost wish I had let that happen because it would have made him look so utterly foolish. I could easily have knocked him down and kicked him in the face (but I'm really glad it didn't happen that way, because I can do without a public enemy).

My reaction to the review when I read it very superficially a week or so ago was "I wonder how Laura will take that." It was indeed more severe than is justified, and yet as I read it I felt that he was not so much attacking your book as using what he regarded as a basically sound job for making a couple of points of his own that he felt needed to be made—not only for your book, but about much of the work of many anthropologists. And I don't think this is an unfair thing to do in a review. I did the same in my review of Dell's book. I don't know Leslie, and I don't even know him by reputation. Truthfully, it has been two years since I read your book and I don't remember the details well enough now to judge just how badly unfair Leslie was. But I did not read the review as a slashing or thoughtless attack. It was no doubt unfortunate for him to be chosen since you had reviewed his book, but it must be hard for a book review editor to keep track of all these things.

I know how you feel, but really a review doesn't make as much of a differ-ence as it seems to. It's like a grade, it seems awfully important at the time but a few years later nobody remembers. Your career doesn't hang on it, you know. In all this I am relying on the idea that you would not expect anything from me except real feelings, and in brief my advice is: forget it.

We are just back from a trip to Philadelphia. We hadn't been there since leaving for the center two and a half years ago, and suddenly it seems that we had a lot of good friends there. We had a hectic four days running around and staying up late talking and gossiping and whatnot. Didn't see Dell, however. It is ridiculously warm here. I'm eagerly wanting to go ice skating, and so far it is nowhere near ice skating weather.

Yours,

Rob Burling
Department of Anthropology
University of Michigan

December 7, 1966

Dear Laura,

Many thanks for the postcard, letter and printed letter. A terribly crowded fall term is coming to a close. I have meant to write you for quite some time, but have had no time to consider ideas for the introduction to the joint vol-ume. I remember well that I promised to jot down something which might be of use to your introduction. But not until today have I had any time to collect my thoughts on what went on at Burg Wartenstein. In a week's time I'll get off some notes. The trouble is, of course, that The Wartenstein discussions in the meantime have paled a bit. What I remember is our walks. But I'll do my best. Concerning a possible introduction to section three on Western Law, I sup-pose that can wait, and most likely won't be called for.

The weather has been incredibly drab, grey, foggy, moist, slushy, dark this fall. It may be part of the penalty for having spent a year in Spain—probably to be explained more in perceptual, than in magical terms (revenge of the Gods). Not that it really helps, but there has been a great deal of talk on the sociol-ogy (or even anthropology) of law in Evian, St. Vincent, Uppsala, and Oslo. I hope that we shall get started on a Scandinavian project on conflict resolv-ing devices, ranging from courts, to arbitration mediation and bargaining. If we do, I think that we should take great care to plan the study so as to allow for much comparison as is possible with anthropological studies of related devices. I'll let you know if, or when, something happens. I mentioned to the sociologists of law in Evian that a future joint meeting with anthropologists of law might be useful, and there was a rather enthusiastic response to that from quite a number of members of the ISA subgroup on Sociology of Law. This group, if left to itself, is running out of suitable topics of discussion. For the moment however, I am more concerned with my own work with organizations. I have promised to hand-in to the Oslo University Press a revised manuscript to a textbook in Sociology of Law by the end of January. When that is done, I'll begin to plan an English edition. At that stage there will be many things I should have liked to discuss with you. There are, for that matter, also at this stage, because I have been spending quite some time working on the Lappish problems. We are seeing some results of our "development" work, and the implications of the investment followed up in detail by sociologists. This ought to be done in Finnmark in a central Lappish district where everybody despairs of lack of possibility to further economic development.

You'll hear from me again very shortly.

Yours,

Vilhelm Aubert
Professor of Sociology
University of Oslo

February 13, 1967

Dear Laura:

I'm glad to see that you are now a full-fledged member of the club of "Those At Whom Gluckman Takes Snipes." I suggest that we incorporate and limit the membership to one of the most exclusive in the whole subject. The *American Anthropologist* doesn't want to print any part of this review, and wants only a very short one, which they will get from Hoebel. I have submitted it, after a total reconsideration and a telephone call from the editor of the *Yale Law Review*, to them, because of the fact that he told me what I hadn't known— that he and some of the other people on his editorial board had taken Max's course during the time that he was there, and he wanted to know what I had to say about the whole subject. It seems that I am not merely a character in several of Gluckman's books, but that I am a question on his final examination. Have to come to the point of thinking it all very funny. However, the review is strictly anthropological. If they do not publish it, I will certainly send it immediately to the *Kroeber Anthropological Society Papers*, and in fact, even if they do, I will ask him if he minds, because the two publications will certainly not overlap with more than half a dozen readers. As soon as I can make it I will get on with the paper for your symposium. I have to give a lecture at the University of Hawaii on the 13th of March about law, and I intend to have it done well before that time so that I can give a version of it out there to a pro-seminar that I have been asked to address. Again, welcome to the club. Yours ever,

Paul Bohannan
Department of Anthropology
Northwestern University

January 3, 1968

Dear Laura:

Apologies for the lateness in returning your *Write Me In*. It came back into circulation and I have my own copy. I hope you haven't needed your copy; I more or less assumed that you would have phoned me if you had. Incidentally, *Gregory's Nigger* is an even better book and one of the most poignant of the Black autobiographies. I'm reading the latter as part of source data for an article I'm in the throes of writing—black/white relations with particular emphasis on black militant students and the problems connected with black identity. I published an article in 1943 on the channeling of negro aggression; now I try to understand the opposite phenomenon. It is not easy!

Hope to be seeing you soon. Happy new year and call me when you are free. Yours,

Hortense Powdermaker
University of California, Berkeley Anthropology Affiliate

January 24, 1968

Dear Dr. Nader,

You may remember my unannounced intrusion last June when we discussed briefly my proposed field research in Kenya in customary law. I thought you might be interested in a copy of my first report to the Foreign Area Fellowship Program, which is supporting me here, on the progress of my research and my future plans. You will see from the report that my procedures and aims vary in some ways from those of your Comparative Village Law Project. Part of this variation is due to my training as a lawyer and part to the particular circumstances of Kenya. I have been relying very heavily on documentary sources so far. I feel this is justified for two reasons. First, the lowest level courts, now the District Magistrate's Courts (formerly African or Native courts) are an established and well integrated institution in Kenya. They have been in existence for over forty years in most places, are geographically accessible to the majority of people and relatively inexpensive, they apply a reasonable facsimile of traditional customary law, over 50,000 cases a year seems clear evidence of their acceptance by the ordinary man as a vehicle for dispute settlement. Secondly, the nearly two thousand cases I have read to date have been by and large literate, well-reasoned, and contain a comprehensible summary of the evidence. Granted that the judgements contain certain distortions from the translation of vernacular proceedings into English, from the western education and legalistic bias of many judges—still, they represent a major 'source' of the law in Kenya. And, because reading judgements is highly efficient way of investigating a legal system, I have learned a great deal in a short time.

On that basis of that knowledge I am in the process of preparing questionnaires for interviewers to use in questioning informants. I may be able to do some interviewing of English-speaking litigants around Nairobi, but elsewhere I will have to seek the assistance of vernacular speakers; although I learned some Swahili before I came neither my ability nor that of most Kenyans is adequate for extensive discussion. I hope to obtain the help of some law students from Dar es Salaam during their forthcoming vacation in March, and later of students from Nairobi. I have found your outlines of vital information and your trouble case questionnaires of great help in developing my own, both to remind me of essential data and to formulate the questions. If the next stage of my research progresses as satisfactorily as did the last four months I shall be very well satisfied with my work here.

I look forward to hearing about the progress of your own much more substantial project, and would be very interested in any interim publications you may put out. I hope to be able to discuss our common interest in customary law again on my return to the states in December 1968 or June 1969, when I will be teaching at Yale Law School.
Sincerely yours,

Richard Abel
Professor of Law
University of California, Los Angeles

April 2, 1968

Dear Laura,

Many thanks for Bennett's article on "American Agrarian Society." I think it is excellent. Most of what Bennett has to say about his Canadian example applies to field cropping anywhere north of Mexico.

I never realized the extent to which the vocabulary which deals with acculturation implies the degradation of the "traditional" society and further implies that this is a bad thing. No matter what view of the process you might take, if you use the customary language to describe the process you are going to sound although you saw it as a loss of cultural flavor, of social and economic autonomy, of satisfying self-self. Bennett's contribution is simply in pointing out that from the point of view of the people involved this loss may be seen as "simply the continuation of desired trends."

Somebody ought to do a study of the socio-economic backgrounds of the major social anthropologists. Whence comes societies, no matter how squalid? It may be in part an obligation to primitive people was to Christianize the poor beggars and put pants on them. There is also a very long tradition in Western thought of the idealization of a simple rural way of life, Western thought having been from its beginnings almost exclusively the creation of townsmen. I expect that any frank attempt to acculturate the negro would be accompanied by a good deal of agonizing over the damage being done to "negritude" and the cultural flavor of ghetto life.

I am going to send Bennett's article to my agrarian society specialist at W.S.U. [Washington State University] and hope that I will get it back. He may have seen it if it is very recent but I am sure that he had not read it the last time I talked to him. Either that or he didn't get the point.

We must carry this important conceptual exploration forward over shish kebab and red wine at the first opportunity. The world is in chaos and time is of the essence. My salutations to Norman and the children.
Sincerely,

William McGregor
McGregor Land & Livestock Company
Hooper, Washington

April 16, 1968

Dear Professor Nader,

I was very happy to receive your letter of April 8th, partly because I have myself recently been looking into the possible anthropological implications of my analysis of adjudication. I enclose herewith a copy of the piece you saw—I suspect you may have received, it, from Yosal Rogat of the Stanford Law School. I also have enclosed an article on labor arbitration which repeats some of the ideas of; the adjudication piece (see espec. pp. 187–43), as well as a short piece on adjudication in international law.

From my slight study of primitive adjudication it would appear that it cannot take place within the restraints I have outlined as characteristic of adjudication in the strict sense as we understand it. Tribal ties and a concept of "corporate" answerability tend to make every dispute "polycentric" in the sense in which I have used that term. (Gluckman speaks, as I recall it, of "multiplex" relations.)

I do hope you will send me copies of anything you write on this or any other problem of legal anthropology. I am going to be giving next fall a course in the sociology of law, and I want to explore all the relevant dimensions of what I call "basic legal processes" which include adjudication, mediation, explicit negotiation and the kind of "half-bargaining" that creates much of customary law. (On this last question, I am an ardent supporter of Malinowski—though I think much of the dispute really turns on an ambiguity in the word "reciprocity.")

I have also included some additional reprints and xeroxed material I thought you might find of some interest. If you are ever back this way, I hope you will get in touch with me, for I like to keep up with what is going on, and what is planned, in the field of legal anthropology (I have of course a copy of your comprehensive bibliography, which I am just beginning to utilize).
Sincerely yours,

Lon L. Fuller
Harvard Law School

October 16, 1968

Dear Dr. Nader:

It was most thoughtful of George Lenczowski to remember my interest in the talk on conflict resolution in Arab societies you gave at Monterey last spring and of you in sending me a copy of your paper on "Communications." I am most interested in the psychological and social barriers to a political settlement in the Near East and spent some time during a visit to Israel this summer trying to make a case for using some social anthropologists as consultants rather than relying primarily on diplomats and politicians for decision-making. I am providing a copy of the paper you sent to my Israeli contact here who seems not wholly to disregard the importance of accepted procedures in moving toward the substance of a problem.
With my best personal regards,

Rodger P. Davies
Deputy Assistant Secretary for Near Eastern and South Asian Affairs
U.S. Department of State

December 28, 1968

Dear Laura:

As you see, I am back in Seoul. I have been meaning to write you since I returned home last September. But the problem of settling down and beginning to teach right away proved to be more time-consuming than I expected or wanted. Now that one semester is over, I can finally sit down and write to you.

How have you been? And your family? I already feel somewhat shut off and isolated from the international community of scholars. Lawrence Friedman tried to bring me over to New Orleans to attend the Association of American Law Schools annual meeting. But he could not find the money. David Bux-baum of University of Washington School of Law has been unsuccessful in finding money to enable me to come to the American Assoc. of Asian Studies meeting in Boston next spring to read a paper of indigenization of Western law in Korea. It seems all the money suddenly dried up. At least, I am grate-ful that I can keep in touch with my friends through letters. It was good of Lawrence to let me have a copy of his paper, "Legal Culture and Political, Eco-nomic, and Social Development," to be read in New Orleans.

I am afraid you have been saddled with my paper on the religious and rural values of the Koreans for the past year. I realize it was wrong for me to burden you with it. I had thought you would just go ahead with some deletions with-out any elaborate editing. If you find the work too cumbersome, please return the M.S. to me. I will tackle it. In any case, I hope you will keep vehicles for its possible publication in mind.

Let me wish you a very happy holiday season and a very happy new year. Please let me be kept informed of all the interesting things you are doing. With warmest regards,

Pyong Choon Hahm
Yonsei University, Seoul

February 27, 1969

Dear Laura:

I was simply delighted to receive your letter of Jan. 22 and the enclosed papers. It was indeed thoughtful of you to send the papers to me. One gets greatly encouraged to know that there are others who are pursuing the same line of inquiry with similar observations and even conclusions. I guess this is what we call an academic "community," a community of shared interests. It is amazing how a scholarly paper such as yours can bring Zapotec, Korean, Brit-ish, Indian and other cultures together. It is simply wonderful.

Since the beginning of this year I have been busy writing the paper on the indigenization of Western law in Korea for this year's Association of Asian Studies meetings. I had to mail it off to David Buxbaum of University of Washington Law School so as to have someone read it at the meeting. I haven't heard as to whom David has chosen to be its reader. Well, I can only hope that it will be someone who can understand what I am trying to say. Being an intelligentsia in Korea, I have been spending a lot of time giving to talks to various groups (including American Women's Club of Korea) and writing adult-education-type papers to various magazines. It seems this is a part of price for being an "intellectual elite" in a country such as Korea.

Thank you very much for recommending my paper to the *Kroeber Anthropological Society*. I hope they will see it fit for publication, your idea of a summer institute on law and social science sounds wonderful. I suppose we have some missionary work to perform.

I am tentatively planning to do a small-scale anthropological study of a couple of villages remote from an anthropological center this summer. I will just live there and take a lot of notes, being a participant-observer. Although my main interest is to make an intensive case study about five court cases in Seoul, I guess I have to limit myself to research that cost me little money, at least of the time being. Your study will be a great inspiration to me.

Wishing all the best to you and your family.

With warmest regards,

Pyong Choon Hahm
Yonsei University, Seoul

April 30, 1969

Albert Hirschman
Center for Advanced Study in the Behavioral Sciences
Stanford University

Dear Albert Hirschman:

From what I can gather I believe Ralph meant the following: the court system is a voice institution. Anyone can enter as a matter of right. You can contrast this with the legislative system in which one can't have a voice—unless elected or unless one has close contact with legislators. All you need to be in order to use the court system is a human being (although some animals have access to the courts!). It is a great case for entrance and exit because you can enter, you can imitate a conflict situation by taking something to court. (The chances of winning are another question.) The Supreme Court decisions have in fact been increasing access to the court system. This increased access in this country is something that other countries are not enjoying. The contingency fee helps in this—anybody—no matter how poor—can hire a lawyer. If he loses he doesn't have to pay. Britain doesn't allow the case of contingency fees which closes the access of course.

Ralph is also interested in the stock market in terms of a voice-exit. The stock market allows a fast exit—he argues that if one couldn't exit so fast it might drive people to claim a greater voice in the system.

Hope this is of interest. Norm and I are looking forward to seeing you both again soon and my thanks again for giving me a copy of your book—a classic. Very truly yours,

Laura Nader

May 12, 1969

Dear Laura:

It was indeed good of you to take the trouble of getting my paper printed in the *Kroeber Anthropological Society*. I have just returned to Mr. Stromberg necessary information so as to enable him to put the bibliography of my manuscript in order.

Under separate cover, I have mailed you a couple of specimens of my recent writing. One is a reprint of an article published here in Seoul. It concerns the early history of the introduction of the Western law into Korea. It is simply descriptive without much originality. The second is a manuscript I have just finished for the Peace Corps here to be included in their orientation handbook for those young people who are coming to Korea for the first time for their work. I have tried to give some insight into the Korean mentality. While I was writing it, I thought of having it published in something like *The Atlantic* or the *Center Magazine*. But I thought of writing a letter to the editors of those publications, whom I do not know, and I have "chickened out." I am at the moment positing a book with the title something like "The Oriental Pattern of Cognition," as a nice goal of life. Well, we will see.

As I pointed out in *Politics of Melancholy*, the Korean way of conceptualizing desirable interpersonal dynamics can never be understood by a Westerner who insists on clinging to the Occidental formal logic. For such a person, one ego plus one ego should add up to two egos. But when you have "overlapping" egos, $1 + 1$ does not equal 2 but rather, something between 1 and 2. Although a Westerner might feel unhappy with the dichotomy of one kind or another and wish to get out of such a structure, he switches to the $1 + 1 = 1$ logic rather than the Korean way of keeping the right hand side of the equation indeterminate between 1 and 2. Thus, for an Occidental Christian, Father and Son become one, the two entities merging into one, but for a Korean, father and son never merge into one identity nor would they be separate, independent entities. It is thus important for us to keep in mind that even the notion of equilibrium, balance or harmony in the Korean milieu turns out to be quite different from the same notion in the West. Needless to say that I have enjoyed your two papers. Since you mentioned the "balance" of young Zapotecs, I am beginning to see the fundamental difference between the two modes of viewing the universe. The inability or reluctance of the Koreans to separate and sharply distinguish all the entities in the cosmos has important reification in behavioral sciences about which I have a chance to discuss with you.

Wishing you all the best.

Sincerely,

Pyong Choon Hahm
Yonsei University, Seoul

July 2, 1969

Gordon Tullock
Professor of Economics
Virginia Polytechnic Institute

Dear Professor Gordon Tullock:

I am very interested to hear of your work. With regard to your point—"are criminals ill?"—do you recall the writings of Merton on this subject? Which suggests they are "super-normal"? You might look at his *Social Theory and Social Structures*, around page 182. Also sympathetic with what seems to be your general orientation is Satz's book on *Law and Psychiatry* (I may have the author's name spelled wrongly). Also, it depends, as Albert suggests, on what kind of criminals are we talking about.

I find your research fascinating but I must confess, I had hoped you might be dealing with two related questions. One would be a cost-benefit analysis of crime from the standpoint of the taxpayer. Specifically, it is being noted by sociologists and criminologists that certain areas of law should be decriminalized prostitution, homosexual offenses, etc. If we realized how much it costs to keep these so-called 'crimes' within the legal, we might be more ready to de-legalize.

A second area I wish some economists would get at has to do with business crime. Does it pay? Are they ill? We've spent so much time studying burglars and robbers, maybe we'd get new insights into the problem if we look at their big-time models.

I hope to continue hearing of your most important work.

Sincerely,

Laura Nader
Professor of Anthropology

September 16, 1969

Dear Laura,

Thanks very much for the copy of your paper, and of the Table of Contents of the forthcoming volume. The former whets my interests for the latter, and I am eager to read more.

I was interested to see a resemblance between some of your ideas and those which Lawrence Friedman set out in the paper on legal culture which he gave to our seminar last spring. Am I right in thinking that "style" in dispute settlement has some relation to legal culture? I find your arguments persuasive that this concept has greater potential value for analysis and comparison than does substantive law, or structure, or techniques. But I am still troubled by its lack of definition. I wonder whether a single style pervades dispute settlement characterized by different styles. Isn't Van Velsen making this latter point in his article at the I.A.I. symposium when he finds a similar style between certain African moots and some American magistrates' courts?

I am also bothered by the idea of "balance" or "equilibrium." These terms seem to imply an equality between disputants which existed before the wrongful act, and which is reinstated by the settlement. But aren't most relations between individuals those of inequality? And doesn't the dispute settlement create a new inequality, which may be different from that originally existing? In the case of the trumpet player (p. 7 & ff.), the trumpeter's original status was higher than that of the drunk, and the settlement left him in a lower position. Thus a disequilibrium (or inequality) caused the incident, and the settlement resulted in another inequality, which the trumpet player intended to redress by covert means. This suggests to me that dispute settlement is a see-saw operation, which may always be seeking equilibrium, but never attains it. (the exhortation by the court in the fourth case—that the son not seek reprisals on his father or stepmother—also indicates that the end result of the settlement was not equilibrium).

Am I correct in thinking that the case reports you present came from the similar written records of the Presidente's court? If so, to my surprise, they are

FIGURE 3. The first Wenner-Gren conference on the Ethnography of Law. Reprinted with permission of the Wenner-Gren Foundation for Anthropological Research, Inc.

remarkably similar in form and contact to those I found in Africa. If anything, to my surprise the African records seem more comprehensive.

I am a little unhappy with the sharp distinction drawn from Aubert between courts and bargaining techniques. As ideal types, these models have considerable values but few institutions in practice are as extreme as either.

I hope my comments will show how stimulating I found your article. I would be very grateful for copies of any further results of your research Sincerely,

Richard Abel
Yale Law School

REINVENTING ANTHROPOLOGY IN THE SEVENTIES

In the early 1970s, Dell Hymes put together a book of collected essays, called *Reinventing Anthropology*, at the invitation of Pantheon Books' "anti-text" series.[1] The field was increasingly getting attention in and out of academia, both here and abroad. A need to study the powerful as well as the powerless seemed obvious to me after colonization and the new independent states, but not to all anthropologists. *Reinventing Anthropology* was about much more—including racism, ecology, community and disciplinary censorship—and it was not universally well received by everyone, as noted by the Chicago anthropologist Fred Eggan.

But local issues such as fluoridation of drinking water also caught my attention, mostly because of the slippery slope involved in using additives in natural water supplies. The antifluoridation scientists were passionate about not putting fluoride in the drinking water for dental care as noted in several of the letters. Innovative critiques by biologists such as Dr. Groth questioning the utility of such policies were being censored, an example of science politics in a closed system, about which I was to learn more later. I wrote letters in his defense, arguing for a more open science.

The longest letter included here was written in response to a query I had put to the Columbia University sociologist Robert Merton about Thorstein Veblen and his use of the concept of "trained incapacity." I had made references to Veblen in an article I was writing for the *Yale Law Journal*, but the editors wanted a specific citation to Veblen himself that I could not locate.[2] In a footnote, I argued to the editors of *Yale Law Journal* that if they insisted on a citation for every idea, no one could write anything new! They asked me to remove my footnote. I said that was censorship; the head of the law review responded, "that's right!" All I could find was something

Merton had written about Veblen after Veblen had spoken at Columbia, although I had researched Veblen's own writings. But Merton took on the challenge, writing the long letter on Christmas Eve and thereby enabling me to support the citation.

Since law was the centerpiece of my interest at the time, I also began to question the role of sociology to understand the way in which white-collar crime escaped the national crime index, and the sociologist James Short took the time to write and document for me the paradigms used that allowed corporate criminals to escape crime statistics. To this day, we mostly speak about crime in the streets, rarely discussing corporate criminal activities that affect all Americans even more than street crime.

Increasingly, I heard from the general public as I was invited to give more and more talks to nonacademic audiences. In the 1980s, I was to give the Phi Beta Kappa lectures, which took me around the country. John C. Lynn, a teacher of incarcerated men, wrote to me about "the sham of corrections." In responding to my permissions letter this year, he told me he was terminated shortly after writing to me, then decided to go to law school. He is now practicing law in the Midwest. Letters to me from death row, jailed persons, and prisoners asking for help enlightened me about our (in)justice system. And after speaking at the University of Southern California Law School, a black law student wrote me, declaring that the problem with the law *is* the law, as he put it.

The criminal justice system in our country is a mess, as policymakers are increasingly noting. But those in the criminal justice system, in our prisons, were already well aware of the problems. So too were young activists willing to give their time to improve situations. Thus the letters from death row, another from a prison inmate, another from a critic of prisons, and more. Why were they writing to an anthropologist? The documentaries, the newspaper articles, hundreds of talks to nonacademic audiences filtered out of the Ivory Tower and into a varied population, including the Department of Justice and the White House.

The range of letter writers expanded. Also during the 1970s, a group of Berkeley faculty and I began to exercise our own academic freedom vigorously regarding the *absence* of academic freedom at the national laboratories. I learned a lot about lab policies from members of my family who worked at the Oak Ridge National Laboratory in Tennessee, at Livermore, and at Berkeley as well. Letters from lab scientists followed—some of which are included in this chapter. I began serving on the Carnegie Council on Children as well as the National Academy of Sciences' Committee on Nuclear and Alternative Energy System project—both interdisciplinary groups. I wrote letters critiquing both projects. More money is often not a solution, and I strongly felt that a rethinking of these projects was needed. Issues regarding experimentation on prisoners were being raised, as well as that of unrecognized experimentation on students (myself included). The Harvard sociologist David Riesman, who had studied law at Harvard before moving to sociology, responded to my work; he was a helpful sounding board. My third and last child was born, and another letter was drafted to the UCB chancellor in regard to maternity leave. And, we *still* don't have federally funded maternity leave in the twenty-first century, despite the fact that most Western democracies do.

In 1975, I received an interesting letter from Edward T. Hall in which he declares our discipline a closed system. Before Hall published *The Silent Language*, he had worked on the Navajo and Hopi reservations and wrote to me about why, from his intellectual vantage point, he would restrict himself to studying his own culture, even though he was publicly castigated for not finding a "primitive" tribe to study.[3]

Other letters from the 1970s came from the American Bar Association, thanking me for my Zapotec film,[4] which they used to train judges; a US Army captain interested in Saudi Arabia and working with Saudi troops and officers from the major tribes in the Hejaz and Nefud regions wanting to connect with a former student of mine, Donald Cole, who worked in the al Murrah region; a Peace Corps volunteer concerned with the dose of radioactive fallout from a particular "incident" on the Marshall Islands that he wanted to challenge through law. Other letters were motivated by discussions about faculty salaries based on contract hours and more in Sacramento and UC Berkeley.

I especially call attention to the letter by Otis Dudley Duncan, a numbers sociologist working with me on the National Academy of Science energy project (CONAES). He was responding to critiques of my report as a political document. Duncan responds, "all our reports are political documents." Such critiques had inspired my off-the-cuff talk at the Mitre Corporation and underpinned the decision by the CONAES group not to publicize my report, "Energy Choices in a Democratic Society."[5] Debate over "more energy" and nuclear cut to the core of our "scientific" debate. Free of politics, of course!

January 10, 1970

Chancellor Roger Heyns

University of California, Berkeley

Dear Chancellor Heyns:

I would like to bring your attention the question of maternity leave on the Berkeley campus.

In 1967 I was told by your office when I enquired as to the policy on maternity leave for faculty women that a) maternity leaves are arranged for clerical help by departmental chairman, b) that women faculty are not entitled to maternity leave, and c) maternity leaves are not considered as part of the University sick leave policy. Apparently, as the late Professor McCown noted, women faculty are supposed to remain celibate.

More than two years later professor Phyllis Dolhinow of our department called your office for information as to maternity leave and essentially received the same response: this is two and one half years later, and no change in policy. Professor Dolhinow is expecting a baby at the end of this month.

I would imagine that it would be simple enough for your office to do something about this question before it is called to your attention by militant women's groups on the campus.

Sincerely yours,

Laura Nader

January 21, 1970

Dear Laura,

Please excuse the informal stationery. I'm out of the standard stuff here at home. But this is an informal request: what do you think of the following idea?

When Pantheon, and its head Andre Schiffrin, read my review of *The Dissenting Academy*, he asked if I would edit a book in the same series! The "anti-texts," of which the first was *Towards A New Past* (historians). I was in England and felt out of touch with what seemed to be a rapidly changing scene in the United States. I promised to look into it once back, did talk a bit with friends like Sid Mintz and Bill Sturtevant, inconclusively. This week I got a letter from Schiffrin, asking me about it again. My hesitation, I realize, had been on several grounds: so far as relevance goes, an issue with which many in *The Dissenting Academy* were concerned, why that's all over the place already in anthropology. And the AAA is not the sort of monolithic establishment agency that has led to the climate of revolt in the MLA [Modern Language Association], etc. We've been more responsive to change and our middle-aged radicals are already part of the power structure. And purely political criteria seemed to endure dismissal of the product.

But I have the sense that the growth and popularity of anthropology is in many ways a response to what anthropology has already accomplished, a superficial sign not necessarily indicating basic health. There is a growing crisis, even if not wholly recognized as such, an unease, the older generation of professionals, remembering when simply to become an anthropologist and to establish the profession as a recognized one was a struggle, often fail to sense the possibility that all basic questions are again open, certainly for the best and brightest students. If anthropology as it now is didn't exist, they might well not feel it necessary to invent it.

So, there would seem a place for a book that was radical in the sense of getting to the roots of raising the question of the justification, purpose, perspectives of anthropology as now practiced. (Think of audience as graduate students in important or central part).

This is "relevance" in part, political perspective in part, but I have some thoughts that cut across any of these lines. The general context would be topics not normally treated in texts, that go on to the root of people's view of what it is to do anthropology and to commit oneself to anthropology.

The question you have been so concerned about this year, what might be called "the ethnography of power," seems to me precisely the sort of thing such a book should contain. The questions of political outlook, social criticism, etc., are there; but you have to raise the issue on a non-ideological, non-sectarian basis, from the basis of pure native radicalism, as it were, that consists of taking a hard look at something others have avoided looking closely at altogether, and asking, can anthropologists tackle this?

To me this gets to the heart of one of the key issues: what is the nature and use of anthropological skill and knowledge? What it has been in the past is increasingly challenged, and the setting in which it goes is rapidly changing. If anthropologists have no skills, no resources for dealing with power—if then, it would seem that the entire field did depend on a certain favorable power relation produced by imperialism—well that's the sort of challenge I see posed by the effort you made to have students work with Ralph, the conflicting responses that others made.

A lot of people might urge the study of the powerful as well as the weak, the oppressors as well as the oppressed perhaps, on general principles. You are the one person I know who can deal with it in really radical terms, in the sense of getting to the root of the matter for anthropologists—what can they actually do in such respects, how does that fit with the ways that they're trained, or need to be trained, etc.

I haven't been able to make up my own mind about the book, about doing it. But if you would be willing and able to do such an article, there would be a clear reason to try it. And I'd appreciate very much your suggestions about others who might participate. I have other tentative thoughts to pursue, but nothing definite enough to report. In general, things going to the root of the question, intellectually, politically, methodologically, whatever, has anthropology a (worthwhile) future? From people asking, what would we want anthropology to be if we did have the chance to invent it now?

All the best,

Dell Hymes
Professor of Anthropology
University of Pennsylvania

February 20, 1970

Dear Laura,

Dell Hymes has tapped me to do a cultural ecology, or something in that line, for the book of radical anthropology he is writing. I am hoping to do something in the way of inventing a radical new social order: *ecotopian* (utopia plus ecology). Like, what use is anthropology if we can't draw on our collective knowledge to invent a new and better culture? Anyway, Dell said I should get in touch and make planning choices, so we won't overlap; he says you are doing ethnography of the powerful, which sounds cool. I would like that fieldwork. Anyway, I doubt if there will be any serious overlap, but I hope I can talk to you about it. Are you going to be at the SWAA and/or Kroeber meetings? I am going to be, if plans work out. Or just call down on the old friendly tie-line.
Good luck,

Gene Anderson
University of California, Riverside

March 16, 1970
Robert E. Connick

University of California, Berkeley

Dear Dr. Connick:

It was a pleasure speaking with you about the D.E.C., its organization, and its possibilities. It has given me an opportunity and forced me to take time to think about campus wide educational problems, rather than dwelling upon the usual departmental and disciplinary educational concerns.

As you said in our talk I am interested, indeed fascinated, with the general problem of how to encourage innovation that could profoundly influence undergraduate education at places like Berkeley. I also questioned the potential of the mechanisms created by the Berkeley division for such task. I believe the organization they have suggested for the task is structurally unsound, and know that if they had explored the functions of the D.E.C. in rather more detail, and in good faith in terms of its functions they could not have come up with what essentially is a Band-Aid, and one with not much stickum at that.

Why are the D.E.C. mechanisms structurally unsound, and why is it bound to fail? Innovative institutions of the sort indicated must have authority that is central, not balanced or diffuse. Try to sail a boat democratically. The chairman of such a committee, especially since he will not have a solid budget apparently, has to have power as well as responsibility. It would then be the chairman that should pick the team he wants to work with him, not the committee on committees or the chancellor, or anybody else. Although there could be certain guidelines such as specific departmental and age distributions. The faculty who participate in such a program have to have incentive: time off to prepare new types of courses, and prestige to offset punitive possibilities that could come from departmental levels—from persons who not only think such courses should not be taught in the department, but not in the university generally. Students should be able to earn credit by taking such courses or by being part of a team that research and organize such new courses. The students chosen by the chairman and his aides would be selected from a panel of students who earned the right to advise on such matters by previous experience.

Unfortunately, as faculty we have only been able to think of additive solutions and none that are designed to restructure outdated modes of teaching. The trouble with additive solutions is that they give hope and then fail. This gives rise to disillusionment and backlash. The D.E.C. may do more. It may stand in the way of departmental reform by acting as a safety valve for conservative departments. Perhaps the 191 vehicle for educational experimentation in departments, and a D.E.C. with a rather different organization than the present form together can begin to have impact.

I thank you for your interest, and am grateful to know that we have a Robert Connick in the Chancellor's office. I would also like to suggest that the talents of Dr. Ellen Gumperz, social studies program, Berkeley, and Dr. Hortense Powdermaker, a well-known anthropologist who has retired in Berkeley might be put to use on this problem.
Sincerely yours,

Laura Nader
Professor of Anthropology

November 8, 1970

Dear Laura,

As you can see, I am now in Bonn. I arrived here with 4 other law professors from Korea at the invitation of the Bonn government. We will be traveling throughout Germany till the end of November. And then, I leave for home via Paris and Hong Kong.

Just before I left Seoul, your letter and the enclosed papers reached me. I had indeed read your "style" paper. At the moment I am concerned with the conflict avoidance aspect rather than conflict resolution. Although I fully realize the importance of studying the style of dispute settlement cross-culturally, I am very much worried that we might be dealing with a marginal or exceptional case. What I mean is that I want to see how a community manages to get by to a large extent without ever being compelled to resolve or settle it.

I am in the process of writing a paper for the 28th International Congress of Orientalists to be held at Canberra, Australia coming January. I will deal more with the conflict-avoidance aspect of the Korean culture and its effect upon the contemporary judicial process. I am not yet clear as yet how to conclude the paper. We will see.

I particularly liked your paper about your first fieldwork. Beautiful! Your observation about the Indians who were living in two cultures with a sense that their indigenous one was inferior to the Mexican one was of special interest to me. It applies equally to the Korean people with their inferiority complex. The "conflict-dynamic" (your prose, Laura!) culture of the West has simply overwhelmed the Koreans. The "passive" cultures of Korea simply disintegrated in the minds of individuals. As you can see, this has created a serious crisis in normative culture of Korea—sans the corruption. Well, I wish you all the best, especially for the newcomer to your family.
Sincerely,

Pyong Choon Hahm
Yonsei University
Seoul, South Korea

September 15, 1970

Dear Miss Nader,

I am presently confined on death-row on the Maryland State Penitentiary, and have been for the past 8 years and 3 months. Recently I came across an interesting article about you. I was greatly impressed.

My reason for writing you at this time is to request any possible help you can offer me by the way of your legal assistance.

I am without proper funds to hire a competent attorney to represent me continually in fighting this injustice through the proper court channels for justice. For five years I was without a lawyer and couldn't get my case before the court timely before some of the witnesses became deceased, making it difficult for me prove a certain point. I am really incapable of protecting myself dealing in the science of law being black, poor and undereducated doubly against me in this society the way the system now operates.

If you have spare time that you could respond and would need additional information concerning my case, I shall be more than glad to send it to you.

I am before the court at this time, awaiting a decision in my case. A favorable reply from you concerning this matter will be much appreciated. Please let me know your decision soon. Any way you can help me would be very much appreciated.

Sincerely yours,

James Omar Tull
Maryland State Penitentiary

Mr. Tull died in prison after Maryland had obliterated the death penalty.

October 12, 1970
Marc J. Swartz

Professor of Anthropology
University of California, San Diego

Dear Marc,

Some days ago your review of *Law in Culture and Society* in *Science* was brought to my attention. I want to thank you for a well written review, and at the same time raise a question you raised with regard to the so-called Gluckman-Bohannan controversy.

As I said to another reviewer who also gave undue space to what I consider to be a totally unproductive argument—the disagreement between Gluckman and Bohannon is not an academic question, but rather a psychiatric one. It is a disagreement that is not academically our business except as an example of wasting scarce resources in anthropology . . . that personalism is a sure sign of decadence. In the special issue of the *American Anthropologist* on law, I tried to put the discussion into perspective by allowing only a paragraph or two for a summary and then pointing out that "how an ethnographer goes about laying bare or describing his society is intimately related to what use he believes can be made of such a description." Practically, I guess I believe that issues of methodology may be raised possibly in a vacuum, may even be discussed in a vacuum, but sure can never be settled without considering particular questions. I will admit however, that many of us can make a living by just such as the above controversy—unproductive though it may be.

Yes, we did discuss this "thing" at the Burg . . . and both members of the "duel" agreed that they did not disagree. It wasn't worth our time to say more than I felt because I am really not interested in Gluckman or Bohannan's psychology but rather in what they can contribute to knowing more. In all fairness to Jim Bohannan, I must say that he made his point with the Tiv book and has really not wanted any part of this ridiculous argument except when he gets goaded into it every now and then. In other words, he thinks he is more productive tackling a disagreement that is not fundamental to the actual work being done in the anthropological study of law. Aubert for example is much more intellectually challenging as are a few other people that I could mention.

Thanks again, it is not easy to review a collection such as this. How are you liking San Diego?

Best wishes,

Laura Nader

October 12, 1970

Dear Laura:

Thank you very much for your letter of September 21 and the book review. I read it with delight! As you know, the American woman has always fascinated and puzzled me. It always strikes me as extraordinary the way the American woman defines her sexual equality in terms of her becoming the "same" as the American man. Koreans tend to take the biological endowment as a "given," whereas the American would try to transcend such "ascriptive factors." Of course, your perspective was much more "moderate" than the other lady. I do not think that somehow we should squeeze in the element of "gracefulness" or some such thing into our balance-sheet of life. A woman may have to become a football player or a bartender for the sake of equality. But for the sake of gracefulness it may not be the desirable thing. I know these are my male prejudices showing up. But we tend to be more "accepting" than the Occidental Prometheus.

Yes, I would love to have a chance of talking with you at the Smithsonian. I plan to reach there by the first of March next year. If you can spare any time, any time after that date will be alright with me. I have no particular preference. I will leave it entirely up to your schedule.

It is always good to hear from you. Best wishes for your new child.
Sincerely

Pyong Choon Hahm
Yonsei University
Seoul, South Korea

November 2, 1970

Dear Laura:

Thank you very much for your letter of October 12. I appreciate your kind words concerning my review of your column, *Law in Culture and Society*.

I can well understand your impatience with the attention given to the Gluckman and Bohannon dispute and your position that it is a "psychiatric" one rather than an academic one. More than that, I agree that methodological issues will never be settled in a vacuum but only with respect to their use in particular cases. However, I am absolutely convinced that anyone reading your volume could not be impressed by the serious question which Gluckman and Bohannon raise in their battle with one another and that they would not view these questions as being due to Max's own particular "hang-ups." The question of comparability is a very serious one which needs to be faced quite squarely and I believe that despite the excellent work that Bohannon did in his Tiv ethnography, his unwillingness to allow a strict operational definition is a limitation on what the findings of particular ethnographers presents a very serious issue. I think that, as you suggest, the only final solution to this problem will come by such definition, but I do not believe that an unwillingness to examine the problems (even in vacuum) is warranted.

I am sorry we cannot agree on this issue. I am really terribly impressed at the high quality of work you managed to get together into your book and I congratulate you warmly on it.

I am having a fine time here at San Diego and am most glad I made the move. This is a very exciting and fast moving department and there is every reason to believe it will remain that way for a long time to come. I hope to see you at the meetings here this month.
Best wishes,

Marc Swartz
Professor of Anthropology
University of California, San Diego

October 6, 1971
Edward Thompson

New York State Supreme Court Justice
Civil Court of the City of New York

Dear Ed:

I thank you for sending me stuff. You're terrific, but I'd like to push harder on you and yours, particularly regarding small claims. More later.
Best wishes,

Laura Nader

January 5, 1972
John Merryman

Professor of Law
Stanford Law School

Dear John:

Thanks for your note and copy of your comments to David. To comment on your comments! Regarding the consequences of lawyers participating in dispute resolution: yet it is so often questioned by non-professionals (particularly those who study societies where there are no such professionals) whether such lawyer types "do" anything that needs doing by them. You're right, the question is not whether professionalism is good or bad; nor is it as you suggest however "what are the proper uses of professionalism?" There are a number of questions that come to mind which stem from a curiosity about the effects of professionalism on the actual and potential consumers of his service. How, for example, has increased professionalization of the American Bar effected the kind of access the "John Q. Public" has to the American legal system? Where you and I part in our questions is that I want to know something about the functions of actual behavior, while you want to talk about an abstract or philosophical discussion as to "proper uses" someday by someone, or never by anyone.

With regard to your comment on "anthropologists focusing on the dispute resolution to the exclusion of everything else which distorts the word." Couldn't agree more. As law school teaching by means of the case method of teaching law distorts the view of the system, anthropologists' exclusive focus on cases has also produced a similar "distortion" if you will. One starts where one can. As I stated in my 1965 piece it is interesting to know what variety of functions the legal system of any society is serving, if only to understand what conditions the law is primarily serving: an ordering versus a conflict management function, and for whom. The reason some of these functions have not been observed, I state, is related to underdeveloped methodologies: how does one study the function of the California Air Pollution Agency when "there are no violations?" At any rate John, the question you raised is one that I raised and tried to answer at some length in the paper I did with Barbara Yngvesson which you were given a copy of at the meeting.

Let's get together and talk about some of this on the West Coast.
Best wishes,

Laura Nader
Professor of Anthropology

March 24, 1972

Professor Laura Nader:

My name is T.K., I had dinner with you and Dean Nelson on February 10th after your speech to the faculty and students at University of Southern California Law School. I am a black man, in my senior year at the law school. I asked you several questions and found your responses of such insight that I would like to communicate with you.

My area of inquiry is: *The Black Man and the Law.* After three years of intensive study, I am of the opinion that law in this country is *the* major tool of racism and oppression—not only of blacks but poor people in general. This may not be new to you, but I have come to this conclusion independent of whatever you or anyone else may have said.

I shall address myself to three broad areas, via (1) economic, (2) education, and (3) political power of the black man in America. My discussion shall be brief, but I believe you may understand basically how I feel about this situation.

(1) *Economic Power of the Black man and the Law*

Black people came to this country in chains. We were denied by law to possess any form of property; more specifically, we were property. The "detached," "intellectual" judiciary participated in decisions such as the *Dred Scott* case. The sins of the law were not sins of commission as much as they were sins of omissions. Blacks were excluded from corporate, governmental, and other economic bases of power without a whimper from the courts. A nation pledged to "equal protection" of the laws, permitted and condoned openly discriminatory hiring and promotional practices. The black man found no help from his dire economic plight from the courts of "justice."

(2) *Education*

The lie that every black student is told is "study hard and you will get ahead." This is cruel. Very little of education is taught in schools, it is taught at home. Black students in ghetto schools are several grades behind their white counterparts (Cf J. Kozol, "Death at an Early Age"). The odds are stacked so high against the average black student graduating from college that attainment of professional status is virtually unheard of. Even the black man that does attain a post-graduate degree finds himself alien to his people; a man in black skin taught to act and sound like a white man. He suffers needless identity problems and is usually ineffective because of his need to "prove" that he is "as good as the white man." This is senseless! *Brown v. Board of Education* was decided in 1954, yet we still have segregated schools. More crushing is Nixon's statement against busing. I do not think given the present context of the business world, that segregated schools can ever be "equal." I believe that schools can be integrated without integrating a people into the sickness of America. The reality here is that blacks are denied the "tools" to compete and the job possibilities to accomplish. In short, the dice are loaded against black people attaining educational (economic) equality within the system.

(3) *Political*

My feelings here are summed as follows: there are one hundred senators in Congress; we are ten percent of the population but we have one senator and he is probably the biggest Uncle Tom in the country! We are equally represented at the other levels of government.

Conclusion

I know much of what I have said has been said before. My purpose is to ask your opinion as to how I may best serve my people. My knowledge of white America is limited. You are established. And based on my brief contact with your intellect, secure within the truths you live. I seek your counsel.
Your Fellow Human,

T.K.
J.D. Candidate
University of Southern California

April 6, 1972

Dear Dr. Nader:

Perhaps you will recall that I rushed up from the audience to commend you for your address before the Southwestern Anthropological Association/Society for California Archaeology Annual Meetings in Long Beach.

In part, this short letter reaffirms the gratitude felt by many members of both associations for the cogent points made during your talk. I would like to say that what you said of cultural anthropological biases toward studying certain "exotic" segments of our own culture is also reflected by the activities of their brethren in archaeology.

Since taking my present position as an archaeologist for the U.S. Forest Service, I have found that the greatest "battle" is waged in the area of trying to break through conceptual biases of just what an archaeologist is. The obvious confusion in the public mind relates to the history of archeology's close relationship with Classics and other branches of the Humanities (not to mention its relationship with paleontology). But a deeper prejudice exists within those "schools" of American archaeology that profess to be the *New Archaeology*. It doesn't involve internal matters, such as theory method or technique, it involves the prejudice of working with prehistoric and early historic native cultures in areas outside of the United States. It is difficult for me to demonstrate to Forest Service personnel and the general public that the archeological record in California is "worth anything." They read the same papers, magazines (*Science* is an apropos example), and watch the same television specials that depict archaeological research in South America, Mexico, and Europe. I believe the lack of press, the lack of large sums of foundation money, and the few major universities involved in North American prehistory to be similar to the heavily skewed bias of cultural and social anthropologists' studies of such "exotic" groups as transvestites, nudists, skid-row bums, and father-daughter incest in our own culture.

I merely wanted you to know that "even" an archaeologist received a lot of stimulus from your talk.

Sincerely,

Donald S. Miller
Regional Archeologist
United States Department of Agriculture

April 6, 1972

Dear Laura:

Through informal channels I have revised and enjoyed your paper *Up the Anthropologist* and wonder what your plans for it may be. I think it far too good and important not to publish, and am glad to offer *Current Anthropology*.

For any audience you should ask yourself what difference it makes to address USA anthropologists and the upside of USA culture, as opposed to Japanese, Mexican, Hungarian, French, Egyptian and other anthropologists and the up-sides of their cultures. I expect that you can and should define somehow the "geographical" (nation-type) limits of your proposal.

I enclose our "Information for Authors" and suggest that you decide if you want the paper referred. Our system permits to accept, but not to reject without refereeing. Refereeing has the great advantage that it gives the author good suggestions before publication it has the disadvantage of costing 6 weeks in time (in addition to what it takes you to take advantage of the suggestions offered you).

If you have not yet committed the paper elsewhere, and want the C.A. treatment for it, please quickly state your preference on freeing and give us the information requested on the enclosed.

With best wishes,

Sincerely,

Sol Tax
University of Chicago

April 18, 1972

Dear Dr. Nader,

I wanted to tell you how very much I enjoyed your talk last night and your company at dinner. For me it was pretty fascinating to consider subjects with which I have a passing familiarity from the viewpoint of a discipline like anthropology about which I know nothing.

Much to my surprise, if I understood you correctly, your instrumental view of law is substantially the same as that of St. Thomas Aquinas in the twelfth-century. Several citations may make this clear: St. Thomas's definition of law: "An ordinance of reason for the sake of the common good " by the authority who has charge of the community and promulgated," (*Summa Theologiae*, la—2ae, XC, 4).

"All law is directed to the common well-being. From this it draws its force and meaning, and to the extent that it falls short of this it does not oblige in conscience," (*Summa Theologiae*, la—2ae, XCVI, 6).

"The immediate end of human law is men's own utility." (*Summa Theologiae*, la—2ae, XCV, 3).

On non-victim crimes: "Human law is imposed on a crowd of men most of whom are not perfect in virtue. Therefore it does not forbid all vices from which the virtuous keep themselves, but only the graver ones which the majority can avoid, and chiefly those that are damaging to others and on the prevention of which depends social stability. " (*Summa Theologiae*, la—2ae, XCVI, 2).

On penology: "In this life there is no punishment for punishment's sake. The time of the last judgment has not yet come. The value of human penalties is medicinal and insofar as they promote public security or the cure of the criminal," (*Summa Theologiae*, 2a—2ae, LXVIII, 1).

Interestingly, the only jurist of any importance that in modern times took the Thomist view of law seriously was the Roosevelt appointee to the Supreme Court, Frank Murphy, of whom his biographer John Roche wrote: "By temperament he was a fighter who was aroused by seeming injustice and did not want to check the rule book before he went into action; by intellect he was an instrumentalist, not in Deweyan sense of being a pragmatist, but in the natural law tradition of viewing all the phenomena of the world about us in terms of a higher purpose, as instruments for the fulfillment of the telos. In other words, Murphy mounted the wild horse of natural law and mercilessly rode down those institutions, traditions, legal precedents which stood between him and his destination—a democratic utopia." He was, of course, detested by his peers on the bench.

Very truly yours,

(Rev.) Stephen C. McCabe, O.P
Berkeley Priory Institute for Thomistic and Ecumenical Studies
Berkeley, California

May 17, 1972

Dear Mr. T.K.,

Thank you for writing to me. Somehow as I read your letter describing the situation of blacks as you see it in this country I could only recall having comparable conversations with my mother, the theme of which was "but the cards are stacked against me"—and she used to smile and say, "Yes, but I believe in you." And I guess that's the way it is. I can't deny what you've said, but I would counsel that you somehow use all those stacked cards as fuel for your tank rather than let them overwhelm you as it is so easy to do.

If I were black and interested in medical research, I'd find out what blacks get sick and die from and go to work on some of those problems. If I were a lawyer, I'd do the same thing. You may know there was interest in getting a top quality all-black public interest law firm going in Washington, but problems came up with recruitment—black lawyers did not want to work for low public interest salaries when corporate law firms were after them. Such information should not discourage you, it should inform you that you're fortunate to be at a good and progressive law school which will, I'm sure, give you strong support. You struck me as capable of having a healthy respect for that which is good and beautiful about black culture while learning at USC. That's capital; don't lose it.

Sincerely yours,

Laura Nader
Professor of Anthropology

June 7, 1972

Dear Laura,

I am glad you could come to the conference, and I am even happier that the weekend is over. Among many other moments I will remember your amazement that we actually put together a conference on injustice. That will stay with me primarily because I was, and am equally amazed that I got involved in such an effort. I had great misgivings from the beginning along the lines of "What the hell do I want to get involved with all this for?"

After a week off, I have started thinking about the conference again. My understanding is that everyone wants to complete their chapters and comments on one another's by the end of this semester. This sounds extremely ambitious, but apparently this deadline was dictated mainly by Ken Boulding who intends to complete his part before leaving this fall for his year abroad. Let me know how this schedule sounds to you. Actually, your paper was closer to being a chapter than the others.

By the way, if you wish I will send on a summary of the reactions of the people in your seminar when it is put together. It might be interesting for you to see how they saw what happened.

In the meantime I insist on taking one more stab at getting my message across. I think it is important that people like Laura Nader recognize that arousing the sense of injustice—by making the inflictor, victim, or observer aware of an injustice—can have all sorts of outcomes. Many of which we would consider undesirable, e.g. condemning the victim even if it is one's self or running away from the victim. One key element in determining the outcome of the power the person has at hand or thinks he has to eliminate the injustice at the time he becomes aware. Powerlessness plus the threat from an injustice is designed to lead to condemnation, avoidance, and becoming cynically alienated like an Irish-Canadian "attorney-plumber" I met once.

Don't believe me? Take a look at the data I refer to in some of the things I am enclosing, especially pages 16–26 in the Chapter I have in press ... don't be misled by the title. The chapter deals primarily with reactions to injustice not interpersonal attraction. If you get intrigued you should then read my tech report—"Deserving vs. Justice," some part of which will appear in the *Journal of Applied Social Psychology*.

Thanks again for coming and making it all happen. The 1st Waterloo Conference on Injustice was a success.

With best regards,

Melvin J. Lerner, Ph.D
Chairman, Division of Social Psychology
University of Waterloo

June 22, 1972

Dear Laura,

Your note of Feb. 1 followed me around SEA [Society of Ethnographic Anthropology] and just got returned to these parts. Your article in *Reinventing Anthropology* was a serious statement, except for the title, but I didn't consider most of the contributors to be anthropologists — despite the blurb. They are entitled to say whatever they want but I didn't like their denigrating what several generations of anthropologists have done so much work to give anthropology its present standpoint.

If someone like Clemmens would do an objective study of the Hopi today he might discover that the greatest threat to the Hopi are the Navajo — the new imperialists in the South West. I've spent some 10 years trying to help the Hopi get their reservation back from the Navajo.

Joan is busy with therapy and photography — we may be by some time in August and will give you a call. In any case we'll be at UC Santa Cruz for the winter quarter of 1976.

Best wishes,

Fred Eggan
Professor of Anthropology
University of Chicago

July 18, 1972

Dear Ms. Nader,

I noted with much interest the U.P.I. [United Press International] article of July 16, 1972 with regard to your devotion toward a more rational approach to our system of justice.

Naturally, I am well aware of your brother's work to securing more recognition and fairness for the average consumer and am proud, as I am sure you are, of his accomplishments.

However, I personally feel (and five years of my present confinement on a mandatory twenty-five year sentence for a first offense wherein no violence, narcotics, nor crime against nature, I believe furnishes me with the experience to express this), that the only way our country can reach a reasonable level of fair justice and law and order will be eventually through the polygraph and the fairly new Psychological Stress Evaluator.

Please believe that we incarcerated persons have the greatest respect for those such as yourself with so much compassion for your fellow man. The very best to you and yours always.
Sincerely,

Paul Kenneth Bowmen
Atlanta, GA

August 12, 1972

Professor Nader,

I have been working as a contract teacher for the past two years at the Federal Correctional Institution in Milan, Michigan. I am at present thoroughly disgusted at the sham of corrections which I have witnessed since employed by the institution. My constructive corrections for reform have been ignored and I can no longer in good conscience compromise my beliefs for the sake of bureaucratic expediency. Somehow the truth about how incarcerated men are treated must be communicated to the public. I read an article in the New York Times concerning your efforts for prison reform and I ask for whatever help or advice you can give me. I have enclosed two items:

(1) A recent evaluation of education and prison procedures written by myself.
(2) A recent proposal to the A.C.L.U. on establishing an Inmate Advisory Board drawn up by myself and two inmates.

Thank you for your time,

John C. Lynn
University of Michigan, North Campus

October 12, 1972

Dear Laura,

I do hope you had a smashing time in Hawaii, we did in the jolly old land! I was going to ring you when we got back, but then I got a frantic cold so I have been more or less enjoying ill health for the past week.

May I ask a huge favour? It's got to do with a remark you dropped when we last saw each other. Something about a "primitive" society where murder is just looked on as a private bother between two people and thus not a specially serious crime, whereas polluting the river harms all the populace and is on the order of high treason.

Anyway, I've got a chapter called "Types of Crime." One bit of it starts something like this: "When is conduct a crime, and when is a crime not a crime? When somebody there—a court, a legislature, a presidential commission—so decrees." Then I've got a bit about abolition of drunkenness as a crime in the District of Columbia because "it was getting to be such a bore enforcing it." So what I'd love from you is something I could quote about the above murder/pollution thing, as it would be very apt in the context. Particularly apt since I had thought (and I expect other people do) that murder is everybody's "least favourite crime everywhere."

That *Cheaper than Chimps* piece has had its ups & downs. The chicken-hearted lawyers for *The Atlantic* seemed to think it was a touch libelous in parts (absolutely not, but publishers' lawyers are always like that in my opinion). So in consequence I had to spend a maddening amount of time revising it to tone it down while not really doing so—if you see what I mean. It is now supposedly set for their January issue.

Did you happen to note it in the paper the other day that Sen. Kennedy is going after the human exp. business? He cited 2 examples the Tuskegee syphilis experiment & another involving newborn babies—no mention of prisons. Why? My guess is he doesn't know.

Do give a ring when you've got time. We should love it if you could both come to dinner soon, so let's set a day.
Best Regards,

Jessica Mitford
Oakland, California

November 15, 1972

Dear Laura Nader:

After your talk here yesterday I felt you deserved an apology. I only mention this now because it is an apology all deserve who study closely, or worse yet live under our system of justice and the social class it keeps. The defensiveness and one-up-manship demonstrated by the law professors was the logical companion and explanation for the system of justice as you described it. If there were not lawyers there would be no law, and with adequate preparation I'm not sure that would be a bad situation.

I was particularly interested in something you had to say after the program had concluded: that the goal of any profession ought to be the elimination of need for it. And I agree in the sense that robust health should be the goal of persons in medical profession, and freedom without conflict should be the goal of persons in the legal profession. Thinking you had in mind something similar to that, I want to share with you an experience in my criminal law class.

The class is conducted as a mock-legislature whose duty it is to redraft the Texas Penal Code. (Revision of the Penal Code is actually taking place in Texas, and the proposals will be cited on in the next legislative session. Any victories as I see it, are of marginal importance, amounting to eliminating the 15th century from our laws). During our opening session I introduced an addition to the section on "Objectives of the Code" which will be considered by the legislature.

What I had in mind was creating a context for class discussion of the idea that our goal as lawyers should be to eliminate the need for lawyers—i.e. create a satisfying life situation in which the kind of conflicts people settle in the courts no longer arise. In the alternative I wanted to demonstrate a visible conflict of interest that the lawyer class charged with the duty of ordering the flow of conflict have a vested interest in continuing the conflict, that is, their jobs are dependent on it. This is even true in the case of criminal law where the state is willing, indeed happy, to incarcerate people rather than eliminate the source of much of our crime.

Sad to say my classroom amendment passed, for none of the reasons I had intended. I attempted to begin the discussion but it quickly waned, and was carried by people who merely like the idea of a "flowery" or "humane" preamble before we got down to the real business of sticking some heroin addict for 200 years.

It's very difficult to keep a hold on oneself in a classroom situation peopled by professors such as those who joined you in the discussion, and by students who largely want to imitate them. Nonetheless there are 3 or 4 classmates who offer support for each other; and I think I am particularly fortunate to have the most important parts of my life outside the law school . . . in the woman with whom I share a life, in our German Shepherd, in our garden. It is helpful to be visited by someone such as yourself—and I would encourage you to continue to make yourself available for discussion with the law students of this nation.

Sincerely,

Ryan Petty
J.D. Candidate
University of Texas at Austin School of Law

January 23, 1973

Dear Laura:

I seem to remember a conversation at Carmel in which I promised to send you references concerning the involvement of social scientists in the history of crime statistics. A good overview is presented in *The Measurement of Delinquency*, by Thorston Sellin and Marvin E. Wolfgang. The book was published by Wiley in 1964.

The book in fact represents an important attempt by the Sellin-Wolfgang research group to measure delinquency from police records. The early history is traced in chapters two through five. One of the most influential articles in this history is Thorston Sellin's, "The Basis of a Crime Index," published in *The Journal of Criminal Law and Criminology* in September 1931. This is the article which arrives at the famous generalization, that "the value of a crime rate for index purposes decreases as the distance from the crime itself, in terms of procedure increases."

I am under the impression that social scientists served on the Committee on Uniform Crime Reporting, of the International Association of Chiefs of Police, or at least they were consultants to that Committee which published *Uniformed Crime Reporting: A Complete Manual for Police* (New York: J. J. Little and Ives Company, 1929). Unfortunately I do not have a copy of that manual, though I did consult it when I was doing my dissertation research years ago at Chicago. I am sure the manual lists members of the committee and probably consultants also.

In any case, Sellin particularly in later writings provided a good deal of the theoretical justification for trusting to the Uniform Crime Reporting system which had been developed by the IACP and adopted by the FBI. Two later works by Sellin are particularly important, his article on "Crime," in the 1935 edition of the *Encyclopedia of the Social Sciences*, and his Research Memorandum on "Crime in the Depression," published by SSRC [Social Science Research Council] in 1937.

I hope this information will be helpful to you. Sorry it has taken me so long. It was wonderful to see you in Carmel in December. Shortly thereafter I managed to break a leg skiing, so I have been somewhat immobilized for a few weeks. It is mending well however, and I expect to be in good enough shape to fulfill a commitment for a week of lecturing in the East next month. I assume you also have been appointed to NSF's [National Science Foundation's] Advisory Committee on Research. Unfortunately, the notice of the meeting on March 22 and 23 came considerably after I had made other commitments for those dates, so I will miss that first meeting. I am sorry to miss the meeting. If you are there, keep them honest. Hope to see you soon.

Cordially,

James F. Short
Professor of Sociology
Washington State University

April 6, 1973

Dear Dr. Nader

It was a pleasure talking with you at Mike Lowy's house. My book, which I mentioned to you, is *Male Dominance and Female Autonomy: Domestic Authority in Matrilineal Societies, Human Relations Area Files, New Haven*. In that, I dealt with female power (or lack of it) in the domestic sphere. In the larger cross-cultural study I hope to do, I shall consider the public sphere as well. Since my interest up to now has been in domestic life, I am not familiar with the literature dealing with women and the political and legal systems. If you should have a bibliography on that subject that you have used in classes, I would certainly appreciate having a copy.

I was intrigued by the highly favorable position of the Zapotec women, as you describe their divorce settlements to me. Do you have any of this material written up? Or would one of your students have similar material? I am editing a book on women at different stages of male dominance or lack of equality or near-equality as well as the other, more familiar, kind. My own paper on the Hopi will be one such example, and I am looking for more. I feel that it is important to dispel the notion that women are always and everywhere subordinate, a misconception held by feminist anthropologists as well as others.

Thank you for suggesting *Women and the Law* to me. I was astonished at the legal disadvantages that accrue to women upon marriage. It is ironic that, in fulfilling her socially recognized and approved sex role, a woman should have to lower her position. In a general way this seems to follow a pattern found in so many societies—that it is only neutered women, i.e., women who, for old age or other reasons are not fulfilling their reproductive and nurturant role, who are granted equal status. It appears that breeding and feeding are without honor almost everywhere.
Sincerely,

Dr. Alice Schlegel
Assistant Professor of Anthropology
University of Pittsburgh

October 25, 1973

Dr. Sterling Wortman
Rockefeller Foundation
New York, New York

Dear Dr. Wortman:

For the record I would like to comment on your report for Task Group 2 on the Peer Review System. Specifically, I cannot endorse findings 1–5 for the following reasons:

1. We have no "hard" data to back the assertion that "in general, the scientific community probably is satisfied with the fairness of NSP treatment of applications for research support."
2. An explanation of the "modest number of complaints" is much more complicated than indicated: any scientific analysis of complaint patterns would have to consider numbers of other variables including the degrees of powerlessness felt in the scientific community.
3. Presentations by the Directors of MPS, BMS, SS, DES, and Engineering were based in great part on intuitions again rather than on hard data and follow-up investigation. Given that people tend to support their institutions rather than challenge them, I found the presentations incomplete and reflected in the rather uninformative statement of our Task Group that the Peer Review System "seemed generally unsatisfactory."

I believe that the National Science Foundation could only gain by self-consciously studying its effect on U.S. science. Such study could be accomplished either formally or informally, by a professional study such as outlined in our report, or by setting up mechanisms within the NSF whereby feedback from the scientific community and the public would be commonplace occurrences that were used by the National Science Foundation to better serve United States science.

Thank you for your kind attention.
Sincerely yours,

Laura Nader
Professor of Anthropology

June 26, 1974

Dear Laura:

Many thanks for the copy of the Groth letter. I began reading it very skeptically since I have been so put off by the anti-fluoridation propagandists, and tend to see resonance to their views as reflecting the kind of chronic paranoid orientation that we used to try to measure with the F-scale. But Groth writes an exceptionally reasonable letter. While I won't take the time to read his dissertation and couldn't evaluate it technically if I did, he is persuasive that the social process by which the fluoridation policy that was adopted was not conclusive to objective evaluation. Furthermore, it is a legitimate worry that massive compulsory treatment was instituted, if as seems plausible from his letter, the case is not firmly proven by usual criteria. Thanks for letting me see this. It did have a persuasive effect. I'd be much interested in how Paul Lemkau responds—as this in his area.

I much enjoyed meeting you at the Linden Hill sessions. It was one of the rewarding aspects of a rather sparse fare.
Sincerely,

M. Brewster Smith
Professor of Psychology
University of California, Santa Cruz

August 5, 1974

Dear Laura:

Thanks very much for sending me the letter about fluoridation. As you might expect, I have been very much interested in the groups which have so strongly opposed fluoridation and the outlandish claims they have made that it is grossly harmful that I have tended to neglect the idea that the basic case has not perhaps been proven. There are a good many reasons.

I think to doubt that the fluorides are harmful, as is noted in this material, perhaps half the people are now receiving fluorides in drinking water and many more in toothpaste and the general death rate or the distribution of causes of death has not shown radical change. The dangers, if they exist, must be subtle.

Fluoride probably coasted into scientific acceptance because it is so closely related to chlorine, which for all I know is equally questionable so far as long term safety is concerned, has been accepted because free chlorine kills certain pathogenic bacteria. The fluoride and chlorine mechanisms so far as health are concerned are, of course, entirely different. One having some sort of metabolic or nutritional effect through the body's chemistry, the other, as noted, protecting the body from harmful bacteria.

I was the Director of Mental Hygiene in New York City when Leona Baumgartner was health officer. We used to discuss how she was to handle the few but vocal and often eccentric people and groups who so violently opposed fluoridation on other bases than those advanced by Dr. Groth. We once worked out a scheme in a semi-humorous vein to the effect that the water of areas with high fluoride naturally was "natural" water, and that the thing to do was to stage a campaign to change New York's water to a more natural state. The only real argument against this is that statistically very low fluoride content of water is more common than very high levels. Mankind has shown no tendency I know of to avoid areas of high fluoride content for which the only punishment demonstrated is that there is greater risk of mottling of the truth.

This late questioning of public health programs which have been accepted as effective in the part is not unusual. I believe there are studies which show that diphtheria immunization can be shown not to have been the main cause of the almost total disappearance of that disease, but the immunization continues. There is to the best of my knowledge, no study that shows that Calumet vaccination against tuberculosis is effective in any important way, yet it continues. Certainly it has had no effect in reducing the prevalence of TB in this country.

One statement Groth makes bothers me: that the use of fluoride is a political matter which implies that the scientist, therefore has no right to speak. I certainly agree that scientists should not decide for society. Such would be suicidal were sciences as "soft" as yours and mine are and as subject to very wide swings of enthusiasm—from permissiveness to behavior therapy in my generation—were to make the decisions for the public. On the other hand, the scientist has an obligation to display the best he has to the public in the best way he can when he believes the public will be helped thereby. I have felt that public knowledge and opinion are the balance wheel that keep us from too wide gyrations of action while allowing gyrations of opinion among those of us in the "soft" sciences we aspire to make "harder."

Thanks again for sending me the material. The length of this letter indicates the concern I have had about problems like this and perhaps also say a quick reaction to your statements in Bethesda.
Very sincerely yours

Paul V. Lemkau, M.D.
The John Hopkins University
Department of Mental Hygiene

October 15, 1974

Dear Laura,

I am enclosing with my letter to you a recent mailing list of the Task Force Against Nuclear Pollution. As will be evident, the Task Force lobbies to try to achieve two goals:

a) Increased funding for ecologically-sound energy alternatives such as solar energy
b) A moratorium on further construction of nuclear power plants plus phase-out of those in operation

I feel that your participation as a member of the Board of Directors of the Task Force would be a great help in this effort. We have direct evidence, as you'll note from the mailing, that this approach to citizen lobbying does not help democracy work. Realizing the busy schedule you already have, the Task Force would rarely ask for much of your time. Your counsel, from time to time, would be invaluable. If I can answer any specific question, I'd be pleased to do so.

Your joining our board would be most welcome.

Sincerely,

John W. Gofman, M.D.
President of the Task Force Against Nuclear Pollution

October 22, 1974
Chancellor Albert H. Bowker

Office of the Chancellor
Berkeley Campus

Dear Chancellor Bowker:

This letter is to inform you that I will be unable to accept your invitation to serve as a member of the Committee on Foreign Students for the 1974–1975 academic year. My position, as I have stated before, is that I no longer serve on administration and Academic Senate committees and will not serve until this campus evolves a reasonable maternity leave policy.

Sincerely,

Laura Nader
Professor of Anthropology

October 23, 1974
Robert Middlekauff

Division of Social Sciences
University of California, Berkeley

Dear Dean Middlekauff:

I request your action regarding a recent news release and report stemming from work at the Institute for Governmental Studies that raise questions as to the action of and the responsibilities of personnel with the University.

Early in September I was asked by Stanley Cost of the IGS [Institute of Governmental Studies] to comment on a draft copy of a report he was preparing with Harriet Nathan on "Fluoridation in California: A New Look at a Perplexing Issue." I agreed to read the draft and was motivated to send a memo to the authors stating my concerns. At the same time I called the Associate Director of the IGS, Professor Todd Laporte, and called his attention to the questions that I had raised in my memo, and later also spoke to Dr. Lee, Director of the Institute.

I raised the following concerns.

1.   Concern that a report that was neither scientific nor scholarly was being released under the auspices of the University.
2.   Concern over the general problem of the University becoming entangled in the adversary process and the consequences that could have for our credibility.
3.   Concern, if the report was neither meant to be scholarly or scientific, but journalistic, over the biased nature of journalism.

I was further concerned, after speaking with the Directors of the Institute and as well with Stanley Scott, that no one was administratively responsible for this particular arm of the IGS. In fact, there was a lack of serious concern on the part of the Directors as to the importance given a busy world, of the questions being raised.

My critique and discussion with Scott unfortunately only served to make his report slicker. I was unsuccessful in influencing him to think through the more basic criticism dealing with the substance and quality of the report. Scott, in a word, was adamant and not capable of understanding why it was important for him to be able to spell out exactly how he had come to take the position he did. LaPorte and Lee were interested but not concerned, or at most thought the "problem" could be ironed out personally between Scott and myself.

I then consulted with Professor Elizabeth Colson of Anthropology who suggested that if I was unable to influence the quality of the report perhaps the IGS would give equal space to the biologist whose most recent work on the subject was given such short shrift by Scott, Dr. Edward Groth III (now at Cal Tech), either as a separate piece or as a comment on the present piece. I made this request and also met with LaPorte and Professor Haas of Political Science to plan an ad-hoc symposium for the campus on the general question of the culture of scientists, which would involve Dr. Groth as a speaker.

The report from the IGS, untouched by any of my substantive suggestions, including the suggestion to award Groth equal time, hit the news media today. As I had expected a new study from the University of California shows that we all ought to fluoridate. Irresponsible, unscientific, unscholarly and reflecting, if not poor management at least a laissez-faire management of the IGS, and indeed more specifically, reflecting the fervor of one author who for personal reasons that we can study, used the University for his own personal soap box.

We cannot afford much more of this in this, or any other University. Science can't afford any more credibility problems. We have got to state our credentials or our absence of the same: why isn't the IGS reporting on the politics of fluoridation rather than the science of fluoridation, or at least on the interplay between the scientific research on fluoridation and politics?

I send this letter to your office as a formal complaint, and request that you, as the University officer most directly responsible for the IGS, will investigate. I would hope that you will not delegate this task to the advisory committee of the IGS for it has been my experience on this campus that such advisory committees are less than unbiased. To specify my request:

1. I would like to have the responsibility of these Public Affairs Reports clarified as neither Director Lee or LaPorte seemed to feel responsible for Scott's work.
2. I request the IGS publish a statement by Dr. Groth on the subject and that his statement-report be circulated to the same people who reviewed the Nathan-Scott study. That you may have some ideas of the matter in which Dr. Groth conducts himself I include a copy of Dr. Groth's letter on the subject of fluoridation to the FDA.

Thank you for your consideration.
Sincerely yours,

Laura Nader
Professor of Anthropology

February 3, 1975

Dear Dr. Nader:

Thank you for your willingness to get me in contact with Dr. Donald P. Cole. I would like your advice and assistance on anthropology courses suitable for a Ph.D. program in Near East Studies at Berkeley. I regret that your busy schedule when we talked about Dr. Cole's address last Thursday did not provide a chance to also discuss your department's Near East courses. I would like to clarify my background and interests in anthropology. I am now an Army officer and moderate Middle East seminars at the John F. Kennedy Center for Military Assistance at Fort Bragg, NC. I served an enjoyable tour in Saudi Arabia in 1971 as a military communications advisor. During that tour I had many experiences working with Saudi troops and officers from the major tribes and often visited several tribes in the Hejaz and Nefud regions. My research then was primarily as participant-observer and recorder of dialectics. Since returning from Saudi Arabia, I have often been Department of the Army escort—interpreter for Saudi and Jordanian military groups visiting the United States for orientation tours or to attend military schools. I have tried to develop some background in Near East sociology and anthropology by studying the works by Field, Polk, Gulick, Van Ness, Patai, and whatever related materials become occasionally available at Fort Bragg.

During the last tour of visiting Saudi Arabian Army officers, I recorded much information, although still somewhat unorganized, about various Saudi tribes, particularly tribal structure, sanction mechanisms, dialect, and integration into the government. I read with much interest Dr. Cole's article on the Al-Murrah in the anthology *The Desert and the Sown*, edited by Cynthia Nelson. I am interested in reading Dr. Cole's dissertation for more insights. I would like to contact Dr. Cole for his suggestions on research methods and local factors he encountered which facilitated or hindered his investigations. There is a strong chance of a second advisor tour in Saudi Arabia, and I feel that his comment could help me in observing and interacting effectively with Saudi counterparts. Please ask Dr. Cole to contact me. I have asked Dr. Molan for general information on his department's Ph.D. programs. He mentioned that his department emphasizes languages, linguistics, and literature, although inter-disciplinary programs are available. I am interested in a strong concentration in anthropology and sociology. Please send me information on your courses and financial assistance, as I would probably enter a Ph.D. program after leaving the Army and use the G.I. Bill and any teaching assistantships or other aid I could qualify for. Do you have programs for overseas studies, either summer-time or full-period?

Thank you in advance for your consideration and assistance.
Sincerely,

Stephen H. Franke
Captain, U.S. Army

February 4, 1975

Dear Laura:

It was good seeing you. I hope you can come up with more suggestions as to directions and people for the second phase of our study. I understand that Michael Sorgen sent you a copy of his latest outline, dated January 29, 1975.

You no doubt saw that the Air Line Pilots Association has got its way concerning radioactive materials. I can think of few actions taken by trade unions on behalf of the public. Then again, this action was as self-interested as any, I suppose. Anyhow, I felt a little better flying back from the Coast, for their efforts and others like yourself who chivvied the airlines about this stuff.

Just saw your review of the Gerzon book in *Harvard Educational Review*. One teeny point. You classify Spock with the "parent-child counselors," rather than the "social critics." Is this fair? I once was Spock's Chicago lawyer. My job was to be with him throughout his Chicago visits in the event that cops, sheriffs, FBI agents, and others who thought him not only a social critic but a dangerous enemy of the people might officially or unofficially hassle him.

In case you didn't see it, I am enclosing a copy of a piece I did on student rights in the December Phi Delta.

Best Regards,

Joel F. Henning
American Bar Association
Division of Professional Education
Chicago, Illinois

July 9, 1975

Dear Laura:

Many thanks, belatedly, for your extensive counsel over the telephone, the essays which you enclosed with your letter of May 25, and the excerpts from Spradley's book and from *Murder in Space City*. Your essays were a considerably out of the ordinary pattern of papers from which we see here, and they proved to be diverting as well as very helpful. They wound up among the very few materials strewn around my desk during the process of drafting an options paper for the President preparatory to the construction of the crime message itself. I have taken the liberty of circulating several of your papers within the White House staff and the Office of the Secretary of the Department of Health, Education, and Welfare.

Enclosed for your perusal is a copy of the President's crime message, together with ancillary materials which were simultaneously released by the Office of the White House Press Secretary. Several parts of the message, such as the paragraph at the top of page 8, are on point with the questions which you raised. I would be quite interested in your reactions to the message.

Per your letter, Spradley did send the Seattle clippings.

I am grateful for your timely counsel and for the perspective which accompanied it. Please keep me current with your writing, and please let me know if you should visit Washington.
Best Regards,

Richard Tropp
Special Counsel
Presidential Clemency Board
Washington, D.C.

August 16, 1975
Kenneth Keniston

Carnegie Council on Children

Dear Ken:

A postscript on my letter of August 3. The more I mull over the more uncomfortable I become about recommendations that are more focused on money as a solution than a change in perspective about children which then would lead one to want to find solutions (money or otherwise). I would be worried if our final report did as Leo points out, just come up with the same old phrase: "if only we had the money." We tried that in many ways in the 1960s, and I do not believe it is where we start with a solution. One could come away from the present reading thinking that what we want money for is to make sure that parents don't care for or that they continue to delegate caring for their children. I would like to ensure that the company becomes aware that what they do affects a man's family, a woman's family, or both. It may be that kind of support which then allows a parent to consider their action from the point of view of children's welfare—after all their corporation considers family in making policy, and so does the government. This kind of attitude does not necessarily cost money and we could probably argue that it saves money in the long run. Shouldn't one of our recommendations resolve around accountability patterns?

I'm sure there will be more later. Best to you.
Sincerely yours,

Laura Nader
Professor of Anthropology

September 23, 1975

Dear Professor Nader:

I was interested in your clipping and I share your dismay that someone such as Mr. Smith could so thoroughly defraud hundreds of people and escape with so little punishment. I am not sure I know why scholars have not followed the lead of Sutherland in doing more research on "white collar crime." (By the way, that is a label that I find quite useless. It is not the color of one's collar that need be taken into account in deciding on either criminal liability or the desirability of research, but the nature of one's behavior.)

However, I am not sure I agree that all theories of crime must take into account business fraud in order to be valuable. The problem arises in the undifferentiated use of the word "crime." It is as if we talked about the problem of "disease." Clearly there are many kinds of diseases; just as clearly there are many kinds of crime. I happen for quite accidental reasons that are not worth repeating to have become interested in street crime that occurs among strangers in public places. (It was an outgrowth of my earlier research on police patrolmen.) I think one can say some true and interesting things about that phenomenon without having to take into account business fraud; although that certainly deserves equally serious treatment since although it rarely involves violence, it certainly involves financial losses that are as great or perhaps greater than those caused by muggers and robbers.

You ask directly the question of what it would take to encourage me to think about this kind of crime. I don't quite know how to answer that since the research I do tends to be the result of accidents of circumstance and place more than the results of carefully thought out plans. However, I am doing research on federal law enforcement agencies and this has brought me into contact with the problem of enforcing laws against business firms and others. I hope therefore to have something to say about this subject over the course of the next few years, but you shouldn't look for anything immediately.
Sincerely,

Dr. James Q. Wilson
Harvard University
Henry Lee Shattuck Professor of Government

October 15, 1975

Dear Laura Nader:

How stupid of me to get you confused with your sister Claire! Since I have kept hearing about you in recent years and not about Claire Nader, I somehow got you mixed up in my head and I am glad you do not mind.

I started at once to read your paper for the *Journal of Social Issues* and thought I would make some comments as I go along, since I do not know when I will be interrupted. (I am glad to see you use what Margaret Mead always tells people to do in her grandmotherly way, which is to mark the margins so that one can refer to specific lines.) A few comments.

1) The American emphasis on fairness seems to me exceptional among cultures. It is an aspect of our egalitarianism; the cry, "Mommy, it isn't fair," is far more common than it would be in any other part of the world: Mommy listens. "Fairness" is usually interpreted as identity; when I see students use the concept here at Harvard College they do not mean, except in specialized cases, justice in terms of individual need but identity: which leads them in spite of their anti-technocratic bias, now to have admission to the Harvard residential houses allotted by computer even though this means that no house is likely to build up a good chamber orchestra, for example.

2) I like your whole discussion of legal pluralism and the conflict between local and national law. Paul Riesman does deal with cattle theft among the Fulani of the Upper Volta, and in the transhumance on which he accompanied the young men into Mali (their resentment at national boundaries and corresponding to tax collectors), but this is not the main preoccupation of the book he wrote on his first field trip, published in Paris and the Hague by Mouton: *Société et Liberté chez les Peuls Djelgôbé de Haute-Volta: Essai d'Anthropologie Introspective* (it will eventually be brought out in this country in English). It is part of the Cahiers de l'Homme published in France in 1973, and if you like I could send you a copy though I do not think you would find much in it of immediate relevance for your purposes, and you might in any case prefer to wait for it to come out in English. In this connection, Ruffini's work sounds marvelous.

3) The Zambian case in Mungule is really fascinating, where taking cattle rustling out of the community led to an increase in the practice, an effort to bring it back to local (would we call it vigilante?) justice.

4) I love Paul Bohannan's phrase, "a working misunderstanding."

5) There is one kind of scarcity in the American setting of which I have become very conscious through having so many friends of varying ages, and former students enter the law with idealistic motives of doing justice. But they have not suppressed their competitive motivations or their desire for variety of experience, and after several years of justice at retail they are tempted to try for justice at wholesale irrespective of the damage that may be done to particular clients. You probably know Harry Brill's book *When Organizers Fail* (which I understand is not popular in the Berkeley law milieu), which deals with this in one instance. I have

talked with Melanie Bellah, wife of a friend and former colleague about her temptations in this respect, and with Louise Cans (wife of Herbert Cans), who after a number of years of legal aid type work gets bored and wants a class action suit even when she is bright enough to know that the results for particular clients may not be happy. Since the federal courts are often better forums for this kind of operation, this leads to nationalization and removal of cases from state to federal courts, and from non-litigious to litigious forums.

6) That is a lovely story about Mexican drunkenness versus American insanity!

7) I began to study social science under Carl Friedrich while I was a student at Harvard, but my first actual foray into comparative studies was in two articles in the *Columbia Law Review* in 1942, entitled "Democracy and Defamation: Fair Game and Fait Comment." They were rudimentary in ethnographic terms, but they were an effort to see why words were handled in different ways in different countries in the European tradition; and I found that people like Robert and Helen Lynd and Paul Lazarsfeld responded with interest to these articles, whereas my law professor friends thought it was odd and interesting but had no genuine interest. It was then that I decided to switch fields. The ethnocentrism of American law was simply too endemic.

8) I love your whole discussion of the relevance of the time dimension. This is of course especially important as you suggest in view of the different time, horizons of various cultures, and within America—subcultures. The assumption that memories will last in this country for the four years it often takes to come to trial (memories of trauma or an accident or whatever) is itself extraordinary.

9) Three years ago at Chapel Hill there were 115 students in a course on environmental law. This was before Watergate and the professor asked the class how many had voted for Nixon—not one hand, and only one said he was not sorry Nixon was President. The professor thought that not all these students would find it possible to practice environmental law as other than what I would myself think of as a kind of class warfare of the well-to-do who want clean air as against the less well-to-do who want jobs and amenities of a different sort. When one gets such class conflicts then of course one tends to have the situation you describe for Zambia: of resorting to national law rather than local means of settlement of complex disputes and trade-offs.

10) I want to continue with this essay and read the other one too but as I feared, I must stop. I wish there were a chance to talk about these

matters. I had at first thought of attending the December anthropology meetings in San Francisco, but now I see there is no chance to get away from here where after a year's leave, I am in effect doing double time. But I will hope to get back to your papers and respond anon. In the meantime, with many thanks and good wishes.

Sincerely yours,

David Riesman
Professor of Sociology
Harvard University

P.S. Could you send a copy of your *Journal of Social Issues* essay to Nancy Jones, a law student at Syracuse University who under the direction of Gerald Grant has been working on a study of Antioch Law School in Washington, D.C. which, as you probably know, attempts to put students into clinical practice from the very outset her address is Syracuse University Research Corporation, Merrill Lane, Syracuse.

October 24, 1975

Dear Laura Nader,

I am sending you under separate cover the talk that I gave at the ASA [American Sociological Association] meetings, and would like especially to direct your attention to my reference to your work on page 18, but of course I would be grateful for your comments and criticisms concerning any of the themes in what has had to be a somewhat truncated paper.

With good wishes.
Sincerely,

David Riesman
Professor of Sociology
Harvard University

October 29, 1975

Dear Laura:

In response to growing concern about past abuses in the use of prisoners as subjects in human biomedical experimentation, the faculty and staff of the Health Policy Program have explored policy options in the regulation of such experimentation. Concerns or the rights of prisoners have led several jurisdictions to ban all such research. Yet little conclusive evidence is available regarding the amount, locations, and conditions of biogenetical experimentation in prisons.

In this discussion paper the authors review available literature and report on their survey of state correctional departments. Suggested regulatory improvements are assessed. A practical new approach is then proposed which assures respect for inmate rights. We believe it offers an opportunity for a principled compromise on this emotional issue.

We hope the paper will be of interest to you. The authors plan further work on the conceptual scheme outlined and welcome your comments

Sincerely,

Philip R. Lee, M.D.
Professor of Social Medicine
University of California, San Francisco

November 4, 1975
Philip R. Lee, M.D.

Health Policy Program
School of Medicine
University of California, San Francisco

Dear Phil:

I just received your piece on *Biomedical Experimentation on Prisoners* and before I read it I have to repeat a comment I made many times to Jessica Mitford while she was writing her last book. Why don't you address the question of biomedical experimentation, and at least concern yourself with the range of areas where it is happening. For example, student hospitals across the country are places of experimentation, serious experimentation. And somehow it strikes me as possibly a worse situation than the one with prisoners, because most of us never knew we were experimental animals at the time, and had no recourse once we found out what happened.

During the sixties students could get embroiled in the question of experimentation on prisoners, but few could admit to themselves that they are also prisoners of experimentation. This is a completely untapped question—is it one that would interest the authors of this paper? As is pointed out in Wildavsky's Oakland project report ". . . we found a distribution pattern than favored both extremes. Some mechanisms were biased toward the rich. Other mechanisms favored the poor. We discovered no examples of mechanisms that favor the middle."

Sincerely yours,

Laura Nader
Professor of Anthropology

November 5, 1975
Charles J. White

Special Committee on Youth Education for Citizenship
American Bar Association
Chicago, Illinois

Dear Charles White:

I have put off answering your letter of August 25 vacillating between tossing the thing out and trying to communicate what I think is wrong with your Teacher Training Notes.

Mainly such memos, outlines, etc., which most professionals churn out are lacking in substantive information, while focusing on procedure and organizations' administration which is a technique like it or not of avoiding why we are doing all this in the first place. Analyze the words in these pages. There is no reference to citizens, to the troubles they face, or to the problems that we as a nation face. A workshop is only interesting if it has a subject matter, who cares whether it is two weeks, three weeks, or more. Who is it that we are teaching? The word children doesn't appear. The reason the guts of the matter don't appear is because programs like ours end up feeding on themselves, while the purpose of the program is to expose professionals like ourselves. That is the problem with schools in general, just look at Berkeley, the second richest school district in the world is in the red with professionals screaming for more.

In sum, if I were a bright teacher and saw this I would have tossed it into the basket.
Sincerely yours,

Laura Nader
Professor of Anthropology

November 19, 1975

Dear Dr. Nader:

I am presently a Peace Corps Volunteer in the Marshall Islands, and though my specific job here is to assist with the formation of a small atoll-wide consumers cooperative and copra warehouse, I have recently stumbled upon something that provides the basis for my writing you stone-cold.

The atoll on which I will spend another year (Utirik) is one of the two populated atolls in the Marshalls which received a dose of radioactive fallout from a so-called "incident" in March of 1951. According to the Atomic Energy Commission (now ERDA), the "incident" occurred because of "wind shifts" which carried the fallout in an easterly direction instead of the predicted westerly direction. And even I accepted this line of reasoning perpetrated by the AEC until I read the 1972 Congress of Micronesia's Report on Rongelap and Utirik which probed a little deeper than the AEIR would have liked.

It turns out that several details surrounding that particular test in March, 1954 have been left unexplained, and for that reason I would like to initiate proceedings for a class action suit against the AEC (and possibly against the Dept. of Defense also), and would be appreciative of any advice you might be able to offer.

To elucidate the issue I will divide the "incident" into three categories (1) the decision to test despite missing wind information, (2) the absence of pre-test warnings and precautions to the nearby local inhabitants, and (3) the delay in the evacuation of those radiated.

By far, it is the first category that remains the most enigmatic even to this day. The nuclear test in question was the second of the hydrogen tests (code-named "Bravo"), and because it was to be a fission-fusion device (instead of the less-powerful fission and fission-fusion devices prior to the hydrogen test series) it was expected to be greater than any of the preceding seventy tests. And it was by a factor of three.

Now comes the peculiar part: The AEC was lacking wind information from the 90,000ft level and above, and despite this vital void in wind information the decision was made to proceed with the test. A statement from a meteorologist at the Nevada Grounds during the time of the 1954 test is quite revealing, and indicates that "with our sophisticated weather equipment we can almost determine where the fall-out will land" (quoted from the Congress of Micronesia's Report). Additionally, the AEC's excuse of "wind shifts" does not make sense, because if there were indeed shifts in the wind that would presuppose their knowledge of the wind's activity. But in fact, they had no such knowledge.

In the second category, it is curious to note that there was no consideration at all given to the island populations near the test site of Bikini Atoll. Several people here and on Rongelap received radiation burns which could have been either avoided or minimized had the people been forewarned to stay indoors or submerged in the lagoon in the event of accidental fallout. In fact, there are reports that some people even tasted the snow-like precipitate to determine what it was. A preparatory briefing with the nearby island populations by the AEC would have reduced the level of exposure, and would have reduced the consequent effects which I will discuss momentarily.

The third category centers around the evacuation of the local inhabitants following the test. It took a full forty-eight hours to evacuate the people of

Rongelap and seventy-five hours to evacuate the people of Utirik, even though the AEC knew "something went wrong" just fifteen minutes after the test. This may be a moot point, but I think perhaps they could have done better.

As far as the medical problems associated with the radiation, all has been relatively quiet until recently with only a few reported cases of stillbirths and miscarriages. About a year ago, a young man from Rongelap died of leukemia, and though the AEC is tight-lipped about his death, they do admit the possible connection between his leukemia and the effects of radiation (I would be curious to see how a similar death would be brushed off so casually with a Beverly Hills family). Also, during the last ten years numerous cases of nodules on the thyroid gland (some malignant) have been discovered, and though only five have been detected from Utirik, (all female. . .) about twenty have been detected in Rongelap. And this from a combined population of only 1,000 people.

Dr. Nader, I am a recent graduate of the University of California at San Diego where I studied anthropology, and having read George Foster's *Applied Anthropology* I feel obligated to scratch the surface of what I feel to be an AEC white-wash. I ask for your assistance, and/or advice with the proposed class action suit, and by now you are probably wondering why I have decided to write to you. Well, I guess a part of the reason has to do with my brother Michael (a pediatrician) having taken some courses through the School of Public Health. He mentioned a few people who he had run across, one of whom was Dr. Margaret Mackenzie, and the other was Ralph Nader's sister/ anthropologist. And in all honesty it was your brother who vicariously tilted the odds in your favor, though I would be anxious to chat with Dr. Mackenzie upon my return.

I have appealed the case to a cousin of mine who lives in Los Angeles. She is a professor at UCLA's School of Law, and shares a private practice with her husband, and they are both anxious to take the case immediately. My only hesitation is with their proposed terms: they will take the case on a contingency basis with a fifteen percent fee. Now, if these people win their case, they would most likely be awarded a considerable sum of money (e.g., the Bikini people now living on Kili were recently awarded a three million dollar trust fund), and I for one would not like to have to explain to the people here about the disappearance of fifteen percent of their money.

Am I being too idealistic in thinking that they could be represented for a smaller slice of pie?

Please let me know your feelings on this matter, and if you cannot find either the time or desire to help pursue with the uncovering of a suspected "can of worms" (e.g. Nixon), I will understand. And on the other hand, if you do decide to help, I (and the Utirikese and Rongelapese) will be very much indebted to you.

Please give it some thought.

Very truly yours,

Glenn H. Alcalay
Peace Corps
Majuro, Micronesia

December 8, 1975

Dear Laura:

Sorry to miss you Friday (Dec. 5). I waited around the Christmas tree in Fairmont lobby from 11 to 11:20 at which point I figured you had been delayed.

What I wanted to discuss with you were your experiences with our discipline as a closed system. It is remarkable when you think of it, that Lloyd Warner started studying American culture and American institutions 45 years ago. It looks as though the field may have gone backwards in this regard.

What continues to amaze me, though I don't know why it should—is that there are practically no (if any) peoples in the world whose lives have not been radically altered by Western technology. Furthermore, most "primitive" people don't want to be "studied" by Western anthropologists. As you suggest there is something condescending about the way we go about it. Some but not all of this antagonism is political, of course. But whatever the cause, who in the devil are anthropologists going to study?

Incidentally, regarding this pressure to conform, once at a large party I was castigated by a leading figure in our field for not doing what other anthropologists do, for not going out and finding myself a "primitive" tribe to study.

I spent several years with the Navajo and the Hopi when I was young under the auspices of a man who grew up on the reservation, in the days when the Indians were still killing occasional Whites and who had forgotten more about the Navajo than all the anthropologists I know put together. His first languages were Navajo and Spanish. At any rate, at the end of the first two years on the reservation it hit me that I not only would never know most of the important things about the Navajo (there wasn't time to learn them), but also that there was no suitable frame of reference in or outside of European anthropology for describing what I did know.

It wasn't until 20 years later that I developed the theories and descriptive frameworks that appeared in *The Silent Language*. Even this is not really satisfactory because each culture must be described in its own terms. At any rate, ever since then I have restricted myself to studying my own culture as its members interact with others around the world.

Do you have a reprint of the article you mentioned in your talk? I enjoyed your paper. All the more encouraging—given the general state of the field. Sincerely,

Edward T. Hall
Santa Fe, New Mexico

October 20, 1976

Dear Dr. Nader:

Perhaps you won't remember me. I gave you my card after your talk here in San Diego's Museum of Man last week. I'm the anthropologist who asked you how we might get a look at the unreleased report by Energy Research and Development Administration (ERDA) which flatly concludes that the U.S. cannot go on expanding its energy-use rate. (By the way, I phoned Marvin Olson at the Battelle Institute in Seattle, a firm doing social assessment work for ERDA and asked him if he had learned about such a report. He hadn't, but promised to ask around. Do you think Alan Cranston could pry it loose?) Trouble is, I do not know how to refer to it.

It was a pleasure to hear your views for a number of reasons. First, I do not feel quite as alone as I have since 1970—in studying such mundane un-anthropological topics as land-developers, community housing, self-sufficiency, crime, and so on (you could do this if you went to some far-off country, but certainly not in one's own university town). Secondly, I felt that the traditional training of anthropologists and their experience with living in small scale communities offered a valuable set of insights. I studied the Papagos of southern Arizona, you studied the Zapotecs. Though this experience did not convince me that I wanted to "go native" after two years, I did feel that they had more real fun, greater peace, less stress, more humility, etc., than any one group I had known. It is not surprising that some pleasant field work experiences lead anthropologists to set forth small-scale communities as really better places in which to live. Why do we want to change them? Why do they want to change?

Finally, your talk sent my mind racing back to Sapir's article "Culture, Genuine and Spurious" (1924) in which he described how an Indian fisherman doing his daily "thing" derived a greater significance and closure to his life in simply fishing than did the girl working on the telephone switchboard in our own culture. This piece by Sapir simply awakened a debate about the meaning of "progress" which I feel every anthropologist must answer for himself. The debate is as old as E. B. Tylor and Matthew Arnold in which to Arnold "culture" with a capital "C" meant mental progress, refinement, humane care, art, etc., but to Tylor it meant more—it meant material culture as well, complexity, etc. (Stocking's Chap. H, "Matthew Arnold, E. B. Tylor and the Uses of Invention" p. 69 in *Race, Culture and Evolution*). But the physicists whom you mentioned as well as many anthropologists believe that in the long run, less energy simply means *less*—both to the developed and under-developed countries. For instance, Leslie White envisioned the world state emerging from nuclear or fusional energy. Though he studied physics, I feel that White would not be as four-square for nuclear energy today as he was in the 1960s.

Well, I enjoyed your visit. Let me know if you learn the title of the ERDA Report or where I can see it.

With appreciation,

Richard D. Jones (Ph.D)
San Diego, California

December 10, 1976
Chief Justice Warren E. Burger

United States Supreme Court
Washington, D.C.

Your Honor:

I was sorry to read that you had joined in supporting Justice William H. Rehnquist's majority opinion on the pregnancy-pay benefits case. Your decision did not place the question in readiness of enlightened and fair legislative action.

I wonder if you are aware that paid pregnancy leaves are provided in most of the advanced countries of Western Europe, as well as dozens of much poorer developing nations of the world. I wonder if any of the justices (majority or dissent) thought about the rights of children. In Hungary the six month full-pay and 2-1/2 year half-pay plans were meant to improve the home environment for children. The United States is the only major industrialized country that does not have a family policy.

In a country where less than 7% are self-employed, we need to think more carefully about the obligations of employers to the well-being of their employees and to the families of those employees. Discrimination may be the legal issues on the pregnancy pay benefits case, but the broader question is, can the law contribute to improving the quality of life for the majority of citizens, and if it cannot, can law survive?

Sincerely yours,

Laura Nader
Professor of Anthropology

June 1, 1977
James R. Brown, M.D.

Director
Berkeley: Student Health Service

Dr. James Brown:

I am sorry not to have responded to your May 10 letter earlier, but the end of the year is associated with a pile of work.

I was somewhat puzzled by your letter. *The Daily Californian* called me just as they had called you—without previous contact.

With regard to our discussion: I did state that I would send you a copy of the preliminary student proposal, and a copy of that preliminary proposal is enclosed. I did say that I would call you prior to proceeding with work at Cowell in order that you might explain the best way to use the time of the Cowell Hospital staff. I would proceed in this way in the spirit of cooperation, and not because I do not view the Cowell staff as free agents. Presently our work does not deal with the Cowell staff, but with students.

Re: your query on whether I believed that students in clinics are sometimes treated like guinea pigs. I was one while attending a prestigious university. There is presently a lawsuit against the University of Chicago for using students as guinea pigs, and as you have undoubtedly read about the University of Michigan case, doctors have been fired from student clinics because they are using students in drug company experiments. The exploitation of students is not novel in and out of the medical field, so why are you surprised?

As soon as classes are over and you have had time to look at the proposal, please let me know. I will be grateful if you could find time for a talk before June 25th.

Sincerely,

Laura Nader
Professor of Anthropology

June 1, 1977

Dear Laura:

Following the recent CONAES meeting I finally found time to read through the May 2nd draft of the CLOP [Consumption, Location, and Occupational Patterns] report. I was rather happy with it, particularly the combination of topics treated and the distribution of emphasis among them. It has certainly taken a much more graceful form than the earlier versions. I was especially happy that you found it possible to retain a generous summary of the comparisons among alternative futurist scenarios. I think this is a most valuable contribution and a counterweight to the vulgar numerology of the main CONAES scenarios which were just aborning (or aborting, as the case may be) as of the end of last month.

I suppose you will have at least one more round of editing of your report. I hope the style can be made a little more consistent from one chapter to another and that you will eliminate the vestigial technocratic locutions, such as "time frame" (for period of time) and "maximize" (for increase).

I noted, with approval, your departure from the conventional assumption as to the gender of the reader, p. 238. Sever and I find it possible to use about equal numbers of "he's" and "she's" in referring to the readers or other anonymous persons such as investigators.

It may be possible to get a little of the "changed attitudes" scenario into the final CONAES report. At least I am prepared to fight to the last ditch for it. Since Brooks and Hollander are determined to have a consensus report, I think I can defend an ultimatum for at least one such topic although it will no doubt be necessary to make all sorts of concessions concerning the language used in presenting the scenario.

You may be interested in this fragment of a conversation:

1.   S. Houthakker: "The trouble with the CLOP report is that it is a political document."
2.   ODD: "Yes, all our reports are political documents."

Best regards.

Otis Dudley Duncan
Professor of Sociology
The University of Arizona

April 15, 1978
President David Saxton

University of California, Berkeley

Dear President Saxton:

I was sorry to note that your argument for the inadequacy of faculty salaries as printed in *The Daily Californian* on Wednesday April 12, 1978 was accompanied by a picture whose caption read: "The men in this picture are some of the early pioneers in nuclear energy. Will rising inflation and low salaries force scholars like those pictured to find jobs elsewhere?" Faculty salaries are in bad enough straits without having to associate the faculty question with the nuclear question which is to say the least controversial in the state. I could imagine a number of people in Sacramento and elsewhere might have read that caption and thought, "We might be better off today if all those men had gone elsewhere."

Another thought that might have entered into people's thinking while reading your argument is: "Has the University considered streamlining its heavy administrative structures in order to transfer funds from administration to faculty support." Have you taken a position on redistribution of funds within the University budget?

Thank you for your attention, and for the work you have done to date. Sincerely yours,

Laura Nader
Professor of Anthropology

May 2, 1978

Dear Laura Nader:

Imagine: an anthropologist demanding "real world" and bottom-up planning from the technocrats (images of Daniel, Jeanne d'Arc, etc.)! Your lecture to Dan Rose's class and luncheon discussion afterward warmed the cockles of this cynical heart.

But the doubt remains nevertheless. This country has a resilient population that time and again has responded or at least coped with crisis after crisis. Your example of the California drought illustrates this well. But can the country be persuaded to implement fundamental lifestyle (to use your loaded word) changes in order to prevent catastrophe 20 to 30 years hence? Planners of all persuasions have to operate with the "oil crisis" albatross around their necks. In other words, short of manufacturing new crises, how do we make people believe, especially when the planners themselves are perceived to be in disagreement? To fight off the always encroaching sense of futility I suppose one has to become convinced on the "nobility" of the cause, and play Sartre's Sisyphus. Who knows? Maybe when someone isn't looking that damned rock will stay up there.

Enough of superficial polemics. I've enclosed a couple of our recent titles to illustrate some of what we've been doing here at the Press. Also included is the recent Meier/Crane article in *Society*. So it can be done; the crux centers on implementation.

Cordially yours,

John McGuigan
University of Pennsylvania Press

May 16, 1978
Dr. John Raleigh

Chairman, Berkeley Division
Academic Senate

Dr. Raleigh:

Given the questions that are being raised as to faculty "contract hours" and outside employment, I think a comparison with the Senate Legislature is appropriate, and I write this letter to call your attention to possible comparisons that could be made in an attempt to clarify the position of the University.

I am aware that certain State legislators, among others, have suggested that California university faculty salaries be related in some way to the hours spent by each recipient in the classroom teaching. The suggestion apparently emanates from a concern that the State paid university faculty members are teaching only part-time. Paying teachers on this basis would be inequitable since classroom appearances are but a small and highly variable portion of a faculty member's responsibilities. Preparation for class consumes far more time than may be spent in the class. Further, this preparation time will vary a great deal depending on the nature of the course, the method of teaching used and even the size of the class. After class work also varies according to these parameters. For example, one cannot grade and evaluate 100 papers while class is in session.

In addition to class preparation outside of class, faculty members have a responsibility to keep current on the happenings in their area of expertise, and to advance the fund of human knowledge themselves if possible. Faculty members are also responsible for much of the governance of the university, serving on committees determining everything from cafeteria planning to curriculum. And faculty members keep office hours to be available to students as counsellors at a critical period in their lives.

It would appear the Legislature could apply the "work for pay" criteria to itself more fruitfully. Perhaps salaries could be pro-rata adjusted based on committee hearings attended or floor votes cast, or some combination of the above. To be sure, such activities are only a part of the legislator's duties, but they would appear to be at least as important to his function as classroom appearances are to a teacher.

Turning to the issue of banning outside employment, here the Legislature has but a clearer mirror to examine. Legislators are now paid $25,555 a year with numerous fringe benefits (see Government Code Sections 8901–8903). Further legislators may pursue outside employment totally unrelated to their legislative responsibilities. (See native implication of Government Code Section 3625).

In the 1971 Fellmeth study of California land use policies, he looked at the State legislator's occupations. From the official biographies of the members of the legislatures (written by them), 25 of the 120 members served as full time legislators. The remaining 95 described themselves as active attorneys, ranchers, contractors, etc. Furthermore, 19 of 25 attorneys surveyed offered their services of their office and of the legislator personally on land use matters. (See Policies of Land by Fellmeth (Grossman, 1975, Appendix 12E p. 668). He found that 55% of the Senate and 60% of the Assembly had some sort of personal profit stake in land use based on outside occupation.

It would appear that outside employment and research by university faculty would augment teaching responsibilities more than occupational conflicts of public interest consuming time, and perhaps affecting viewpoint on matters of public policy would complement a legislator's proper function.

I think it about time that the UC faculty change its defensive posture to one that examines questions raised about our status in some broader context. Sincerely yours,

Laura Nader
Professor of Anthropology

June 20, 1978

Dear Professor Nader,

Our study on the "Future Conduct of American Foreign Policy" has been officially launched. I am convinced we got off to a good start. The Advisory

Council discussions held from 10:00am to noon July 14th were lively and most helpful.

The attached booklet spells out the scope of our study. We followed the agenda as shown herein, but the discussion ranged far beyond this agenda. Several subjects not mentioned on the agenda will be considered for possible study in the future.

Senator Fulbright felt that we should examine in a thorough and fundamental way the whole question of Soviet intentions. Consideration was also given to a task force studying the question of illegal immigration from Mexico into the United States.

There was a good deal of discussion about making international economics an integral part of the overall study. I was pleased to announce that the Honorable Paul McCracken has agreed to serve on our advisory panel.

Following the morning meeting and luncheon a well attended press conference was held in the AEI conference room. The attached press release will give you some idea of what went on.

I am sorry you were not able to attend the meeting, but everyone certainly understood.

If the attached information raises any questions please drop me a note to the above address or give me a call. I am not in this office very much, but Ms. Jennifer Fitzgerald can get hold of me promptly.

More later, but you will be pleased to know that Senator Bob Griffin of Michigan has agreed to join the Advisory Council.
Sincerely,

George Bush
American Enterprise Institute for Public Policy Research
Washington D.C.

December 24, 1978

Dear Laura,

Your short note of inquiry about Veblen's notion of "trained incapacity" taps a longish chapter on the transmission of ideas. Your asking whether the idea-cum-term has been passed on by oral tradition hints that you might suspect this to be the case. Since others have asked me about Veblen's compelling term, and since as a sociologist of scientific knowledge I've long been interested in patterns of the transmission of ideas, and since this case in my own backyard exemplifies one such pattern, I'll indulge myself at your expense during this holiday season by going into far more detail than you need or want if only to get this story transformed from the oral to the written tradition (some quasi-sorites!).

To begin with, and so far as I know, the term "trained incapacity" appears only once in the entire corpus of Veblen's writings. I had come upon it during my graduate student days and was at once impressed by both the idea and the evocative term which says much in little. When I began my teaching at Harvard in the mid-1930s I drew upon the powerful idea, and tried to put it to work in connection with processes of socialization and social change. Thus, so far it was wholly a matter of oral transmission of an idea. It was not until 1940 when I put one of these lectures into print—"Bureaucratic Structure and Personality," which was reprinted in *Social Theory & Social Structure*—that part of the oral tradition was converted into print.

I run a bit ahead of the story. Once I encountered Veblen's largely unelaborated idea-cum-term, I naturally searched the "literature" for discussions of it. For a time I had no success at all. Joseph Dorfman's magisterial biography *Thorstein Veblen and His America* had just appeared (my copy of it gives a November 1934 publication date), but though J.D. carefully summarizes each of Veblen's books, he takes no note of "trained incapacity." Kenneth Burke alone referred to the notion in his *Permanence and Change* (1935), along with references to Dewey's "occupational psychosis" and Warnotte's "professional deformation," both of which were entirely new to me. Since Burke had collated this trio of related ideas, I cited his usage of "trained incapacity"—the only one to have picked up Veblen's idea in so many words. Because neither Burke nor I gave specific page references to Veblen, we apparently became the main conduits for the passage of Veblen's term-cum-variously-implied-and-applied concept into later writings which make use of it. One basis for this inference is my having often come upon allusions to "trained incapacity" but never with a specific citation to the one place (so far as I know) in which the term appears in all his voluminous writings. A second more specific reason for assuming this mode of transmission is the frequency with which the term has been ascribed to me in print. Although I expressly introduce the term in the paper on bureaucracy by referring to Veblen's concept of "trained incapacity," the term has ever since been ascribed to me with embarrassing frequency. It is not too far-fetched an inference then in light of this misattribution, and the absence of specific citations to Veblen's only explicit use of the term, that it has had a largely mediated rather than direct transmission.

Simply for the record of this abbreviated case—history in the transmission of a socio-psychological idea, and at the cost of a hidden blush of embarrassment, I note a few of these misattributions that appear in my files on palimpsests (about which another few words later):

> "Unburdened, in other words, with the trained incapacity (as Merton has put it) that afflicts so many of us today," (E. Digby Baltzell, *American Sociological Review*, June 1965, 434).
>
> "Merton's notion of 'trained incapacity' (Merton, *Social Theory & Social Structure* 1957, pp. 197), may also be applied to the profession of journalism," (Karl Erik Rosengren, Peter Arvidson & Dahn Suresson, "The Barsebäck Titanic: A Radio Programme as a Negative Summary Event," *Acta Sociologica* 1975, 18, 318).
>
> ". . . the theoretical social sciences . . . are not mature enough to create a basis for reliable practical recommendations; they develop excellent cognitive skills but are subject to what Robert Merton calls 'trained incapacity.'" (Adam Podgorecki, *Practical Social Sciences*, London: Routledge Kegan-Paul, 1975, 104).

And for one more marginal rather than pure case which hints at this mediated transmission without misascribing the term . . . see the informative analysis of "traditional" and "participatory" models of client-professional relationships (in a sample of some 60 cases of legal handling of personal injury problems); "Unreflective routinization of non-routine tasks has been referred to as the 'trained incapacity' of certain workers. Robert Merton, 'Bureaucratic Structure and Personality,' in his *Social Theory & Social Structure*, rev., ed., . . . 1957, 197–8" (Douglas E. Rosenthal, *Lawyer and Client: Who's In Charge?*, N,Y: Russell Sage Foundation, 1977).

What we seem to have at work here is something I once dared describe as a "palimpsestic syndrome" (palimpsest properly defined would have been better): . . . in the transmission of ideas each succeeding repetition tends to erase all but one antecedent version, thus producing what may be described as the anatopic or palimpsestic syndrome (*On the Shoulders of Giants*, 1965, 218; also 218–9n). With some medieval to modern cases in point, I propose much too briefly, even elliptically how it is that "the altogether innocent transmitter becomes identified as the originator of the idea when his merit lies only in having kept it alive, or in having brought it back to life after it had long lain dormant or perhaps in having put it to new and instructive use" (OTSOG, 219n).

The reconstruction of the process in that passage refers however, to the special case of a palimpsestic error of attribution, the case in which the name of the originating scholar does not appear at all in the course of transmission;

thus: "Naturally enough, most of us tend to attribute a striking idea or for-mulation to the author who first introduced us to it. But often, that author has simply adopted or revived a formulation which he (and others versed in the same tradition) knows to have been created by another. The transmitters may be so familiar with its origins that they mistakenly assume these to be well-known. Preferring not to insult their readers knowledgeability, they do not cite the original source or even refer to it. And so it turns out that the altogether innocent transmitter . . ." (see the preceding II of this letter for the rest of this passage).

But in the cases of the palimpsest pattern in the transmission of ideas, the originating author explicitly referred to as with Burke's and my allusions to Veblen's idea of "trained incapacity," or (to continue this letter for the files) as with this case in point:

Here is Charles Sanders Peirce noting by mere juxtaposition of the first mediating passage, and later paraphrase how his term "pragmatism" has been fathered upon another who obfuscated its actual parentage. Peirce sets down the following pair of quotations:

> ". . . the whole subsequent argument has already had its main lines mapped out by our introductory discussion of that Weltanschauung which Professor James has called 'pragmatism'—F. C. S Schiller" (in *Personal Idealism*, ed. by Henry Cecil Sturt, 1902, p. 63).
>
> "The passage of Professor James here alluded to is as follows: 'Mr. Charles Sanders Peirce has rendered thought a service by disentangling from the particulars of its application the principle by which these men were instinctively guided, and by singling it out as fundamental and giv-ing to it a Greek name. He calls it the principle of pragmatism,'—William James" (*The Varieties of Religious Experience*, 1902, p. 444).

(This engaging and potentially instructive case of palimpsestic misattri-bution can be found in the *Collected Papers of Charles Sanders Pierce*, ed. by Charles Hartshorne & Paul Weiss, Harvard U. Press, 1965, V, 9n.).

All this only serves to narrow down the problem of the palimpsest in the transmission of ideas. For the time being, I'm prepared to accept that my supposal about the types of cases in which the intermediaries assume that the origins of an idea are so well-known that they do not refer to it to avoid insulting their readers' assumed knowledgeability, and to preclude their own embarrassment at stating a presumably universal bit of information. It would be downright embarrassing to most of us I suspect, to find ourselves putting into print:

"To be, or not to be; that is the question" as Shakespeare has Hamlet ask in a famous play.

And so it is that readers or listeners coming upon a howsoever well-known phrase or idea for the first time are inclined to attribute it to the author who first introduced them to it, especially when said mediating author has not referred to the presumably "universally known" originator. This form of the palimpsest was adopted by the immortal P. G. Wodehouse in all those many Edwardian comedies featuring Bertie Wooster and the unflappable Jeeves, as Bertie is forever attributing to his learned valet aphorisms and turns of phrase that enjoyed evident distinction. Consider these few which I have on tap from the hundreds or like kind:

> ". . . my brow was sicklied over with the pale cast of thought, as I have heard Jeeves put it."
>
> "I remember Jeeves once saying that sleep knits up the raveled sleeve of care. Balm of hurt minds, he described it as."
>
> "He looked at her with what I have heard Jeeves call a wild surmise."
>
> "'Tis not as deep as a well nor as wide as a church door, but 'tis enough, 'twill serve,' I said, recalling a gag of Jeeves's."

[This handful being from *Jeeves in the Offing*]

Again, in *Right Ho, Jeeves* Bertie Wooster ascribes to the inexhaustible Jeeves what Alfred Lord Tennyson might have liked to claim as the beginning of his *In Memoriam*:

> "I remember Jeeves who . . . has always had a neat turn of phrase, once speaking of someone rising on stepping stones of his dead self to higher things."

Or yet again, from *The Code of the Woosters*:

> "I remember Jeeves saying to me once, apropos of how you can never tell what the weather's going to do, that full many a glorious morning had he seen flatter the mountain tops with sovereign eye and then turn into a rather nasty afternoon."

To appreciate the Woosterian metaphrastic, one need only call to mind the lines from the Thirty-third Sonnet:

> "Full many a glorious morning have I seen flatter the mountain-tops with sovereign eye,
>
> > Kissing with golden face the meadows green,

Gilding pale streams with heavenly alchemy,
Anon permit the basest clouds to ride,
With ugly rack on his celestial face,
And from the forlorn world his visage hide,
Stealing unseen to west with this disgrace."

Tho' master of high burlesque reminiscent his special friendly way of the *Memoirs of Martinus Scriblerus*, Plum Wodehouse must not be allowed to divert us from the sobersided pattern of authentic cases of misattributions in scholarly work. It is notorious that parody often bemuses as it amuses.

It was probably a mistake to import Wodehouse's parodies into this account: too severe a change in tone and all that. But if you will allow them to fade into the remote background, I in turn will get on with patterns of misattribution in the transmission of ideas in scholarship and science, with the case of "trained incapacity" as our point of departure. In the simplest model, differing frequencies and kinds of misattribution of ideas are thought of as functions of the explicitness of citation. Again, for the sake of simplicity, let's consider only two attributes of citations to the source of an idea (or, in this case of 'trained incapacity' as is often the case, the source of a term-cum-idea): the originating author is explicitly mentioned or not; the exact citation to the source is provided, or not.

Originating Author Exact Citation to publish source
Explicitly stated (book or journal pages, etc.)

1.	Fewest misattributions	+	−
2.	Tends towards palimpsests	+	−
3.	Null case	+	+
4.	OBI ("Obliteration of source by incorporation in currently accepted knowledge)	−	−

First, a few words about the simplification into dichotomies (originating author; + exact citation; +). We know that there are intermediate gradations of these attributes which cross-tabulated would generate more fine-grained distinct situations; for example, the case of citation to a particular book but without specific page numbers. But these are matters of successive approximation, and in any case, here we are on page 6 of a response to your one inquiry, and I'm not at all certain that you are still with me. If you are not otherwise occupied, and are following this non-linear account with me, let's agree to save such finer discriminations for another time.

Next then, a few more words about the four logically generated "types" of citation and reinforcing behavior which it is being conjectured, should lead to differing rates and kinds of misattribution. (As you will have noted, in the limiting type 4, this involves non-attribution rather than misattribution).

We eliminate type 3 as an empirically non-existent case; if an exact citation has been given to the original source, then ipso-facto the originating author will have been indicated.

Type 1 citation behavior in which both author and publication source are explicit would presumably lead to the lowest rate of misattributions. Yet we know that even under these conditions, as in the case of the attribution of pragmatism to James rather than Peirce, such errors of attribution can occur. I won't set down some obvious conjectures about what might bring about these (presumably) occasional misattributions even under conditions of full citation to the originating source. (Time as well as space now run short as we approach the festive eve).

Type 2 in which the originating author is explicitly identified (e.g. my reference to "Veblen's concept of "trained incapacity"), but where the specific reference is not given, will produce the-most misattribution. This will take the form of palimpsests in which the later usage effaces the original usage. Many readers do not make the considerable effort required to track down the original source—as you report "neither the young man assigned to the review nor I have been able to trace the original cites that you refer to on pp. 251–2 (most recent edition). I have checked your earlier editions and the Burke reference also with no luck." Few make the effort, and the others know nothing more about the originating treatment of the idea beyond what they have read in the work which called the idea to their attention? Not having read the original source they cannot know whether the idea has been faithfully transmitted, whether it has in fact been misrepresented, or developed, or generalized, or put to new and instructive use. Under these conditions the marginal memory trace of the mentioned originating author fades, and the author who introduced them to the received or developed idea is remembered as the originator. Nor can the distinctive contribution (if any) of the intermediaries to the development of the idea be identified and understood. The palimpsest may thus represent a double error in understanding the development of an idea in the course of its transmission: the misattribution means that the originating author of the idea gets lost to view, as do the cognitive changes taking place in the biography of the idea. And to the extent that the reward-system of science and scholarship calls for credit to be given where credit is due, the palimpsest represents a flaw in its operation.

Since the case of "trained incapacity" as term-cum-idea is clearly a type-2 situation (the originating author explicitly stated but without exact citation to the work(s) in which it can be found), I'll want to get back to it—promptly and specifically. But first a little more of the type-4 situation in which both the originating author, and the specific citation are unstated. This is a pattern which has interested me for the last dozen years or so, ever since I came to recognize it as a pattern akin to that of the palimpsest. As you see, this is described as a pattern of "obliteration of source of ideas or findings by their incorporation in currently accepted knowledge"—obliteration by incorporation, or OBI for short.

The notion of OBI emerged in connection with a problem which has long interested you anthropologists: the forms of selective accumulation that take place in various branches of knowledge. In the interest of conserving time and space and of precluding possible errors of paraphrase, I reproduce the formulation:

> "Because the theory and findings of the fairly remote past are largely incorporated into cumulative present knowledge in the more exact sciences, commemoration of the great contributors of the past is substantially reserved to the history of the discipline. Scientists at their work-benches and in their papers make use primarily of the more recent contributions which have developed these earlier discoveries. The result of this practice is that earlier and often much weightier scientific contributions tend to be obliterated (though not without occasional and sometimes significant exceptions) by incorporation into later work. In the humanities, by direct contrast each classical work (poem, drama, novel, essay, or historical work) tends to remain a part of the direct experience of succeeding generations of humanists. In short, firsthand acquaintance with classics plays a small role in the work of the physical and life scientists and a very large one in the work of humanistic scholars" (*Social Theory & Social Structure*, 1968 ed., 27–28).

In the process leading to the obliteration of the original source of the idea and of later developments of it, the number of explicit references to the antecedent contributions declines in the papers and books making use of it. To the extent that such cumulate obliteration does occur, itself an empirical question that is only beginning to be examined, ever explicit citations do not indicate the lineage of scientific work. Luckily, for at least the commemorative function of citational behavior as I have had occasion to note:

> "Every scientific discipline has some practitioners who take pleasure in keeping green the memory of developers of ideas though none, to my knowledge, more so than Paul Samuelson, master constructor of those freight-trains of eponyms which instantly catch up main lines

in a genealogy of ideas. An exact Hume-Ricardos-Marshall model of international trade can serve as an example of the hyphenated variety though a longer search would surely uncover as long a freight-train as the adjacency type exemplified in economic theory of index numbers associated with the names of Pigou, Kflnus, Keynes, Staehle, Leontief, Frisch, Lerner, G. D. Allen, Wald and my own theories of revealed preference" (*Sociological Ambivalence* (N.Y.: The Free Press, 1976, 130n).

But as we have seen with the misattributions of the palimpsestic type in which all antecedent formations but one are effaced, we cannot count on the "literature" regularly affording us the Samuelsonian kind of eponymous chain that succinctly registers the lineage of a historically evolving idea. After all it requires a detailed knowledge of the biography of an idea to provide those mnemonic links in the eponymous chain of cognitive development; a degree of retained information that is not given to all of us journeymen and journeywomen of science and scholarship.

The process of obliteration of sources through non-citation may operate particularly for certain kinds of knowledge. As intellectual influence runs deep it becomes less readily visible. Such profound influence may stem from acceptance of a tacit as well as explicit theoretical framework, or through long standardized procedures of scientific inquiry. As Joshua Lederberg once observed, "The work that everybody knows . . . is hardly cited at all!" (this, in his Foreword to Eugene Garfield's, *Essays of an Information Scientist*, Philadelphia: Institute for Scientific Information Press, 1977, xiii). In short, it may be canonical knowledge, the kind that is distilled in textbooks, that is most subject to obliteration of source.

But since the infrequent dual holiday eve draws ever closer (we are reminded that Christmas Eve and Chanukah Eve coincide only every 19 years), I shall give no further musings about OBI. In the improbable event that this pattern in the transmission of ideas might hold some interest for you, I substitute for further meanderings this short bibliography on the subject of OBI (including for your convenience items rendered redundant by prior citation).

You will infer, and rightly, that I have put this list of writings together by reaching out for materials on OBI which are immediately at hand. Still, I'll not extend the bibliographical search. Instead, I bring the context-bearing prelude to a close and now get directly, or almost so, to your query about the locus of Veblen's idea of "trained incapacity."

When Kenneth Burke in the first instance, and myself in the second were much taken with the idea of trained incapacity, (this back in the 1930s) we took care to identify the term-cum-concept as one of Veblen's characteristic ideas. We did not then have access to the supposition which I've stated a few pages back—that crediting an idea to an author without supplying an exact citation to its formulation leaves ample room for later misattribution of its source. It is proximately, if not ultimately clear why Burke provided no citation to Veblen's short explicit discussion of "trained incapacity": there are no such citations in the whole of Burke's *Permanence and Change*; and though we cannot account for his adopting this practice of general allusion rather than definite citation, we can understand that no exception would be made in the case of Veblen.

Nor can I reconstruct the reasons, if indeed there were reasons rather than only causes, for my not having provided an exact citation to Veblen's only use of the term "trained incapacity" that I knew of then (and the only one I still know of). And whatever the reasons or causes for my not having done so when I first published "Bureaucratic Structure & Personality" in 1940 after having lectured on the subject for several years, those reasons would not hold for the three editions (in 1949, 1957 and 1968) of *Social Theory & Social Structure* in which that article with its use of the idea of trained incapacity was reprinted. I might of course have revised the allusion and supplied the exact reference in these successive reprintings. But the plain fact is that I never got round to revise any references and citations in those enlarged editions. As a result, the reference to Veblen's concept of "trained incapacity" remained untidily general rather than operationally specific. And to the best of my knowledge, so it remains with all subsequent published allusions to the concept. None gives a specific reference to what is still for me the lone appearance of the term "trained incapacity" in the Veblen oeuvre.

This sustained silence about the specific location of the term presents us with a puzzle which differs fundamentally from the puzzle of the origin of the aphorism: "if I have seen further [sic], it is by standing on the shoulders of giants." There the originating question was whether the widespread attribution of the aphorism to Newton was correct. And of course it could scarcely have been more mistaken. The search for the actual genealogy of that idea with all its many implications for an understanding of the selective accumulation of scientific knowledge, took us through centuries of learning. But in the case of "trained incapacity," the general provenance of the term is undeniable. We know its creator. (Indeed, to put it even more strongly, if the powerful historical context of this phrase did not preempt our attending to its literal meaning, we might say that we know its onlie begetter.) Here, the puzzle is rather: why the fairly widespread reference in print to "trained incapacity" with nary a precise citation, so far as I can tell to Veblen's only explicit use of the term?

And having introduced the puzzle, I freely confess that I cannot solve it. Not at least in these waning moments of the pre-festive afternoon. That the term-cum-idea was largely transmitted in mediated rather than direct fashion, as some of the evidence suggests, may account for part of what we observe in the matter of non-citation. But this leaves much unaccounted for. Surely, many a generation of reader, including some destined to be scholars and scientists of one stripe or another, must have read Veblen's book in which the term appears. And I like to think that some of these in turn resonated to the term-cum-concept enough to make use of it. Why then the seeming evidence that they typically came upon the term in one or another mediated form rather than directly? The puzzle remains, and I'd be indebted to you for indicating the form of its solution.

Here then is the specific answer to your query. To the best of my knowledge, the term "trained incapacity" appears only once in Veblen's writings: in *The Instinct of Workmanship: And the State of the Industrial Arts* (New York: The Viking Press, 1937, p. 34).

I give you this edition because it is more accessible than the first edition published in 1914 by Macmillan. The text remains wholly unchanged in later printings. The context of the usage is provided by a theme to which Veblen adverted repeatedly in many of his dozen or so books: the basic irreconcilable clash between industry and business, production and profit-making, even workmanship and salesmanship—between the "industrial incompetence of the "financial captains of industry" and the industrial competence of the engineer. Here is the passage in which the term appears:

> "Of course, all this working at cross purposes (in the 'community at large' as well as particular sections and classes of the 'industrial community') is not altogether due to *trained Incapacity* (emphasis supplied with retrospective wisdom) on the part of the several contestants to appreciate the large and general requirements of the industrial situation; perhaps it is not even due to such inability, but rather to an habitual, and conventionally rightful disregard of other than pecuniary considerations. It would doubtless appear that a *trained Incapacity* (emphasis inserted) to apprehend any other than the immediate pecuniary bearing of their maneuvers accounts for a larger share in the conduct of the businessmen who control industrial affairs than it does in that of their workmen, since the habitual employment of the former holds them more rigorously and consistently to the pecuniary valuation of whatever passes under their hands; and the like should be true only in a higher degree of those

who have to do exclusively with the financial side of business," (*The Instinct of Workmanship*, 347–8).

But though the term appears only in this one passage, much of the idea condensed in the term recurs in most of Veblen's books. At least, as it seems to me somewhat unsurprisingly. It is fair to say that Veblen set out practically all the major themes of his lifework in: his early writings *The Theory of the Leisure Class* (1899) and *The Theory of Business Enterprise* (1904), as well as the now special work *The Instinct of Workmanship* in 1914. The rest of his life was given over to developing the varied applications and extensions of these ideas.

One of Veblen's long lasting interests was in what he liked to call "training," what later sociologists and psychologists would describe as "socialization." It is possible to show that the thematics of "training," as developed by Veblen, led him to problems in diverse fields; in the sociology of knowledge (with differing "propensities," "perspectives," and "traditions" deriving for example, from differing relations of businessmen and workmen to technological processes of industry); in the psychology of recurrent behavior patterns; and of most immediate interest, in maladaptive as well as adaptive socialization (i.e. training).

And so it is that although the term "trained incapacity" appears that once in *The Instinct of Workmanship*, the thematics which gives the term its explicit and tacit conceptual interest appears repeatedly. Your patience and my time having been just about exhausted, I won't develop this interpretation of Veblen's notion at length. But for the sake of future ready use, I'll collate in what has evolved into a non-linear memorandum for the files, just a few of the many places in which Veblen enlarges upon both the term, and the concept of "trained incapacity."

Thematic Resonances To "Trained Incapacity" in Veblen

"The mere mechanics of conformity to the schedule of living implies a degree of *Trained Insight* and a facile strategy in all manner of quantitative [sic] adjustments and adaptations, particularly at the larger centers of population, where the routine is more comprehensive and elaborate" (*Instinct of Workmanship*, 314).

"And then the 'money power' comes in as a third *Pecuniarily Trained* factor . . ." (Ibid. 347).

"The point of immediate interest here is the further bearing of the machine process upon the growth of culture—the disciplinary effect which this movement for standardization and mechanical equivalence has upon the human material. If this *discipline* falls more immediately on the workmen in the mechanical industries, and only less immediately on the rest of the community which lives in contact with this sweeping machine process . . ." (*The Enterprise*. NY: Scribners, 1934, 306 7ff).

"It is safe to say that such habituation (to machine work) brings a change in the workman's habits of thought, in the direction, method, and content of his thinking, heightening his intelligence *for some purposes and lowering it for certain others*" (Ibid. 313n).

"The thinking required by the pecuniary occupations proceeds on grounds of conventionality, whereas that involved in the industrial occupations runs, in the main, on grounds of mechanical sequence or causation, to the neglect of conventionality. The *institution* (habit of thought) of ownership or property is a conventional fact . . ." (Ibid. 318–9).

"The spiritual attitude given by *this training* in reasoning derived from pecuniary premises to pecuniary conclusions is necessarily conservative . . . the intellectual activities of other classes such as soldiers, politicians, the clergy, and men of fashion, moves on a plane of still older conventions, so that if the *training given by business employments* is to be characterized as conservative, that given by these other, more archaic employments should be called reactionary" (Ibid. 321).

And now, ten years before the term "trained incapacity" appears in *The Instinct of Workmanship*, is the essential idea though still in a static rather than dynamic sense of adaptation to one set of conditions meaning maladaptation to a significantly different set:

"Aptitude for the matter-of-fact work of the machine technology means, in a general way, ineptitude for an uncritical acceptance of institutional," (Ibid. 352).

And again, just a few years after use of the term "trained incapacity," Veblen applies the essential idea to the diverse competences and incompetencies of scientists and businessmen: which presumably develop from diverse "training" (i.e. socialization):

> "The *training* given by these two lines of endeavor (science and business) is wholly divergent; with the notorious result that for the purposes of "business enterprise" the scientists are the *most* ignorant and incompetent class in the community. They are not only passively out of touch with the business spirit, *out of training by neglect* but they are also *positively trained out of habit of the habit of mind indispensable to business enterprise*. The converse is true of the men of business," (*The Higher Learning in America*. Viking Press, 1965, 77.ff).

I should think that this might especially germane to your immediate purpose

Three years later, in *The Engineers and the Price System*, first published in 1918, the thematic idea appears in renewed and somewhat extended form. In effect, the idea states that the training, or more generally socialization that produces a capacity to perform one social role can serve to produce an incapacity for other social roles. In the course of these ancillary observations, Veblen creates a vocabulary of cognate terms:

> "*Trained* ignorance," (pg. 117) the disqualifications of having "been *trained* for business" (pg. 137).
>
> "Training in businesslike ways of thinking leaves them incapable of anything like an effectual insight into the use of resources or the needs and aims of productive industry . . . by *trained propensity* and tradition" (Ibid. 137).

And so there you have it, at least the barebones of the genesis and diffusion of the term-cum-idea of "trained incapacity." It begins with the lone appearance of the term (this always subject of course to so-far-as-I-know) in 1914 in *The Instinct of Workmanship*. After an apparent lapse of two decades the diffusion begins first with Kenneth Burke, and then with my own use and generalization of the concept. "Trained incapacity" is taken to designate in effect, a type of maladaptive socialization.

As a general concept of this sort, it is of course not confined to the trained incapacity of bureaucrats or of any other particular role; rather, it is a concept that alerts us to types of socialization that create perspectives, preferences, and perceptions which are adapted to the performance of one type of role and maladapted to the performance of others; in two-words, maladaptive socialization. Burke's and my explicit reference to Veblen's concept of "trained incapacity" both helps make for its diffusion and invites the kind of mis-attribution found in palimpsests.

Now all this will enter a new phase. When you cite the precise book and page for "trained incapacity," this will be again, to the best of my information, the first time that the citation will appear in print. A moment for the estimable *Yale Law Journal*. We shall have a degree of curiosity about this phase in the transmission of the idea.

Incidentally, the generic idea applied to social change rather than to co-existing, and structurally induced differences in capacities and perspectives emerges even earlier in Veblen's work. There it appears in the form of the collateral idea of "cultural lag" (if I may anachronistically adopt the term which would be introduced some years later), and perhaps quite independently of Veblen, by William F. Ogbury. But that as they say is another story, and surely not a story for this day.

With every good wish for what remains of the holiday season.

Yours,

Robert K. Merton
Columbia University
New York, NY

February 23, 1979

Dear Dr. Nader:

This office, the educational training branch of the Minnesota State Supreme Court, recently exhibited your fine film *To Make the Balance*. I am writing now to thank you for your help in securing the film and for making the film.

The film was shown at our 1979 Judicial Institute. That institute was designed as an initial orientation for all of our new trial judges. It attempted to give a primer on all aspects of the judicial role. Course offerings included sections of Traffic and DWI Matters, Conciliation Court, Probate Court, Civil Commitments and Judicial Demeanor.

Your film was shown as part of the Sentencing Seminar. It was used to show the very practical aspects of sentencing, and to display the rudimentary principles of the sentencing function. The comments of the Judges were that it caused them to reflect that although they consider the service of judging as one of the highest callings, stripped of all its rules and trappings they are in the business of determining what is right, fair, and equitable. It had a humbling effect which was quite positive.

The movie was previously shown here in 1975 to members of the Select Committee on the Courts of Minnesota. One of the members of that committee recommended the film as "one of the best he had ever seen." The Select Committee was informed of the film by a Minnesota State Senator who saw the film at a conference.

We found the film enlightening and extremely helpful in starting our new judges out with the proper perspective. Thank you for making the film.

Sincerely,

M. Kyle Aiken
Associate Director
Continuing Education for State Court Personnel
St. Paul, MN

November 13, 1979

Dear Professor Nader:

I found your presentation at the Georgetown Law faculty seminar on November 7th to be stimulating and informative. As I mentioned at the seminar, the adjudicatory process for occupational safety and health violations is a reasonably "closed litigation system" with several extra-adjudicatory mechanisms available. These mechanisms include labor-management grievances and collective bargaining generally, as well as closing conferences between labor, management, and the Labor Department when allegedly violative conditions have been identified during an inspection. In the past few years, employers have resorted to the adjudicatory process with increasing frequency as measured by the rate of contested inspections and the absolute caseload. Concurrently, settlement rate of cases in the adjudicatory process has increased. I am currently compiling the raw statistical data, and I would be glad to discuss the process in more detail if you think it might be useful in your study of litigation rates.

Two other topics arose during the seminar that deserve additional mention.

1) Attorneys and adjudicators have constructed an ideal model of the adjudicatory process—particularly the parties' expectations. However, the legal profession has given too little attention to the parties actual expectations regarding the adjudicatory process. For example, how do parties and the public prioritize expedition and timeliness of decisions as compared with dispositional thoroughness and informative decisions? More specifically, they are the actual expectations of the parties.

The number of cases initiated by employees and labor organizations are too small to draw any statistically significant conclusions, though there seems to be an emerging trend in employee participation in terms of the quality of the adjudicatory work product. In terms of expectations, do the parties differentiate between trial and appellate forums or different types of forums (e.g., U.S. Supreme Court, federal appeals court, and federal adjudicatory agencies)? How do institutional expectations conform, complement, modify, or negate these actual expectations of the parties? An understanding of these and related expectations is important in understanding the impact of various efforts to limit access, allocate adjudicatory resources, and implement docket management

2) Your comment on footnotes for your journal article was particularly interesting. I suggest that there are several additional reasons for the windfall of footnotes. Both of these relate to a basic search for authority.

Historical distance from the enabling charter such as the Constitution or an enabling statute requires judges to find authority to support propositions that may not be self-evident to their colleague or a reviewing authority. In addition, there is the need to find authority in order to counterbalance the erosion of public confidence in the institution's integrity. Finally, some footnotes are an attempt to break free from the constraints of an extremely limited adjudicatory issue in order to reach the actual controversy in dispute between the parties. This second type of footnote is more typically judicial dicta.

I regret that I was unable to join you for dinner after the seminar but I hope that we will be able to discuss these issues at greater length sometime in the future.
Sincerely,

Bertram Robert Cottine
Commissioner
Occupational Safety and Health Review Commission
Washington, D.C.

UNCOVERING ACADEMIC MINDSETS IN THE EIGHTIES

A Syrian physicist, Dr. Bizri, confirmed my points about science mindsets for his country after he read my "Barriers to Thinking New about Energy" piece.[1] Professor Clark Bullard writes that the "Barriers" paper is useful in teaching engineering. George Wald, a well-known Harvard biologist, speaks of changing attitudes in science since the beginning of the twentieth century. Others speak of the irrationality of scientists on discussions of energy, and Albert A. Bartlett comments on the "growth religion." Arno Penzias notes the lack of independent intellect among hard scientists. Jonathan Rowe, an investigative reporter, heard my talk when it was read on the radio. Claude Ginsburg speaks of the "technocratic establishment" and in 2018 wrote that he more than agreed with the young man who wrote the letter many years ago. C. Arthur Compton commented on physicists as technicians. A. B. Zahlan wrote from Lebanon that scientists in agriculture do the same. And I still get comments today on that Mitre talk!

Not all who wrote agreed with the "Barriers" critique. An Israeli physicist, Asher Peres, conflated support for solar energy policies to ancient beliefs in "sun gods," and dismissed concern over nuclear energy safety. Other rebutted comments were published in *Physics Today*. And when portions of my talk were published forty years later in the *Industrial Physicist*,[2] letters to the editor by engineers who strongly disagreed with my positions were both personal and emotional. My letter to the editor responded in the context of *longue durée* and human survival.

On another subject, my letter to the economics professor Roger Noll followed attendance at a conference on regulation during the Reagan years. The backlash against the 1960s consumer movement was starting. The paper I had presented, co-authored with my sister Claire Nader, was not well received.[3] In fact, one Berkeley sociology professor spoke up immediately: "I'm sorry you wrote this paper in a spirit of alienation." The move to the right in the United States spotlighted regulation. "A Wide Angle on Regulation" was for me basic anthropology. So we had a conflict of disciplines: economists thought of regulation as governmental, while anthropologists include a wider range of human behavior. The letter I wrote to Noll was about publication. When it looked like Noll did not want to include our article, I sent the piece out for parallel reviews—to anthropologists and law professors. The four-page letter from the Wisconsin law professor Stewart Macaulay was a comprehensive argument for why a wide angle was important—noting the reviewers lacked understanding of the subject matter: private government. Lawrence Friedman of Stanford Law followed suit, while the anthropologist Paul Bohannon suggested a more subtle approach. Ashraf Ghani, the current president of Afghanistan, examined Noll's economic research agenda. In the end, the piece was included in the book, and a book review of the collection selected our article as being of particular interest. The fact that during the 1980s I continued serving on the Carnegie Council on Children as well as the National Academy of Sciences Council on Nuclear and Alternative Energy Systems (CONAES) added to the diversity of the subject matter for letters to and from.

Apart from the cluster of letters on energy policies and regulation there were sporadic letters from fellow academics and the public on questions ranging from the anthropological debate over Derek Freeman's book on Margaret Mead and Samoa,[4] to prisons, dispute resolution policies, specific materials on cancer rates, and national laboratories.

One example was Pedro Mascheroni, a physicist at the Los Alamos National Laboratory, who wrote to me regarding the lack of academic freedom in university-affiliated laboratories. His employment had been wrongfully terminated when he went against the grain by pursuing research on a cheaper alternative to laser technologies that were favored by the laboratory management at the time. Before a review of his work had concluded, which ultimately found his conclusions to be sound and recommended that further research be conducted, he was "laid off" by the managers who were in favor of a competing technology. Although he was reinstated at a later date, he was then fired and stripped of his security clearance—effectively silencing him. All of this occurred after he brought his grievances to upper management and continued to advocate for further research, which had been halted despite the recommendations of the review panel. He reached out to university faculty in an effort to establish protections for academic freedom in the national laboratories. At the same time, Berkeley scientists formed a group called "Ousted Scientists" in an effort to do something about academic freedom in the labs as well.

In the end, after being permanently fired, Mascheroni was entrapped by the FBI and found guilty of revealing secrets to a foreign country. He spent several years in jail, as did his wife for co-conspiracy. By 2018, he had completed his sentence and is looking to redeem his reputation now in his eighties.

Around the same time that I received the letter from Mascheroni, I wrote to the biochemist Bruce Ames asking how he arrived at his cancer statistics, because in our earlier phone conversations his position was concerned with rising cancer rates. Chief Justice Burger's antilaw movement had taken off, and letters were coming in either praising or critiquing the Alternative Dispute Resolution (ADR) movement, which aimed at taking disputes from the courts into forced arbitration or mediation—freedom to roam in a four-cornered cage. Neil Gold, a practicing lawyer, makes a careful argument about dispute resolution and negotiation, as does Sheila Harty, a corporate initiatives director, and Donald Black, a professor of sociology.

The academic meets the practitioner on issues of ADR, with some, like Robert Mann, arguing that to deny that the United States is unusually litigious will not be convincing. Islam and Islamic law come up in Ashraf Ghani's letter on Pakistan, as well as when George Sfeir writes about work on legal reform in Saudi Arabia, as law and development programs move into full swing. A stunning four-page letter from Professor Ben Anderson of Cornell succinctly summarizes the personal proclivities of Clifford Geertz as they influenced 1970s anthropology—an era of Cold War warriors in Indonesia and elsewhere. History is often forgotten.

Speaking of history often forgotten, the 1980s was still a time when pay equity was an issue. My letter to Chancellor Mike Heyman is included here, as are a few comments from my colleague Elizabeth Colson to the chancellor, which provide further context to the issue.

February 12, 1980

Dear Laura:

You were kind enough to say that I might send you pieces I had done on Chinese law, and I am unkind enough to take you at your word. I am sending an article I wrote some years ago on traditional law (Ch'ing law), and a talk I gave last year on the same subject at the American Oriental Society which carries it a little further. I am working on a translation of the Ch'ing code and hope to work this material into an introduction. I am also enclosing an article and a review-article on modern Chinese law that use somewhat the same approach.

It seems to me that at present in the West we have two principal approaches to law; the Anglo-American which concentrates on process or dispute settling, and the continental which concentrates on conceptual analysis of substantive law. When I first got into Chinese law I intended to use the former method, but at that time (ten years or so ago) there did not seem to be available data nor any hope of acquiring them. Now it looks as if such a study would be possible at least for modern China.

However I have opted for the other approach and I think it can be useful. I think one starts by looking for the societal model within the conceptual system. (Every legal system, or ideology as you phrased it, is in part a way of looking at society). In western law this has been made quite explicit, particularly in the German Civil Code. We take an individual (the person) as our center. It is not explicit in Chinese law, but I think one can find it. It takes the Emperor or possibly the Government as its center. One can apply either grid to the other society. The social institutions are frequently similar, but they are viewed from different perspectives. The Chinese had a law of mortgages though it never occurred to them that they did. They were interested in collecting taxes from landowners, not in settling disputes between them. We have a law that deals with the commerce of the nation as a whole quite separately from individual buying-and-selling transactions. But we tend to analyze even such statutes as the anti-trust laws in terms of their application to particular cases. I have the feeling that Hebrew law, in a similar way, saw its society as consisting primarily of aspects of man's relation to God. Incidentally it considered contracts, usury, crime, etc. Hindu law, I would assume, would also look at its society from a religious perspective—but that of a very different religion.

I run on. I won't burden you further, but I would appreciate any thoughts you might have on approaches that might be useful. I think you are right in viewing anthropology as the discipline that is best equipped to enable one to view one's own discipline from a certain distance. Economic analysis has given us some interesting insights into law, for instance, but the anthropologist's view of economists and lawyers might be even more interesting. That's one of the reasons I would like very much to read your energy study. I think you gave me all the relevant information on how to get it when it appears, but I don't seem to remember it. I would appreciate it if you could let me know the necessary bibliographical information so that I can be sure that we get it and that it is routed to me.

Your visit was very exciting—much too short for us, but plenty long for you I'm sure. You are very good to go round and talk in the way you do.

We need stirring up in the way that only personal contacts can accomplish. Sincerely yours.

William C. Jones
Professor of Law
Washington University

April 11, 1980

Dear Dr. Nader,

I read the report of your contribution to the CONAES work in this week's *Nature*, and presumed that you are unaware of the Earth Enterprise project; despite the NAS [National Academy of Sciences], and despite a recent exchange with Harvey Brooks who said he hadn't been aware of it 'till my letter of 25 January this year informed him.

The key analysis of the energy problem was written in early 1973 by a management consultant's report to the Board of the enterprise in which everybody is entitled to a seat to the shareholders (everybody) for the proper management of the company's resources. The Shareholders are also trustees for future shareholders, and everybody is an employee and a customer. This business notice in which everybody has to wear several hats provides a whole new way of allowing everybody to understand the ramifications of decisions, everybody to participate in the discussion, and the action on the basis of a common understanding of the essential facts.

The Earth is viewed as a business in which energy equals finance; with the sun providing the "income," the fossil fuels, the "negotiable reserves," and nuclear energy—the "strippable fixed assets." "Expert" opinion is invariably based on the unsound assumption that reserves can be treated as revenue, that the income isn't worth collecting, and that assets-stripping is such a contentious business, that it will develop an unstoppable momentum long before the "experts" reach agreement on it.

"What is the relationship between experts who assess probabilities and those who assess their consequences?" and they're all wrong! Since space is limited, perhaps I should refer you to Dr. Stephen Brown, lecturer in epidemiology at the Epidemiology Research Unit at Berkeley, to whom I have explained at length the fundamental unsoundness of playing with figures before you understand the relationship between all the facts and factors, and the flaw in prediction, before you understand the sensible reason for incorporating Murphy's law in nature.

Could I also refer you to "Is Science a Business?" in *Physics Bulletin*, October 1976, which should provide some clues as to how I succeeded in integrating the behavioral sciences with the physical sciences in the "energy business" structure.

The theory unifying all the disciplines making sense of the human condition was discovered simply by explaining the problem of the world's energy accounts to everyone, from first principles taking everything and everyone in account. We are designed specifically with the capacity to learn how to manage the world's resources successfully. The formula for success includes a set of rules called the "Energy Economy," which are little more than the rules for sound long-term financial management applied to the management of energy.

The energy problem is not "unbounded." The basis for intelligent discussion and action has to be a firm framework of established fact, and that I provide in my "report to the Board," showing clearly that the case for the "Energy Economy" is a case for common-sense versus nonsense. As for "life-styles," I neither preach nor predict but simply take my own medicine. Please read my report and join the "Board Meeting" currently discussing it. Business is transacted normally in writing, which forms its own minute.

Yours sincerely,

Miss J. M. Pick
Surrey, United Kingdom

February 25, 1981

Dear Laura Nader;

I loved your article that just appeared in *Physics Today*. Not only the semis and the macho and the number running to use a phrase. When I got into this business (originally I was a physicist), I was amazed at the number-fascination of the social scientists, and the structuralist concoctions of the anthropologist, and how fieldwork and description were thought soft and un-scientific, and unconvincing, and "feminine." The current idolization of the country's problems as economic ones, in terms of inflation and re-industrializations, is a similar concretization of the political/economic problems.

Nice job.

Sincerely,

Martin H. Krieger
Massachusetts Institute of Technology

February 26, 1981

Dear Laura,

I just read your magnificent article in *Physics Today*. It's great that they ran it, and just there however tardily.

Yes, that's the way it is. It's well guided by an unexpressed but well understood system of rewards and punishments. But things have run down badly in the enterprise of science that has changed entirely since the end of World War II.

In the first half of this century we had a generation of monumental physicists—Einstein, Bohr (both of whom I knew), Heisenberg, Pauly, Schrödinger, and on, and on—all of whom knew that what physics is about is reality, and that physics (science) can explore only part of reality, and by far the smaller part. That kind of thought is now virtually forbidden in scientific literature. . .

Sincerely,

George Wald
The Biological Laboratories
Harvard University

March 3, 1981

Dear Professor Nader,

I enjoyed reading your recent article on thinking about energy in the February issue of *Physics Today*. It is one of the more thoughtful pieces I have seen concerning energy policy.

I am a physicist and have worked on various aspects of energy technologies. For some years I was involved with materials problems for future fusion reactors and I am now working in the area of photovoltaics. I have noticed over the years an apparent irrationality on the part of many colleagues when it comes to discussing matters relating to energy. All the data in the world cannot bring about a change in energy strategies once the person has decided on a particular cause. This is all the more strange as many of these people are competent and intelligent scientists who are usually willing to alter their view in the light of new data.

What seems to be happening is that many scientists who work in energy policy and energy technology have different social and personal values and their values are rationalized by appeal to numbers and data. Many of the disagreements I have witnessed about energy policy, or one technology vs another is really a disagreement over values.

Normally a disagreement over values would be stated as such, but I think physical scientists are uncomfortable in the subjective realm of values. This inability to recognize the true source of conflict leads to nonsensical and ridiculous statements you mention in your comment.

I have come to realize that to understand in any serious manner the energy question it is important to gain some comprehension of the social and human dimensions of the problem. This is particularly true for scientists and engineers. I hope you will continue to contribute your valuable

expertise as an anthropologist and your clear thinking to this very important, very confused issue.
Sincerely yours,

Alan Sweedler
Professor of Physics
San Diego State University

March 3, 1981

Dear Professor Nader,

Your article in the February issue of *Physics Today* was superb. It is greatly appreciated.

I too encounter marvelous mindsets in the energy field. The enclosed article documents many of these under the heading of "Horror Stories." The subject of the long article is also the subject of a talk I have given with great success in Board Rooms, University Colloquia, and in Junior High-School lunch rooms. After giving the talk (on the arithmetic of growth) to a class of Junior High students a couple of the students came to a tie and said "We can understand what you said!"

It's pretty easy. Why can't grown-ups "understand it?" I answered that growth is the "American Religion," and a religion is something you accept without subjecting it to analytical scrutiny. The growth religion is rare among the religions because with the growth religion one can predict the consequences of courses of action.

But the true believers don't wish to see the predictions made. When someone does make the study of the consequences of the growth religion the high priests don't want to hear, heresy.

Again, my thanks for making a marvelous contribution to the literature of physics.
Sincerely yours,

Albert A. Bartlett
Professor of Physics
University of Colorado at Boulder

March 5, 1981

Dear Prof. Nader:

My copy of the February 1981 issue of *Physics Today* arrived one hour ago. I think that your comments entitled "Barriers to Thinking New About

Energy" is one of the finest articles that ever appeared in this journal. I have received this journal for 33 years. Your views indicate that you conform to my conception of an educated person.

I am a retired physicist and a one-time meteorologist. During my active career my colleagues probably at best rated my technical competence as mediocre. In my youth, meteorologists seemed to me to lack an understanding of logic and were extremely sensitive to fads and the current "authority." An example of the mode of thinking that is still current is "the low pressure system will not move into the local area because it will be blocked by a high pressure system." This seems to me to be saying that the pressure tomorrow will not be low because it will be high.

Physicists are generally of much higher caliber, but the education of physicists even in their own field appears to lack two important elements. First, physics texts present the subject matter in an orderly manner but usually fail to indicate how the present concepts developed. Few theories were eagerly adopted when the theories were first announced. In Bell's "History of Mathematics" Bell states that when a new theorem was announced mathematicians mostly said that the theorem was not true. A few years later the truth of the theorem was accepted, but mathematicians stated that it was a trivial consequence of a theorem they had proved years ago. After more years passed the mathematicians then admitted that the new theorem was an important one and that they knew it all the time. Physicists have been much like this. Second, physics students are given problems with known answers. They are not trained to be original.

A final point I want to make is that physicists work in groups and often for large organizations. If a young physicist asks fundamental questions about the main work of the group, he does not make a favorable impression upon his superiors. I have known cases where young talented physicists have had to change fields because reviewers for journals ("old authorities") did not approve of the young upstart.

At one time in my career as a physicist I worked with five other physicists. One day when I was in the office of the head of the project, I noticed that he and one of my colleagues were using a foolish and time consuming method of converting the tracing on a chart to numbers for a table. Immediately my five colleagues recognized the truth of my observation. Four of them laughed but the project head did not think that it was amusing. He stated that the reason that I noticed the foolishness of the procedure was because I always wanted to take time to think. He said that he was too busy doing research to take time to think.

For the first three years of our study there was a lively controversy between our leader and theoretical physicists from other organizations. Our measurements did not fit the theory. One day when I was bored doing what I was supposed to be doing, I decided to determine the cause of the difference between theory and measurement. I decided to go over the steps of our procedure. At step one I found that a coefficient that we used was obtained from a table published long ago. In our great rush to do research the wrong value was read from this table, and no one had checked the reading of the table. When the current number from the table was used our experimental results agree with the theory. In the great rush to do research three years of heated argument was found to be useless. I was not awarded a gold star for this little piece of work.

I will not tell any stories of stupid mistakes I've made.

Sincerely,

Edward V. Ashburn
Physicist
Granada Hills, California

March 11, 1981

Dear Dr. Nader:

I read your guest comment in *Physics Today* with considerable interest and agreement. As a nuclear scientist I too perceive a significant problem engendered by the hard science establishment. Unbeknownst to the general public, the leading physical scientists are not Einstein-like characters, but are more likely intelligent bureaucrats largely intent on building or maintaining their empires. Those of us who would seriously question the scientific goals of our peers face an ultimate blacklist from our profession by the entrenched establishment. The general public can also not question this scientific elite because of a language barrier that convinces most people that because scientists discuss complex topics they actually understand what they are talking about.

I have given some thought as to why this is so. The experience in most universities is that many students enter stating a preference to study hard science yet only a few succeed. Those that leave science do so because they fail to survive the implied and actual rigors of the technical curriculum. Thus, a strong selection process for narrow academic brilliance is in effect. The most creative students often resist the scientific dogma they are taught and fail to survive to graduation. This happened to Einstein and is still true today. The best of the survivors, judged entirely by their academic performance, go to graduate school where they evolve complex yet very narrow research projects, ultimately incomprehensible to everyone but the student for which they are awarded a Ph.D. At this point they have become incompetent to do anything of practical value so they: 1) go into industry where they are retrained; 2) join a research group in a national laboratory; 3) teach; or 4) continue to work on the same narrow research project. At this point purely social factors take control as the scientist realizes he will not generate any new, earth-shaking ideas. Thus, he 1) enters management and becomes a research group leader; 2) becomes department chairman; or 3) writes a gigantic research grant proposal to the government. Thus in the final analysis money and power become the end of scientific enquiry. The construction of a large accelerator becomes a highly visible project which can generate great respect for the scientists involved irrespective of the scientific worthiness of the venture. What people do not realize is that very little scientific consideration goes into the generation of most large research projects.

Those of us who survive this system with our creative juices intact work quietly in the background living off the droppings of the elite establishment and trying not to rattle our cages too loudly. The "leading scientists" on the other hand, get invited to energy conferences where, unable (or unwilling) to think their way out of a paper sack, they play their power games. The people you met were not concerned with the energy problem so much as getting a piece of the action. You must have appeared indeed strange to them because those panels were being used for lobbying efforts and who would give an anthropologist energy money?

I hope you will remain active with your energy panel involvements. It may be up to the social scientists to unmask the deceit of the physical scientists because I don't see a revolution brewing from within. My advice is to seek hard scientific advice from the younger, less polluted physical scientists who do not yet have an institutional axe to grind. Above all, get at the scientist-students in their formative years when the universities can (and should) demand a broader education. Don't settle for the platitudes and condescension that you hear, but demand clear and comprehensible science. Hold the scientists accountable for what they say and do, and if you don't get reasonable responses keep pressing the issues.

Sincerely,

Richard B. Firestone
Staff Scientist
Lawrence Berkeley Laboratory

March 16, 1981

Dear Professor Nader:

I was on the point of discarding my most recent copy of *Physics Today* when I came across your stimulating article. I have a deep personal and professional concern about the use of human ingenuity in the improvement of the human condition. It is clear that when a group of people think alike, most of their brains are redundant. Group thinking has become (maybe it's always been—I don't know) so common in the "educated" parts of our society that it's almost funny.

Consider the statement: "since a minority of experts in the field have expressed strong reservations about possible long-term health hazards its use ought to be avoided." The almost universal agreement (or disagreement) with that statement, (depending on whether "it" refers to nuclear power or marijuana) in one culture is exactly reversed in the opposite one.

As far as I can tell, the educational process does little to enhance original thinking and a great deal to stop it. I'm sure that I'm not the only parent who has noticed that the child's habit of asking endless questions disappears shortly after kids start school. When these kids come out of the other end they have acquired a great many tools, but not a sense of independent intellect they must have in order to make use of them.

As a manager of a research enterprise, I try to help create an environment in which creativity can flourish. There isn't all that much that I can do, but that doesn't keep me from looking for ways to help the process along.

One point in your article that struck a personal resonance was your observation of the lack of diversity among the scientists at a meeting. Some time ago, a friend of mine claimed that if there had been a black man on the Ford they would never have gone through with the Edsel. At the time I argued with him, but my experience in the intervening years has made me see that he was right. Your view of physical scientists paints a harsh picture, but the message contained therein is something we must listen to. We don't have to agree with all of it in order to learn from it. I'm very glad that *Physics Today* saw fit to bring it to the attention of a wider audience. If you have any further published material in this area I would very much appreciate a copy.

Best wishes,

Arno A. Penzias
Executive Director of Research
Bell Laboratories

March 19, 1981

Dear Dr. Nader:

I found your commentary in *Physics Today* provocative, thoughtful, and generally "on the mark." Like any very good anthropologist, your observations of "homo-scienticus" in his natural habitat are accurate.

I think the interpretation of your observations would be clarified by the following anecdote.

In about 1965 John U. Campbell, then editor of *Analog* (Science Fact and Fiction) *Magazine*, became interested in dowsing the location of underground water. He reported in the magazine, preliminary experiments which convinced him that certain techniques for dowsing really worked.

He then visited a large Eastern technical university (I believe it was MIT) to try and interest someone in more formal research into the technique. The Geology Department decided that though it involved underground water, the essential phenomenon must be electromagnetic and hence beyond their purview. The Electrical Engineering Department felt that since it worked equally well with bent copper wires and green twigs from a sapling that the problem was clearly psychological (i.e. not theirs). The Psychologists directed him to the Biologists who sent him to the Civil Engineers, etc., etc. The only point of unanimity in the disparate departments was that there being no government money available to fund research, the problem surely belonged somewhere else.

I think there are two characteristics of the scientist embedded in the story which are quite pertinent to your commentary. The first unites the scientist with the rest of humanity: cupidity all other things being equal, there is greater opportunity for personal gain working on billion-dollar projects than on thousand-dollar projects. (I'd wager that the version of solar sometimes called "the power tower" had fairly staunch defenders in scientific or at least engineering circles). The second distinguishes the scientist from the rest of humanity: specialization scientific education is an extended process of focusing, learning more and more about less and less. The scientist in marked contrast to the humanist (with all apologies to C. P. Snow), knows what he doesn't know, and frequently the better the scientist the more carefully he restricts his field of expertise (in effect so long as they had to confront a solar collector on a residence, they had no greater skill than the random homeowner).

Please be assured that this is only a minor quibble with your commentary. Even when your observation stung (I worked at the Oak Ridge National Laboratories for a decade and consider myself "establishment" on the subject of power generation), they admirably fulfilled the R. Burns injunction to "see ourselves as others see us."

Very truly,

Gordon L. Love
Vice President
Sprague Electric Company

March 25, 1981

Dear Professor Nader:

I want to congratulate you on your fine "Guest Comment," an article in the February 1981 issue of *Physics Today*. I think the points you make are very important, and I hope they'll receive the attention they deserve.

I'm sorry you live so far away, because I have a great deal of material here that could perhaps be helpful to the cause you are trying to promote. Enclosed are three sample items that provide a little background for my belief in that possibility. Sincerely yours,

Theodore M. Edison
West Orange, New Jersey

March 27, 1981

Dear Dr. Nader:

I found your commentary in the February 1981 issue of *Physics Today* on "Barriers to Thinking New About Energy" fascinating, depressing, and important. Such insight needs greater exposure in the hope that prevailing attitudes will change and be changed. I would appreciate a copy of the article and any similar material you may have written. I am not a regular reader of *Physics Today* (never before, in fact), but fortunately the text of your commentary was read over the air on KPFY Pacifica radio's *Science Connection* program a couple weeks ago. Sincerely,

Michael H. Horn
Professor of Zoology
California State University, Fullerton

April 3, 1981

Dear Prof. Nader:

I have just finished reading your "Guest Comment" article in the Feb. 1981 issue of *Physics Today*. It is the most refreshing article I have read in some time and gives substance to feelings I have had about the way our scientific programs develop.

Temporarily, I am a liaison scientist here in London at the Office of Naval Research. However, my permanent position is Professor of Physics at the Naval Postgraduate School in Monterey. Recently, I attended a conference in London on "Future Energy Concepts." Several of the things you mentioned were also apparent there. One speaker expressed the opinion that the era of zero-growth in energy use in Britain (similar to your 70–70 scenario) was already here. This was based on analysis of data of the last 10 years.

Conservation was given lip service on several occasions, but always the subject was dropped after being invoked. In fact one person remarked: "it isn't sexy," and others pointed out the lack of intellectual challenge.

After reading your comment I think my understanding is strengthened. My wife is a dedicated women's liberationist and I am sure she is in agreement that engineers and scientists are "macho."

Perhaps when I return to Monterey next year you would consider talking about this subject at a physics colloquium. Not before, because I would like to hear more from you.

Sincerely,

John R. Neighbours
Liaison Scientist
Office of Naval Research, Branch Office, London

April 6, 1981
Dr. Harold Davis

Editor, *Physics Today*

Dear Dr. Davis

To date I have received 9 phone calls and 27 letters from your readers of my "Guest Comment" (February, 1981). The letters sent directly to me came from physicists, chemists, astronomers, geologists, engineers, urban planners, biologists, zoologists, and from three science and technology publications.

The responses to my commentary indicate that there are a good number of people who are concerned with thinking new, who are concerned with the use of scientific knowledge in improving the quality of life, and who are just plain curious about "homo-scienticus." The letters to be printed in *Physics Today* are concerned as well.

Dunning is concerned that power centralizers might interfere with the development of energy technologies from the bottom, a perspective I share. McKelvey comments on my scolding, lamenting, and complaining, and misses the point which is that open debate on national energy policies have been censured by cultural and organizational factors built into what one of the letter writers called the natural habitat of "homo-scienticus." Mr. Pay, who as a specialist in radiation protection would not be expected to understand about cultural and organizational factors, is correct in expecting consistency on safety concerns, although his comparison of nuclear safety and wind safety is like talking of onions and oranges.

Finally, I remind Mr. Thelen that attribution of the remarks I quote, which could be forthcoming from myself or a number of other CONAES participants, would serve to personalize an issue which I argue is structurally and culturally determined—that is, it is behavior that is selected for, learned, and transmitted from generation to generation. We have to break that cycle. Sincerely yours,

Laura Nader
Professor of Anthropology

April 16, 1981

Dear Laura:

I missed you very much at our meeting last weekend. In many respects, it was a depressing meeting because of all the awful stuff that's going on with the present administration. I'm afraid that instead of trying to buoy up the Committee (like a good chairman should have done), I gave in to my depression and anger—especially when we were visited by a representative of the Dept. of Education (an economist) who prefaced his remarks by letting us know that we were referred to at DoE as the "touchy-feely" committee, and that the only reason that we exist at all is because Bill Lewis insisted! Anyway, my recollection is that I behaved badly. We could have used your special kind of wisdom in that situation, and I missed it deeply.

We did discuss Bob Axelrod's letter. Personally, I am hot to write something protesting what's happening at DoE in particular, or with the Reagan administration's general efforts regarding both conservation and the social sciences. However, it was the sense of the Committee to hold off for just a bit. The general feeling is that our best shot will come from the work that we are doing, especially in terms of a book with wide popular distribution. We need a second year of funding in order to write that book, and it was the Committee's feeling that we should work hard to get that second year of funding as our first priority. Similarly, we decided that it would be premature to schedule our next meeting until after.

Paul Stern and his new assistant Richard Hofrichter have taken a whack at writing something sensible which incorporates the thinking in some of the snippets.

Let me know if you have any reaction to all of this. I'd certainly be interested in hearing from you.

Cordially,

Elliot Aronson
Professor of Psychology
University of California, Santa Cruz

April 28, 1981

Dear Professor Nader:

I read with great interest your article in *Physics Today* of February 1981. Since you are an anthropologist, I suggest the following topics of research about superstitions and taboos in Northern America, during the last quarter of the 20th century:

North American natives (mostly white and literate) seem to believe in "solar energy." Is this related to some ancient rites of Sun worship by their forefathers? So strong is this belief that tribal leaders are allocating lots of taxpayer money to promote what every scientist knows is a hoax. (Of course, the corporations employing these scientists are happy to make a fast buck).

These naive people are also afraid of nuclear power. What is the origin of this fear? Ancient superstitions about witchcraft and sorcery? In particular, try to imagine a "scenario" of what would have happened in Northern America if a single person had been killed at Three Mile Island. Or just injured.

Sincerely,

Asher Peres
Professor of Physics
Technion—Israel Institute of Technology

April 30, 1981

Dear Dr. Nader:

I read your article in the February *Physics Today*. I was very pleased that the editors chose to print this article, even though it was probably to bolster their image of "scientific objectivity."

I am a physicist and engineer. For years I have felt like the ultimate minority. I have been characterized by my peers as illogical, a kook, and other assorted categories. I am glad that you have brought up the pathological blinds of the "technocratic establishment." I now feel that I am not irrational. I merely refuse to include human beings as numbers in sets of equations.

I know better than most people the dichotomy between words and action in government. I went to graduate school intending to train myself as a solar energy researcher. After I got out however (during Carter's administration), I found that there were plenty of solar conferences to attend but no jobs. After searching for six months for employment in the solar area, I have three degrees with a 3.84 final average, I gave up.

I have often compared the attitude of physicists and engineers to cowboys; the only difference being that cowboys get drunk and run over people in their jacked up pickup trucks. Scientists get drunk on technology and may run over us all with their dangerous toys.
Thank you,

Claude Ginsburg
Seattle, WA

May 7, 1981
Mark R. Gibson

Strategic Planning
Branch Solar Energy Research Institute

Dear Mark Gibson:

Before I leave for a meeting on "Energy and Equity" and the Australia and New Zealand AAAS [American Association for the Advancement of Science], I want to send along some brief comments on the SERI/Solar/Conservation Study.

I found the work forward looking and reflective of a trend towards the use of different mixes in solar and conservation. Its strength is that the study doesn't rely on things that are not already developed, and its illustration, again, that predictions have not been very good in the transition range.

A few other comments. I wish these studies carried indexes. It would make them much easier to use. On page 3 you should strengthen the following sentence: "One would not commonly think of an investment in building insulation as an alternative to an investment in an oil well, but the two kinds of investments can have precisely the same outcome."

I would quibble with the word "precisely." Fortunately, investment in conservation has a much superior outcome if only because it can save the oil for use that cannot be substituted for. One final comment: the study focuses heavily on the economic view; as you know a subject such as energy needs diverse intelligences working on the problem just to keep us all in check.

Thank you for the good work.
Sincerely yours,

Laura Nader
Professor of Anthropology

June 18, 1981

Dear Professor Nader,

Sometime before the publication of your report on *Energy Choices in a Democratic Society* (1980), you gave a talk on the Public Broadcasting System in which you made a series of striking analyses concerning the relation between design criteria in technology and various social factors. I recall for example, that you made reference to the possible role of male machismo as a factor among many engineers. You also called attention to the readiness to take high risks and to design for complexity that is well beyond reliability. You called attention to the likelihood that engineers have been undergoing a wrong kind of training. Accordingly, you said there is an unprecedented problem: how to retrain "the experts, the problem solvers."

When your report appeared from the National Academy of Sciences, I hastened to get a copy hoping that the analysis along the lines included above would be contained at some point in the report. Alas, there was nothing of the sort to be found.

Therefore I am writing to you even at this later date, in the hope of getting a copy of the full text of what I thought was your remarkably interesting discussion on the Public Broadcasting System concerning these matters.

I'll be most appreciative of your help in solving this question.
Sincerely,

Seymour Melman
Professor of Engineering
Columbia University
Defending a colleague.

July 26, 1981

Dear Dr. Nader:

My December 1979 copy of *Psychology* arrived the other day in a box of magazines, and I just now read your article on "Complainer Beware." I just had to sit down and thank you and also tell you more horror stories. Being that I live overseas most of the time, mine are compounded by the distance and the inability to follow through. Here are my main stories:

(1) IRS: Three huge fights. The first included 50 unanswered letters and finally a letter to my congressman with fast action and the payment of money overpaid. The second included some extreme trickery and lies at the time of the *Reader's Digest* articles on IRS. A letter at the advise of *Reader's Digest* to the congressional committee lead to a slow but complete settlement. The 3rd I handled myself, and I must say that the IRS has changed considerably. I was able to meet with the IRS people and talk reasonably and settled for half of what I wanted, but I admit it was not the clear-cut case of the others. My cost? Audits every year for 14 years in a row. On my last I told them that I would make a complaint of harassment if I were audited again over the same questions and I have now gone two years without one . . . so far.

(2) American Motors. I have bought two new cars in my life, both AMC and junk. The first was a long time ago but the latter was in the mid 60s. They even wrote me a letter laughing at me when I tried the C of C [Chamber of Commerce] in Toledo. Everything in that car that moved was replaced by 25,000 miles and it was an expensive Wagoneer. I took it with me to Vietnam when I worked there and the VC blew it up, so that solved the problem.

(3) Pathway Products. The point here is that C of C of Verona, NJ said the company was good and I bought a franchise. When I had made complaints to the company and the C of C, as I saw it as a fraud, the C of C distributed information on the company saying it was good. I know because I had a relative write them for information about Pathway after I had written my companies to the C of C, and she reviewed a letter with a clear bill of health for the company. It folded within a few months. I lost over $4,000.00 on that deal.

(4) My Local Drain Commission. They came to my property and cut down hundreds of trees. They lied in telling me that they had come to dig out a small creek to make it carry more water. I discovered that they trespassed

on one piece of my land and started suit. Once the suit was commenced we discovered that they had no right of way at all. Won $14,000.00 but the ONLY reason I could do this was because I found an attorney willing to take it on shares. He took 1/4 and I got the rest which was most fair. We never hit the final courtroom. If we had he would have gotten 1/2.

(5) Aldens. Bought a Hot Point window air conditioner designed to self-destruct. It did so within 100 hours of use. A letter brought a form letter saying take it to my dealer. Problem? I bought it from Aldens in Chicago but was in Liberia by this time. Subsequent letters brought no more answers. Took it back to the US with me when the job was over. Wrote to the Illinois Customer Complaint and would like to know what the lady said. Aldens had me a check in HOURS for more than I paid. Time spent . . . over three years!

(6) Mayflower Cartage. I shipped my goods to Liberia, and shipped them so that they would arrive when I did. Weeks after I arrived, I reviewed a letter stating that I underpaid them $300.00 (it was their figure, of course), and that they were holding ALL my shipment until the $300 was received. I had paid them almost $4000.00. However, the local company DID ship everything but my car right away. The car arrived months after I did, and I can easily claim that had it been sent when it should have been, it would not have been ripped off the boat as it was. I got it running a month before I left, three years later. I demanded damages from Mayflower . . . not for the dropped car, but for the loss of the use and the expenses from not having my materials on hand when I arrived. They denied any responsibility for misfiling me. I tried the BBB to help settle and they told me that since it was an interactional carrier they could not help. I gave up since the amount was less than $1,000 and I was too far again.

(7) Commodore Business Machines. I bought a computer to take to Liberia with me. It never functioned. A letter elicited a suggestion that I buy a repair kit. I did, but I could not get it to work even with the kit. For all three years I wrote trying to get further help. They never answered again. I took it back with me, and wrote the A.G. of California, the BBB and the C of C. The Atty. General's office was totally useless. The C of C never replied, and the BBB did what they could but this was not much. Commodore finally did call me and offer a new machine. Since I had bought it to make calculations in LIBERIA and now had the MSU computers at my disposal, I did not want another computer. Also, by then it was out of date. We had an impasse. Then I was sent here and

wanted to settle somehow. They finally offered to send a mew machine HERE and I agreed, sending them the old and the various tapes and kit. They sent a new machine back to my house in Michigan minus the other items. I wrote the BBB and they gave me the name of an attorney who was willing to again, work on shares. Otherwise I could not handle it at all. Just this week I got a copy of his brief and he has filed a suit for $1,075,000.00—I love him even if he doesn't win a cent. I also had the joy of walking into an office in the Republic of South Africa with money in my hand to purchase a computer system with USAID monies and saw the word COMMODORE mastered across the front of their machine. I still have the money and the promise of the very frustrated sales manager to write Commodore telling them why he just lost an $8,000.00 sale.

(8) Sears Roebuck. I have had several arguments with Sears because I buy a lot from them. 100% of the time they have lived up to their slogan of satisfied customer. 100%!!!

I think that making possible for attorneys to go to court on shares of an amount that is worthwhile to them is one of the real possibilities for helping the consumer. At least it is the only thing working for me
Most sincerely,

Jack Down
Maseru, Lesotho

October 22, 1981
Elizabeth Colson

Lusaka, Zambia

Elizabeth,

Burton is wrong. Anthropologists have always written about the things that "everybody knows." It is the attention via analysis that has made the difference. I suspect that as with other subjects that touch on controlling processes and power, you made some people uncomfortable either because they were not part of the development network themselves, or even more aware than you or I, or the political meaning of the development business. As one person said to me, "That's just the rural picture and maybe true, but governments would have toppled without development projects."

Anyways it all reminds me of the work I did with energy experts where people were either saying that it wasn't true, or that it was a terrible choice of subject given the importance of alternative subjects, but it touched a chord and gave others courage to speak up afterwards. Women are good at that. The reason I suggested *The New York Times* magazine section is my thinking that it would follow in the tradition of many good pieces by Barbara Ward that have the same flaw—of saying what everybody knows out loud.

Sincerely,

Laura

November 25, 1981

Dear Prof. Nader:

Your comments published with my letter in *Physics Today* (October 1981) inspired me to write a rebuttal.

You said that my comparison of nuclear safety and wind safety was like talking of onions and oranges. I don't believe that is true. A person is just as dead whether the death is caused by a nuclear accident, an automobile accident, or a windmill accident.

Tom Wicker of *The New York Times* wrote of the "unmatched" potential of the Three Mile Island accident, which was described as 48,500 immediate and future deaths 2,951,000 immediate and future injuries. In 1977 automobile accidents caused 4,000–9,500 immediate deaths and 1,900,000 immediate injuries (some of which should be expected to cause future deaths), and $50.5 billion in damage. I had to call the National Safety Council to find the figures on auto accidents; they are not reported in newspapers any more. The difference is that the nuclear accident deaths could occur within a short time, and that such an accident (like TMI which caused no deaths) receives nationwide publicity while auto accident deaths occur by ones or twos and are rarely reported beyond the small localities in which they occur. I think the difference is cultural and organizational.

I think the difference between wind deaths and nuclear deaths in the public perception is also cultural and organizational. Without strictly enforced safety regulations on windmills, I believe wind deaths will far exceed nuclear deaths.

It is because of the cultural and organization misconceptions that I believe regulations applied to individual windmills or wood-burners to be unenforceable if they are applied. For the same reasons I believe they will never be applied.

Centralized power plants, for cultural and organizational reasons, will be much easier to regulate. I believe the present cultural and organizational attitude is anti-safety and anti-environmental despite the great protestations to the contrary. I have been trying to fight that attitude because I find it anti-rational.

Sincerely,

James H. Ray
Irvington, New York

January 6, 1982
James H. Ray

Irvington, New York

Dear James Ray:

Forgive me for delaying my response to your letter of November 23, 1981 regarding my comment on the comparison of nuclear safety and wind safety as talking of onions and oranges.

Your point of view that "a person is just as dead, whether the death is caused by a nuclear accident, an automobile accident, or a windmill accident" is of course true, but it's only part of the picture. Death by automobile does not change the genetic composition of a population, or add numbers to death by increasing disease, such as death through cancer. Death by windmill will not irreversibly change the local (and not so local) environment for thousands of years due to increase of radio-activeness and other toxic consequences. Thus the difference between wind deaths and nuclear deaths is more than cultural and organizational, it is biological and environmental.

Windmills and wood-burners should of course, be regulated by improving design and like mechanisms, and this will also only prevent some deaths. As to whether the present cultural and organizational attitudes are anti-safety and anti-environmental, there is no evidence for saying that (except of course in referring to the present Administration) and polls that say the opposite.

You are certainly correct that it is anti-rational to be anti-safety and anti-environmental, but that is what we must try to understand—the irrationality.

Thank you for your interest.

Sincerely yours,

Laura Nader
Professor of Anthropology

January 25, 1982

Dear Dr. Nader,

I really did enjoy your article in *Chemtech*. Not being a scientist myself, I seldom find anything in there that I can understand, but you write so well that it is a joy to follow your thinking!

For years I have been wondering why everything has to be "bigger" in order to be "better," so your 70~50 scenario answers this question for me. Perhaps this is so because I am a child of the Depression years.

Personally, I do not favor nuclear energy—why keep on making disposal problems for ourselves? I think it particularly wasteful to continue stockpiling nuclear as well as other types of armaments when "we now have more than enough to destroy civilization as we know it." Maybe you can help convince some of our brilliant male thinkers to divert their energies to a more constructive line of activity.

I agree that most conferences spend more time talking than doing, and that now is the time for constructive action
Sincerely,

Mary H. Hartford
Charlotte, North Carolina

January 30, 1982

Dear Dr. Nader,

If the paper you presented at M.I.T. last Wednesday is available, I would welcome a copy. I doubt if any of us truly enjoyed all that you said about the profession, but it was important to hear, and I hope we can listen to charges even when they hurt a bit. I would like to give my colleagues here a chance to enjoy your challenge even if only through reading it.

I hoped to catch you after your talk, but pressures to catch a plane forced me to miss even the third presentation of the session. Perhaps I can make a few comments here.

I regret that your analysis of physicists is probably all too appropriate, and perhaps the blindest of all are those of us in public schools who somehow tend to perpetuate the very worst elements of the enterprise called science. As I. I. Rabi said in his remarks on Tuesday, physics used to be done by people—people with first, middle, and last names. Now it is done by laboratories (Brookhaven, Fermi, etc.) and the individual people are largely faceless—hence not specifically responsible. Having come from a family of physicists of Rabi's vintage, and having known many of the men whose names were legend in their times even as they are remembered now in the history of science accounts, I sometimes suggest in full seriousness that most of the practitioners whose attitudes (and blindness) you properly decry are not physicists at all; they are technicians, perhaps very good ones, but technicians nonetheless. And so I wonder, as Rabi wondered in the talk, whether the age of physicists is over. If it is, then maybe we can understand the kinds of myopia the profession seems to perpetuate and which you called to our attention in your presentation.

On a more positive note, I was amused that in passing you mentioned Jim Conant (on whose living room floor I used to play with electric trains), and the eastern institution you had visited, naming your example Harvard College. I am not of that institution myself, but my daughter is in her second year there, having shifted her area of emphasis from biology to anthropology.

My point is that a neighbor at the session spoke out, asking you whether we shouldn't bring societal issues into our courses. Mine was the voice that spoke out "too late," urging that the effort had to begin lower down in the educational ladder. Al Bartlett ended that sparring match by suggesting "it is never too late to begin." That exchange illustrated I think, part of the physicist's problem; they always seem to think in terms of courses. Let us put some ethics into our physics classes and make our physicists ethical. I doubt the fishermen you described learned their wisdom in classes; they got it from family, the community, and the veteran fishermen with whom they worked.

Which brings me back to Haverford. It occurs to me that much of what I suspect you hoped to find in those institutions (and which I and my wife hoped to find also), does not come at Haverford via classroom work or any other visible curriculum. There as in your tribe, the real learning which may border on wisdom comes from the "family" or community, the give and take as faculty and students meet as friends (not necessarily also as *friends*). I suggest that which is learned through this all-pervasive curriculum far exceeds anything that can be transferred through class work, although the work in classes must be supportive of it. I think my daughter learned more about physics, and physicists as they should be, through house sitting for her astronomy professor, or having lunch with the instructor of Icelandic Sagas, than she could have got from even my physics course. I cannot say that this invisible curriculum comes with smallness; there are small colleges where it does not exist. But smallness may help—which makes one worry about the influence of these large national laboratories.

This is not a defense of Haverford, but a comment on your presentation and continued effort to put us in a position to have to accept your challenge. Changes cannot come through course work alone, and we as a profession must learn that. They will come only as we change our methods, our own behaviors, and our own attitudes toward science. That will take more than conference presentations and redesigned courses. And Al Bartlett notwithstanding, there are those who fear it is indeed "too late." But we must try. Thank you for challenging us, our preconceptions, our unadmitted reliance on mysticism, and our ineffective answers to the dilemma we have created.

Very sincerely,

C. Arthur Compton
Department of Science
Phillips Exeter Academy

February 8, 1982
Dr. Roger G. Noll

Chairman and Professor of Economics
Division of the Humanities and Social Sciences

Dear Roger:

Thank you for your thoughtful letter of February 1 to which this letter is not a response. From my personal point of view, the conference was most certainly a success since it stimulated me to think about regulation and those that write about regulation. I did not think that the summary comments were up to the standard that the papers your chair had set for the conference, but beyond that they did stimulate a worry. An anthropologist can handle the assignment "think new," but not the additional directive "but use our categories." Not that you're saying that but others might.

Some of your concerns might be taken care of if I spell out the anthropological perspective which allows us to quite naturally think of regulation as either public or private, and which allows us to quite appropriately talk about the political government and the economic government in the same paper just as apparently your knowledge of the literature suggests that others have done. But if I do that in the best possible way it still might not lead to thinking about dispute resolution models as a central solution. Know that dispute resolution is a fad now with the Chief Justice and all, but prevention might be better and cheaper.

Claire and I are happy to rework the paper—it doesn't meet our standards yet. But I have to feel that I can write this paper in free spirit, and that it will be refereed also by a free spirit, or at least one where there isn't too much of a technical mind-set problem. Can you give us some idea of who the referee audience is?

Thank you for your reprints. I will value reading them. In return I enclose a piece that was published in *Physics Today* which deals with the mind-set problem in another field, and my piece in the *Yale Law Journal* in the United States. My book *No Access to Law* goes a good deal further in policy recommendations, but the Yale piece presents the necessary background.

Sincerely yours,

Laura Nader
Professor of Anthropology

April 23, 1982

Dear Professor Nader,

I was browsing through *Chemtech* recently and came across your article "Barriers to Thinking New About Energy." I would be grateful if you could send me a copy of your original address to the Mitre Corporation, so that I may circulate it to my colleagues. The comments you make about engineers reflect a stereotype which I believe we have left behind over the last ten years or so.

It is some dozen years ago since I first questioned the general energy growth assumption before audiences of students, engineers, and the public. Naturally, I was ignored or laughed at, but my general thesis that "the growing demand for energy reflects lack of ingenuity and imagination rather than a real need" is now listened to politely. Even engineering myths and taboos change with time.

Yours sincerely,

Harry Dickinson
Department of Electrical Engineering
University of Edinburgh

June 23, 1982

Dear Dr. Nader,

I am writing to thank you for coming to speak to us at the Nuclear Chemistry Gordon Conference. We call ourselves a community of sorts but do not really think of ourselves as members of a culture with its own customs and mores. Your perspective will help us to do so and to thereby function more effectively inside the culture.

Some of the reaction to your talk astonished me. A week ago I would not have thought mere facts and observations could so immediately arouse some of those people. Many kept their objectivity and faced you with reasoned objections to what you said, what you were perceived to have said, what you implied, or what you were perceived to imply. Many others however, just stormed off with hurt feelings and defensive anger and recited incantations ("that's the standard anti-nuke line," or "she's anti-everything . . .") to one another until they felt their image of the world was again secure. As another student said, the formal discussion turned into a Phil Donahue show. It was a little disillusioning, but no worse than the revelations I got when I first argued semi-taboo subjects with Dr. Seaborg. Now we mostly talk football, because what with the thesis and all, I am not up for controversy with my research director.

It did not seem to me that we extended to you the degree of courtesy we insist upon for one another. If someone has access to data and observations that others do not, and is presumed to be expert at analysis then we may ask questions to confirm the validity of the data and analysis, but we may not deny them without presenting proof of better data or analytical methods. We certainly do not allow one another to misperceive what is said. A fellow student said, "She made it clear from the beginning that she didn't like me," based I presume, upon your expression of dislike for the scientific culture, and made that his reason for denying your entire presentation. He apparently took it as a personal insult, and began watching for "further insult," stopping up his ears to the development of the points you were trying to make. It was a typical reaction. I am sorry we were so quick to leap out of our objective receptive scientific characters. I think you should have been recognized as a member, at least for the purposes of the meeting, of our little culture, and thus protected from anything but rational attack of your observations and conclusions, and of course others thought so too, but some did see you as one of those "Whatevers." Few of us really know "jack" about social science, and our relative expertise is comparable to what an intelligent student of the humanities knows about physics—enough to survive and/or fulfill graduation requirements. Perhaps we read a SciAm article on the subject for recreation. The so-called "softness" of social science perhaps fools us into presuming more.

I do have some arguments and comments about your talk. I don't think the energy culture is as comparable to basic research culture as you implied (or seemed to imply?). Although I recognized some parallels, I found the subject of the interrelationships of centralization and democracy, which you exemplified by the nuclear energy industry regulation in France, very thought-provoking. Because we nuclear scientists do find ourselves, often inappropriately, in the middle of nuclear energy debates, and we have been thrown together with nuclear energy since day one in the government administration, but it is not our field. We researchers do not interact with the energy people at all unless we become administrators at some level overseeing both and we don't like for whatever reasons being equated with people so shamelessly "applied." If you could have followed up with a more relevant example, it might have been more directly helpful to us. Also, your quotes attributed to "Nobel Laureates" would have carried more weight with me if you had identified them by name. Some are more credible than others in their ventures far outside their field of specialty.

As a result of your talk I will see my social environments more from an "anthropological" view, and this will help me make more sense of my professional and outside world. Perhaps I will even be able to resolve some of the many contradictions and dilemmas that arise in my mind when I go from one to the other. As all the best lessons do, yours demonstrated a new way of thinking about our same old situations. I am glad you don't subscribe to a "non-interference" policy, but are trying to educate people who are subject to the rules and regulations of cultures we don't even realize exist. Also, I feel better about being a little controversial myself in my group; I have been reminded how important it is for a person to not deny her own senses just for the sake of peaceful lunches.

Thank you again for taking the time to come talk to us.
Sincerely,

Rose Marie McFarland
Derry, New Hampshire

November 22, 1982

Dear Professor Nader:

I enjoyed your television program *Little Injustices* which appeared on KCET this past Saturday. The enclosed article on California justice courts which appeared in the December 1982 *California Lawyer* reminded me of the more informal dispute resolution procedures you described in Mexico.

As a lawyer, I am acutely aware of the practical impediments to the quick and economical resolution of disputes in our judicial system, whether the problem is major or minor. However, I don't know that it is entirely fair to lay responsibility totally upon faceless corporations. For example, the California

Supreme Court, which generally has been in the forefront of expanding consumer rights and remedies, in *Gordon v. Justice Court* substantially weakened the justice court system in California, a system which was not entirely dissimilar to that of the small village near Oaxaca. Americans are also much more litigious than many other people, and we have the unrealistic expectation that social problems can be solved simply by passing a law or have courts decide disputes over social policy.

The American consumer on your program apparently attempted to get satisfaction directly from the manufacturer. While the manufacturer may be the party, who should ultimately be liable? I think in many cases consumers ought to take their complaints to the retailer. This is the party they dealt with on a face-to-face basis, and the consumer should be able to get the retailer into small claims court without difficulty. Then let the retailer go after those higher up in the distribution chain.

Anyway, I really enjoyed your program and agree that we must come up with better ways to cure the "little injustices" of life.
Very truly yours,

Thomas Larry Watts
Rosenfeld, Meyer & Susman Law Offices
Beverly Hills, CA

November 24, 1982

Dear Dr. Nader:

I watched with interest bordering on awe, the P.B.S. Odyssey Special *Little Injustices* based on your experiences in Talea, Oaxaca. I was interested because I work in a legal services program, and your American witnesses sang a familiar litany and awed because on sober reflection I realized that I'd much rather do this job in Talea.

My work is exclusively devoted to the representation of old men and women, and my clients have ceased to be consumers in the accepted sense of the term. They buy shelter, heat, light, food, and communication—nothing more. Their lives hinge upon a more esoteric system of consumerism. They contract for one product only—that being survival, and the faceless producer is the government! When the product doesn't measure up the result is tragic. They live on retirement benefits, widows' benefits, disability benefits; Supplemental Security Income benefits such as: Medicare, Medicaid, Food Stamps, etc. They live in a world where simple seasonable clothing becomes a luxury, and any real comfort becomes a fantasy beyond dreaming.

Often adrift in the society, they are prey to deadly events to be sure, but few can be more frightening than the actions of their own government—their protectors. The computer hiccupped, a regulation changed, or some bloody local functionary is not as alert on any given day as he should be. There is an administrative push to cut costs, or to collect old debts, or to review cases with an eye to less "liberal" interpretation of needs or assets. And then there is the letter: "Due to mumbo-jumbo as interpreted by the blah-blah-blah, you have been overpaid in the amount of. . . " or "your grant is reduced to . . . " or "the medical service you solicit will not be covered." "You have of course, the right to appeal."

The appeals process is designed to be simple. The whole premise of administrative hearing in entitlements and grants is to maintain an informal arena wherein the appellant can represent his own interests with a reasonable chance of success: a "fair" hearing, a good-faith effort to keep it local like Talea. The sticking points become obvious after only the briefest foray into that arena.

The Judge that you face is paid by the agency which has denied you entitlement. The agency itself will be represented by its professional representatives (i.e. case managers, supervisors, directors or legal counsel). You only have yourself.

Your reinstatement or denial may hinge on a single regulation, or some case law that you've never heard of, or some question that was trickily put and guilelessly answered, or a single word or sentence buried in pages of dossier. Even if you knew what to look for, you (my dear average arthritic octogenarian) would be hard pressed to figure out where to look, or how to interpret to the advantage of your claim. So you do the only likely thing in the circumstances— you lose.

And then you suffer. The consequences of such losses are incalculable. They can mean the difference between warm, secure housing, and the drift into the slum; they can mean cans of dog food on the shelves of people who keep no pets; they can mean the administrative removal of a free human being from the community into a life of unwilling institutionalization because that soul has simply had all other options foreclosed from "above." The meanest act of an increasingly mean society may have been to prolong existence without prolonging life.

The worst part of the process is that it can prolong itself over a year or two, or more. It produces tremendous anxiety; it is embittering and disillusioning. It produces mental stress as well as physical and emotional devastation to suddenly discover that the last of life can be a defeat instead of a realization. And if you finally win (and you only win with expert assistance) the victory is pyrrhic at best.

One of my clients, a gentleman who I am sure has always considered himself a good hardworking solid citizen, said upon being told that there was no help for his particular problem "isn't it a shame that the young man didn't finish the job?"

A reference to our latest assassin. It is depressing that this last generation of true believers should be driven to such despair that they should indulge in that most foreign (to them) of all trades—non-directive frustration-born radicalism.

We are as your documentary points out, a consumer society. But we are something else increasingly. Our present unemployment, as wicked as it is, bodes a changing future according to economists, sociologists and science-fiction writers. We are becoming an automated society. The majority of the presently unemployed may remain unemployed because the need for them will disappear. With this their ranks may swell. How we deal with that future as a governmental or a fiscal entity is a discrete matter. How we come to cope as a societal entity with a large, nonconsuming public reliant on community support for existence is precisely germane, and worth intense study.

We still set out welfare populations into neat slots as a manageable minority, and we feel little social compunction about the hoops we put them through, and little obligation to alter the manner of redresses available for these "small injustices." But if we do not look to their frustrations now, what shall we do with the future when they may be the majority?

I kept wishing while I watched the program, that my clients could have been on that screen. While I felt sorry for the ladies with the lemon car and the defective Bendix, they had two things guaranteed them to which most of my clients cannot aspire—a good dinner and a buying future. Perhaps a critical study of the small injustices against the aged minority will have some use against the day when we go to bed as a consumer society and wake up as a welfare population. The Talean process seems exquisite by comparison to the present possibilities. Sincerely,

Louise McMillan
Paralegal Counselor
Legal Services for the Elderly Project

February 2, 1983

Dear Laura;

Last summer at the Institute on Law and Social Structure in the Near and Middle East we discussed Weber's concept of Islamic law, and upon my criticism of his work you suggested that I write a paper on the subject. When I returned to the states, I discovered that Bryan Turner has already written a book on *Weber and Islam: A Critical Study* which came out in 1974. This work has only confirmed further my belief that Weber did not know what he was talking about when he described Islamic law as irrational.

I have been working on the concept of *istihsan* for my S.J.D. dissertation at the Harvard Law School in an effort to show that Islamic law is a rational system of law. Enclosed is a paper which I have just finished on the subject and which I thought you might be interested in reading. I have submitted it to the Articles Editor for the *California Law Review* at Berkeley, although I am not sure that Islamic law has yet grabbed their fancy.

Vildan Akan, Nazzan Forrest, and I are still waiting to hear word on our submitted project proposal concerning "The Effect of Law No. 44/1979 as an Instrument for Dispute Resolution within the Family Structure." Vildan has written me twice from Turkey, and all three of us are quite eager to continue with the project. We hope to hear from the Subcommittee on Law and Social Structure in the near future.

I hope all is well with you, especially during this time of stormy weather out West. We have had unusually good weather, albeit rainy as usual, but I suspect that the cold weather is about to set in.

With best regards.

John Makdisi
Assistant Professor of Law
Cleveland State University

February 23, 1983

Dear Laura:

A very quick note on the run as usual. But I wanted to pause one moment and thank you again for the opportunity to talk with you and your class. Next time I'll be more to the point and leave more time for discussion! In any event, I thoroughly enjoyed this opportunity and discussion, as well as the pleasure of seeing you again.

I am planning to do a repeat performance at Harvard Law School in April, schedules permitting, and again in Moscow in the fall. I have just received an invitation to the Institute of U.S. and Canadian Studies to speak on "legal imperialism," as well as American foreign policy in Latin America, etc. They have reviewed the book, so it should be remarkably interesting—especially as I engage and criticize Marxist interpretations of law and change (these are discussed most thoroughly in the chapter on Chile). As you will recall, my discussion suggests that American "law and development" paradigms very poorly explained what was going on, just as Marxist "law as a super structure of oppression" paradigms lacked explanatory power given the much more complex and interactional reality of multiple types of law interacting with each other and with social change. In any event, I'll look forward to this discussion; it should be remarkably interesting.

The immediate impetus for this note is a collection of materials actually sent to me from colleagues at the Ford Foundation. Several quite familiar: "legal assistance" initiatives are apparently underway, but the "international development law" discussion presented perhaps the purest form of déjà vu. I have attached a copy for your interests. My friends at Ford tell me there apparently is life after death, even for "law and development."

I hope all goes well with you, Laura. Please do keep me in touch with your research. You are always welcome at Lewis and Clark, and in the Gardner home. Warmest personal regards.
Sincerely,

James A. Gardner
President
Lewis & Clark College and Law School

May 19, 1983

Dear Laura Nader,

Since Derek Freeman sent me a copy of his letter to you, I thought I should send you a copy of his to me. I think I won that round . . . he was even more vitriolic to me than to you! I also had a hate letter from a Dr. Katz at the UCLA School of Medicine.

I am going to stay silent because I just fear he may seek even more publicity by provoking rejoinders to rejoinders, but I wanted you to know how glad I was to be in such good company as yours in earning Freeman's displeasure!
Sincerely,

Colin M. Turnbull
Department of Anthropology
George Washington University

June 14, 1983

Dear Laura,

Many thanks for the comments on *Private Government*. While I would not claim to agree with every comma in every article you've written, I always read your work. We do tend to work the same side of the street. If I did agree with every comma, I'm not sure you would be happy; the disagreements tend to be one of emphasis. For example, I like lawyers better than you, and I'd probably get along better with law professors.

Yet most of what you say about them seems to me to be right on target. I will look forward to reading Nader and Nader on deregulation in "field A" leading to increasing regulation by "private" governments. Just the idea seems right to me from your statement in the letter. I suffer from having Nelson Polsby on the SSRC committee reviewing my manuscript. He won't let one suggest any merit to what he calls a "non-decision" approach. I think he is just wrong—or he is overstating some doubts far beyond anything he can justify. Yet at some point one gives up and tries to get a manuscript published or rejected so one can get on with other things. Please send me your article in whatever form it exists when you have something to pass along. I am sure mutual reinforcement will be the result.

You mention trying to please economists. Have you seen my colleague Neil Komesar's *In Search of a General Approach to Legal Analysis: A Comparative, Institutional Alternative* (79 Mich. L. Rev. 1350 1981), "All legal decisions . . . involve a choice among imperfect alternative decision-making institutions." For a University of Chicago trained economist, Neil seems a breath of fresh air. Undoubtedly, he has been associating with bad companions here.

I also enjoyed the book reviews you sent. Here, I cannot even find any commas to object to. If comparative law (in the old fashioned law school sense) isn't impossible, it is so close to being impossible as to make it hard to justify the time spent on attempts. I think that looking at another society is valuable, but more as a sensitizing matter—a kind of Rorschach inkblot to prompt imagination and questioning about one's own society. I remember for example, your observation that third world nations send their 2nd class professionals (inexperienced or dumb) to the provinces to deal with the people; the few good ones escape to the big city leaving the time servers in place, etc. Then I wonder how do we allocate lawyers for cities and counties in Wisconsin—who becomes an Assistant D.A. in Eau Claire, Wisconsin?

I don't think the process is the same as in Mexico or Chile, and yet it is true that the Eau Claires of the world find it hard to draw people with what passes as the badges of talent in our society.

I also enjoyed your questioning of the litigation explosion position in the 2nd to last of the review—Derek Bok's report was a strange document. He denies there is such an explosion but then jumps on too many lawyers, too many complex laws, and calls for simplification and access. My favorite expression of this now fashionable view is Terry Cline's *The Attorney Conspiracy* (Arbor House, 1983). This is a badly written thriller. You see the Soviet Union is behind the whole explosion of law and lawyers. In the story they create a very wealthy man who backs any candidate for office as long as he is an attorney.

In this way capitalism will be brought down. I find all of this funny because I see this attack as so very conservative—what rights are being asserted by whom that bothers anyone? Wouldn't it be "nice" if Blacks would go back to "their place" as they were in 1953, if consumers would just accept the junk pushed out as they did before *Unsafe at Any Speed*, if women would get back in the kitchen, etc., etc. And the Japanese analogies are just wild, but they are very revealing. The Japanese, in our fantasies are a harmonious and happy people without problems. But what did they do when they wanted to block the construction of a new airport? I find so much of the writing revealing an attitude of "I've got mine, and these trouble makers should just shut up and accept their fate."

Isn't that what the "Public Interest" is all about?

I have to teach a summer school class. It was good hearing from you. I hope you enjoy Wellesley and Cambridge.

As ever,

Stewart Macaulay
Professor of Law
University of Wisconsin—Madison

June 15, 1983

Dear Professor Nader,

I am writing to thank you for allowing me to look at the manuscript *Regulatory Policy and the Social Sciences* edited by Roger Noll, as well as the correspondence between you and Prof. Noll regarding the piece you wrote with Claire Nader on "A Wide Angle on Regulation: An Anthropological Perspective." I have read said piece, as well as chapters 1 and 2 authored by Prof. Noll, and chapter 10 written by Lawrence Friedman. The following are my remarks.

I discern two sets of explicitly stated objectives in Noll's research agenda. On the one hand, he is concerned "with offering a set of policy recommendations on the issue of regulation-deregulation on the basis of the present state of research in the social sciences." On the other hand, he is attempting to "offer a comprehensive theory of the politics and economics of regulation in the United States." To avoid ambiguity, I will briefly quote Noll on these two goals.

Citing his own work to buttress his assertion, Noll writes that "the research literature on the effects of regulatory agencies reaches generally harsh judgements" (p.13). Therefore, instead of evaluating the empirical literature on the desirable "economic effects of regulatory agencies," he "presumes that agencies do have such effects" (Ibid). The practical implications of this assumption are spelled out in chapter one. He argues that "an important question is how and why many poorly performing regulatory policies were turned around in the late 1970s, and what can be done to the structure of government to assume that this is not a temporary phenomenon" (p.7).

Although your piece does not explicitly take issue with these goals, its thrust is clearly in opposition to them. But you are not alone in questioning these assumptions. Friedman in a striking phrase asserts that "a good deal of what economists regard as efficient, the public finds immoral" (p.529). Furthermore, he argues that "political argument and struggle lie behind all major statutes" (p.542) and that "economic analysis (or sociological analysis for that matter) is useless unless it confronts the legal system as it is, not as described in the books" (p.550). Friedman's analysis in my opinion nicely complements your call for a model that is holistic and interactionist.

Noll himself, calls for the need for theory to come to grips with complex reality. In his critique of "simple cartel theory," he demonstrates that "only by adopting a more complicated model of society as a complex combination of numerous interests can one explain the diversity of regulatory institutions" (p.31).

In his concluding remarks, Noll acknowledges that "the theory of regulatory behavior is rudimentary and fragmentary" and that "empirical work is almost non-existent on the kinds of issues of interest to policy makers" (p.94). On this basis he identifies the actual working of the regulatory agencies, and the factors that influence their performance as the "most productive areas for further scholarly research" (p.95).

Given the fact that this is the state of the arts in the study of regulation, it is important to shun a narrow economic definition of the tasks facing the social scientists. We have to insist on a holistic interactionist framework of analysis. Your paper makes a significant beginning in this direction. Therefore, I strongly agree with the evaluation of the anthropologist who refereed the paper for the press—insisting that it should be published. I am quite at a loss as to how a serious scholar could have called it "silly." Furthermore, I simply cannot believe the fact that the same person who praised Friedman's work, and who described your analysis as "useful anthropological perspective" in

one sentence could in his/her next sentence claim that your analysis verged on "babble." Arrogance can be blinding.
Sincerely,

Ashraf Ghani
Visiting Professor of Anthropology
University of California, Berkeley

June 19, 1983
Stewart Macaulay

Professor of Law
University of Wisconsin

Dear Stewart,

I so very much appreciated your letter, and it's reassuring to know that some people still know how to write letters like that. In addition, what you say further confirms my hunch about creeping censorship centered around a clique probably consisting in the main of political scientists of Democrat/ liberal origin like Nelson Polsby. Indeed, when I began looking into how the Jeanne Kirkpatrick thing came to happen at Berkeley I found Polsby at the heart of that as head of a faculty committee that brought her here, and before she came spelled out the "scenario."

In the light of your experience with "Private Government" I decided to send you the version of the regulation paper that was turned down by Noll and the reviews he sent along. As you can see, the "reviews" consisted of vitu-peratives until Noll responded to my complaint that this was not review, but censorship with his three pager followed by his editor's response as well. Our paper suffers as Elizabeth Colson remarked from trying to please too many audiences which is of course the trap one falls into when you are trying to get at least the idea you have included in a volume like this. I won't do that again. By the way, I also had the whole thing looked at by a scholar I very much respect that is also included at the end of the letters.

I see this as one of a series of cases that I mostly don't know about. The *UC Press* a few years ago did review the thesis of a graduate student of mine—on a comparison of insurance regulation in Pennsylvania and California. First, they promised to publish, then a political science review said it wasn't scholarly— it is in fact the most interesting work on regulation that I have seen, and indeed predicted what was to happen under the Carter administration. But based as it was on participant observation and the analysis of the participants as workers it was too much for the formalists. By the way, the fellow who did this work had had enough—being peripheral in choice of topic in anthropology then not accepted elsewhere, and eventually he dropped out. I did get him a contract through *Cambridge University Press* with a promise to publish after some cleaning up of thesis language but it was too late.

I add these experiences on regulation study another this time with the study of power more directly. I was involved in putting out a volume jointly with two other authors on the concept of *Power, Structure, and Ideology*—a volume to come out in 1984. An academic press was to publish it. We had an enthusiastic verbal contract. The volume was copy-edited and ready to go when the editor called me to say that the President of the academic press refused to sign the contract. When I called him to enquire he went berserk. The calmer I was the more hysterical he was screaming at me on the phone, "I don't have to publish this book," and refusing to give me a clue as to why. A change of policy on multi-authored books?—no. Change on policy on social science?—no. Content not up to snuff? He simply did not have to give a reason. By the way this was the same fellow who wanted me to delete the disacknowledgements from *No Access to Law*. Yup, times have changed.

You're quite right about the strangeness of the Bok report, and I'll have to get the Terry Cline book you mention—maybe the only way we can tell it like it is today is to write fiction!

Anyways Stewart, if you can find time to send me your criticisms of this paper we would appreciate it. I'll probably recast it for the *American Anthropologist*, although for anthropologists the point of view would be considered bland.

Best wishes,

Laura Nader
Professor of Anthropology

June 24, 1983

Dear Laura,

"A Wide Angle on Regulation" and the collection of reviews arrived this morning. I meant to skim what you had sent then because I was preparing to teach a 2 hour class this afternoon. Of course, it was better than a detective story, and I had to read everything then and there.

First, my overall reaction is one of anger and confusion. Your paper is not a revolutionary manifesto. If anything, it might better be criticized as a statement of what obviously is the case. In the absence of the reviews and what we know about academic factions, one might wonder what you (and I in "Private Government") are making such a big deal about. "It is marred, as usual in Nader's work in the U.S., and by a serious loss of objectivity verging on babble." Translation: "I (the reviewer) know the truth. Nader sees things differently and disagrees. Therefore, she is not objective. Moreover, I do not understand her, and so her writing verges on babble. I am so smart, famous, or whatever, so I am entitled to make assertions without the slightest argument or example." Notice that Roger Noll has to write a brief to support the reviewer(s), and it seems to me that he struggles a bit.

Indeed, most of his points seem to me to be the kind of thing which a sympathetic editor would raise and which could be taken care of by very modest revisions. For example, take his first point. Couldn't you have responded in a few sentences somewhat as follows (this is rough but I hope it makes' the point): "Choice is always constrained. Relatively self-sufficient farmers might have faced floods, infestations, raids by outlaws and the like. However, these could be seen as either natural hazards beyond the control of people or the sort of thing within the control of individuals who could arm themselves or enter into forms of defensive alliances. Moreover, government recognized their plight and at least promised (and sometimes provided) the army to deal with outlaws and Indians. When people moved to the city and worked for wages they faced a new set of constraints with which they were, and still are to a large extent, ill-equipped to cope. Moreover, our accepted ideology long denied there was any problem. Competition, the rule of law, and simple ideas of free contract were said to make everyone free. Whatever limits these factors placed on power in the long run, many workers and many observers perceived their situation as one of restricted choice and powerlessness." To take a modern example, in the long run perhaps Ford has been disciplined by the market because its Pinto was knowingly produced as a rolling people incinerator. However, this offers little consolation to anyone except a University of Chicago economist (all of whom should be sentenced to drive Corvairs in the morning and Pintos in the evening while being followed in large trucks by the parents of children killed in those cars who might just decide to ram them from behind). You see how I am always objective?

His second point shows that he doesn't know the historical literature—he is stuck on Kolko. Of course, any strong statement such as Kolko's conspiracy theory will prompt a reaction—young scholars make their reputation by trashing older ones, even radical older ones. I have the citation in my class notes at the office if you ever think you need it. Of course, Noll's position serves both radicals who think regulation cannot work, and conservatives who think that it just injures the purity of the free market. How many cases could

I find where without a push from consumers, business got itself regulated in its own interest. Airlines and perhaps trucks are the major examples, but even they are very mixed cases. Even the most cynical conspiracy theorist might admit that business made use of consumer power in some, if not most cases by conning consumer reps into thinking that regulation controlled business when it could be transformed in the future into a cartel. But is all this central to your argument, or only a point to be handled in a phrase or a sentence?

His third point suffers from any idea of symbolic politics. Isn't part of the problem with dioxin and kepone that government has promised to deal with such things, but has failed to do so through discretion, underfunding and overload, appointments to agencies, etc. The public has been led to believe that it both is and ought to be protected. Most probably draw an analogy to public health in general. In the U.S. you can drink the water, eat the lettuce, and buy cheese, ice cream and the like without a thought. In such a society, we just expect government to protect us from dioxin and the like—lomotil won't cure that. Moreover, the market won't work here for the reasons he cites. Finally, the interaction between parts of public government and corporations may mean that dangerous chemicals were developed in response to public contracts.

You could develop your regulation of the poor by business argument in terms of the growing reaction against free immigration which kept expanding the pool of cheap labor. Historically, this seemed a neat substitute for slavery— legitimated with the symbols of streets paved with gold, etc. Yet it was a factor in producing big city bosses and the fear of democracy by the old WASP elite. Threatened with the votes of workers, steps had to be taken to avoid loss of position. Welfare measures were part of a package to buy off potential social revolution. It went with the reality/myth (both of us are beneficiaries of some of the reality) of opportunity for those who would work; this of course, sold an individualistic or family oriented ethic rather than a collective one.

His last points are harder to deal with. You might get through to people such as Noll if you took a concrete example (say an article by Noll) and showed how it is flawed by a failure to see the regulation of private government. But this is a question of editorial judgment which would have to be answered by thinking about who you are trying to write for, what their assumptions are likely to be, and whether they would respond to a particular example. I'm not saying that this is entirely missing in the paper, but you could do more in this direction if you thought it worth it. The difficulty of course is that you might have to learn a lot about an area only to feel safe in trashing a particular article, and it might not be worth the effort.

Barry's letter also is troubling. I think again that one can ask for examples when his/her work is called "ungrammatical" or "slack." Even Barry once in his life, I would wager, has made a grammatical slip. These are the kinds of things I try to avoid but which I hope secretaries, reviewers and editors will catch. And what is "slack" writing? I assume it goes back to the claim that the paragraphs follow one another arbitrarily. Since I had no trouble at all following you—I am at a loss.

However, he seems to have missed the point badly in several places—so badly that I wonder what filter he has before his eyes. Why is regulation "normative control" over behavior in some due process law professor sense? Acme Paper Co. decides to dump chemicals into the river. Those affected are too poor to hire lawyers to sue, and Acme is the largest contributor to the state Democratic Party so state officials do not try to regulate. Acme thus has ruled how much gunk will be in the river along which those affected live. On the other hand, suppose Acme applies to the Dept. of Natural Resources for a permit to dump so much gunk into the same river, a hearing is held, and a permit is granted. The amount permitted is exactly the same as Acme dumped in the first instance. In terms of the power to dump gunk into the river, Acme held it in the first instance while the DNR did in the second. In terms of those affected, the amount of gunk has been regulated. Of course, for various purposes it might make a difference to distinguish whether an agency subject to due process, or one subject to administrative procedures needed to issue cease and desist orders was in control or it might not. But this just raises research questions.

Enough. I don't have time to write this letter, and you probably don't have time to read it. Nonetheless, I was annoyed.

I wonder what it does represent. Censorship could connote that the Polsbys of the world consciously decided to limit access to publications likely to be read by those outside certain academic ghettos. I think it more likely that Polsby, Noll, Barry, and the unnamed reviewers all are honorable people who think they are acting in good faith. In a way that makes coping with it so much harder. When you charged censorship, you provoked lots of pages from Noll and Barry. But they can satisfy themselves they are being objective, and in these cases they are both defendant and jury. On the other hand, the public/private distinction is so much of a background assumption that people don't have the ability to cope with it. Noll keeps saying that he agrees with you, but then cannot understand the implications of this concession. Your Martian anthropologist sees so many things in ways new to him that he cannot handle it again and again. I read you as saying (sometimes explicitly; sometimes implicitly) that here are some interesting parallels; here is a different way of looking at public and private regulation, of seeing that the absence of public regulation does not yield some state of nature without constraints.

What differences does it make? One difference is that our ideology denies there is any such unchecked private power—"the market" just takes it away. It may be that the very denial of such power itself is a major cause of problems. You and I, and the guys at the bar near the plant are aware of the gap between promise and performance.

Instead of censorship in the crude party-line fashion, the censorship may be that of people who are rewarded for holding a general position which they manage to believe.

The story about our U.N. war criminal and Polsby is grand—so bad that it is good. Jackie and I watched Joan Baez and her trip to Latin America on public television last week. There was Jeannie K. being interviewed in Santiago about Gen. Pinochet—"very agreeable, very strong, very honorable."

I suppose I think she ought to be able to speak, but I think free speech implies at the very least that a university act in ways not to grant its stamp of approval to her views. Those who feel as I do might have some access to the audience. You are right that it seems set up now to give her the status of a victim in the cause of free speech. And yet the British Parliament deals with Margaret Thatcher by commenting as she is speaking—"shame," etc.

There are virtues to blind reviews I suppose. Nonetheless, why do you have to put up with this kind of stuff? Why don't we have real informal sanctions which work that force one with the power given by not having his/her name disclosed to act responsibly? At least Barry had to subject himself to your judgement, and my judgment of what he said.

It is 1:30 a.m. and I have to get to bed because I have to get up. Nonetheless, I couldn't have gone to sleep without writing this letter. As you can tell, I think you have been treated badly. University professors might almost make you learn to love lawyers? Well, arrogance is arrogance.

I am sending a copy of "Private Government" to your brother. Did you see my latest on lawyers and law schools? You might enjoy some of it.
All my best,

Stewart Macaulay
Professor of Law
University of Wisconsin—Madison

July 31, 1983

Dear Laura:

I have finally managed to read the article that you and Claire wrote about regulation. I find it interesting and relevant. But let me tell you some of the things that might have put off some of the readers. First of all, you insist on an anthropological approach. My own conviction is that this is a mistake. Just do it and they will never know. You can even quote Malinowski by saying that the point you are making isn't exactly new, and then letting them figure out that Malinowski was an anthropologist and that yours is an anthropological approach. Then if you like, in quite another context you can say what you have done. I have found that people do not want to hear "anthropological approaches" (or any other kind of approach when it is marked by a disciplinary label), but rather they want to hear about the subject.

Second, you (like all anthropologists) have to somehow defend yourself against the charge that anthropologists talk about everything and won't allow anybody else's boundaries to stand. Of course that is so . . . indeed that is our point. Our job is to change the context. But people react to it better when you tell them straight-out that you are charging and altering the context to get a new kind of look at the subject. When you tell them (and unfortunately, you have to say it every time because they never remember) that their contexts and their premises are blinding them—only then are they alerted not to judge whatever you say according to their own previous premises.

Third, there is in it a mixture of scholarship and admonition that might almost be designed to put academics off. I happen to agree with you on all your points, but that is not what you want to hear. It is a stylistic matter: reading it gives me the impression that you first analyze a situation, and then point an accusing finger without ever giving a program for correcting the difficulty. I think this is the major difficulty. Is there any way that you can separate out the analysis from the admonition?

I think that it is the admonitory tone that is getting the reactions that I see in the letters you sent. Of course, academics do not know when they do this kind of thing—they only know they don't like something, so they find something specific to hook their dislike to that may or may not have anything to do with it (it is like selection committees who turn down good research proposals that unconsciously threaten them, but do it on the basis of their methodology).

Finally, there is another matter. When a scholar becomes senior, he or she also becomes visible. That makes you a very good target. There is not a thing any of us can do about that. People get brownie points for shooting down the prominent. At least in their own eyes.

I hope this helps. You see, I too have had a lot of trouble with publishers, with the result that I have more or less pulled back from "scientific contribution" and have gone my own sweet way. It has probably cost me a lot, but it has also netted me a lot. I too have been screwed by the *University of California Press* (so help me God—the stuffiest in the business), by their reviewers who did not understand what they were reading, or were more likely threatened by it.

The point of all this is don't give up. But particularly on the admonition point—you might want to look at the piece again.

I hope this is helpful. Best of everything.

Yours ever,

Paul Bohannan
Los Angeles, California

August 9, 1983

Dear Laura:

No, I haven't forgotten that I promised to look over what you wrote for Roger Noll. What happened was that after returning from a trip, I was immediately plunged into a complex tangle of problems which are too long to go into here, but which I will tell you about sometime. Anyway, things are back to normal now.

I am not very satisfied with my own piece, even though it didn't suffer the same fate as yours. In the last couple years, I have done a number of short essays on subjects I didn't really feel comfortable with. But I was persuaded by a combination of money and the argument that people needed a fresh, outside look. What I discovered, or should have known, is that people think they want a fresh look, but they really don't—it's hard to be taken seriously outside of your own field.

Generally speaking, I find your point of view useful and an important corrective. The economists emphasize the distinction between regulation and market processes, and on this basis they have built up what is in many ways an impressive body of theory, but they need to have their knuckles rapped as often as possible. And they need to learn precisely the perspective that you put forward, that is that rules for regulating social behavior can emanate from any source of organized power.

I have become more and more convinced that the distinction between public and private regulation tends to be irrelevant in many contexts. A person who is treated unfairly hardly cares whether the unfairness is governmental or non-governmental. This means that I am of course basically sympathetic with what you have tried to do in your piece. I am not saying that I wouldn't have changed some things here and there, and perhaps the organization leaves something to be desired.

I have the impression that Roger Noll's letter of June 4 does have some valuable suggestions for improving your paper, and would have been on the whole a constructive letter if the end result of all this had been different. That is, that your contribution would have been accepted with changes.

To sum up: I think that you make a contribution. I would have definitely kept your article, though with some revisions of course. I think you were badly handled, even rudely, and the whole thing is unfortunate. You spoke in your letter about "reality testing." You have strong views and are not afraid to assert them. You get a lot more done and make a lot more of a difference in the world than those of us who are more mealy mouthed and "even handed." You have many friends and admirers, and I would say to you keep right on going. That doesn't mean that you shouldn't listen to people who are critical in a constructive way—of course you should. I myself have some doubts about some aspects of your argument, but so what?

Have a good summer and forget about this mess.

Regards,

Lawrence M. Friedman
Professor of Law
Stanford University

Kathleen Gough was a politically outspoken anthropologist who was "let go" from Brandeis University for her outspokenness which was cast as her not being a "good teacher."

November 12, 1983

Dear Laura,

I have thought of our brief meeting in August many times. I was so pleased to see you and to hear your courageous paper. David and I saw Valery Tishkov that evening and he said how much he had liked your work, even though we agreed that we do not believe in two comparable "superpowers."

It was about this that I promised to write you. I delayed because events came so thick and fast that I seemed too breathless, but I have had it in mind. I'm enclosing the article I wrote in 1962, surprised that so little has changed in 21 years.

Beyond that, I wanted to try to make the following points.

1. I think that ever since the invention of the first atomic bombs, it has been the U.S.A. that has created new weapons of mass destruction, with the U.S.S.R. following with similar weapons a year or a few years after. This suggests that the U.S.A. is the primary aggressor, with the U.S.S.R. acting mainly defensively.

2.   There are countless works documenting the fact that transnational
     corporations and the governments of the "core" capitalist countries
     garner huge profits from investment and trade in the Third World.
     Although they usually camouflage it, the capitalist governments often
     admit that the reason they go to war is to safeguard their profits and
     property. By contrast, I think the U.S.S.R. gains only small profits from
     its international relations, and indeed is probably on balance a major
     donor to poorer countries. The Soviet Union may get some profits
     from its trade with Eastern Europe and India, although I am not even
     sure of that. East Germany, Hungary, and probably Czechoslovakia
     for example, seem to be better off than the U.S.S.R. Certainly, India
     shells out far more in profits, interest, and unequal trade to the U.S.A.,
     Britain, West Germany, and Japan, than it does to the U.S.S.R. On the
     other hand, the U.S.S.R. is the donor to Cuba, Vietnam, Laos, Cambo-
     dia, Afghanistan, Angola, South Yemen, Nicaragua, Ethiopia, and until
     recently, Grenada. I think none of these countries could keep afloat
     long without Soviet aid. The U.S.S.R., for example, gives at least 3 mil-
     lion a day to Vietnam.

It is true that the U.S.A. also gives capital goods to some countries (e.g.
Israel, probably South Korea, etc.), to which it is on balance a donor. However,
I think it does this in order to protect its investments elsewhere—giving a little
to some in order to get much from others. We must also look at which classes
profit from this aid. In the case of the U.S.A.'s debtors, they are the capitalists
while the poor languish. In the case of the U.S.S.R.'s debtors, the common
people have by and large improved their conditions a great deal since their
revolutions. So all in all, I think the U.S.S.R. does act largely out of "proletar-
ian internationalism," while the governments of the U.S.A., Britain, etc., act
and make war to gain or retain profits.

The many wars since World War II have not been started by the Soviet
Union, or very seldomly so. Most of them have been revolutionary wars begun
by indigenous Third World peoples trying to get back control of their territory and property from Western governments and corporations. The wars in
China, Korea, Vietnam, Laos, Cambodia, Angola, Mozambique, Zimbabwe,
Nicaragua, Cuba, El Salvador, Lebanon, and the Palestinian assaults on Israel
have all been like this. The U.S.S.R. is secondary—it comes in to give aid sometimes, although sometimes too little and too late. It is not the main aggressor.

I can't prove these points here, but I think there is a great deal of research
that does support them, and that they have to be considered—otherwise the

basis of the peace movement arguments is false. Although it may be hard to put the correct arguments (assuming I am correct) to some people, and useless to put them to some governments, I think they have to be understood if we are to act reasonably, and that it is possible to persuade increasing numbers of their truth.

Much love and thanks for the work you're doing.

Yours,

Kathleen Gough

December 19, 1983

Dear Professor Nader,

An article based on an address you delivered at the Mitre corporation has recently come to my attention. The article was titled "Barriers to Thinking About Energy," and it appeared in the January 1982 issue of *Chemtech*.

Although I am one of whom you refer to as physical scientists in your article, my more recent involvement with energy research and planning activities, and in ministerial committees here in Syria has opened my eyes to a number of the shortcomings you mentioned in your article as exhibited by scientists in this country, and in other countries in similar stages of development.

I am writing this letter simply to let you know that the experiences you outlined in your article correspond very closely with my own more recent observations in our rather special setting, and that I am full of admiration for the clear and direct manner in which you put your views on this subject.

I should be happy if I could get to know more about your other contributions in this field through reprints, or merely references to your other publications.

Yours sincerely,

Dr. O. F. Bizri
Scientific Studies Research Center
Syrian Arab Republic

February 9, 1984

Dear Ms. Nader:

Thank you for writing to express your dismay at the Reagan Administration's actions regarding the forced resignation of Peter Bell, the President of the Inter-American Foundation.

I certainly share your concern. In my view, this is just part and parcel of the Reagan Administration's mindset toward Latin American problems—particularly demonstrated in its approach toward Central America. No one has raised any objection to Mr. Bell's competence, integrity, or record. But his approach is evidently not compatible with the Reagan Administration's philosophy, and the resulting loss of his considerable talents at the I.A.F. is symptomatic of the Reagan Administration's policy failures toward Latin America.

You may be certain that I shall continue to do my best to moderate the Reagan Administration's approach.

Sincerely,

Christopher J. Dodd
United States Senator
U.S. Senate Committee on Foreign Relations

September 19, 1984

Dear Laura,

Thanks for sending me the copy of the paper by Mary L. Foster. I plan on using it in my class to teach engineers to listen and read more carefully.

You may also be interested in knowing how useful I have found your *Physics Today* article: "Barriers to Thinking New About Energy." It is an extremely perceptive and thought provoking piece that serves as a basis for very productive discussions in my class of seniors and graduate students in engineering. I use it as part of a series of readings aimed at developing students' appreciation of the ways people in different disciplines go about framing a given problem. Naturally, they are particularly blind to the types of value judgements implicit in the engineer's approach to framing problems. Your article provides them with insights into a mirror that most engineers don't even look at until they enter those relatively safe years just prior to retirement.

Very few of the engineers in my class have had a course in anthropology. By the time they are seniors, most of them have developed an attitude I call "technocratic arrogance," resulting from the rather elementary nature of their introductions to the social sciences and humanities via "101" courses. But your article makes a tremendous impression on them, it gives them a genuine appreciation for the intellectual contribution anthropologists bring to the framing of what they previously perceived as purely technological problems. Later in the course as they trace the evolution of a variety of technological developments such as nuclear power, they frequently cite concepts from your paper as they analyze the successes and failures of various technologies.

As a former DoE Office Director, I am aware that funding for such investigations is scarcer now than it ever was. So in lieu of cash, I hope you will accept these words of encouragement and continue your excellent work. It is certainly making a profound impression on a significant fraction of the new generations of engineers graduating from the University of Illinois.
Sincerely,

Clark Bullard
Director
University of Illinois at Urbana-Champaign

March 14, 1985

Dear Laura:

I was glad to hear from you just before your departure for Cairo, where I hope that you will have time to see some of the antiquities that you may have missed on former trips. Our daughter Alice and her husband the oceanographer recently returned from their first trip to Egypt and were fascinated with it.

You were kind to send me your essay on "Ideology as Covert Power," but I must admit I have not been as interested as you clearly are, in ideology and power as they are applied to social change. I have been so absorbed by medical science all of my life that I have had no time for anything else.

I must admit that recently I have been absorbed by my struggle to protect radical mastectomy and the scientific background of facts that support it. I see examples all around me in medicine in which physicians blandly ignore well established and not very complex facts and data. The only explanation that I can find for them is that their will to power is so great that facts are very secondary and power comes first—although they may not themselves realize it. Ideology is a far away land that they never think about.

Did you ever read the interesting book, about Richard III written by Josephine Tey, and called *The Daughter Of Time*. It illustrates as well as anything could how social facts and history are distorted. A wonderful example of the distortion of facts, or rather the lack of them in the minds of the physicians concerned, is the article on the front page of *The New York Times* today announcing the "discovery" that lumpectomy for breast cancer is just as successful as radical mastectomy, and that my operation need no longer be performed. This is endorsed by the American Cancer Society and the director of the National Cancer Institute.

I have finished the revision of my textbook, and Alice has found a publisher for her local history—so we are both happy. Please write me when you get back from Egypt.

With our love to you,

Cushman Haagensen
Department of Surgery
Columbia University

May 22, 1985

Dear Laura:

Reading your responses to questions posed in the *Dispute Resolution Forum*, the theologian in me felt the need for some sort of "apologia" to my new job as Director of the Corporate Initiatives Division of the National Wildlife Federation. Of course, it was the only job offer I got in eight months of uncompensated unemployment! Nevertheless, I am persuaded on its motive and rationale as a "bridge building" process (this is a non-fundraising effort). I've enclosed some of our material for your interest.

I did not think I was doing "dispute resolution" work because I understood that reference to mean alternatives to the judicial process for citizens—as I first learned the term through your work. However, a Jesuit priest at Boston College invited me to address his seminar on "Dispute Resolution" on my division's agenda for building bridges with corporations. So when I read your comments in DRF, I wished I had the opportunity for discussion.

Admittedly, this effort of ours fits more into your "organizational expansion" and "professional profitability" concepts. Still, I think you would also recognize the "macro-prevention" aspect of trying to structure a productive process of prevention for the environmental problems endemic to industrial growth. I'm using a "carrot," but I can justify that colleagues retain the stick. Children—and indeed we are a toilet training industry—need to be acknowledged and rewarded when they make their beds and help their siblings, even if the rest of our expectations are disappointed.

I have met senior environmental officers in corporations who are environmentalists and I can work with them. One former Exxon Vice President for Environmental Affairs told me that he always viewed himself as the "Ralph Nader of Exxon." That comparison is more than amusing to me, but that was the man's perception of himself. If we don't support and reinforce him in his work, he may mitigate his advocacy to accommodate his colleagues' suspicions or disgruntlement. We want to provide him with a support system that encourages environmental quality over economic priorities.

I don't know if you have the time or interest for a dialogue on this. But I did want to write you about what I was doing after reading DRF. What do you think?

Sincerely,

Sheila Harty
Director—Corporate Initiatives Division
National Wildlife Federation

October 10, 1985

Dear Laura,

Many thanks for your note of September 30, your outline, and the two publications that you sent me. I very much enjoyed reading your article "Barriers to Thinking New About Energy." I have been involved in a very large scale project in agriculture and I find identical problems. We have been attempting to look at the agricultural sectors of Jordan and Sudan through the eyes of the farmer. And to my absolute horror and amazement, I discovered that in the Sudan the farmer is never in the picture. That is, planners and agricultural scientists and agricultural researchers practically never remember to even think of him. They study every aspect of agriculture, but make absolutely no reference to the miserable person who is supposed to be producing the food we eat. In Jordan the situation is significantly better although not perfect. As a result of research work in Jordan we were able to introduce a fairly dramatic change in perspective, and now it is very much "in" to talk about the farmer and his problems. Maybe I should send you copies of the volumes on this type of research. Since most of them will probably be of interest to you, I've enclosed a small brochure on the publications. Please select the ones you would like to receive.

I look forward to your participation in the workshop in March, and I am sure it is going to be very interesting. For your information, you are the only lady in the group!

I am looking forward to receiving your paper in the near future. Please do not be late. End of November at the latest.

Very best wishes,

A. B. Zahlan
London, United Kingdom

October 15, 1985
Ira Michael Heyman

Chancellor
U.C. Berkeley

Dear Chancellor Heyman,

At your suggestion this letter summarizes my conversation in your office yesterday, and my appeal which, was prompted by your September 9, 1985 letter which included the aggregate summary of reviewers' evaluations of my recent case for advancement to Special Salary Status to be effective July 1, 1985.

First, a brief background note: In my 1979–80 review, the Department requested Special Salary Status. I received Step 6 with advice from Dean Hooson to come up for Special Salary again in the Fall of 1980. Since I was at the Wilson Center in Washington, D.C. 1980–81, I waited until my return to be put forward again, and again the Department requested Special Salary. I was given Step 7. In 1984–85, once again the Department presented a case requesting Special Salary; it was denied.

As I said yesterday, the aggregate summary contained unscholarly and prejudicial material, and suffers problems of omission. For the moment, however, I will dwell on the root of the matter in order to unravel the problem. Years ago, my unfinished Zapotec law monograph (10 chapters completed) got highlighted in my record at a time when I thought it was central to my work. In fact, the Zapotec law monograph forms a part of my work—a piece of a global question dealing with the disputing process. In addition, I felt no hurry to publish what are basically political materials until these materials were well-distanced from the time of data collection due to developments unfolding in Mexico.

The Budget Committee, however, focused on the Zapotec monograph and locked themselves into a mechanical posture on the case. In fact, the Budget Committee got so focused on what I should be doing that they have not looked at what I have done and what I am doing. Note that *No Access to Law*, research covering ten years of effort, was completely omitted from the aggregate summary. *The Disputing Process*, a research effort of 15 years, was referred to as "a collection of pieces." In both research projects (The Berkeley Village Law Project and the Berkeley Complaint Project) there was a research design with specific objectives which were achieved. The research on law and the disputing process has been part of an ongoing research strategy I have been working out for 25 years (working first within one society over time—the Zapotec, then cross-culturally—*The Disputing Process*, then cross-nationally—*No Access to*

Law), a strategy which is now directed toward understanding the evolution of law (Wenner-Gren Conference, Bellagio, Summer 1985).

Basically, I am a patient and reasonable person, and I feel diffident about having to make my own case. However, over the years I have raised grievances and the responses to these have not been straightforward. Let me list a few: When it is said that my service to the University is negligible, have reviewers adequately considered the 15-plus years of service that I gave at the NIMH, the NSF, the NAS, the SSRC as a representative of the Berkeley campus—service which resulted in considerable support for our students? In the creative sphere, has the Budget Committee weighed the two film contributions as comparable to published work (To Make the Balance, 1966; Little Injustices, 1981)? Has the Budget Committee considered additional teaching (I have always taught more courses than required when there has been need)? I participated in one of the most important of national energy studies (CONAES) and I was given no university support in conducting this research (*Energy Choices in a Democratic Society*, 1980). My Honors are treated as etceteras, as if they happen to everyone. The recognition I receive does not lead me to believe that. For example, when I was invited to participate in the SLEP seminar in Oklahoma (Spring 1985), a seminar composed of carefully chosen outstanding people across the country, I was Informed that X was the second anthropologist chosen over a ten year period; the other was Dr. Sherwood Washburn of Berkeley, a University Professor. When I was invited to participate in the Nebraska Symposium on Motivation (Fall 1984), I was informed that in 40 years or more of that Symposium's existence I was the second anthropologist to be selected; the other was Dr. John Whiting of Harvard University.

I am recognized for at least three major contributions: first, I have taken a relatively insignificant sub-field in anthropology (the anthropology of law), and have raised it to significance in both the scholarly and policy arenas, through national and international meetings and by means of the published volumes that followed. Second, I have played a major role in initiating a second look at the proper unit of analysis for social anthropological research ("Up the Anthropologist" and "The Vertical Slice"), arguing that by limiting ourselves to a residential unit we may be overlooking the interesting questions and needlessly limiting our development of theory, third, my work on energy and then on the process of doing science has set a model, one in which the anthropologist defines the important questions for anthropological research, which I believe is necessary if we are to carry out interdisciplinary efforts with integrity. This is an important position in relation to policy issues and why I believe I am often the only social scientist to be invited to address law trained people on questions relating to Alternative Dispute Resolution. I do not try to do what the physicists or lawyers can do better, rather I do what anthropologists do best.

Finally, I would address the salary inequity problem. I am not being given equal pay for equal production as you would glean if you were to have my record compared against the superscales in anthropology and right across the University. And this in your administration which has dedicated effort to improve the position of minorities and women!

Your letter of September 9 depended on staff for an aggregate summary of my work. In the light of our conversation, I would appreciate having your evaluation. I thank you for your kind attention and look forward to hearing about your reconsideration of my case.

Sincerely yours,

Laura Nader
Professor of Anthropology

May 15, 1986
Ira Michael Heyman

Chancellor
U.C. Berkeley

Dear Chancellor Heyman,

Please accept this letter as a response to your letters of January 10 and May 15, 1986 which still do not address the core of our conversation of last Fall.

First, I requested last Fall that my entire production be reviewed. I produce books, articles, films, and reviews. My request was not honored. If a scholarly review of my work was made, it has not been made available to me.

Second, let me remind you that it was your office (letter of Jan. 10, 1986) that made the explicit comparison between my case and the case of my colleague in anthropology. My letter of October 15, 1985 made no explicit comparison with any particular Berkeley faculty member. Once the comparison was raised by you, and then responded to by Prof. Colson in her letter to you a response to this issue of equity was required. In your January letter you point out that the colleague in my department who was advanced to Special Salary had produced scholarly work that was "considerably more numerous" than what had been found in my record. In fact, your statement is wrong. While it is considered improper to make a direct comparison, it seems entirely proper to compare my record and my colleague's record to the same standard, I can only say that I am not alone in this department in feeling confused as to what that standard could be.

I feel that I need to comment on your observation that Anthropology has "consistently requested advancements . . . in excess. . . " It would seem logical that a department that was nationally ranked number one would request and receive advancements on merit. It may also be the selection patterns of the campus (not the department) that is fortifying the folklore regarding advancements in excess.

Let me conclude by saying that I am grateful for your attention and expression of friendship. At the same time I am obliged to express the view that the system is not working right, and that this is not to the advantage of the University. Although I speak about my personal case, I am trying to point out that these disinterested set of components deserve attention they are not receiving. My questions are straightforward. Why was my complete record not under review? What criteria of scholarship were used to advance my colleague that I did not meet?

Sincerely yours,

Laura Nader
Professor of Anthropology

Elizabeth Colson was the first woman chair of the Budget Committee. In a letter she wrote to the Chancellor in 1986, she said:

> "Professor Nader has been judged not on her distinguished record but on the things she has not done. On that basis, most of us would fail . . . Professors Nader and Benedict are both friends of mine . . . both have fine records, though their strengths differ. Professor Nader stands above Professor Benedict in terms of national and international reputation for sustained scholarly publication, pioneering innovation that continues to open up new questions for research, and overall impact upon Anthropology and related disciplines. But to advance one and not the other puts in question the equity of the reviewing process."

—Elizabeth Colson January 27, 1986

July 2, 1986
Bruce Ames

Professor of Biochemistry
University of California, Berkeley

Dear Bruce:

In several conversations we have had over the past years, you have made reference to the downward movement in cancer rates in the U.S. Could you

please send me the citations of the studies on cancer rates that you are referring in order to verify whether the public perception of rising cancer rates is
erroneous, or whether the data are being collected in ways that would lead us
to believe that both the public and scientific views are correct.

Thank you very much for your help on this. I enjoyed dinner very much
with you and Giovanna the other evening.

Sincerely yours,

Laura Nader

July 24, 1986

Dear Laura:

What I said about cancer rates is: 1) Lung cancer has been going up for
years (and epidemiologists attribute essentially all of this to smoking: there is
only a tiny amount of lung cancer in non-smokers and most of that is thought
to be due to radon). Smoking also contributes to bladder and some other
cancers, and of course to 25% of heart disease. 2) Stomach, uterine, and liver
cancer rates have been coming down for years (a likely explanation for the
decrease of stomach cancer is a better diet and less salt). Most other cancers
haven't changed very much.

I enclose the latest graph from the American Cancer Society and a recent
newspaper article. Of course, since cancer is also a degenerative disease of old
age, if you don't correct cancer rates for age, they are going up because we are
all living longer every year (see my enclosed paper on aging and cancer, which
also shows why living is the same as being irradiated). Epidemiologists always
age-correct of course, as in the American Cancer Society figures.

I also enclose an article by Richard Peto which lucidly discusses the latest
information. The definitive review on the causes of cancer is by Doll and Peto.
Sir Richard Doll is the leading epidemiologist in the world, and I think that
Peto is the smartest guy in the field.

The idea that cancer rates were going up was sold to the environmental
organizations by Sam Epstein on the basis of some bad science on incidence
rates that was later demolished by Doll and Peto (Appendix C in Doll and Peto
book, which I'll send you if you want to read it).

Sincerely,

Bruce Ames
Professor of Biochemistry
University of California, Berkeley

July 29, 1987
Derek Freeman

Professor of Anthropology
The Australian National University

Dear Professor Freeman:

Thank you for your letter. It is always stimulating to know of your latest research efforts, and to know more about your sequel to Margaret Mead and Samoa. Controversy in science is a topic that interests me as well. In this regard I enclose a piece "Barriers to Thinking New About Energy" published in *Physics Today*, February 1981.

Re: my review of Margaret Mead and Samoa published in The *Los Angeles Times*. Let me repeat in a somewhat briefer form: Derek Freeman is a first rate anthropologist who wrote a bad book which should not have been published by a good press.

Re: "Nature, Nurture, and Behavior," an editorial written by the current editor of *Science*. I have followed the Koshland editorials since he took over the editorship of *Science*. This piece on nature and nurture is written in the same sloppy style as all the rest. Of course nature and nurture are both involved in our behavior.

With all best wishes to you in your research efforts.
Sincerely yours,

Laura Nader
Professor of Anthropology

July 29, 1987

Dear Laura,

You have sent on two batches of mail which I have not acknowledged, though the second reached me a couple of weeks ago. You are sending exactly what I need. Thanks indeed for taking care of it, I know it is just that much more on a busy schedule. The reason I haven't written before seems to be over involvement in other things. Late June I finally spent a night down in Sinafala, and that was wonderful even though it was cold, and at one point I wondered if I weren't beyond the age of enjoying sleeping curled on the backseat of a car without enough blankets. Then, Bonnie Keller and some friends of hers went to the Kafue National Game Park over the long weekend early in July—alas poachers had been before us, so we saw no elephants and were told the herd there had been wiped out and other herds were much diminished. But the birds were wonderful, and we did see various kinds of antelope, lions, leopards, hyenas, jackals, and one beautiful wild dog. Plus tons of hippopotamus and more crocodiles than I was interested in. Then Jonathan arrived just over a week ago.

Since then I have introduced him around the Institute, taken him to shops and banks, taken him down to Musulumba for a few hours where we ran into hordes of people assembled to complete the funeral of a man who died last September—people from 23 villages were there. Fine chance for me to see various ones and for Jonathan to be introduced. I have also taken him down to the Gwembe District Office (140 miles from here) to introduce him to the District Governor and District Secretary so they know who he is when he is reported down in the villages.

I think he thinks this is somewhat of a slow start, but I am busy at the university and can't take off much time during the week. And if I had not been here he would be spending much more time getting himself organized, especially as far as transport is concerned. This weekend is another long weekend, when Bonhie and I have arranged to go down to a campsite in a game park in Zimbabwe said to be rich in game. We will take Jonathan with us and give him one chance to see a side of Africa he probably won't see again. Gwembe now has little game. During one long trip in July—starting at 5 a.m. and ending at 7:30 p.m., over miles and miles of Gwembe South which was only rocks, hills, sand, and busy, we saw only 2 bands of baboons and one mongoose.

Jonathan won't have an easy time when he does start on his own. There is real hunger, and the delivery of bags of meal isn't anywhere near meeting the demand so far, even though various international agencies are getting into the act. The morning paper reported that a woman in Siameja, one of the census villages, was hospitalized with broken ribs while 10 others were injured when they stampeded to buy meal being delivered by a truck—about 1,000 people are said to have charged forward, fearful that the bags would run out before they got something.

I've been to a wedding reception—the bride and groom, and most of the 400 or so people present were mostly from Western Province (old Barotseland), but I gather the reception was standard Zambian, with its combo band and loud speaker system blaring at its loudest. When most of us got there it struck up "Here Comes the Bride" in rumba rhythm, and in danced the two flower girls, groomsmen in dark suits, and probably assorted relatives. Everyone jumped up on tables and chairs to get a good view, while women shrilled and most everybody clapped—I had to leave before the cutting of the cake. My ears are not susceptible to that much noise, but even some of the young

Zambians complained. During the admonitions to the bride and groom by various relatives, we could get only an occasional word given the loud-speakers' determination to reverberate everything from ceiling and all walls.

Please don't send any mail after September 1st. Given the slowness with which some of it arrives, I might be gone before anything mailed much later can come through for I leave here October 3rd, returning by way of England where I shall spend a few days in London. Before I leave Jeanie Kayser-Jones may come here for a week or ten days. She wants to see how the elderly are treated in places such as Zambia.

I do hope you are feeling energetic and are completely over the thyroid virus. I know you are working full out on the lectures for New Zealand. You should be getting back about the same time that I am. It will be good to see you and hear all that has happened. I know you will enjoy New Zealand, and have enormous pleasure in taking your mother into new experiences. But before you go, if the opera tickets have arrived, arrange for that first ticket for "Tosca" to be used—Nadia might find it worth hearing.

My best,

Elizabeth Colson
Department of African Development Studies
University of Zambia

July 31, 1987

Dear Laura,

Another packet of mail has just arrived sent off in early July. Many thanks. Yes, you are sending right things, but again don't send or have anything sent after September 1st. You haven't said if the check for $1,000 I sent you in early June for repairs on radiator covered the cost of repairs, or indeed if it arrived safely (I hope it did).

Haven't heard anything more from Seteny, and I don't know if she has found someone to stay in house after she leaves. But I have decided not to worry.

The packet of mail contained a letter from University of Adelaide asking for reference for Nancy Williams who has put in for the chair they have advertised. I had told her to alert them to my current address, but apparently that didn't sink in—perhaps with her, or perhaps with the people at Adelaide. I sent it via fax. The investigation at U. of Zambia produced information they had never heard of such a means of communication. Telex does exist, but one would have to drive a mile or so to Vice Chancellor's office to make use of it.

I'm enclosing envelope for Women's Faculty Club and would appreciate it if you would drop it into the Campus Mail.

Thanks for everything. It's wonderful to have a trustworthy person at the other end.

Best,

Elizabeth Colson
Department of African Development Studies
University of Zambia

August 13, 1987

Dear Laura,

Two letters from you. Thanks for thinking about the house—any of the people you suggest sound all right, though I would particularly like Gabriella Bozzini if she would be willing to occupy. The Grinnell student as an unknown quantity is least appealing.

Wonderful to see the Zapotec book so near completion. I am anxious to read it, and of course to see the Auckland lectures once they are done. I am amazed that you have been able to work on three different writing projects at once. When I try even two, one usually interferes with the other and I get blocked.

Too bad about the Youth News and all—Nadia has put a great deal into it the last two years, and she must be very sad and very much at loose ends as she decides where next to invest herself. Probably she and Tarek are having many long thoughts together in his breaks from the garage roof.

But you must also be thinking about this year next time when Rania too will be leaving for college. As you said, your family is in a stage of major transitions.

It is depressing about Cathy Witty. When we had that lunch before I left she seemed happy and assured about where she was going and the possibilities of the job. Give her my best.

Jeanie Kayser-Jones is due to arrive Sept 1 and depart Sept 8. Jonathan has been introduced in Gwembe South, including at a meeting when the Assistant District Secretary and the Senior Gwembe Chief—each expatiated on the importance of this work and told people to help him because it did so much for Gwembe. An interesting idea. This coming week I shall take him to Gwembe Central and leave him for about 10 days on his own so he really gets into the swing of things. While I get on with some of the other things I want to do in the few weeks left out here.

I hope Suzanne has found something in Washington. It is good news that JoAnn is teaching for a term, even if the pay is iniquitous, and it was a labor to get her appointed.

No doubt each member of the department immediately thought of a student whom he or she wanted to have teach as soon as they heard that any finishing student was being considered.

How good you are going to have Carmen, Jose, and their daughter with you for a little bit now—should release you to concentrate on Auckland and all that goes with such a long trip.

Again my thanks for all you are doing.

Best,

Elizabeth Colson
Department of African Development Studies
University of Zambia

August 25, 1987

Dear Laura,

I take my car to Automotive Unlimited on Addison Street, just south of Shattuck Avenue. Sorry that you have had to hunt for letter—not something you need in the midst of trying to get off for New Zealand.

As I wrote, I would be delighted to have Gabriella Bozzini stay in the house until I get back October 9th, and for that matter, if she wants to share with Jenny Beer the two of them can occupy it. Seteny said that Alice Horner would be prepared to look in, but I would much prefer to have one or other of your students. The last time I left the house in Alice's care she used my car against my express instructions, and the explanation that my insurance was no good if car driven by anyone under 25.

Alice always thinks she knows best, and frequently she doesn't. Alas, there is only one opera ticket. In the past I used to have seats with a friend, and when she didn't get back in time I used her ticket along with my own. But in the last few years I have gone on my own on a Sunday afternoon and so have only one ticket to hand on to someone else.

I do hope that the New Zealand trip is a release, and a lift for both you and your mother. I know it will be strenuous, but you will also enjoy the honors, the new people, the new environment. I hope they take you to the mountains where you can sit and listen to the birds sing.

Yes, I did say Katie could use the car—you had suggested that I make the offer.

My best,

Elizabeth Colson
Department of African Development Studies
University of Zambia

September 26, 1987

Dear Prof. Nader:

I am sorry we were not able to meet during my visit to California earlier this month. But I am planning to relocate to your lovely part of the country by the end of this year when I hope to have the pleasure which I missed on my last trip. Meanwhile I would like to appraise you of my work on the reform of the law in Saudi Arabia, and see if there is ground for us to cooperate in an interdisciplinary approach.

As you may know, the oil boom and the public development projects of the past two decades generated a surge in the statutory enactments to deal with the expanded economic activity in the country, independently of the traditional Islamic Law (the Sharia) which constitutes the basic common law of the land. The result has been a clear dichotomy in the law, and the settlement of disputes between equally valid sets of rules which Lon Fuller would describe as "two forms of positivism"—a fascinating case for legal theory had it not at the same time created in practice problems of choice, chicanery and conflict not only to the administration of justice, but to the budding economic institution of the country as well. (I have developed this issue of duality in the Saudi legal system in an article I submitted recently to a law journal). However, since I do not subscribe to the notion that the study of the law can be divorced from the rest of the social condition (Richard A. Posner has written on "The Decline of Law as an Autonomous Discipline," Harvard L. Rev. vol. 100, Feb. 1987 pp. 761–780), I believe that with a better understanding of the Saudi legal situation and the future course of the changes now taking place, this can be achieved by a combined approach of the legal, anthropological, sociological, and cultural disciplines.

As you probably know, the Sharia does not distinguish between law and society. As the word itself indicated, it is the righteous path for the faithful to follow in their daily lives, and remains in the public domain the source of legitimacy for governmental power and the law. The new statutory enactments (invariably referred to as nizam (plural nuzum)—that is ordinances rather than quanun—that is canon or law), and their respective tribunals were primarily intended to regulate the activities of foreign contractors engaged on governmental projects, while the local people continued to adhere to (and have more affinity with) the traditional rules of the Sharia. Today, banking disputes over the payment of interest on loans would fare differently if brought before a Sharia court or a civil tribunal. Consequently, the authorities in the hope to preserve the conventional banking system which the new regulations sanction, have recently ordered that such disputes be brought before a committee of the Saudi Arabian Monetary System (SANA) rather than the Sharia courts; apparently believing that conciliation at the hands of the committee would diffuse the obvious legal impasse created by defaulting borrowers which, because of the recession, refuse to pay the interest (riba) on the ground that the Sharia prohibits it. In a crunch, the statutory enactments represent to them imported tools for achieving economic ends, while the Sharia rules are intrinsic elements of their Islamic faith.

The distinction between the Sharia courts and the civil tribunals is more than a matter of competence, while the former have general jurisdiction in all matters "except those excluded by regulation," (the Judicature Act, article 26) they nevertheless continue to adhere to the traditional quasi-justice whose goal is compromise as long as the moral precepts of Islam are safeguarded.

The civil tribunals on the other hand seek to uphold the new rules which more often than not are single purpose legislation uncorrelated and unrelated to the customs and traditions of Saudi society. Even for a modern law, such regulation of economic life is a far cry from the evolution of the "Law Merchant" in Europe and of "Blackstone notion" of the law in general as "ancient and long established custom" distilled by judges into "the perfection of reason," (quoted by Prof. Thomas C. Grey of Stanford in his review of *Law's Empire* by Ronald Dworkin, The New York Review of Books, Mar, 12, 1987). The diffused and discordant rules and regulations in the commercial prompted me to develop a plan for the codification of the regulations with annotations which has received the blessings of the Saudi Ministry of Commerce.

What I would like to consult with you about and have your reaction to is a revival of course 264: "Modern Islamic Law," previously given at the School of Law, or the launching of a new course dealing with the law in the Middle East in which you and I would cooperate in presenting an interdisciplinary approach to the issues attending the transformation of law in an Islamic society. At the same time, we would cooperate on research into the purposes and problems of law reform in Saudi Arabia in particular, again using anthropological, sociological, and legal tools of analysis. Such course and research span the School of Law and the Departments of Anthropology, Sociology and Middle East, or International Relations. During my graduate studies at the University of Chicago Law School in the fifties, I worked closely with Karl

Llewellyn, father of the U.S, Uniform Commercial Code and well known to you as the co-author with Prof. Hoebel of *The Cheyenne Way*, which was often discussed in his courses on jurisprudence. In the ancient law field I also did work with Prof. Redfield, particularly on Bedouin law. Since my major was Comparative Law I worked with Prof. Max Eheinstein during the period in which he was engaged on editing Max Weber's *Sociology of Law*, where I participated through seminars he conducted on the subject. My doctoral dissertation was a socio-legal study of the institution of personal status in the countries of the Middle East, with particular emphasis on Lebanon where the institution assumed its more consummate form.

I mentioned this academic background to assure you that although my training has been in the law, my scholarly interests and research invariably crossed into these other related disciplines.

I look forward to hearing from you, I know academic institutions move slowly to react to situations. The importance of Saudi Arabia to the strategic and economic interests of the United States is such as to provide an incentive to do so, particularly that the internal stability of Saudi society in the present fundamentalist wave will greatly depend on the development of a genuine legal culture in which legal process rather than radical forces constitute the level of social change.
Sincerely yours,

George N. Sfeir
Chevy Chase, Maryland

October 5, 1987

Dear Laura Nader,

I was disappointed not to hear from you after I left the package of documents on genetic engineering: I hope you weren't overworked during your stay with us. Bernard Brown tells me you mentioned some interest in my old mentor Calvin. That intrigues me. If there's anything I can do by mail please let me know.

Denying that the U.S. way of life is unusually litigious is not going to convince many I predict—I for one was startled by that denial. The relative triviality of alleged grounds for lawsuits, and the relative size of amounts sued for in the U.S.A. are widely seen as extreme compared with those in British Commonwealth countries. And your attitude to the promotion of conciliation was remarkably one-sided. Can it really be all that unrelievedly wrong to promote negotiation (even if it is Berger and friends spearheading the move)? Was restricting tobacco-smoking in railway carriages an error just because it was a U.S. Supreme Court judge who made the big move on it? The lack of record is also not an unrelieved disadvantage of negotiation compared with litigation.

I realize you must have more people asking to hear from you than you can readily answer. Nevertheless I do hope to hear from you if you think we might usefully pursue mutual interests. Meanwhile, I enclose some recent writings of mine and hope they will interest you.

Thank you again for the inspiration of your first three lectures. I'm going on talk-back radio about genetic engineering this week, partly on the basis of that inspiration. You have my best wishes, and many others', for your continued radical courage.

Sincerely

Robert Mann
University of Auckland, New Zealand

July 6, 1988

Dear Laura:

It was wonderful to hear from you again. I am looking forward to reading your manuscript on "Orientalism and Occidentalism." The delay in sending you the enclosed material, for which I apologize, was caused by my having to secure a copy of my piece on Orientalism from the Library of Congress, as I had misplaced my copy of the journal. It was something that I wrote in 1977, and it reflects the concerns of a group of us at the time in Afghanistan. I read the paper in a conference on Afghani, where my friend proposed holding the first congress of occidentalists in Kabul.

I am also enclosing a copy of my interview with Eric Wolf, and an incomplete manuscript on Islam in Pakistan to give you some indication of my projects on history of anthropology and on Islam in Pakistan. The project on history of anthropology will entail doing 25 life histories during the next three years. After reading the corpus of an author's writings I conduct in-depth interviews for a number of days with her or him. The tapes are then transcribed and after review by the anthropologist concerned I make my selections for publication.

My aim is not merely to provide a history of the discipline, but to treat the present moment of the discipline as history in the making. The criterion of selection is therefore not age, but impact on the direction of the discipline. I sincerely hope that you will agree to a series of conversations during 1989. I will be able to come to California or somewhere else should it be more suitable for you.

My goal in the project on Pakistan is to provide a processual analysis of Islam in the context of the colonial and post-colonial state. To avoid the pitfalls of reification I resorted to a method of controlled comparison during my fieldwork, focusing on different institutions in two cities. I am now engaged in work in archives to unravel the relations between these institutions with the state, the elite, and the financial institutions.

Should there be a possibility of going to the Center at Stanford, I think the academic year 1989–1990 would be the most suitable for me. I will be able to finish these two projects and get ready for fieldwork on domestic organization in Egypt—which is my next project.

Rula, Miriam, and Tarek are well and join me in wishing you, Norman, Nadia, Tarek, and Rania all our best. We hope that whenever you are in the east coast you will let us know. We would love to see you again.
As ever,

Ashraf Ghani
Johns Hopkins University

October 17, 1988

Dear Laura:

It was a pleasure to meet you, and a great pleasure to hear you. The fadism that has accompanied the perplexing and problematic dispute resolution through a war of mechanisms is, has, and always will be a varied and somewhat personal process. That the public has a stake in dispute settlement is evidenced by our historical faith in government agencies, especially the courts, to assist us to do what we have seemed unable to do on our own. But the public has viewed the public role of courts from the narrow purpose of settling disputes with the force of government behind the judgement: public declarations of practice, principle, and policy; public support of those who symbolize high ideals (in particular justice); and the educative role of judges in explaining why it is that human relations should be governed in particular ways have been developed. Forcing any dispute to be a particular way is probably problematic, and while courts are suited to particulars, and have been developed for public purposes, they are unsuited to many—especially for private purposes. Like everything else, context while not being everything is quite a lot. Needs and priorities shift, and sometimes value is at stake. That the A.D.R. movement should have missed contextualizing and ignored fundamental principles is regrettable, but no real surprise. In an effort to make the case for change, context requires us, too often I fear, to say that the present is no good at all—for how else do we justify expenditure or change unless it is greatly needed?

The discussion which followed your talk permitted you to clarify that you too were not taking an extreme traditional liberal position. That we be conscious of what we are about whenever we are about (whatever it is), and that this consciousness requires us to account to the principles which we hold most dear, is a critical and fundamental reminder.

Mahatma Gandhi, as a young lawyer in South Africa, then as now a fractious society, saw his role as bringing together those whom he described as "riven by strife." This healer role may not be for the purpose of peace alone— for a peace which is a cover-up of real problems is not a true peace at all. But peace is a value, even if it means accepting differences of opinion, value, belief, point of view, and even on occasion factual finding. A peace that is a real peace in the sense of persons understanding the disagreement and division, and accepting it is I think acceptable both in principle and necessarily in practice.

There is a private place more powerfully important to dispute settlement and negotiation than mediation rooms. Lawyers' advice giving process undoubtedly affects the nature of disputes more than any other single component besides the parties own preferences, predilections, predispositions, and orientations. There in the lawyer's office, a private sanctum of a special professional wisdom, clients' problems are framed, reframed, defined, revised, and sometimes rather dangerously changed. These private places then, when they are peopled by professionals, require sensitive, understanding, perceptive, insightful, humane, and profoundly disinterested from the point of view of self-professionals.

In short, and I have gone on too long! Your talk, discussion, and dinner conversation were provocative and helpful to my own inquiry. Perhaps I have not proceeded too far along the path to really understanding what you said— but I am working on it.

Thank you.

Sincerely,

Neil Gold
Dean
University of Windsor School of Law

December 30, 1988
Paul Feyerabend

Professor of Philosophy
University of California, Berkeley

Dear Paul,

To celebrate Paul's Birthday lineally is impossible for me. Paul, we always meet on the path where your interests and mine overlap in a laugh as you encourage the

freeing up of procedures, and shake my dutifulness a little bit in the process. My students and my children tell me that yours is the only theory that is intelligible— "that's good," said Rania "because then more people will read him than the others." And thank you for coming together over food every once in a while—again to remind me and mine that categories are not sacred, and that there is probably more "real" about soap operas than what we experience daily at the universities. Thank you for being Paul, and may you have many, many happy returns.
Your friend,

Laura

December 31, 1988

Dear Laura,

Thanks again for the wonderful dinner. The night afterwards I dreamt I lived in a house made of the crumble cake (or whatever you call it) you served, and whenever I felt like it I took a bite out of the wall. It was like heaven. You also have very nice friends, and the juniors are a riot, and not only that they are well informed about things of the matter where your own knowledge seems to be sadly deficient: movies, mystery writers, novels, and so on. And the idea that chemistry is all made up—well I could not agree more. Which may emerge from the enclosed paper, which alas, is very abstract, and most examples are from physics and astronomy, and I argue in a line what took me years to realize (or to think that I realized something). I also enclosed a few pages from my book where I argue for a replacement of expert authority by the judgment of citizens initiatives. And now in return, can you send me a copy of your article in *Physics Today*? And, thanks again for cake and company. Sincerely,

Paul Feyerabend
Professor of Philosophy
University of California, Berkeley

March 28, 1989
Bob Guccione

Editor-in-Chief
Omni Publications

Dear Editor Guccione:

It has been a long time since I have read an article like "The Importance of Hugging" by Howard Bloom (*Omni*, February 1989). It is hardly possible that it could have been written in ignorance. Anthropological knowledge is rich on the subject of physical vices, yet Bloom's use of that knowledge is both simplistic and distorted, indicating a propagandistic style. A propagandist selects his data: Bloom mentions that anthropologist Abu-Lughod's father is Arab, not that her mother is Jewish. Bloom says that Abu-Lughod did not report on the relations between Bedouin and their children when she had written about the children who are "held, coddled, and adored." He asserts that Islamic cultures do not hug their children, and uses Abu-Lughod's observation that Arab men do not hug Arab women in public as evidence. He notes that "Bedouin culture is the mother of all Islam" when Islam is urban in origin. What can I say except that *Omni* should do better if quality reporting is important to your reputation. Sincerely yours,

Laura Nader
Professor of Anthropology

April 13, 1989

Dear Laura:

Crosstalk happens. A student in my introductory biology class mentioned you to me today with the reference being lack of controversy in science, homogenization of opinion, etc. I agree . . . it's there in spades. It came up because I had the AIDS question discussed by Peter Duesberg here, and also by an epidemiologist from UCSF (Nancy Padian) who takes the standard view. It is a nice example of pressure to maintain party line but also of the difference between ways of thinking. The epidemiologists think statistically and can only point in the direction of causality. The virologist gets the message and defines causality in terms of mechanism. They do not really talk to one another . . . especially when defensive.

Anyway, as I get older I am tending to teach more. I have a lecture about some of this and would be happy to interact with you—guest lecture or something.
Sincerely,

Dick Strohman
Department of Zoology
University of California, Berkeley

June 9, 1989

Dear Laura:

Thanks very much for sending your Windsor paper. I'm sure many people would find it provocative. You should send it around.

For me however, the big question is why. Why an ideology of harmony now (or any other time or place)? Insofar as you address this question, your answer has a somewhat conspiratorial ring to it—as if the elites are trying to pull a fast one on the masses.

I would be more inclined to look for the answer in the changing structure of American (and other western) social life. I hinted at this in my bureaucracy paper which I trust you saw.

Thanks again.

Best,

Donald Black
Department of Sociology
University of Virginia

August 9, 1989

Dear Laura:

I have finally finished a readable draft of my chapter on law and order. A copy is enclosed in hopes that you want to read it. Certainly if you do I'd much appreciate comments and especially criticisms both about the ideas, and about what students will put up with reading.

Politics and religion are not only controversial topics, they are for me difficult topics. The struggle on religion continues. At least I am over my life-long hang-ups on the subject, and I have indeed decided that when this textbook is finished, I will do a book on Tiv religion. It will be in that area that I will consider the whole matter of comparison. The first (short) part will be about what ethnography is about and what comparison is about. Part II will be at the ethnography of Tiv religion. Part III will be a comparative study.

The problem with comparative studies is that you have to ask what it is you want to know and what you want to know it for. The context of comparison seems to me to be unequivocally in the milieu of social science, which I simply cannot consider as important a context as the context of an ethnography. Ethnography interests me far, far more than social science.

I'll call you one of these days. Meanwhile, if you have time to read this, thanks.

Yours ever,

Paul Bohannon
Three Rivers, California

4

THE IVORY TOWER IS NO MORE IN THE NINETIES

The 1990s was a time when Alternative Dispute Resolution (ADR) or the anti-law movement was being vigorously sold to the American people—a subject for much of my correspondence and public talks. Professor Kagan wrote about formal adversarial litigation. Another law professor, Stewart Macaulay, weighed in on the arguments. The Navajo leader James Zion expressed his perspective, and comparisons arrived from Ota Shozo on ADR in Japan. The *San Francisco Chronicle* weighed in on my theory of "coercive harmony" via Norman Larson, and George McGovern wrote apologetically about the tort reform (or deform) battle. I wrote to David Hamburg of the Carnegie Corporation explaining the double-sided nature of harmony, while the lawyer Ann Sayonara discussed a case involving the same while asking me for advice. As I noted, ADR dominated my correspondence during the early 1990s, crossing lines between academic disciplines and between the university and the public.

The publication of my Mintz lecture on Controlling Processes came in 1996.[1] "Controlling Processes" stimulated correspondence between me and psychologists who specialize in cults and the deprogramming of people who are caught up in them. Paul Bohannon was apparently so inspired after hearing me give a talk on the subject that he wrote me a three-and-a-half-page letter on self-destruction in US culture and society, a special kind of anomie that was antisurvival. Another letter came from a former student who wrote on how controlling processes work in Japan.

My letters commented on disparate issues—hospital closings; advice to younger anthropologists like David Price, who was dealing with the taboo subject of militarism and anthropology while coping with academic censorship by those whose history of anthropology dealt only with issues internal to the discipline while the interference of the CIA was still staring us in the face. I wrote to UC President David Gardner about student fees and CALPIRG—Public Interest Research Groups at UC Berkeley. I wrote to a scientist about causes of breast cancer beyond genetic inheritance, stressing the need to examine environmental factors. She did not reply, I was told, because she was too outraged by my suggestions. Central as well was the role of higher education and in promoting democracy during the Cold War—outside of academia. Human rights surfaced regularly, as well as a letter to me on biological factors in mental illness by the University of Pennsylvania anthropologist Anthony Wallace, saying that Margaret Mead called his a "destructive hypothesis."

The New Press had published a book on *The Cold War and the University* in 1997 in which I had an article on "The Phantom Factor: Impact of the Cold War on Anthropology."[2] The Cold War had a large impact on academia in general, as well as anthropology specifically. Thus I had an exchange with Richard Lewontin of Harvard University about his comments in the book on whether the Cold War had negative or positive impacts on the academy. The anthropologist Sandy Davis wrote to me noting how his own fieldwork in Latin America was affected, although he had not realized it at the time. The effect of the Cold War on physical anthropology and notions of race were central to Jonathan Marks's letter, followed by an exchange between me and the anthropologist George Marcus on issues of development. The archaeologist Alice Kehoe wrote about conservatism in American archaeology. My article was a wake-up call for some, and apparently still surprises others: so ingrained was the belief that the Ivory Tower was insulated from outside factors.

Apart from the clusters of letters regarding ADR, Controlling Processes, as well as the Cold War and academia, several letters on indigenous rights were important. Alejandro de Avila wrote from Mexico about government exploitation of indigenous land among the Zapotec and Chinantec, using satellite data to develop long-term plans for regional resource extraction. In early 1991, US Attorney Carol Gillam wrote about monolingual Zapotec being flown into the United States illegally as plantation workers. Apparently, there are no border walls for private airplanes. She was trying to develop arguments for prosecution of the company she thought responsible. The indigenous people brought to California had no idea where they had been taken, and they didn't speak Spanish. "Big Science" was also present in exchanges I was having with the anthropologist Gene Anderson and others.

In 1999, I received a ten-page letter from John Borneman, then at Cornell University. Borneman had been in the field in Lebanon and wrote about Lebanese who live in Germany going "home" for the summer. Borneman was explicit about what Lebanon looked like nine years after the end of the country's civil war. The Syrian presence was still there as Hazef al-Assad had helped end the war principally to favor Syria's economic interests. Borneman visited the infamous Sabra and Shatila camp, site of a 1982 massacre, and everywhere people spoke about departing from violence. Who could hear his suggestion? As he writes, the Israelis were bombing East Beirut and Hezbollah territory. His most poignant observations were about the young. In giving permission for this letter, he noted that forty years later, he found himself in Germany studying Syrian refugees fleeing the devastating Syrian Civil War.

February 11, 1990
Margaret Singer

Independent Psychologist
Affiliated with UC Berkeley

Dear Margaret,

Re: our conversation on what is in-between the macro-forces that have an impact on what I call mind controlling processes are the following:

- teaching of trust in schools but not distrust which was certainly part of the Jeffersonian agenda (e.g. school games where the kids fall backward and expect that an acquaintance will catch them).
- invention and nourishment of the generation gap by marketing techniques which breaks the communication between generations. Wisdom is out. Now anthropologists have documented societies where there is a break between children and parents, but in same societies its every other generation—child/grandparent.
- the taboo on making judgements ("you're being judgmental")—a linguistic stopper which as you know is powerful.
- harmony ideology or the movement against the contentious
- moral minimalism.
- the marketplace definition of self, sexual conduct, beauty standards, etc.

What these controlling processes achieve is isolation, a flattening of values, and normal self-defense mechanisms which are prime for predation.

Let's talk in more detail. I hope by the time you receive this that your health is better.

Best to you,

Laura Nader

February 21, 1990
President David Gardner

University of California—Office of the President
Oakland, CA

Dear President Gardner:

I call to your attention the attached article in the *Daily Californian* of February 21, 1990, and hope that there is no basis to the fears it evokes of funding for CalPIRG being jeopardized. While the winds of change may blow democracy into Eastern Europe, we should note that our democracy is increasingly non-participatory. Higher education has an important role—to encourage participation in governmental processes, and to actively remove obstacles to citizen participation. Otherwise, how might we respond to questions now coming from the Soviets and East Europeans—"how do you do democracy in the US."

Thank you for your attention.

Sincerely,

Laura Nader
Professor of Anthropology

March 22, 1990

Dear Laura,

It's the crack of dawn (actually it's well before the crack of dawn) and I know you are still at Vivian's, but I am writing this instead of calling because I want to think more slowly as I go. Reports of ethnographic research in process are sometimes interesting, but seldom disturbingly interesting (indeed, threateningly interesting) in the sense that your material is. Although I have heard you talk about some of the things you said last night, always before it lacked the wider context that you could give it in a more formal presentation. And only with that context can the full impact hit.

For years I have been fighting the idea that our society is mired in anomie. I held that a new form of society was emerging, and that we had to understand it in its own terms—not in terms of analysts like Max Weber (not to mention Marx) who had had a quite different social context in which to work. Anomie in this sense is a deus ex machina that actually explains nothing. I still think that.

But after hearing your presentation last night, I now also think that I had oversimplified anomie. It seems to me this morning that there are two (or more) kinds of anomie. There is the simple anomie of what used to be called "social disorganization." It doesn't explain much, but rather only gives us something to rail at.

You are finding (or perhaps I am only just coming to realize) that there is also another kind of anomie that results when a society totally misunderstands, and therefore misinterprets and woefully misapplies its own values. We need a special word for that kind of anomie. Neuropathic anomia won't do, but it's in the right direction.

What you made me realize last night is that the society that is emerging may in its very form be anomic, in the sense of anti-survival, without being in the least disorganized. And the irony is heavy: the anomia comes from the very values that people thought would be liberating. It's something like the divorce law: in an admirable attempt to get rid of the awful choice of having either to dedicate one's life to a particularly horrible anguish, or else to perjure oneself in court and be branded as a failure and almost a felon by one's peers, we set ourselves up for extensive poverty, and a set of family forms that do not work (at least they don't work if we don't totally rethink the family).

What you are doing is providing the insight that the emerging society may be built on the kind of nomopathic anomie that results from misunderstanding and misapplying one's own values. It does not threaten the establishment, but rather (if it spreads far enough beyond the American and perhaps European heartland) it threatens the species. This too will undoubtedly pass, but the spoor it leaves may make it difficult or even impossible to find a road to social health (whatever that is).

One of the most astonishing aspects of the emerging society is the absence of hierarchical authority as you have shown. The systematic if unthought destruction of authority, where the baby is thrown out with the bathwater of hierarchy. At some political levels, that fact is helping to create new kinds of control based on single interest groups with television as a mode of communicating concern (the anti-nuke movement or anti-abortion movement are using this mechanism with great skill). The emerging form puts on the individual the immense burden of "getting it all together." The social structure used to provide the glue, but now each of us has ourself to provide the glue. Moreover, this new form however well it adapts to protest and criticism, can seldom be used to build something. What do we do when there is no replacement for hierarchy which admittedly has its own kind of tyranny? What is the tyranny of the emerging forms of non-hierarchy?

Because of the startling (if not shocking) dimensions of the ethnographic material you presented at the end of your talk, people lost sight of what you had said about freedom earlier in the evening. Erich Fromm was worried about the all-too-human tendency to escape from freedom, to buckle under authority, and to compromise in the interest of harmony. You are uncovering a very different situation; one in which freedom (unlike Fromm's freedom) has been unconsciously transformed (in the linguist's sense) to mean normlessness. That is a failure on the part of Americans to understand that autonomy per-se does not necessarily imply normlessness. Autonomy, the way it was being pushed by the psychoanalysts, meant that one chooses one's own prison—or better that one paid what one had to pay for the support one got. Autonomy meant to them, standing up for your rights (an adversarial, non-harmonious position) within the context of stability and predictability. Some of them added that if it wasn't worth the price, you could push off (fight or flee). However when the great American value of self-reliance was turned loose on that idea, it came to mean that each of us, being self-reliant, had to give up on traditional support for groups like families and communities. As a result, we had to turn to the new single interest support groups that had to be invented to take up at least a little of the slack. Autonomy in the good sense means that one is not constrained into crippling compliance by outside factors or outside people. It has been transformed to mean that everybody must "stand on their own two feet," which turns out to mean unconnected.

What you are finding is that the psychoanalytic view of autonomy has been totally misconstrued by the American public. It is something like oat bran: when it was discovered that soluble fiber can lower cholesterol by naturally blocking the liver's making cholesterol (which is a life promoting-function, but which the liver, poor dear, cannot help making too much of in the absence of soluble fiber), oat bran was transformed by the general public, almost instantly, into a magical yellow-brick road to eternal health (read "happiness"). Most people pushing oat bran said that you had to accompany it with lowered fat intake. It became instead a magical formula. The people who knew the facts had never said that oat bran by itself would lower cholesterol. Even the cereal ads didn't say that (although they didn't say anything responsible about oat bran or other soluble fiber as part of an altered diet either). Thereupon some fool medical researchers come along and say that oat bran doesn't work. What they meant and should have said was that it doesn't work magically by itself. Of course it doesn't work if it is lifted out of context and if you don't follow the entire program. Then the binary principle strikes again: instead of being a good thing, oat bran became a hoax—something that didn't work and therefore is a bad thing. They said that they had been gulled again. The destructive binary opposition and the oversimplifications of pop-science had struck again. We have done with autonomy what we did with oat bran.

The major question as I see it this morning: do ideas of control and controlling adequately set out the context of the ethnography you have been gathering? Controlling by lack of control? It gets subtle—perhaps too subtle. You have here another example of Americans (like all other people to one degree or another) being their own worst enemies. They are simplistic. They want it binary. No gray. That enforces the "don't worry, be happy" syndrome. If you are not happy, you must be miserable. Being miserable, you are rocking the boat—threatening the only kind of insecure stability people can achieve. This is a very subtle sub-sort of bottling it up in the interest of harmony.

I think we need a concept for cultural situations that set us up, ironically to destroy ourselves with our very own best petards. As we mentioned yesterday, Jules Henry wrote about it. I believe Skip Rapaport wrote an article about destructive culture some years ago, although I don't remember where. But all these ideas have not recently been brought together (although, interestingly enough Francis Hsu's old *American and Chinese* touches a little bit on it—his Chinese side). Realization of the destructive side of culture, and realizing its amorality may be as important for our day as the idea of utopias was for an era of the early industrial revolution. In culture lies the seeds of destruction as well as salvation. Pessimistic? "Don't worry, be happy."

Thanks for getting me turned on about all of this.

Yours ever

Paul Bohannon
Three Rivers, CA

April 15, 1990

Dear Laura,

Thanks very much for your incredibly quick response to my interest. Of course I am always delighted to see anything you have written. I hope we can keep in touch.

The science articles seem very good to me. I can't add any really helpful editorial comments on the draft—I don't know enough about the problems. The quotes from the scientists seem to show that most people recognize the problems of modern "Big Science," but don't have comments about what to do about them, or an organization that could do anything if there was a consensus. The postmodern predicament: everything's so multi-vocal, contested, deconstructed etc., that no one can act.

Anyway, I sense a lot of interesting questions under all this about what science is. Malinowski used it to mean "empirical stuff" as opposed to "stuff that anyone can see isn't empirically grounded," to oversimplify a bit. In this sense, the Trobrianders necessarily have had a working sense of the differences: they could see that there was a connection between hooking a fish and hauling it in that there was not between fishing ritual and canoe safety. Now, in the science you study that is not the situation. Rarely do modern physicists have the fortune to see what they are talking about. They see cloud-chamber traces, or columns of figures, or gauge measurements instead. These they take as "neat" but not perfect indicators.

But more to the point, "science" in the US is several things, none of them very empirical.

Science in the classic sense, and the way I use it, is search for more accurate, thorough, efficient, or predictive explanations and models of things.

Science as an institution, the way most of the people in your article are using it, is science as a bureaucracy with its personnel, funding sources, institutional culture, and other Weberiana. In the U.S., the Republican government gets more and more power at defining the agenda. The A.A.A.S. is now run by conservative Republicans, or at least they're the men writing the editorials in *Science*.

Lastly, Science as a set of methods to arrive at empirical knowledge, specifically the following (more or less established by Francis Bacon): open publication and open debate, test (by experiment or data collection) to see which side of the debate is more correct. This self-correcting aspect that criticizes it can be seen in looking at individuals or institutional practice!

So here we have five things that are not only different, but they are not even comparable. Process, institution, methodology. . .

Now, what you are describing in these papers is a mix of science as an institution and science as "what scientists do." The institution, duly bureaucratized, has all the problems of every good Weberian bureaucracy, and that is what your interviewees are complaining about. It is the nature of the Weberian bureaucracy that its problems emerge in spite of the fact that everyone in the bureaucracy is trying to stop them from emerging. There is no hope. Meanwhile, the scientists are also busy being human—i.e. being biased, seeing all the evidence that confirms their biases, ignoring all the evidence on the other side, etc. As Francis Bacon pointed out, everybody is full of personal and cultural biases, and therefore the only way that any search for truth can work is by open debate between people holding contending viewpoints. Now of course, what has happened is that a bureaucracy hates open debate above all things (it "rocks the boat," etc.), and thus bureaucratization is deadly to science in the first and fifth senses above.

Most of the current "critiques" (read: snide, uninformed put downs) of science are based on the cheap shot of showing that individual truth, and saying that this one has perfect, absolute truth, and saying that this disproves science. Of course this sort of critiques does not touch science of the Baconian sort. At best, it's a critique of doing science badly, not of science itself (this is the same cheap-shot critique that people like Clifford and Marcus level at ethnography. I guess some of these guys mean well, but I doubt if most of them do, the misunderstanding and misrepresentation of both science in-general and individual ethnographers is so extreme and so blatant that I believe they are intentionally distorting the situation just to score points. See the comment by Fredrik Barth and the following few pages of debate in recent issue of *Man*).

A far more serious critique is the one we (you and I, and our like-minded colleagues) have so often done—looking at institutionalized science and seeing how it gets warped farther and farther from the search for truth, so that it can instead serve the interests of whoever is running the show. Here of course, the whole scientific enterprise is completely corrupted, instead of being a search for truth it becomes a search for lies. But it isn't a critique of masquerading as science.

I think this makes my own mind a lot clearer, but you probably know all of this already. I think the agenda of open publication and debate is the best thing that ever happened to humanity—a more important invention that all the technological stuff. What is happening is that we are all in one of those periods of stagnation when such things get too dangerous to the status quo.

Meanwhile, I see an intensely right-wing agenda as one of the less savory currents in postmodernism. It is the current that comes from the lifelong dedicated Nazi Martin Heidegger, via the Nazi Paul de Man and other lunatic-fringe rightists. It has become enormously persuasive in the U.S. This is basically the following set of loose ideas:

— Reality is anything you damn well please (or at best anything you see and experience). Thus, science is what scientists do as institutional science only not a search for truth.
— Thus, the will constructs reality. Reality isn't given out there, nor is knowledge of it constructed through progressive experience of anything external. We (individuals and cultures) construct what we please.
— Thus, there are very different realities—varying by individual, gender, and culture—and these are what really matter. They are virtually non-communicable.
— Moreover, human groups are so rigid and so essential that there is for example, a black science that is different from, incomprehensive to, and just as valid as the "hegemonic master-text" science, and women's literature that is utterly different from men's but somehow linked around the world. (This can get confusing when Zora Neale Hurston is a "black" and when is she a "women." It never occurs to any of these people that she could be a person, and one who studies with Franz Boas, at that.) This is basically an utterly different concept from our own anthropological take on culture. Recall that all the scathing analysis of Nazi "rassenkunde" by Boaz, Sapir, and others.

I like a lot of the postmodern bag: Foucault and Bourdieu have become major influences, but I sure don't like this Nazi input. Postmodernism is so "multiboval" that nobody seems very bothered except old-time radicals like me. I must say, when UCI hired Hillis Miller (de Man's star student) at a six-figure salary I felt like I should protest, but was too cowardly to do so.

Anyway, the whole business of invalidating the search for truth, going for pseudoscience, and essentializing cultural/social differences scares me.

This is all crazy enough surely—but what to say? The world is crazy. I'll try to get more up to date on conservation organizations and who's doing what. There are so many now that I can't keep track.

All the best,

Gene Anderson
Professor of Anthropology
University of California, Riverside

Paul Feyerabend was a Berkeley Philosopher of Science and was most outspoken regarding the hypocrisy among science institutions.

April 17, 1990

Dear Laura,

Thanks for your letter which reached me today, here in Switzerland. It is an interesting subject, but I can't see myself at a conference, giving a speech. Besides, I won't be in the U.S.A., I should be in Rome (most likely) or in Switzerland. I have just resigned from Berkeley. I have two reasons, I want to be close to Grazia and I want to be far away from any earthquake. End of July will be my last semester in Zurich—and then I should be poor, but free.

When I was little people asked me, "what do you want to do when you grow up?" My reply was "I want to retire," and I had good reasons: all the retired people were sitting in the park when I played and were talking in the sun. The others were rushing about with fine briefcases in their hands and a hurried look on their face.

So retirement seemed to be a good choice for a grown-up. It still does. Incidentally—do you know of Cardinal Ratzinger? He is the ideologue behind the conservatism of Pope John Paul II. In March he gave a talk in Parma about the situation of the Church, and he pointed out that despite earlier indications to the contrary the Church would not revise the procession of Galileo. And whom did he quote in support of this decision? ME. So I am now a pillar of the Church.

In December I'll be back in Berkeley for a few days, so I'll ring you then. Did you get our postcard from Rome?

Love,

Paul Feyerabend
Zurich, Switzerland

FIGURE 4. Paul Feyerabend, my friend and colleague from the University of California, Berkeley Philosophy Department. Photograph from author's collection.

May 14, 1990

Dear Professor Nader:

Thank you for your letter of April 9, 1990, and your additional comments about CalPIRG. In this instance, we will have to agree to disagree on the democratic nature of the negative check-off method of collecting fees for voluntary student organizations.

I do not believe that this mechanism is appropriate, and feel strongly that collection of voluntary student fees in support of student organizations should be achieved through a positive declaration on the part of each student that he or she actively wishes to make this contribution. I would add that CalPIRG is unique among student organizations in having established this method of fee collection. Further collection of student organization fees through negative check-off is not in my view a proper use of the registration process.

We are in agreement about the fact that the University of California faces many other pressing issues. I am pursuing this one because the Chancellors and I would like to see this matter resolved in an acceptable manner once and for all. As you know, after lengthy discussions with students and with the Chancellors of the four campuses with CalPIRG chapters, I have referred the matter back to the campuses for further consideration. Each is now in the process of assessing the merits of existing and alternative mechanisms for collecting fees on behalf of registered campus organizations. I look forward to receiving campus responses on how best to proceed and am sure that whatever the resolution is it will be in the spirit of more direct democratic choice, rather than less.

In appreciation of your writing again, and with all good wishes, I am. . . Sincerely,

David Pierpont Gardner
President
University of California

June 20, 1990
Dr. Philip H. Abelson

Scientist
American Assoc. for the Advancement of Science (AAAS)

Dear Phil:

Your editorial on "America Bashing" caught my eye because I have just finished teaching a graduate seminar on how the East and West write and think about one another. We used "The Japan That Can Say No" as one of the readings.

That authors of this book are "America bashing" seems obvious if one is defensive. On the other hand, as the title indicates it is an attempt to build Japanese self-esteem by asserting (as Edward Said has taught us) an old technique—that of "positional superiority." In a world which is increasingly dependent however, it seems foolish to think that the "focus of change" simply moves from the U.S. to the Eastern Pacific. A more constructive model would be based on interdependence. The U.S. is better at democracy, while Japanese have shown what's possible by use of a coercive harmony and organization of a more determinate sort.

The shocking aspect of the book for me was to realize that we are dependent on the Japanese for defense technology. Much of what they say is good critique, but I was as ready as you may be to pass the mantle. I prefer the U.S. vision, ideal though it may be, rather than more authoritarian structures, and so might the Eastern Pacific outside of Japan. Finally, we might get rid of the word "bashing"—to say we should have the right to buy Japan if they have the right to buy the U.S. is not "Japan bashing." Equally, to criticize the U.S. for a loss of will as exhibited by our leadership is not "bashing," but useful critique.

Thanks for the editorial. I look forward to seeing you next February in Washington.

Sincerely yours,

Laura Nader
Professor of Anthropology

July 27, 1990

Dear Laura,

I hope that this letter finds you in good health. The last academic semester was very busy for me. I have just finished with the students' final exams
and other works. But besides these activities which take a lot of time, I have
started with our common project of comparison. Our discussion made me
think more explicitly about the comparison in relation of hierarchy and hegemony. With the help of Dumont's work, I have addressed new questions to the
problematic of egalitarianism and difference, universalism and relativism in
both contexts of modern society and modern anthropological thought.

The example of Islam and Maghrebi immigrants in Europe, and especially
in France, helped me to address these issues with a new pertinence. I choose
as indicators of the hierarchical comparison that we observe in both popular
culture and scientific thinking: the veil, the exclusion, the spaces of Islamic
cults, the factories and other places where Maghrebi immigrants work, the
associative and communal institutions, the public schools, the civil and political rights. In the context of secularism, the ideology of "Human Rights" and
"Universal Values" inherited from the Enlightenment, which characterize
contemporary France, the problem of integration and rejection of the Arab
immigrants appear as good a field to test and discuss the validity of some rela-
tivistic propositions like "all differences are equal," "equality with respect for
diversities," etc. It is also a "good" field for discussing the universalism which
sustains "modern ideology" (in the sense of Dumont, but also the project of
anthropology) and for thinking it as inherently hierarchical and universal,
especially when the concern is the relation between Orient and Occident.

In order to treat these different aspects of the problem I need more time.
First of all, I have to collect additional information of the field, especially
after recent controversy in France about the port of veil by young Arab girls
in the public schools. This controversy has taken a national dimension and
concerned all groups of the French, Belgian, and Swiss population (citizens,
politicians, scholars, media, religious authorities, etc.). The issues addressed in
this debate are the conditions of integration of Maghrebi and Islamic populations in France and other European countries, as well as the way in which this
very integration has taken place, the status of Islam in secular society, the place

of Arab women, etc. On the other hand, I have to work hard this summer in order to finish my manuscript on the oasis. The editor just cannot wait anymore. For these reasons I cannot send you my paper before fall.

Did you receive any news from Guita? I will be happy to read something new from you. Look forward to hearing from you.

Sincerely,

Mondher Kilani
Professor of Anthropology
Université de Lausanne

May 25, 1991

Dear Dr. Nader,

I would like to take this opportunity to thank you again for allowing me attending your classes last fall in "Comparative Society," and this spring in "Controlling Processes." In this session, although I could not perform well due to my poor understanding of American culture, I truly enjoyed your class. Furthermore, it meant a lot to me as a beginning anthropologist who has the same interest in Japanese society, to learn from you. In the future, I eagerly hope that I can conduct further cross-cultural research between Japanese and American education. For a term paper for an "Education and Culture" class taught by Dr. Ogbu, I discovered many opposite results in the same problem of education between these two countries. Also when I took your "Controlling Processes" class, I recognized many ways of control which I cannot implicate into Japanese society directly. I am assuming that there are some different styles of controlling processes which originated from cultural traits between Japan and America. For example, there is a different marketing technique in headache medicines between these two countries. In general, Japanese people do not experience "headaches" as much as American people do. Because Japanese people have different idea to describe the discomfort of headache symptoms from American people. Japanese people say "headache" when they start to feel real pain, whereas they refer to lighter headache symptoms, which American people call "headache," as being "tired" or having "heavy head." Japanese people do not use a headache medicine for "heavy head" symptoms, thus there are less demand of its medicine than the American market. As a result, corporations are trying to sell headache medicines as tie-in sales such as: Buffering and Aspirin being sold for a headaches and common cold symptoms, while Excedrin is sold for headaches and P.M.S. In addition, all of these medicines are from America, sold by Japanese companies (also in my knowledge, P.M.S. is not a popular way to refer to symptoms in Japanese language.

Mostly, it's just called a menses pain). I suppose that corporations are using their controlling processes on Japanese customers in different ways than they use on American customers in order to fit into Japanese society. This is due to cultural discontinuity, even though they sell the same medicines.

If it is possible, I would appreciate it if I may discuss this issue with you someday over the summer. Wishing you have a wonderful summer and get well soon.

Sincerely yours,

Tatsuya Fujii
Former Student
University of California, Berkeley

July 24, 1991
Wayne Cornelius

Institute for Regional Studies of the Californias
University of California, San Diego

Dear Wayne:

A copy of *Profmex Policy News* (Spring 1991) just reached me. I don't know what your influence is or where your responsibilities lie, but perhaps you would be interested in my observation.

The news reads like self-serving propaganda, and not even subtle propaganda at that. If Mexico's environmental pollution is due to its poverty, how do you explain our pollution? Pages 8 and 10 on the question of "free" trade are examples of advocacy without scholarship. The concerns raised are about the state of health of Mexico, which I applaud, but not without consideration of how "free" trade will impact on the poor in *both* the U.S. and Mexico. The pages of *Profmex Mexico Policy News* might better be published by a Chamber of Commerce or corporate office rather than a university.

What's your view as an insider?
Sincerely yours.

Laura Nader
Professor of Anthropology

August 27, 1991

Dear Dr. Nader,

I was happy to speak with you by telephone last week about the possibility of helping us in prosecuting a slavery case involving abuses of migrant workers. As I had previously mentioned, I am the lead prosecutor in the case *United States v. Edwin Mitchel Ives* et al., CR 90–400 (B)-CBM, filed in federal court in Los Angeles. The trial is now scheduled to begin February 4, 1992 against 12 defendants. This has been a well-publicized case brought by the United States against a wealthy flower grower and his foremen. I enclosed a copy of the current indictment, which as you will see, charges slavery, racketeering, and numerous other violations of federal law.

Many of the victims who are named in the indictment come from two remote villages in Oaxaca and are Zapotec Indians. The vast majority have never traveled outside Oaxaca before they were brought directly up to the ranch in Somis, California. The cultural differences between these men and the usual federal court witnesses are, as I'm sure you know, profound.

I am aware of some of your publications, including the recent book *Harmony Ideology*, which I am halfway through reading as I write this. I am also aware (from Don Brenneis and others) that you have been involved in migrant worker issues in addition to doing fieldwork in anthropology.

You have expressed some interest in exploring the possibilities of defining a role for you in this case, and agreed to meet with me in mid-September. As soon as I can finalize details of my itinerary, I will let you know.

In the meantime, if you have any further questions, please feel free to call. I will be in Mexico September 4–9, and should return to the office September 10. I sincerely look forward to meeting you next month.
Yours very truly,

Carol Gillam
Assistant United States Attorney
Los Angeles, CA

June 25, 1992
Rajesh Choudree

Principal Legal Officer
Aboriginal Legal Service of Western Australia (Inc.)

Dear Mr. Choudree,

Thank you for your letter of January regarding Mediation and ADR amongst indigenous peoples. I understand the conflict you speak about. From what we know cross-culturally mediation only "works" between people of relatively equal power. Between parties of unequal power mediation has a conservative effect with a bias towards the powerful. That generalization is widely supported by hard data. The fact that it is ignored leads one to suppose purpose other than ideal.

Sincerely yours,

Laura Nader
Professor of Anthropology

August 10, 1992

Dear Laura:

I've recently agreed to do some pro bono work for the New England Council relative to a new layer of fishery management analysis that is being considered (translation: the government has it out for consideration and review, and will move to initiate the process, regardless of what such a review reveals, once the federal guideline "paper tiger" has been respected). Since the document and "guidelines" are a horrendous example of bureaucratic stupidity compounded by blatant hypocrisy, I thought you would be interested in glancing at it and my partial analysis, as well as comments to the Council. The Executive Director of the Council staff agrees with the thrust of my analysis, and has circulated copies to the Council members. We both agree however, that nothing the Council or anyone else does will change what appears to be the inevitable imposition of the procedure of Social Impact Assessment under review here.

As an aside, I might also add that this brings up one of the lesser attended binds confronting anthropologists who don't conform to the mode of applied work. On the one hand, I've been invited by NMFS [National Marine Fisheries Service] on several occasions to submit a grant proposal to do the kind of social impact assessment being "considered," and have rejected same on the grounds that other studies with which I'm familiar have been either ignored, or worse, used to help frame government directives in ways to vitiate the thrust of findings negative to the government's intent. On the other hand, both my effectiveness as a critic, and my ability to pursue my research, are hampered by my refusal to be co-opted as a paid researcher/consultant. I've sent copies of my letter to the Director of NMFS (the same William Fox I speak of in the paper I prepared for you), whose response was to send me the usual "thank-you-for-your-input" form letter sent to "the public" as part of the public hearing process.

I grow more despairing of being able to effect a management process that both resists the growing capitalization of industry and increasing predation on the stocks, both of which are leading to the disappearance of the small scale, family firm fishing vessels, and to communities that they support.

Any comments or queries you might have time to make would be welcome. Sincerely,

M. Estellie Smith
Professor of Anthropology
Oswego State University of New York

October 30, 1992

Dear Laura:

I want to thank you very much indeed for your article in the October issue of the *Family and Conciliation Courts Review*. As usual, you get right to the meat of the issue instead of the fluff with which we are constantly afflicted.

I think I am a little, but not much "wetter" than you appear to be on mediation, and possibly on other policy issues in family law. But yours is a significant, important, and overdue contribution. I wish I had read your article before I completed a recent article I was asked to do for the *Denver University Law Review* on "No-Fault Divorce and the Best Interests of Children." In it I endeavor to touch upon some of the points you correctly raise but without the same penetration.

(I wish I had been aware of the unpublished Fuller, Claeson, and Dart, whom I gather were your students. They look as though they might be relevant and interesting to my struggles in trying to identify the influence and limits of the law. The references from them make your classes sound interesting indeed and cause me to wonder: What raw red meat do you feed them)?

Last year after the first symposium on "Family Law and Children" initiated by the American Bar Association, I took the liberty (without your permission) of proposing that you be invited to attend the proposed continuation of the project.

The intention of the project was and is to bring together a multi-disciplinary group to look into the questions: What do children need for their optimal development? What framework of law can best foster those needs? The intention is that the group, meeting from time to time, come up with recommendations for legislative change and then lobby for them. I find it difficult to articulate what the project is all about.

I hope it can avoid the committee imposed platitudes of the Carnegie Endowment work on children of some years ago. In our society, thinking about children and platitudes go too easily together.

A first and "trial" symposium was held at Ripon College, a most delightful place, in April, 1991. Forty were invited: the usual assortment of judges, lawyers, legal academics and anthropologists, child development specialists

(Brazelton, for example, but who was sick at the last moment), psychologists, educators, ethicists, physiatrists, social historians, and so on. Some were good, and some were not. You are needed.

The enthusiasm of the group was greater than I have experienced, and all of us went away with the most sincere good intentions. Translating good intentions into concrete action is difficult and this what we are trying to do.

What makes me so enthusiastic about the project is that for the first time anywhere in the U.S., Canada, and Great Britain, there is at least an opportunity to consider family law reform (and its interrelation with all the other social and economic phenomena) from fundamentals instead of from dogma. It compels us to not only think about the limits of the law, but also how the law stands in the way of other beneficial development as well.

It needs (and this is difficult in a multi-disciplinary group) the discipline of recognizing and focusing on what is doable. It needs the input of those rare persons who can stretch their minds beyond the intricacies and immediacies of their own disciplines without loss of scholarship. In other words, it would be right up your alley.

Besides, I think (or, at least I argue) that what our nations are now doing to our children is not acceptable and that we must do something about it. A change in family law, if it were fundamental, addresses but one part of the problem—though I argue that it is an important part.

Since the initial symposium, the committee has been sporadically scrambling around searching for its mandate (which now is on a firmer footing) and looking for funding. There is going to be a meeting of the steering group in Chicago next week, and I hope that we will now be able to come up with something concrete. The committee is headed by a feisty judge from Milwaukee, Marianne Becker.

Are you at all interested? If you are, I think I have some but not a conclusive influence. You ought to be in on developing the agenda, but I doubt that that is possible for the time being.
Best regards.

Donald S. Moir
Moir Associates
Vancouver, Canada

March 4, 1993

Dear Laura,

I very much enjoyed seeing you in Columbus, both because your talk and our conversation was so stimulating, and because it reminded me how special the intellectual environment in Berkeley really is. I brought students from my 4 p.m. seminar on environmental law enforcement to your lecture, and then we spent the second hour talking about your ideas rather than the assigned readings.

Your criticism of harmony ideology is important to me because, as indicated by the enclosed article, I have become increasingly critical of one alternative— formal adversarial litigation. I come to that view not because of nostalgia for a nonexistent golden age, or dislike of legal conflict per se, or attraction to mediation. But rather, I come to it as a result of a growing conviction that where litigation is especially slow, costly, and unpredictable as in the U.S., the resulting *inefficiency* is a *major* source of injustice. One must compare alternative modes of decision making not only with adversarial litigation as it works at its best, for the few cases that get to trial. One must compare it to the system as it works for the bulk of cases, which are not adjudicated because the parties, especially those who are trying to change the status quo, can't afford it (in terms of money or in time), and therefore must surrender legally valid claims or defenses.

In case you read the case study on Oakland harbor in the article, I'll bring you up to date: in October/November, Phase I of the dredging project finally occurred. The sediments were deposited near Alcatraz, the site originally chosen over five years ago, and probably the least environmentally desirable choice.

Best regards,

Robert A. Kagan
Visiting Professor
Ohio State University

April 25, 1993
Mary-Claire King

Professor of Epidemiology
University of California, Berkeley

Dear Prof. King;

I write in reference to the story on "Researchers Close to Finding Inherited Breast Cancer Gene" in *Science*, the *S.F. Chronicle*, and a couple of U.C. sheets including the *Berkeleyan*. I find my outrage increases each time I see the headlines and write to you in the hopes of clarifying some issues.

From my limited understanding it appears that breast cancer(s), like many other diseases now claimed to have a gene, is a simplification of a complex state of affairs neither befitting the research scientist, nor respectful of the lay public reading about such matters. The hubris embedded in the quotes attributed to you, and the arrogance that a "scientific truth" can lead to a "registry of all women found to be at high risk for breast cancer . . . so that their progress can be followed and their choices assessed," indicates no apparent concern for the civil liberties issues, nor is there any humility about the risks involved in medical care such as screening. It's a big ball of wax and simplification for media purposes, and can only hinder the long run goals that we undoubtedly share. Background to my concerns may be found in T. Duster's book *Backdoor to Eugenics* (1990), and Ruth Hubbard's book recently released by *Beacon Press*.

Any clarification on the above issues would be appreciated as a prelude to discussion about priorities, prevention, and the contrast you recognize between inherited breast cancer and its opposite which we might for the moment call "cultural breast cancer."

Thank you for your attention,

Laura Nader
Professor of Anthropology

June 17, 1993

Dear Laura,

It was good seeing you in Berkeley a few weeks ago. I still remember our conversation at the Law and Society Association meeting in Boston a few years ago. We sat down to talk and spent the afternoon together. It was great fun, and unfortunately very unusual for me.

The introduction to *The Cheyenne Way* brought back memories. First, I saw Karl in action when Marc Galanter and I were Biology Teaching Fellows and Instructors at the University of Chicago in 1955–56. When I began teaching contracts, I discovered that I didn't know the literature in my field. (This is a big difference between someone with a Ph.D in almost any field and an assistant professor of law who has just been to law school). So I worked my way through the greats. Llewellyn's writing delighted and baffled me. I didn't expect poetry and the lack of stuffiness typical of law professors, but I learned a lot.

Last January I gave a paper at AALS [Association of American Law Schools] about "the jurisprudence" of the Uniform Commercial Code. I called for an empirical view of how this law might be used and by whom. Of course, most people paid attention to the law and economics types who called for objective, non-qualitative default rules so that parties would not have to incur the transaction costs involved in spelling out everything in a contract. As you might expect, I was skeptical that such a body of law would serve anyone but those who could hire the largest law firms and who had sufficient bargaining power to impose their will in negotiations. The organizer of the panel was very nice. He said I did just what he wanted because I was "the spirit of Karl Llewellyn!" I guess I am in a group of law and economics types.

Malinowski also brings back memories. As far as I can remember, *Crime and Custom* was the single book that most impressed me as I was working on my 1963 ASR [*American Sociological Review*] article. Perhaps it is why I noticed what I noticed as the business people told me stories. You mention that his style was "literary." Indeed! This book is just plain fun to read.

You note that Llewellyn and Hoebel neglect power and domination by white society. Llewellyn wasn't a radical or even a New Deal liberal. He really liked people such as elite appellate judges. This was a good society with a few problems, and intelligent realist judges and law professors could fix them. You are certainly right to signal both the strengths and weaknesses of the trouble case method. I always wondered how much L&H really knew about the Cheyenne.

At the end you are very kind to "Critical Legal Studies." Only a few really use an ethnographic technique. Too many of them are the law professors who get their data from God or the ceiling tiles. But you are right, some of them are very good on legal education—particularly Duncan Kennedy. Have you seen Granfield and Koenig's two articles or their book? The articles are: "The Fate of Idealism: Accommodation and Ideological Work at Harvard Law School" (39 *Social Problems* 5, Nov. 1992), and "Learning Collective Eminence: Harvard Law School and the Social Production of Elite Lawyers" (33 *Sociological Quarterly* 503, No. 4, 1992). Their story rings true and disheartens me very much.

As I would expect, your introduction to the reissue is an excellent one. You bring the people to life, but of course you have a rare talent for an academic—you can write. From "Legal Process to Mind Processing" is one of those articles that I find myself laughing with: that is, I so agree with you that I start looking for something to object to. You are saying what I would have said had I thought about it. Albeit much better of course, but still we have the same reaction to the romanticized view of ADR. I've gone around with several social workers on this one a number of times. I remember people saying when I was a Stanford undergrad (when dinosaurs roamed the world?) that all problems of international conflict would be ended if we only could understand each other. I also remember thinking at the time that if we really did understand each other, we might really have something to fight about. Of course, a lot turns on what we mean by "understand." If I see the other as a human with his/her own slant on things, it may be harder to drop bombs on him/her.

Jackie and I are off to Japan at the end of July. We've never been there. Setsuo Miyazawa teaches sociology of law at Kobe, and we met at Ontario a few summers ago. They want me to do my contract law number. I found a passage that delighted me. Have you seen it? Wagatsuma and Rosett say: "The Japanese live by the illusion of harmony, while Americans live by the illusion of autonomy and self-sufficiency . . . the attitudes of the Japanese toward business transactions and contract which are regarded as uniquely Japanese . . . are also found in American society although the significance of that behavior may be defined differently by each culture."

The Law School just received a lot of money to set up a named chair—the Theodore Brazeau Professorship. I was very flattered to get the award. The honor is nice, but it means that I will have money for trips such as the one to Japan as long as I can make some claim of a connection to academic work. And Brazeau turns out to have battled for workers compensation when he was a young state senator in Wisconsin.

Did you happen to see Jamie Boyle's "The PC Harangue" in the latest issue of the *Stanford Law Review*? (45 Stan. Law Rev. 1457 May 1993). Here is a critic who can write, and he is pointing out important things.

Enough! I do ramble on, but this should suggest that I really enjoyed reading your letter and the two reprints.
Sincerely,

Stewart Macaulay
Theodore W. Brazeau Professor of Law
University of Wisconsin, Madison—School of Law

July 20, 1993

Dear Doctor Nader:

This is a fan letter. Over the years, I've read your articles on alternative dispute resolution, and I particularly appreciate your continued insistence that we must focus on morality and "justice for the masses." I also like your perspective that Indian people have offered methods of addressing dispute resolution.

I want you to know that your thinking is affecting the work of the Courts of the Navajo Nation. We have the Navajo Peacemaker Court, which is a method for court-annexed dispute resolution using traditional Navajo methods. At present, we are working on court access policies to attempt to serve the public without lawyers. We are trying, as you put it, to do macro-justice.

If you have a bibliography of your work I would appreciate having one. I thought you might like to know that there are some people out in the legal world who like your ideas, and who are putting them into practice.
Sincerely,

James W. Zion
Solicitor
Navajo Nation—Judicial Branch

August 4, 1993

To Whom It May Concern,

The purpose of this letter is to recount the events that led to the loss of my job, loss of funding for my research projects, withdrawal of my Ph.D registration and supervision, and finally to attempts (some of which were successful) at private and academic "blacklisting." All of this happened because I chose to challenge a system of sexual discrimination, and then continued to speak out against what I felt were violations of basic human rights, and fair and equal treatment—actions which simply did not conform with "how a woman should act."

This began with my employment at the University of Auckland in 1988 as a Senior Lecturer in the Department of Management Science and Information Systems—at the time I was the only woman in the department. Although from 1986, the University had a stated policy of equal employment opportunity, I observed and experienced unequal pay and research funding early on. Because of the University's policy, I felt it appropriate to address my concerns to the Dean of Commerce, Professor Alastair MacCormick. He warned me that it would be unwise to try to interfere with the system.

Not heeding Professor MacCormick's warning, I continued in the ensuing weeks to request equal treatment for all, and to question decisions that were being made within the School of Commerce. As I pressed my complaints regarding these inequalities to Professor MacCormick, his warnings became threats. When our discussions reached a point where I advised him I was left no recourse other than to file an official complaint, he responded that if a complaint were made I would never finish my Ph.D.

In late 1981, I presented Professor MacCormick with a letter for his signature. The letter was requesting outside grant money for my research. As he held his pen over the paper he asked, "If I sign this do you promise me peace and quiet from now on?" My response was: "I don't do blackmail." He looked annoyed, but he then signed the letter.

In a subsequent conversation when we were discussing funding for my research, Professor MacCormick enquired as to how I could continue if I were to lose my job at Auckland. I told him that I had lots of experience and would simply find another job. To this he replied, "I'll see to it that you never work again in New Zealand."

Naively believing that academia was one place were such actions would never be tolerated, I filed my first complaint with the Human Rights Commission (HRC) in the latter part of February 1989. Up until this time my Ph.D. progress reports had all been satisfactory. Negative reports began in the first review following the filing of my complaint. Research funds were withheld by the University from that time forward. And in the latter part of 1989 my Ph.D. registration was officially withdrawn.

In addition, although I was promised two two-year appointments, my employment was not renewed at the end of 1988. Despite my enquiries to the Registrar, I was never able to determine the grounds for my not being renewed. Despite efforts of one or more people at Auckland, which are related later, I was able to obtain employment at Victoria University in 1990 (having worked there in 1987), and was (in 1990) hired in three different departments.

In April of 1989, I spoke with the head of the Department of Computer Science at Auckland University. This was concerning a job application for a post in that department. Initially, I was advised that he would have to check on my application because I was in litigation with the University. Subsequently, he informed me that they had given the appointment to someone whose "research interests are more in line with those of the department." I had occasion to speak with a member of the department who, unaware of my application, told me the department had wanted to appoint a woman, but that "none had applied." At this time, I also applied for an advertised position at Waikato University. Subsequent to my interview I was told by a source, who because of fear of reprisal desires anonymity, that my application was dead because: "MacCormick talked to the Vice Chancellor."

In April of 1990 (while I was employed at Victoria University) an article about me appeared in the *Dominion*. It described me as an American who would not allow herself to be pushed around. The article went on to say that I taught this to my students, and that I encouraged them to stand up for their rights. This was followed by a letter to the Vice Chancellor at Victoria from the former Prime Minister, then Attorney General, enquiring as to how it could be that someone like me could be employed at Victoria.

When I applied in late 1990 for another position at Victoria, Professor MacCormick called Dean Mann and stated that I was trouble. Dean Mann has described this intervention in statements made during the investigation of my second complaint to the HRC. By this time my consulting jobs came even less frequently, and although I had conducted courses which received positive evaluations, the repeat sessions were cancelled. The position at Victoria was given to an applicant who did not meet the advertised minimum criteria. Ultimately, I felt I could no longer survive economically in New Zealand, and thus in May of 1991 I retreated to the United States.
Sincerely,

Patricia "Max" Vandervort
Atlanta, GA

September 21, 1993

Dear Prof. Nader:

Thank you very much for sending me a copy of your fascinating article on the ADR movement in the U.S. I apologize to you for the delay in response. I was out of town for the summer vacation.

The political use of "harmony" to promote ADR without empirical foundation of ADR's usefulness, nor of the so-called "litigation explosion," as you describe in your paper, reminded me of the rhetoric used by many Japanese businessmen and some scholars in explaining Japanese way of behavior. Stereotypical explanations are: "Japan is a homogeneous society . . . people are living together in peace and harmony." These rhetorics are used to oppress opposition, e.g., managements use them to control workers: employees are de-facto forced to work until late at night without extra payment (this "voluntary" work is called "service zan-gyo," but be careful in reading statistics by the Ministry of Labor because this type of "voluntary" work is not counted!), people are told that "all of your colleague are doing this, so should you," and active union members will often be segregated as disturbing the "harmony." Companies formed a sort of membership club where cartels and collusions are made and executed under the name of "harmony of the industry." Not only politicians but also high officials of MTI, the Ministry of Agriculture and Forestry, etc., are the coordinators of these industrial collusions—those bureaucrats sometime call them "Peace Keeping Operations."

Interesting thing is that many people who are actually disadvantaged also believe in the fallacy. In other words, "harmony" and "homogeneity" are shared beliefs in this fallacy. In other words, "harmony" and "homogeneity" are shared common illusion, but nobody knows empirically whether it is true, or how and to what extent it is "Japanese." I can say that the "harmony" extends to the "insiders" only, where insider-outsider distinction is made by those who have the power in the "inside group." Usually, those who oppose or cast some doubt on the illusion will be excluded and become an "outsider." To the extent the relation between insiders is intimate (or appears to be intimate), the relation between an insider and an outsider is hostile. It has been said by some political/sociological scholars that Japanese do not establish "individuality" or "self," but people fear very much losing identity by becoming an outsider. In other words, they identify themselves to the "homogeneous" group instead of establishing their own self.

The shared illusion explained above may be restated this way: people tend to overestimate interdependence. This over-estimation leads to the excessive function of peer-effect. Going back to ADR, I would say the same rhetoric has been and is mobilized in establishing ADR in Japan, especially when the administration (government & bureaucrats) takes the initiative of it in cooperation with the business. Behind the rhetoric arguably lies the intention to exclude those who will be disadvantaged by the informal procedures from the decision-making process (e.g. consumers and the under-represented). The bureaucrats are motivated to pursue this line so that they obtain more discretionary power (i.e. control).

ADR is also used as "moratorium," by which I mean the way to postpone social decision making (which is usually legislation). There is a widespread "illusion" that the law, if enacted, is the end of the story to everybody (i.e. the winners take all and the losers lose all). Therefore, solving socially important problems through legislation is quite difficult in Japan. When legislatures face these types of problems, they often choose not to decide. The administration, who plays a major role in legislative process in Japan, even larger than the legislature, does not want to decide either, especially when legislation would affect the industry over which it has jurisdiction. By being public officials, bureaucrats cannot appear to be hostile to the general public either. Thus, the administration looks for a way to postpone decision making. The solution is to establish ADR so that there is no immediate loser nor winner.

Thus the ADR movement in Japan led by the government and business is, in reality, not necessarily oriented to "harmony." But they use the rhetoric because Japanese people have propensity to avoid law, and they hate litigation so ADR is the best way for Japanese people to solve disputes.

Having said all this, I still think it is not a bad idea to promote ADR in Japan. The reason is simple efficiency. The court system does not work because of the lack of resources (i.e., number of judges, courthouses, and lawyers), and the budget for judiciary expenses are all extremely small. When I consider the political climate, I do not think it is easy to improve the kaput judicial system soon. In this circumstance, I think that ADR is one of the feasible options.

You may say that Japan's ADRs are not functioning very well in that although there are a lot of complaints coming in (actually much fewer than in the U.S.), the majority of these cases end up unilaterally. In other words, very few people go as far as bilateral procedures like mediation and arbitration. Some scholars argue that it is because people do not want to solve their problems by themselves, instead they want the government to solve their problems for them. Others claim that it is because the people do not want to face the opponents in person and to discuss unpleasant topics. Persons in charge of ADR may claim that it is because they give satisfaction to the claimants at the unilateral stage. Unfortunately, nobody knows the truth.

Thank you very much again for your kindness. I'm looking forward to seeing you in the near future.

Sincerely yours.

Ota Shozo
Graduate School of Law and Politics
The University of Tokyo

October 18, 1993

Dear Laura,

A short while back a friend of mine from the bay area sent an article about you that was from the *S. F. Chronicle*. I found this article to be very interesting and that is what prompts me to write to you.

I have enclosed a self-addressed postcard and I would appreciate it if you could write any dates in the near future that you will be making a speech or participating in a discussion on this topic of "coercive harmony." I'd also be interested in articles.

It has seemed to me that for quite some time now that people in general have been reluctant to speak out or confront those things that they would normally challenge.

As a teacher at the high school level there appears to be a concerted effort to keep people from speaking out and somehow make them intimidated to take a counter position. I think that all this works something like this: The principal of the school talks about "his" staff and the "team" that we are all on—this is done both verbally and in written communications from him. For example, he'll thank the team for the wonderful job they did during a fire drill that we had. Not that we haven't had many very uneventful fire drills in the past, but now they are extremely all well done and this is because we are all pulling together as a team for the benefit of the students and the community.

I don't know why it is, but it seems to me that teachers as a whole are of such a psychological makeup that they need a lot of reassurance from the "boss" and they like very much being part of the team. Anyone who speaks out now is somehow considered to be a rebel or some sort of misfit and can't get along with their colleagues. And worse, they are not doing their part as a team member. The problem is the only game in town *IS* the game the principal runs—he owns the ball and the bat and sets all the rules. If one does not want to be counterproductive, then they must play the game the principal and the rest of the staff (through the principal's efforts) wants. The merits of the "game" are inconsequential.

I agree that we are now in an era, for whatever reason, when going along with the main flow is very important and societal pressures to go along with the flow are great. Unfortunately, this trend diminishes individuality and allows those who are in a position to "coerce" to have their way no matter how harmful or misguided.
Sincerely,

Norman A. Larson
Lompoc, CA

April 6, 1994

Dear Laura,

I read your argument in favor of electing the regents in the February 1994 issue of the *California Monthly*. I couldn't possibly agree with you more. The U.C. system is faking the citizens of California. When I was a student at U.C. Berkeley in the early 1950s the fee was $60 a semester, about 1% of my father's annual salary who himself was a 1925 graduate at Berkeley in engineering. At today's rates, my son can attend an out of state (Oregon) for only a little more tuition than today's fee at Berkeley. My father and I always agreed that the U.C. system should be available to all qualified applicants cost free.

At last somebody has articulated my complaints, and very well at that.
Very truly yours,

Donald R. Wells
U.C. Berkeley Class of 55'

August 30, 1994

Dear Ms. Nader,

Thank you for your letter of June 10, 1994 regarding the securities arbitration process. For your information, I am enclosing copies of legislation that I introduced earlier this month, as well as my statements on this subject.

The bill is entitled the "Civil Rights Procedures Protections Act of 1994." This legislation would make arbitration of all employment discrimination claims voluntary. As you know, in the securities industry and others arbitration of employment claims are often mandatory. This bill would reinstate the civil rights of employees in the securities industry and other business—rights which are granted to every American under the federal civil rights laws.

Thank you for contacting me about your views on this important issue. Please do not hesitate to contact me again if you have any further thoughts on this issue.
Sincerely,

Edward J. Markey
U.S. House of Representatives
Committee on Energy and Commerce
Subcommittee on Telecommunications and Finance

January 6, 1995

Dear Laura,

Here's a copy of my Zapatista proposal with a sample cover letter. I hope I'll be finished this by summer 1995. If I can get the funding together in the next several weeks, that should be no problem. I'm very interested in your film project and would love to work with you on it. Have you seen any of my work? I'm a journalist with an artist's eye, and would be happy to show you some. Let's talk soon about your plans. Your schedule is probably fuller than mine, so why don't you figure out a time that's convenient for you to meet and then give me a call? It can be anytime in the next several weeks, as I am not planning to do any traveling before mid-February.

I'm a former ABC News cameraman and television producer with a long-standing interest in indigenous cultures. I need your help to finish an educational video documentary about the political economy of Chiapas, Mexico. This project is aimed at classrooms, community groups, and lastly a general broadcast audience. It deals with human rights, agriculture, trade, and native cultures. As you may know, the "unpleasantness" in Chiapas last January was the biggest Indian uprising in the Western hemisphere since the Mexican Revolution in 1910. This documentary explores the underlying causes and looks at some possible solutions to the crisis there.

We want to make a program with a long shelf life that can be used to illustrate the general case of indigenous peoples in tropical zones all around the globe, and particularly the problems they face organizing themselves to meet the challenges of the next century. Unless native peoples turn things around and begin to thrive in places like Chiapas, they will continue to stream northward creating illegal immigration problems here in the U.S.

I've tried to be thorough without overwhelming you with paper. The gist of the proposal is this: I've raised and spent about $10,000 and need another $12,500 to finish the production shooting. I've raised a challenge grant of $2,500, and Edward James Olmos has tentatively agreed to narrate the project. The Institute for Food and Development Policy (Food First) has pledged to raise $4,000 of the-post-production money and to distribute the finished program. While the bad news is that we need $12,500 and don't have it yet, the good news is that since most of the resources are already in place or promised, we only need this relatively small amount to bring this worthwhile project to a successful completion.

The Mayans of Mesoamerica are an endangered species, and this film explains why. Trouble is again brewing in Chiapas as I write this, and as you know, anti-immigrant hysteria has carried the day out here in California. Understanding how these two phenomena are related, and what should be done about it is the educational goal of this project. Thank you very much for your consideration.

Best,

Peter White
Freelance Journalist

March 3, 1995

Dear Dr. Nader,

I read with great interest the paper you lent me entitled "Protecting Indigenous Peoples' Privacy from 'Eyes in the Sky.'" Do you have the information on where it was published?

As the author discusses briefly, GIS data *can* be used to bolster indigenous claims to lands. Furthermore, they are enormously valuable in communal projects of sustainable use of natural resources. Based on my experience in Southern Mexico, I can document two notorious examples:

The Zoque communities of Santa Maria and San Miguel Chimalapa on the Oaxaca-Chiapas border, own collectively over 600,000 hectares of forest—the largest tract of pristine tropical ecosystems remaining in Mexico. Cattle ranchers and loggers from Veracruz and Chiapas have been encroaching on Zoque lands in the last decades. The government of Chiapas has fabricated a boundary dispute in order to exploit over 100,000 hectares of forest. The brother of former governor Absalón Castellanos of Chiapas was actually caught robbing timber, and was taken prisoner by the Zoque in 1988. The Zoque allied themselves with environmentalist groups, most notably Maderas del Pueblo, and have unilaterally declared their whole communal lands a campesino ecological reserve. Mexican environmental authorities have lagged in granting official recognition of Chimalapa as protected area within the national system of nature preserves. With the endorsement of the communities, Maderas and SERBO (Sociedad para el Estudio de los Recursos Bióticos de Oaxaca, the non-profit group which we established) have obtained the LANDSAT satellite images to map out accurately the extent of Chimalapa forest and classify the different vegetation types present. A GIS system is simultaneously being developed that will provide the basis for a communal forestry plan—some areas within the campesino reserve will be set aside for strict conservation, others will be harvested sustainably for both timber and non-timber forest products.

The Zapotec and Chinantec communities of the district of Ixtlan are using data derived from satellite images and aerial photographs to develop long-term forestry plans. Their timber extraction schemes of the past decade were based largely on the old taxonomic studies from the time when the forests were concessioned to Papelera Tuxtepec, the government cellulose industry. Seeking to generate communal employment rather than large-scale profit, the timber-extraction rates and management schemes of the communities are radically different. Some of the communities (particularly Ixtlan, Comaltepec, and Calpulalpan) are also concerned about conserving some areas for watershed regulation, environmental tourism, and the protection of genetic resources (a bioprospecting initiative, funded by the Swiss pharmaceutical company Sandoz, was just initiated in Comaltepec, involving microbiological sampling; several communities in the area are also gathering "matsutake" mushrooms and *selling* them communally to the *Japanese* market, for a very high profit—the species requires mature pine forest, a further incentive for forest conservation). Like the Zoque these communities are working with SERBO and ERA (another NGO in Oaxaca, specializing in forestry) to learn to use satellite data applications to natural resource management. SERBO has obtained recent LANDSAT images for this region, and has made the data available to the communities.

Regarding the paragraph on Chiapas in section 4 of the paper, I think that the situation is much more complex than the author presents it. Although it is true that PEMEX has prospected in Chiapas, I have not read of any displacements of indigenous peoples as a result of oil extraction. My understanding is that the lands in northern Chiapas where PEMEX has active wells had been taken away from indigenous communities long before oil was discovered. It is in neighboring Tabasco and southern Veracruz where the infringement by PEMEX on the agriculture and fisheries of Chontal, Nahuat, Popoluca, and non-indigenous communities has been well documented. I feel that Madsen's connection between oil production and the Zapatista rebellion is grossly oversimplified and misportrayed—not that oil is not an issue, as we discussed, but the causal connection is not as mechanistic as he presents it. In any case, I do not know of any evidence to back his supposition that GIS data may have been instrumental in locating petroleum reserves and displacing Mayans off their land in Chiapas. There is one NGO active in Chiapas with remote-sensing technologies that will surely be knowledgeable on the history of this and may be able to provide us with the documentation you request: it's called Ecosfera and is based in San Cristobal las Casas. They have used satellite images and aerial photographs to map out forest areas in both northwestern (El Ocote) and northeastern (Selva Lacandona) Chiapas. Their interest is natural areas and wildlife populations. I believe they are the only group in southern Mexico to use Arcinfo, a quite sophisticated (and expensive) GIS system. They also use elaborate geographic-positioning technology for fieldwork. I know two people at Ecosfera we could contact if you wish to pursue this.

I hope my comments are useful to you. It is a fascinating topic, but one prone with controversy—the greatest challenge perhaps, is to provide viable proposals on how to enforce indigenous rights to collective privacy. Look forward to your thoughts on this.
Sincerely,

Alejandro de Avila
Ph.D. Candidate
University of California, Berkeley

March 16, 1995

Dear Prof. Nader,

Thank you for taking the time to send me a thoughtful letter and the excellent articles by you on our civil justice systems. My apology for being so slow in responding. . .

I should probably have not been drawn into the tort reform battle as a non-lawyer, but it did seem to me that excellent as it is our civil justice system does need some corrections. I regret that my support for this general position has been interpreted as an inducement as the Gingrich agenda now pending in Congress. *The Washington Post* will soon carry an op-ed by me setting forth my views more intelligently. . .

Respectfully yours,

George McGovern
United States Senator

May 3, 1995

Dear Professor Nader:

I was profoundly impressed by your skillful debate with former Judge Renfrew (whom I know and regard as a personal friend) as reported in the current issue of *California Lawyer*. I have no doubt there has been for at least 15 years a concerted movement by corporate America to reduce access to the courts so as to reduce accountability. I also firmly believe that "ADR" is but one of the more subtle but no less effective weapons in that movement's arsenal.

Renfrew was not able to rebut any of your points. But what I particularly liked (as a lawyer) is that a sociologist could defeat a lawyer on this issue without having to resort to the one legal argument Renfrew would be unable to rebut: the First and Seventh Amendments together accord us the Constitutional right to petition our courts for the empanelment of a jury to hear and decide our grievances. If there are those who believe we have "too much" civil litigation for our own good, let them seek repeal of those Constitutional guarantees. Of course it will never happen because they are essential to a peaceful democratic society. A dispute not resolved in court mustn't be resolved in the streets.

Yours very truly,

Eugene Crew
Townsend and Townsend Khourie and Crew Law Offices

May 22, 1995
Dr. David Hamburg

President
Carnegie Corporation of New York

Dear David:

Recently I received the Carnegie reprint "Education for Conflict Resolution" for which I thank you. While I applaud the direction that this document

reflects, there are some dangers that I have been examining over three decades or so. Harmony and harmonizing are double-edged, I have studied this phenomena among the Zapotec, in freshmen dorms, in alternative dispute resolution and in numerous other settings. I enclose two short pieces on the subject: one, the Brazil talk which has appeared in four different places in Latin America but not in English, and the other in relation to the law as practiced in California. One cannot put anger into a box without feeding explosive behavior. As I said the last time we spoke, I would have liked to speak with the Carnegie people about this matter. At the moment, all I can do is fight against education for conflict resolution as described in your pamphlet.
Cordially yours,

Laura Nader
Professor of Anthropology

July 7, 1995

Dear Professor Nader:

Re: *Badie v. Bank of America* San Francisco Superior Court Case No. 944916 California Court of Appeal, First Dist., No. A068753.

Thank you very much for speaking with me the other day. I was very impressed by your comments to *California Lawyer* in the article "Coercive Harmony" and very much look forward to receiving the articles you have written.

Enclosed is the recent article by Professor Mark Budnitz that I promised you. I found it very helpful.

I will be sure to send you a copy of our opening appellate brief, which we expect to file on September 5, 1995.

You may be interested in a brief summary of our case. Bank of America unilaterally imposed a mandatory arbitration clause upon existing checking account and credit card customers, which was contained in a billing insert mailed with checking account and credit card account statements in June, 1992. The insert contained incomplete and misleading language, requiring absolutely no affirmative consent by the consumer. The Bank's own readership survey conducted before the mailing and introduced into evidence by the Bank at trial made it clear that less than 4% of its customers would read "stand alone" inserts. The Bank failed to mention the new arbitration term altogether in the personal letters sent to more than 5.2 million former Security Pacific checking account and credit card customers in June 1992. These personal letters, informing customers acquired from Security Pacific as a result of the purchase of the bank by Bank of America that their existing accounts would be changed to a new one without interest, required those customers to sign affirmatively and tear off an agreement at the bottom of a letter to switch to an interest bearing account. The Bank clearly had the option of these tear-off signature agreements with respect to the arbitration agreement, but chose instead to simply insert a notice in billing statements it knew would not be read by the vast majority of customers. The trial court found that ADR is favored by California public policy, and that the ADR Clause is therefore within the reasonable expectations of the Bank's customers, the notice given was not deceptive or unfair, and that the Bank retained as a matter of contract, the right to modify the credit card agreements to add the ADR Clause. The Court issued this opinion despite its findings that the notice was not "the best possible notice," and that it was not designed to achieve "knowing consent." The Court equated "knowing consent" with hostility to arbitration. There has been wide-reaching disapproval of this decision and we believe the likelihood of reversal is strong. We have determined the key issues on appeal to be as follows:

1. The California policy favoring ADR does not extend to non-consensual, unilateral, and mandatory imposition of ADR. The unilateral imposition of ADR which imposes involuntary submission to arbitration by disputants who do not choose it violates California public policy. ADR must be mutually agreed upon to be mutually beneficial. It is incorrect for a court to find that because of ADR's favored status, the scrutiny to be given to provisions adopting ADR is less in determining whether an agreement exists.

2. The premise of ADR is that it is consensual; volunteerism is a basic principle of all non-binding forms of ADR. Specifically, consent must be manifested by a signature in a contractual document which (already) contains the provision. The trial court's application of the meaningful choice test to an ongoing stable business relationship was erroneous and entirely unprecedented. Traditional contract principles of offer and acceptance govern. Since there is no manifestation of mutual assent, no contract exists as to arbitration or reference.

3. Assuming a contract was created, the ADR clause is unenforceable because it is unconscionable. Under *Graham v. Scissor-Tail Inc.* (1981) 28 Cal. 3d 807, the issue is surprise or whether the agreement was outside the reasonable expectations of customers. The court's standard for determining unconscionability as whether the clause lacks "minimum levels of integrity" was incorrect. The secretive adoption of ADR certainly was a surprise and was outside the reasonable expectations of customers.

4. The trial court erred in not applying the standards set forth in *Wheeler v. St. Joseph Hospital* (1976) 63 Cal.App.3d 345 of (1) consent, (2) a notice that fully and completely informs, (3) an understanding by the customer of the implications of arbitration and reference.

The notice given was inadequate to meet the requirements imposed by the Constitution and by contract law:

1. The right to jury trial is inviolate and a waiver of that right requires a voluntary act and a knowing consent.
2. The notice itself was unclear, terse, and its validity is substantially undermined by the stark contrast between the language of the actual insert and the Bank's explanation of its meaning in its trial briefing. B of A's attempt to add ADR provisions to the existing terms of the credit card agreements violates the duty of good faith and fair dealing since the uncontroverted testimony at trial was that the notice was likely to be read by only 4% of the Bank's customers.
3. The court ignored the fact that B of A's credit card agreements are adhesion contracts and that unclear terms therein must be construed against the Bank. The term "change" as used in the agreement must, if fairly construed, be limited to purely price terms for already existing services. This is how Bank employees themselves interpreted the agreement. The term "change" cannot reasonably be deemed to be the equivalent of the word "amend" so that "change" would include "add" or "delete," "revise," "replace," or "modify." The contract did not allow modifications to provide for ADR. *Perdue v. Crocker Nat. Bank* (1985) 38 Cal.3d 913, appeal dismissed (1986) 475 U.S. 483, does not allow the Bank to add a provision for dispute resolution as a "change of terms."
4. The court failed to distinguish appropriately between arbitration and reference. As to reference, absent consent, it violates the Constitution for a referee's decisions to be other than advisory only to the trial court.

Please feel free to call me in the meantime if you have any questions or if you care to further discuss the issues raised by the imposition of mandatory arbitration in the commercial setting.

Very truly yours.

Ann Sayonara
Sturdevant & Sturdevant Law Offices
San Francisco, CA

August 27, 1995

Dear Laura,

The paper "Biological Factors and Cultural Factors in Mental Illness" was indeed published (long ago in a collection of papers edited by Francis Hsu, *Psychological Anthropology: Approaches to Culture and Personality* (Homewood,

Ill., Doresey Press: 1961, pp. 225–295). I am afraid I don't have any reprints but I am sure you can find it in the Berkeley library. If you have trouble, I can make a xerox for you.

This paper earned a rebuke from Margaret Mead in a review in (I think) the *American Anthropologist*. She said that my suggestions that hysteria might be a symptom of calcium deficiency was a "destructive hypothesis!"
With best regards,

Anthony Wallace
Professor of Anthropology
University of Pennsylvania

February 20, 1996

Dear Laura,

Thanks very much for your incredibly quick response to my interest. Of course I am always delighted to see anything you have written. I hope we can keep in touch.

The science articles seem very good to me. I can't really add any helpful editorial comments on the draft—I don't know enough about the problems. The quotes from the scientists seem to show that most people recognize the problems of modern "Big Science," but don't have a consensus about what to do about them or an organization that could do anything if there was a consensus. The postmodern predicament: everything's so multifocal, contested, deconstructed, etc., that no one can act.

Anyway, I sense a lot of interesting questions under all this about what science is. Malinowski used to mean "empirical stuff" as opposed to "stuff that anyone can see isn't empirically grounded," to oversimplify a bit. In this sense, the Trobrianders must necessarily have had a working sense of the difference: they could see that there was a connection between cooling a fish and hauling it in that there was not between fishing ritual and canoe safety. Now, in the science you study that is not the situation. Rarely do modern physicists have the fortune to see what they are talking about. They see cloud-chamber traces, or columns of figures, or gauge measurements instead. These they take as accurate but not perfect indicators.

But more to the point, "science" in the US is several things, none of them very empirical like science in the classic sense.
Sincerely,

Gene Anderson
Professor of Anthropology
University of California, Riverside

April 5, 1996
Dr. Richard C. Lewontin

Museum of Comparative Zoology
Harvard University

Dear Prof. Lewontin:

Andre Schiffrin was kind enough to send along a copy of your paper on "The Cold War and the Transformation of the Academy" to the other contributors in the Cold War volume. I was deeply disturbed upon reading what you had to say. Indeed the academy was transformed by the Cold War, but your piece is so decontextualized as to constitute a revisionist history—one that denies the parts of the picture that were not so benign.

I have always admired your work and your manner of reasoning. On this one I cannot agree that the "extraordinary sum of public money . . . has provided academics with a degree of control over the conditions of their employment." You who is so good at qualifying forgot to qualify—to include those who lost control of the conditions of their employment. Have you read my piece?

I am left with the question . . . what happened? Should we talk?
Sincerely,

Laura Nader
Professor of Anthropology

April 15, 1996

Dear Laura Nader:

I was chagrined to get your letter, but I must say it was not unexpected. I think the problem is largely a rhetorical one. I did not expect André to send out what was a first draft to people, but he did. My guess is that you will not be the only one who does not see what I am driving at because of the rhetorical weight of various parts of the article.

I do say in the very first page that people's lives and careers were ruined by the Cold War, and I do not intend to say a great deal more about that because your article and others cover it so well. I can see that I just let the statement lie there without working it into the rest of the article. The point however, is that although the lives and careers of numerous people were ruined by the Cold War, the academic profession as a whole did indeed achieve immense prosperity and control over the conditions of its own work as a consequence of the Cold War. That contradiction between the benefits received by the large majority and even the institution as a whole, and the sufferings of a minority is a contradiction not confined to the academic workplace and the Cold War. It is part and parcel of the history of unionization for example, in the history of American labor. The successful struggles of American workers to unionize, especially in the case of the crafts unions, was the direct cause of the immiseration and exclusion of a fraction of the working class that had previously found some employment.

Craft union organization in particular fell heavily on Blacks and other minorities who, over and over again in various sectors of the country, were excluded from union membership, and therefore became totally excluded from the possibility of work.

The purpose of my article is precisely to rub the noses of the academic community in the real truth: which is that although they would not like to admit it because it would seem cruel, or because if they are on the right, they think everybody really got what they deserved and the students got too uppity, they really benefitted from the Cold War. Far from decontextualizing, my intent is to make the contradiction as strong as possible. It seems clear to me from your reaction to the piece that some rhetorical work has to be done, and I had already realized that in the second draft that I had fixed up. Nevertheless, I do not want to spend a lot of time on the material that you and others have so well covered in the book. If André insists that my piece be the first piece in the book then, of course, I will have to spend a bit of energy pointing to other essays on the severe damage done by the Cold War to some members of the academic community.

What worries me most about your comment is that you think I have decontextualized the problem. On the contrary, my whole purpose was to contextualize the other essays by reminding us that the Via Dolorosa along which some of us, our comrades, our friends, and our relatives were dragged to their crucifixion, was also the highway to success for the vast majority of academics. Discussions of the persecutions of the Cold War and the distortions of intellectual agendas must be seen, in my view, in the context of the general prosperity that the Cold War brought to the mass. I suppose one could say that one person's text is another person's context.

I do not know whether I have got at the issues which are bothering you.

I certainly see the necessity of some expansion of my remarks to make it clearer. If I have not touched the point that disturbs you, then we ought to discuss it more, and I certainly would welcome that.

Yours,

Dr. Richard C. Lewontin
Museum of Comparative Zoology
Harvard University

May 4, 1996

Dear Laura,

As you can see, I am far from home. Your thoughtful note and attachment of long ago, affording me the end product of your lecture, languished for some time before reaching me. I must also apologize for my own sluggishness.

I was honored by your visit with us, and thrilled by your lecture. Having something named after you that way is slightly embarrassing, at least to me. But the lectures are so splendid that I am reassured each year that the cause is just.

I'm here teaching, doing a bit of research, and being enlightened. I'd wanted to see this place once more before you know what. My research is on piscophagy, a favorite Hong Kong (indeed, South Chinese) diversion. It may sound fishy, but it's a great research topic.

I continue to enjoy teaching, and the students here are keen, industrious, and much fun. It is a young institution, its character more reminiscent of my Alma Mater than of Yale or some manual laborers; and yet they all seem well equipped to become as middle class as (well, to what should I compare them?) me. What lies in store for them in the next year or so however, is by no means entirely clear.

The campus is mountainous, but somewhat contrary to what people think about JK—it is also sylvan. The weather is now beginning to warm up; it gets awfully hot quite soon.

I hope that you are well and enjoying life. Thank you again for visiting us; thank you for your fine paper.

Sincerely,

Sydney W. Mintz
Professor of Anthropology
Chinese University of Hong Kong

September 2, 1996
Richard C. Reuben

Stanford Law School

Re: "The Lawyer Turns Peacemaker"

Thanks for faxing the piece. Enjoyed talking with you. As for the piece you sent, I am not yet able to accept the degree of raw propaganda published in our trade journals. What you call mainstream I call propaganda—pure and simple. Some of the figures you quote (i.e. from Harvard) knew nothing about this subject before the Pound conference ... within a week they became instant experts. Even Goebels would be impressed. Sorry—but at least you can count on a straightforward response.

Best wishes,

Laura Nader

October 9, 1996
Richard Blumenthal

Attorney General of Connecticut
Hartford, CT

Dear Attorney General Blumenthal:

I write to you because of my concern for the future of the Winsted Memorial Hospital, and as an anthropologist who for over 40 years has been studying the role of law in the United States and elsewhere. In addition, I have been directing a three year study of health management for the California Wellness Foundation in a small California town not much larger than Winsted.

The Winsted case raises two points of concern. The first has to do with the role of the attorney general to act on behalf of the public in the absence of private attorneys general. The second has to do with legal culture as it has developed since Chief Justice Berger's decade long war against the law in the 1970s.

As you know, the function of the adversary system is to equalize unequal parties before the court. An important function of the attorney general's office is to represent the unrepresented, especially in cases of utter disregard of community interests. Certainly your first statement to the court fit the public image of what an attorney general should do.

What happened between your first statement and the appointment by Judge Walsh of a receiver was less a part of law than a part of the contemporary culture of negotiation that has now spread from Litchfield to the Gatt offices in Switzerland. It is a style of negotiation in which the weaker party loses. There is mounting evidence that in such negotiation the weaker party seeks to adjudicate while the stronger pursues negotiation.

The negotiation that took place between the hospital board and your office, which led to the judge's decision to validate an agreement to further disenfranchise the Winsted community, falls in the category of anti-law. The most interested parties were eliminated from the negotiation. The Winsted Memorial Hospital case should be debated in public and in court. Why?

The American health system is changing rapidly into a for-profit industry. The U.S. health care sector has undergone formal rationalization (or "McDonaldization") which includes among other things: the corporatization of hospitals, the rise of HMOs, and the emergence of a class of bureaucratic managers (not physicians and not patients) that make decisions about delivery of services. People with a stake in the for-profit medical industry should not be appointed as receivers. The Winsted case must be seen in this larger picture for you to imagine how broadly significant your actions are.

Sincerely yours,

Laura Nader
Professor of Anthropology

October 27, 1996
Ira Michael Heyman

Chancellor
University of California, Berkeley

Dear Mike,

Your letter of last summer caught up with me just as university was opening and it has lain on top of my correspondence for answer. Noting that you are joining us at the AAA meetings in San Francisco moved me to the typewriter.

There was much both in your letter and in your talk to the curators that calls for response. The fact that I don't know quite where to start is why I put out the book *Naked Science*—it takes more than a few paragraphs. But for starters let me say that I do not believe that either you or the American Chemical Society understood Molella's exhibit, although I'll bet a majority of the viewers did. For me it was not an evaluative exhibit. It was "Science in American Life" from the point of the viewer and not from the point of view of Nobel Laureates. It did not have to be "balanced" in the sense you indicate. Indeed, if it were to balance the exaggerated glorification of science we often suffer in this country, it might have been even "more so." In that context, I thought it interesting that you mention the absence of mention of increase in life span in the 20th century, presumably crediting science with that achievement. I wonder if you have ever read Rene Dubois's *The Mirage of Health* in which he, himself a distinguished scientist, credits the increase in life span to the use of glass windows, the use of cotton underwear, and sanitary engineering rather than medical science.

I do not think that curators should learn from lawyers how to present balanced exhibits. They could help in the debate over what constitutes balance perhaps, and what to do when there are more than two sides—say five. One would have to consider power in such constructions and include in talk to curators pressures from donors like the American Chemical Society. Your comments on curators vs. academics and the question of attribution make a point worth pondering, but I kept coming back to your comments on "balance" and "two sides," and I ask myself if I could construct a two-sided, balanced exhibit on the holocaust—I could not. Life is not about two sides and balance. In fact, the central theme of my Zapotec and U.S. work has been on the concept of balance as control.

Perhaps we'll bump into each other at the meetings. If not I wish you a productive time with the natives. Best wishes to you and Teresa.
Sincerely yours,

Laura Nader

March 9, 1997

Dear Laura,

Thank you for thinking of me and sending me a copy of your article "The Phantom Factor: The Impact of the Cold War on Anthropology." I read the article with a great deal of interest, remembering that you had mentioned it to me in a telephone conversation over a year ago. Having lived through many of the events you describe, I found the article quite insightful, and I want to congratulate you on the courage which it must have taken to write the essay.

I particularly liked the personal tone of the article and your description of what it was like to be a graduate student in anthropology at Harvard in the 1950s. Having gone to Harvard more than a decade after you, and then having taught there for a short period in the early 1970s, I now recognize how little any of us really understood the broader context in which we were studying and conducting research. Because anthropology was so inward looking, it was difficult to understand either the intellectual or political field in which our work took place. We did not have great admiration for the "sociology of knowledge" at that time, and even if we had strong ethical positions, we seldom placed them in the wider context of the Cold War, or American society and culture.

One of the things which I found striking when I returned from fieldwork in Guatemala and two years of teaching in Brazil, was the rediscovery of the history of anthropology. Jack Stauder and I were close friends during that period, and all of us were rediscovering the roots of anthropology: especially British social anthropology which so greatly influenced our graduate studies. At the same time, the book which you contributed to, *Reinventing Anthropology*, was published and it provided some inspiration that perhaps there was a way to reinvent the field. However, at the same time the so-called "academic market" for anthropology was shrinking, and many of us were looking in other places (some to Community Colleges, others like myself to Advocacy Groups) to use our anthropological skills. Somehow, we may have been less a product of the ideological currents of the 1960s (the Civil Rights Movement, the anti-war movement, the women's movement, etc.) than that of the economic changes taking place in America in the 1970s (an overabundance of people trained in a field for which there was little room for employment). But that may be too materialist an interpretation.

At the same time as I read your article, I wish there was more discussion of the "cultural" and "intellectual" field as well as the wider political economy in which anthropology in the final decades of the 20th century evolved. For example, much of the criticism of British anthropology by Stauder, Talal Asad, et. al., if I remember, had to do with ideological currents (functionalism, social integration, failure to deal with class and conflict) as it was a reflection of colonialism itself. And, this may have also been true of American and French anthropology, the former going toward cognitive psychology, and the latter entering the realm of symbolism via Levi-Strauss. As Bourdieu and others have made clear, it is the ways in which power affects the "intellectual field," as well as the power relations within the discipline itself and relation to the wider society, that affects the trends in a discipline. You touch on these in a very interesting way at the end of the essay when you deal with "post-modernist" anthropology via Marcus and Fischer, and I wish this analysis in the essay had more depth.

But I am just rambling here and I want to congratulate you on a fine essay, one which does make a great contribution to the history of anthropology, as well as American intellectual history. I am sure the essay sits well with others in the volume.

In hopes that this letter, written with much haste in the midst of a busy work schedule, finds you well.

With best wishes.

Sandy Davis
Falls Church, VA

April 6, 1997

Dear Dr. Nader,

It was a fascinating experience going through your book, *Naked Science*. I have come to archaeology through my research in paleo-climate and physical dating techniques. But I belong to Kumaun, Central Himalayas and therefore have grown up in the absence of local folklore. I have been impressed by their knowledge of ecology, effects of snowfall, changes in wind directions etc. And the folk ecology management in North East India has impressed some of our best Western trained ecologists so much that they have returned back humbler after learning from them, rather than teaching them!

But what intrigues me most are the Muauni Jagars. There are rituals through which the Jagaria (Shaman?) calls departed souls to descend into some media (dangaria). The spirits are cajoled, entreated, made benign, and finally installed in some rock to immobilize them permanently—thus freeing them from their eternal wandering. Being possessed by spirits and getting excised is universal, but calling the spirit, making it descend into a medium, and seeking its advice and help is quite unique. The ritual is an elaborate and very solemn occasion for the village folk. The dangaria levitates and then behaves like a zombie. Usually, the departed spirit is a woman who committed suicide due to torture at the hands of the in-laws. The in-laws also attend the ritual and beg forgiveness of the spirit and pay compensation to the bereaved family. Thus the ritual also serves the purpose of social reconciliation. By what intrigues me more is the real significance of this ritual. Is it some traditional technique to tap the unconscious, to come to tell of what Vaclav Havel called the unknown, the illogical, the mysterious parts of being (mind you, I am not a superstitious man but a materialist to boot!).

I am a novice in this field. Your comments would be very useful to me. I am sending a reprint for your comments. If I get your email address, I would like to send a reprint of my paper for your valuable comments.
Yours sincerely,

D. P. Agrawal
Ahmedabad, India

May 1, 1997

Dear Laura:

Thank you very much for your continuing concern about "Science in American Life." The political furors seem to have quieted down for the moment, though I am sad to say that we are having financial problems with the exhibition ever since the American Chemical Society decided, in its wisdom, to pull out support for the exhibit's very popular hands on-center, an activity that they once strongly supported. But because they had taken such a public stand on the "politics," as they saw it, of the exhibition, they decided they could not save face and still maintain the hands-on center. Talk about cutting off your nose. . .

At the same time, I am quite intrigued by a budding sociological industry based on "Science in American Life." A number of articles about the exhibit now seem to elevate it to the status of historic artifact. There is hardly a mention of any curatorial or human agency whatsoever in the development of the exhibition, but I guess I shouldn't let that bother me. Yet, it is difficult to see the exhibit disappearing into the realm of high abstraction.

Not having seen Sophia's reviews, though I can easily imagine her approach, I am baffled by the leftist response to her work. I have been in touch with her, but she has not told me about the Smithsonian Institution in Washington, DC—her latest contretemps. This is really puzzling. As for *Naked Science*, it seems to me some greater public attention is due. I noticed in the latest *Newsweek* that there is a two-page spread on the science wars, dealing of all things with the internal controversy on scientific "subjectivity." I wish I could tell you how to get the attention of those editors, but as you know I have spent a lot of my time just avoiding public attention and laying low. So I may not be the best judge.

I am indeed in good spirits, thank you. At a recent event related to the Lemelson Center that I am currently directing at the Museum, I was very happy to run into your brother. It looks like there may be some opportunities to collaborate on our upcoming conferences on environmental technologies.

I was glad that he did remember some of the problems that we experienced with "Science in American Life" as well. I owe a great debt to the Nader family. Again, thanks for writing and please do keep in touch.
Sincerely,

Arthur P. Molella
Assistant Director
National Museum of American History

May 7, 1997

Dear Professor Nader,

Thanks for the speedy transmission of the two papers and the second readers report. I've looked them over and here give you my rather off-the-cuff reactions. I liked your paper very much: it has a nice personal feel, doesn't make claims it can't back up, and doesn't sound mean-spirited. I agree with almost everything in it. I was hoping to be able to say the same for Price's essay, but alas I can't. It seems to me virtually the opposite of yours.

There's no doubt in my mind that Geertz was in many ways a product of the Cold War (and who wasn't in his generation). But he wasn't a standard Cold Warrior on the model of his Chicago friends like Ed Shils, David Apter, and so on. If you are interested in my view of him, you could look at the longish review of *After the Fact* I did a year or so ago from the London Review of Books, or the essay "Research and Method in the Study of Indonesia in America," in Audrey Kahin, ed., *Interpreting Indonesia: Thirteen Contributions to the Debate*, which we put out here as a Cornell Modern Indonesia Project volume maybe ten years back. Price doesn't cite or mention the book that made Cliff's reputation: *The Religion of Java*, which was and is a terrific book, in which "interpretivism" and subjective narrative already appear well developed. It is a book still to be read with a profit, and it remains rightly influential. It is only if one reads Bob Jay's less grand volume on one "mojokuto" village that one sees how Cliff sidestepped the Indonesia Communist Party (Bob deals with it very nicely). The later work hasn't worn well. Mark Hobart blew up the cockfight piece by pointing out that a part (central) of it hinged on the "fact" that the Balinese word for penis is the same word as that for rooster; yet this word is an Indonesian word, and the Balinese word for penis is quite different: i.e. Cliff never mastered the Balinese language that would be the necessary foundation for an analysis of Balinese culture. The *Negara* book was fatally flawed for the same reason—Geertz didn't/couldn't read the indigenous Balinese manuscripts of the 19th century which would have given him a good idea of what Balinese really thought about their politics in the precolonial era. *Agricultural Involution* has also been shown to be fatally flawed by many serious agronomists and demographers. What happened to Geertz after the success of *The Religion of Java* was that he was brought to Chicago by Apter et al., and quickly found a position for himself as the anthropologist of choice for the late 1950s social science regime, and then a broader public. The most Cold War of his texts aren't actually the Indonesian ones but the "general" essays that you find in *Thick Description*. They're mostly unreadable now.

What Price doesn't realize is that in 1963 Geertz ceased doing fieldwork in Indonesia, and his texts published in 1963–65 all came out of his 1950s work. Cliff himself explains why: in 1958 he found himself caught in West Sumatra with his wife (very ill) and two small kids at the time of the CIA backed PRRI regional rebellion. They got out with difficulty, and it's clear that he didn't like the growing violence of Indonesian life, indeed he avoids violence pretty consistently in his work—as a topic. So all his substantial work on Indonesia, including the *Negara* of 1980 was "done" in the 1950s long before the massacres of 1965. He decided in 1963 to move to study quiet Morocco. Then in the late 1960s he describes himself as appalled by the campus uprisings, the Chicago convention, the Black Panthers, and so on, and took the chance for a quiet, non-student surrounded life at the Princeton Institute for Advanced Study. He likes the quiet life! What strikes me always has been his "apoliticalness." He doesn't even mention the Vietnam War in *After the Fact*, and always refuses to lend his name to campaigns about political prisoners, torture, East Timor, etc. But he wasn't "triumphalist" about Suharto's regime and the kind of development Suharto sponsored either. He said nothing substantial about it at all.

One can tell something from looking at the friends he kept most closely to in Indonesia. Almost all of these were connected with the tiny Socialist Party, an inbred group of intellectuals and publicists who abandoned socialism early, but were fluent in English and felt themselves the representatives of Western nationalism in a sea of radicalism, nativism, and so on. Very anticommunist in a second international kind of way. It is interesting however that in 1965 he wrote in *Encounter* a sharp protest against Herbert Luethy's violently Cold War attack on Sukarno and his ideology.

I think the Cold War side of him that matters is best represented by his attachment to Weber and occlusion of Marx; and a Parosnian version of Weber at that. He's always been I think, a rather timid man and an American-liberal-conservative. I started studying Indonesia in 1958 and went to the field in 1962 just as Cliff was leaving it. I remember thinking how odd it was that Indonesian communism was almost wholly "off the map," since the party was huge and legal, and one ran into members all the time. It might be that this was also a consequence of McCarthyism—my mentor George Kahin suffered a lot, was denied a passport for some years, and was regularly smeared as Red. I think that this had an effect on Asianists, who mostly kept their heads down if they didn't become fully-fledged Cold Warriors. But you might note that the Ford Foundation and Rockefeller helped start the Cornell Indonesia Project exactly at the time when Kahin was passportless. There were people who fitted Price's picture, such as the Rand Corporation's Guy Pauker, but he was regarded hostilely by most Indonesianists of my generation, almost all of whom felt themselves to be critical of American policy, all the more so as the Vietnam War deepened. I don't think there was any comparable hostility to Geertz, more a certain sadness, and as time passed, a feeling he wasn't really relevant.

I think Price has generally presented an unsatisfactory account of the Cold War and scholarship. It seems to me that up to 1960 there was a real degree of consensus, post-McCarthy cold war liberalism, "development" in a naive "new nations" way, and not a great deal of money around except for selected high prestige institutions like Chicago, Berkeley, and Harvard. I was a grad student from 1958–1962 at Cornell, and in those days there were simply no fellowships— all students practically worked as TAs every semester because teaching was the only source of funding. Then came Sputnik, and a panic about being left behind. The NDEA [National Defense Education Act] Speech Movement, Civil Rights, SDS [Students for a Democratic Society], the War, Camelot, and so on. Price's view of things make the vast upheaval in the academy against many aspects of American activities—and just when there was a huge amount of money floating along—incomprehensible.

Indeed in that period it was precisely people regarded as Cold War scholars, justly or unjustly, who were pillorized and humiliated. This was the era of the vogue for Maoism in Sinological circles, for Paulo Freire in Latin American circles—Marx came back in with a vengeance, and so on. The 60s last till the end of the Indochina War, and then the reaction in every sense sets in. The third Cold War era is Reagan-Bush, but also the era in which the younger radicals of the 1960s had moved up the academic ladder into senior positions. But this was also the era in which Levi-Strauss has his post-Geertz moment, followed by the wave of Foucault and Derrida—hardly agents of American consumer capitalism.

It started to be in this era that one noticed a major bifurcation. In SE Asia, you had SSRC type funding for anthropology (socio-cultural), history, soft political science, some psychology, where the style was clearly critical of American hegemonism, and you'd never have gotten money for Rostowian projects—the selection boards would have laughed you out of court. On the other side, applied anthropology, rural development, rural sociology, and agronomy went over to AID contract work, and were naturally very conformist. We used to joke about this—dull conservative students would get Fulbrights and smart lefties would get SSRCs.

One could look at it in another way. Who in the general field of anthropology were the really influential people? Mead, Benedict, Schneider, Geertz, and Sahlins perhaps from the U.S.; Levi-Strauss and Dumont from France, Leach, Douglas, Goody, Turner from the U.K. (People born between 1900 and 1930). Gluckman, Redfield, Lewis a few others. Very hard to describe any of these as a real cold warrior, and the most influential weren't even American!

Back again to Price. The reviewer's specific comments I think are 90% right. Price doesn't know anything about Indonesia; gets basic facts wrong, including chronology; relies on very sketchy sources; makes a mass of unproven and I think often unprovable general assertions. It is never really clear why he singles out Geertz for so much of his attacks. He never addresses the obvious counterfactuals I've sketched out above. One might conclude with this question. Until a year or so ago, only two Southeast Asian specialists in any discipline held chairs in the U.S. One is Jim Scott, whose outstanding career has been built on a sustained critique of development, of agribusiness, and state destruction of peasant communities, and in the defense of tribals, poor peasants, and so on. The other is myself who has been banned from Indonesia for 25 years, and who has repeatedly testified in Congress against American support for the Suharto regime and the brutal annexation of East Timor. How did we get these chairs, children of the Cold War that we are, and how come neither of us had any real difficulty in getting the modest funds needed to do field research?

Well, I've gone on too long. I don't think the Price essay is acceptable—though I wish it were, since a well-researched and nuanced analysis of the American scholarship during the Cold War is a topic desperately needing to be undertaken. But grant "funding" is only a part, and I think a relatively small part, of the story—McCarthyism, fear of the Soviet Union, American exceptionalism and ethnocentrism, the multiple crises of the long 1960s are at least as significant. In my view the most important aspect of funding, in any case, has never been grants but salaries. When I came to America in 1958, my department had 6 faculty, today it has five times as many. The annual budget of my department must be close to $2 million dollars. Annually speaking, field research grants are a tiny fraction of this. These salaries, the vast expansion of higher education, and the powerful protection of the tenure system, are the foundations on which the financial system of Cold War scholarship was really constructed.

Well, I've gone on far too long. I'm really sorry to have had to come to these conclusions. But there it is.

With warm regards,

Ben Anderson
Department of Government
Cornell University

September 22, 1997

Dear Laura,

Thanks very much for the article on the "Cold War and Anthropology," which I devoured (in spite of the fact that the xerox had cut out the bottom two lines of each page). It seems to me that in physical anthropology the most direct influence of the Cold War era involved the issue of race. I know Carleton Coon had been some kind of intelligence officer during WWII, and aside from the ignominy of his *Origin of Races*, his sentiments during the civil rights movement are pretty appalling. (I spent some time reading his mail at the Smithsonian last summer). Here's an excerpt from a letter from 1962 to Harry Turney-High, a member of the Sociology and Anthropology departments at the University of South Carolina:

> As I have suggested to others, it seems to me that somebody should do [two] things: (1) investigate the communist influence on American anthropology via Bella Dodd, Boas, and the Boasians. Bella Dodd has already testified to this, it is in the congressional record, I believe. I read it in the NY Times some years ago. It is strange that no one has used this material. (2) find out why Ashley Montagu changed his father's name retroactively in Who's Who, and whether or not he has ever carried a card.

He fed those same accusations to his cousin Carleton Putnam, who publicly aired them in *Race and Reason* (1961) and *Race and Reality* (1967). Apparently Coon made a point of telling everyone within earshot that Montagu had changed his name from Israel Ehrenberg as a student. I noticed also that you didn't mention the anti-Semitism angle in your article; but wasn't there a widespread equation of "commie" and "Jew?"

Coon, curiously, could also write to Putnam, (10 July 1960):

> The role of the professor is responsible one, like that of a minister, doctor, or lawyer. As he is in charge of teaching he should strive for the truth and not engage in movements nor join pressure groups. He is free to publish what he likes as long as he remains non-partisan. Anything that he has published can be quoted by anyone interested. Professors are not supposed to be for or against anything. They should not be on anyone's side, but should give their advice, if they wish, to both or any number of sides.

At the same time, of course, he was arming the segregationists with scientific arguments!

Certainly after the flap over *The Origin of Races*, biological anthropology becomes increasingly abstracted and trivialized (the hot areas became monkeys and fossils, neither of which is particularly threatening), which is in my opinion what allowed *Sociobiology* to happen. I think also that the attraction of sociobiology generally to physical anthropologists is two-pronged: On the one hand, there is a constant historical striving of physical anthropologists to be like "real" scientists, hence the attraction of the American Eugenics Society in the 1920s for Hooton and Hrdlicka, and the lure of the Human Genome Diversity Project now; and on the other hand, biologists can indeed draw on more resources than anthropologists can, and as a result their research programs become attractive. For all the sociobiological crap that comes out these days, we have to bear in mind, it gets funded!

Sincerely,

Jonathan Marks
Professor of Anthropology
University of California, Berkeley

November 26, 1997

Dear Laura,

I've just read your paper on the Cold War in the latest GAD [General Anthropology Division] Bulletin, and while (as you know) I strongly applaud your effort to diminish your discipline's general astonishing naiveté, I can only regret that the circumstance of UC Berkeley archaeologists being politically conservative (or as Jeff Fish puts it so well in his article accompanying yours, so "American"), left this subfield out of your focus.

More to the point, American archaeology has been an extraordinary social phenomena in that it is only now yielding to the social revolution inaugurated by the G.I. Bill. Not until the 1980s were non-WASPs recognized in the profession. Look at Gordon Wiley's 1988 *Portraits in American Archeology* and you will see nearly all the subjects were photographed by Yousuf Karsh—you don't need to read to figure out that they come from U.S. aristocracy. The one exception is James Ford, with whom Wiley published landmark research so that they couldn't ignore him, but in the vignette Gordon marvels at Ford's "lower-class" Mississippi origin. Aside from Wiley's book, which in our library is located literally on the same shelf as *The Education of Henry Adams*, even those leading archaeologists who weren't Boston brahmins (e.g., Emil Haury, Waldo Wedel), came from highly conservative families. The next generation, that of Lewis Binford, was in the mold; Binfold himself grew up a Virginia fundamentalist who in 1954, during Army service in Okinawa, interpreted archaeological data as evidence of the Noachian deluge. In his autobiography (1972), Binford railed at the elitist gentlemen dominating archaeology (he names Braidwood), but is entirely oblivious to political factors.

The most significant aspect of the sociology of American archaeologists is the point made by Val Pinsky (Boas' great-granddaughter), originally in her dissertation, that following the failure of the 1919 censure against Boas, American archaeologists retreated de facto from anthropology, maintaining 19th-century racist evolutionism as well as excluding all but well-connected WASP men from the profession. In my book due out from Routledge by May, *The Land of Prehistory: A Critical History of American Archaeology*, I show that this racism has been powerfully reinforced by Manifest Destiny ideology (a point made independently by historian Roger Kennedy in his *Hidden Cities*, 1994). The Cold War has been but the recent phase of this ideology integral to mainstream American anthropology since Morgan.

Sincerely,

Alice B. Kehoe
Professor of Anthropology
Marquette University

April 19, 1998

Dear Laura,

It was a pleasure to meet you finally, after so many years. I enjoyed your presentations and was especially sorry that my class schedule did not allow me to see how you handled the irritation your perfectly calculated talk to mediators caused. I will ask those who were able to stay.

I write now mainly to burden you with some of my own work because I got a sense that we have been coming to a similar point from quite different angles. Of course, as my wife Pilar told you, we also have a fortuitous connection via Oaxaca. While I was learning how to do fieldwork on the Stanford program in St. Maria Guelaze, we met a man who was a school teacher in either Talea or Juquila and who knew you. He was married to a local woman and was making a point of knowing you to show me I was not the first anthropologist he had met. Many years ago and far away, but I remember the pleasure it gave me to read your study of those communities.

Anyway, remembering aside, I sort of knew that our paths were crossing again and again in recent years. In 1983, while tasked with running the Center for International Studies at Cornell and trying to keep my brain from dying as an academic administrator, I had the good fortune to be asked to help William Foote Whyte in a study of the labor managed cooperatives of Mondragon in the Spanish Basque Country. As someone who had worked in the Basque Country from the late 1960s, I was asked to help with the project aimed at understanding how these Basques had created the most successful labor managed cooperatives in the world (32,000 member owners as of now). So began my work in "industrial anthropology" but also so began my work in action research. Since that time, I have found no way to turn back. The combination of epistemological and methodological strength and of democratic values transformed me into a full-time action researcher but also into someone even more alienated from anthropology than before.

One of the things that most struck me about your talks is your strong anchor in anthropology and your apparent commitment to the discipline. I love anthropology and respect our approaches, but I don't love the profession and its "lapdog" status, along with the rest of the social sciences. I look for more, both epistemologically and politically. Because you are one of the few persons I have run into in anthropology who seems more interested in "getting it right" than in impressing colleagues, I wanted to share a bit of work with you and get your sense of what meaningful next steps are. Until I heard you, I have been inclined to simply pursue action research and let anthropology wallow in its own self-pity, including the whining of applied anthropologists who feel ignored by their "betters."

To this end, but trying not to overburden what I take to be a very busy life already, I am sending you a draft commentary I wrote for a session on theory and practice in anthropology organized by Carole Hill and Marietta Baba, and the first five chapters of a book that Morten Levin (an engineer and Ph.D. in Sociology at the Norwegian University of Science and Technology, Trondheim) have written on action research and that will come out from *Sage* this November.

I hope you will find these things interesting and I would also value your thinking about what are meaningful next steps. For instance, I am not attending the AAA this year, having reached a point of alienation that I cannot deny. Instead, I will use my travel money to go to the conference on Participatory Design in November in Seattle where a huge mixed group of scientists, engineers, and social scientists will meet to talk about the role of participation and action research in the companies of the future. In my estimation, the latter was a better use of my time and resources. I suspect from your talks that you would imagine that the AAA still deserves attention. Is that right, or did I misperceive your views?

At any rate, a bunch of pages to read is not much of repayment for a pair of good talks. Sorry about that, but kindred spirits are hard to find.
Best Wishes,

Davydd J. Greenwood
Professor of Anthropology
Cornell University

June 3, 1998

Dear Laura,

I really enjoyed the piece. I thought the issues you bring forward about the media, and the very interesting alliance suggested between more popular forms of media and the academic press were provocative. With all of the fallout from this Sokal affair, few people have commented on this. I'm wondering if there are other people out there who would like to comment in this vein. Also, the point you make about the American one-sidedness of the issue also merits further comment. As an American who experienced these "wars" from the U.K., I have to say I find it unsettling to hear stories like the one that you invoke in your opening section. I'm tempted to make a general call for musings along these lines. My hesitation is that I don't want to pander to more "war-mongers" who seem to be getting a lot of mileage out of this (i.e. Bruno Latour and Alan Sokal have a roadshow which is coming to the London School of Economics soon). I also have seen some pretty sappy proposals along the lines of "why can't we all just get along here in the academy." Actually, in the U.K. we are now struggling with a political movement called the "public understanding of science" which the NSF has also tried. Basically, it is an attempt by scientists, with government funding backing to appropriate social scientists, to do research on why the masses cannot understand science. But there have been a number of sociologists who have re-appropriated the field for themselves. A real comparison of multinational interests in this field might shake out more pressing issues.

Do you have any suggestions along these lines? What might prove an adequate forum to discuss these issues with real efficacy? I'd appreciate your thoughts if you have a moment sometime soon.

Anyway, it was a pleasure virtually meeting you and I think the exchange with Gunder Frank will be readable and provocative (which is what all journal editors want, right?).

Regards,

Joan Leach
Editor
Social Epistemology

September 7, 1998

Dear Laura,

I really enjoyed talking to you during my visit last week—I'm glad we had the chance. I read your Cold War piece with much interest and benefit along with the follow-up piece in the GAD newsletter. I would love to talk to you about it (debate it with you) sometime. I'll just offer some overall thoughts here which can't be that satisfactory. Certainly, this essay could be a study for a short provocative book or memoir. What would need to be fleshed out of course would be how this little history in anthropology fits into the larger history of the left since the 50s.

I love the idea of the phantom factor, but it is very undeveloped in your essay. It cries out for an anthropological/ethnographic account of how it works. In the absence of really demonstrating the phantom like connections, particularly from the time of the new-left onward, and how it permeated academic work later. There is a linearity to your account which I think is a problem. The crux is how the old-left/new-left break occurred specifically in the realm of anthropology. Was the fear that invaded the old-left directly imparted to the new-left equivalents in anthropology? I think not; rather I think the younger generation in anthropology was inclined to dissociate itself from that earlier period, even forget it—especially aided by the wave of and thorough immersion in the post-Marxist, post-structuralist influences from France (you know—Foucault, Lacan etc.), which was of course a completely different set of intellectual influences than the main actors that you discuss ever really grasped—for better or worse of course depending on your perspective.

It is like (and has some intellectual genealogies with) the divide between Western Marxists versus classic Marxist thinkers—the latter viewing the former as effete idea types, having lost the activist edge of the Marxist project. In short, while clearly you don't like what happened in the 80s and use us (ACC and WC) to contrast then (and afterwards up to now even) with the straightforward activism of the late 60s, I don't think you can explain us in such linear terms as you do. You just need a whole lot more micro-history in there.

I dunno . . . maybe the result is the same . . . the sort of activist anthropology which you champion did indeed get derailed and this cannot be denied. But how and why this happened can't be explained in the frame that you use. By the late 70s already, the Stauder critique, the anti-corporate capitalism, the anti-colonial critique etc., was already irrelevant. For a moment, the attention to anthropological authority in its language construction cut to the chase very effectively for a broad spectrum of anthropologists and renegotiated the center of the discipline toward its peripheries, and I think you will agree this was long overdue, however much we might disagree about the exact intellectual mode. Like you, I don't like much the way things have gone since. But as you could gather from my talk, because anthropology means so many things to so many people, it is always redeemable.

For details, we should talk. I am sending along a paper by a very good student of ours from South Africa on "exposé anthropology" and its fate during and after apartheid. It begins a little archly, but the central discussion is useful to what we are talking about here. Of course, I'm afraid what he does have to say has the telltale signs of hanging around us here.

Anyhow, very provocative piece that deserves wider circulation among anthropologists—it restarts a discussion much worth having at a moment of generational transition.
Cordially,

George Marcus
Professor of Anthropology
Rice University

September 19, 1998
George Marcus

Rice University

Dear George,

Thanks for your letter. Re: "The Phantom Factor" paper. Just a few comments in return or as a prelude to talking about such things sometime in the future. I was struck with references in your letter to the left (old and new), and realize that I just don't think in those terms. Maybe that is my problem. In "Up the Anthropologist" I spoke about "Perspectives Gained from Studying Up," and about scientific adequacy and democratic relevance. I don't much care for censures or boundaries about what we should study or not. I noticed that some things were rarely studied, and that it certainly made for poor theory and poor ethnography here as well as in the third world. I am described by colleagues at times as doing activist, applied, or policy work. I don't think of what I do as an activist—while I do think of it as interesting or even pioneering. I certainly have never done applied work, as I understand the term, and if one wants to call the energy work policy that's ok, although I don't much like the word or the connotations.

As to an account for how the phantom factor works, that is easier said than done. As I think I mentioned to you, it took over two and a half years of digging to get my hands on enough materials to spell out what I did. Here are anthropologists who are digging through CIA and FBI files trying to fill out this period: maybe they will. I think if you want to understand how these things work David Noble's *America By Design* (1977) is a good place to start, but you know about that.

As to what has happened in anthropology since the 80s. I think a lot of good things have happened, and I mention them in my "Post-Interpretive

Anthropology" article. Mainly things got freed up and we began to ask more interesting questions. What I don't like is the denigration of an anthropology that doesn't fit a party line—again, censures and the consequences for the institutional base of anthropology in the U.S. I think you probably care a lot about anthropology otherwise you might not have done what you have, but I also think the manner of doing the work, the anti-disciplinary pull in many quarters, has stood in the way of institutional support for anthropology. I think the folks at Stanford probably had good reason to disagree, but I also think they're thinking of their own happiness rather than some strategy for the discipline. One thing I have learned watching law professors—no matter how much they fight inside, that is where they keep it. They are smart in that they have a sense of survival. As to expose anthropology—I use different categories—it is either competent or not, then I break it down. We were "interdisciplinary" when I was at Harvard, but the rock we had our foot on was that of the discipline. Soc. Rel. was a disaster.

Enough for now. Again thanks for your comments. I enclose a copy of a recent paper in case you have not seen it.

All the best,

Laura Nader

December 8, 1998

Dear Professor Nader,

It was a pleasure to meet you, however briefly, at the AAA meetings. In your session on paradigm shifts in legal anthropology I asked about the use of legal and legislative pacification strategies to discourage conflict which end up having the opposite consequences. From my experience in corporate agricultural research, politics and policy, and court cases in the U.S., particularly in Iowa, I have observed a number of such efforts resulting in more conflict. You asked if I had any data on such events, but I have not quantitatively tracked such trends. However, I can offer a number of concrete cases and related literature which I've enclosed.

I am familiar with three types of state laws that have recently been used in an attempt to prevent conflict resulting from rural community or neighborhood objections to corporate livestock facilities in the Midwestern U.S. These include: 1) preemption of local control laws that usurp the authority of local governing bodies, e.g. county supervisors, zoning boards, boards of health, from establishing rules concerning the siting and operation of corporate livestock facilities; 2) laws requiring mediation or arbitration before a suit against

a corporate agricultural operation can proceed; and 3) the establishment of
nuisance suit protection laws that remove common law based recourse for
neighbors who have had their property or lives infringed upon by a neighboring large-scale corporate livestock operation. Michael Stumo can perhaps
provide additional insight on the nature of these and other laws. I can sketch
how these laws have had an effect opposite to the desired outcome of squelch-
ing conflict as they relate to the proliferation of industrial corporate livestock
facilities that have created an uproar in the rural Midwest and other parts of
the country.

1. *Preemption of local control.* The movement of capital and corporate
    hog production technology throughout the U.S. is accompanied by the
    movement of corporate lawyers and lobbyists into state legislatures to
    establish laws that preempt local governing bodies from doing anything
    about how these hog factories are sited or operated. As Robert Morgan
    (former U.S. Senator and state Attorney General from North Carolina)
    points out in Chapter 8 of our book *Pigs, Profits, and Rural Communi-
    ties* (see enclosed book), corporate operators quietly and effectively
    amend state laws to keep local governing bodies from doing anything
    about them. This same legislative process has been repeated, and con-
    sciously so, in places such as Iowa and Utah to specifically squelch con-
    flict brought to local government bodies by neighbors and community
    members. It has often had the opposite effect. In North Carolina, rural
    residents were so outraged that they mobilized, picketed the state legis-
    lature, used creative public health strategies to sidestep restrictions on
    their zoning authority, and eventually succeeded in getting the state to
    establish a moratorium on the building of large-scale hog operations.
    It should be noted that Senator Lauch Faircloth, who recently lost his
    reelection bid in North Carolina, owns interests in large-scale corporate
    hog operations in North Carolina.
2. *Mediation requirement.* State law in Iowa requires a Mediation Release
    before a lawsuit against a large-scale livestock operation can be carried
    out. In the case I enclosed marked *Rutter et al. v. Carrolls' Foods of the
    Midwest, Inc.*, a group of neighbors, primarily family farmers, recently
    filed suit to protect their area from environmental damage. The purpose
    of the suit is to seek injunctive relief through an innovative anticipatory
    trespass legal approach, and to provide another constitutional challenge
    to a form of nuisance protection law on the books. I was at the farm of
    the lead plaintiffs in this case the day of the required mediation hearing
    (Sept. 9 of this year). The mediation process itself simply infuriated the

husband and wife farm couple since it prolonged the court process and cost them $50. This case was taken on by the Iowa Civil Liberties Union, as well as a Des Moines attorney who used to work for Robert F. Kennedy. It's worth pointing out that the lead plaintiff is a long-time republican who feels betrayed by his party.

3. *Nuisance protection laws.* The 1995 Iowa legislature passed a law widely known in the state as House File 519. It effectively prevents neighbors of corporate hog operations from filing suit. The legislation changed the burden of proof from the traditional common law nuisance to one of proving negligence. I have enclosed an Op-Ed piece written by William Hines, Dean of the College of Law at the University of Iowa (the computer version was an advance copy of the piece which ran in the Des Moines Register on Feb. 9, 1997) which conveys the absurdity of this law (I should also note that Dean Hines is a rather conservative Republican). Rather than reducing conflict, the law actually resulted in a number of constitutional challenges from neighbors. Earlier this year, our conservative 9-member state supreme court voted 7–0 that the law was patently unconstitutional. It should be noted that one Supreme Court justice excused himself from hearing the case because he was fighting a corporate hog operation near his home in southwest Iowa.

On February 3, 1997, in a packed hearing room, I testified before the Iowa House Agricultural Committee. In addressing the issue of rural conflict I made the following point:

> "Community divisions are created and frequently become disruptive as the result of large-scale swine operations. Various types of organizations have emerged in Iowa, North Carolina, Missouri, Kansas, Minnesota, Illinois, Nebraska, Utah, Colorado, Ohio, and other states, to resist the construction of these facilities. The common denominator underlying the emergence of these grassroots organizations is a view that their rights to enjoy their property and family have been violated. More fundamental than any single issue is the deep-seated frustration these people feel from the lack of adequate local means of problem resolution. The lack of control results in an escalating social pathology in many rural areas. A continual recurrence of discords and repeated attempts to find an outlet to resolve problems has led to a pattern of community distrust that is at odds with core values of rural Iowans. Several studies suggest that the conflict itself may have a more enduring effect on the quality of life at the local level than the actual operation of the swine

facility. In addition, intense conflict of this sort acts as a pressure cooker; with no outlet, attitudes and behaviors that resonate with isolationism and extremism can develop. In my view, the evidence is compelling that the social health of our rural communities depends in part on providing a mechanism for local control and conflict resolution."

My work does not specifically focus on tracking conflict and/or conflict resolution. I am most often involved in helping the plaintiffs assemble expert witnesses and crafting their case with the appropriate science. I have enclosed a copy of an unpublished paper entitled "Piggeries and Politics: What Scientists Aren't Telling You" that provides a better sense of my involvement, what is happening with the corporatization of U.S. agriculture, and why anthropologists should get off their duffs and start attending to these issues (you may have seen an article Paul Durrenberger and I wrote in a recent AAA newsletter on "Coming in from the Margins"). I know you won't have time to read through all of this, but if you decide to pick and choose, I might suggest you read the chapter by Laura DeLind in our book. It may be interesting for you because in it she describes how a community won their legal battle to purge itself of corporate hog operations, but as a result became forever disillusioned with the prospects of ever getting involved in legal battles or political processes again. This is the most frightening consequence of these conflicts.

Thanks again for all your work over the years, I have admired it greatly. It was a breath of fresh air to have a cultural anthropologist actually ask for data. Sincerely,

Kendall M. Thu, Ph.D.
Associate Director
Iowa's Center for Agricultural Safety and Health

March 19, 1999

Dear Professor Nader,

Thank you for sending me your article about ways justice is being "traded for harmony" in various practices of the law. And please do send me the article you mentioned in your letter, about teenagers and healthcare bureaucracies in rural California. Your arguments do parallel the arguments that I make in my writing about the aftermath of the Bhopal disaster. Like the advocates of ADR you describe, environmentalists (of all political persuasions) often exhibit a strong allergy to conflict models of the world. In corporate environmentalism particularly, the overt goal is to "move beyond blame."

I think Byron Good's reference to my work was to an article I submitted for review by *Culture, Medicine and Psychiatry*—which I include here despite not yet having done much needed revisions. It should give you a sense of the material I am working with and of the shape of my argument—though the latter definitely needs refining before publication. A critique of momentum toward harmonization is also an explicit and recurrent theme of the book manuscript I am now completing, on a number of registers. As a whole, the book challenges dominant articulations of environmentalism and political advocacy—because they presume harmonization as the logical or desired goal. I've included a very brief overview of the book that shows how I draw these critiques together.

I've also included here the chapter from my book manuscript about "green consultants," who provide the logic and rhetoric of contemporary corporate environmentalism. It builds an argument related to yours about covert forms of control, pacification and burnout relation to harmony ideologies and cultures. Contemporary corporate environmentalism works by diluting all opposition. Chemicals are described as natural (rather than as synthetic saviors from the rampages of Nature, as in the 60s); interest and value conflicts among "stakeholders" are read as communication and attitudinal problems; disastrous pasts have been fully and finally settled (in the Bhopal case, both literally and metaphorically). Like legal mediation, control is exercised through the definition of problems and of appropriate forms of speech, and by designating what "counts" as relevant for the public record. And the stakeholder model of participation, by creating a facade of equality, in practice erases social context. One result is the burnout experienced by so many community environmental activists. Like the consequences of mediation you describe while discussing Trina Grillo's work, corporate environmentalism "flattens the desire to seek redress." Insistence on harmony in contexts of hierarchy—whether in corporate law practice, family conciliation or environmental risk management—is indeed exhausting. Therapeutic modes of redress won't suffice.

Environmental politics generate particularly acute needs for effective engagement with dissent because of uneven distributions of risk, because of the extraordinary stakes of chemical companies, because of the uncertain, dispute-ridden science of toxics, because environmental issues demand so much of democratic institutions, because environmental crisis now operates in a globalizing/far from harmonious world order. So I want to continue working out how cultures and ideologies of harmony operate, and look forward to learning more about your work. Thank you again for getting in touch. I'm sorry it took so long to get back to you.

Sincerely,

Kim Fortun
Department of Science and Technology
Rensselaer Polytechnic Institute

June 4, 1999
Linda S. Wilson

President Radcliffe College

Dear President Wilson:

I was most dismayed to receive your April letter the "historic agreement" between Radcliffe and Harvard. For me it symbolized the end of the 20th century woman's movement. No matter how many times the word "excitement" was used, it was clear that Radcliffe needed stronger negotiators. Radcliffe College had money, property, and a history of stunning graduates with which to negotiate.

Personally I do not value an institute that is "concerned with women, gender, and society" as a central mission and absent other missions. Radcliffe women that I know and value are doing biology, anthropology, physics, writing—all of which may have nothing to do with women, gender, and society. I would have been happier had Radcliffe negotiated a woman president of Harvard, or chairs in the valued subjects. What is it in the proposed agreement that guarantees that women will have 50% of the power?

In closing I must admit to the nostalgic—women of the early 20th century woman's movement were tougher, stronger.
With all good wishes.

Laura Nader
Professor of Anthropology

June 9, 1999

Dear Prof. Nader:

For some time, I have been working on a conference paper on the reciprocal view of Eastern and Western civilization. From Edward Said's *Orientalism*, I came to find out something on its Arab other, namely Hasan Hanafi's "istighrab" on which he published a large volume in 1991.

In that context, I also read your 1989 paper from *Cultural Dynamics*—"Orientalism, Occidentalism and the Control of Women" which I found very fascinating. In my attempt to reconstruct an archeology of the very term "Occidentalism," which consequently was used both by the American-anthropologist James Carrier and the Chinese literary historian Xiaomei Chen, I could not reach further back than your paper. There you mention that you had started reflecting about Occidentalism after conversations with Ashraf Ghani and others. At the same time, you introduce the difference between Orientalism and Occidentalism which were brought to your attention "through a fruitful discussion of texts that were written in Arabic on the West." It would be very interesting for me to know more specifically which Arab authors inspired your reflections and from which intellectual background these came. Would it still be possible for you (at a decade's distance, I admit. . .) to specify this part of your subsequent theoretical elaboration?

I also found that there was a previous, apparently widespread use of Occidentalism in the Latin American post-colonial context (with which Hasan Hanafi seems to have been familiar), so it appears that the whole notion, though probably coined independently in different settings, has had some gravitational effects tying together various threads.

Is it asking too much if I repeat my question about your Arabic sources of inspiration?

I happened to see on the internet that you are going to be in Germany this summer (and actually, in the same region of Lower Saxony), so it might even be possible to communicate over a shorter distance. Unfortunately, I could not find your e-mail address, but I do hope that my letter will reach you before you depart for Europe.

I would be very grateful for any of your kind advice.
Sincerely yours,

Professor Rainer Brömer
Georg-August-Universität Göttingen
Institut für Wissenschaftsgeschichte

August 5, 1999

Dear Laura,

I am writing to you in your role as a wise elder with hopes that you can offer me some advice. I submitted the enclosed paper to *The Anthropologist* about a year ago (9/8/98) and received a split review (I will dig these reviews out at home and mail them on to you in the next day or two), with two reviewers concluding it should be accepted, and two wishing to see changes. The requested changes had to do with adding more commentary and historical context.

At that time I spoke with Bob Sussman and explained to him that I had written this piece with a low-commentary narrative so that these delicate events could be described without preaching. I told him that I believed that if I added more commentary it would probably decrease the chances that *The Anthropologist* would publish it. Sussman then told me that the best thing to do would be to just add a few more pages describing the historical context of these events, and to add a few comments relating to the meaning of these events and to resubmit the paper. I did make such changes, resubmitted the paper to *The Anthropologist* in early April, and today have just received their second rejection/invitation for revision.

You know the issues that are involved in all this better than I do, so I won't go on about my perception of the importance of the issues raised in this paper for the discipline. Perhaps I am wrong, but because of the political nature of all this I do not believe that any editor of *The Anthropologist* could ever reject (as opposed to send back for revisions) a paper documenting covert relationships between the AAA and the CIA. At this time I am quite hesitant to add more about the individuals involved in this episode—not because I lack information, but because the discussion that would follow would surely generate more heat than light (this is what I had communicated to Sussman last March, and I thought he had agreed with me on this point).

I would welcome whatever advice you could offer me in this matter. I just received this latest rejection a few hours ago and have not clearly thought through my options, but am currently considering submitting it (with some style and format changes) to *The Nation*, to *The Newsletter*, or making some revisions and resubmitting this to *The Anthropologist*. What do you think I should do?

All in all, things are well with me and I have completed a few more chapters this summer in my "Cold War Anthropology" book (are you interested in making comments on the chapter I have just finished discussing the FBI's extensive surveillance of Oscar Lewis?).

I hope things are well with you,

David Price
Professor of Anthropology
Saint Martin's College

August 26, 1999

Dear Laura,

I wrote this rambling letter on August 2 as my stay drew to a close nearly a month ago, but have been out of reach of a printer, hence have waited until

I returned to Ithaca to send it to you. I was unfortunately unable to reach Etel Adnan (who my new friends here are also eager to meet), and among your other friends I have met only Samir Khalaf and saw him but once. Nonetheless, I got a feel for the place and plan to return again in February and again in August.

The plane from Berlin was full of babies and mothers living abroad but going "home" for the summer. Approximately 15 million Lebanese live abroad, but only 3.7 million in Lebanon, a 4/1 ratio. Some estimate that 1.5 million Syrians work/live in Lebanon. And then there are 365,000 Palestinian refugees, the original wave driven from Israel in 1948, for whom this place is an exile. I sat next to a Sunni Muslim couple. When asked by the female border guard in Budapest to take her white scarf off at the border control; her husband responded: "that's impossible," but the guard insisted before she would let them pass through the metal detector, and she did take it off, grumpily, in front of us all. Very talkative, she works as doctor's aid, has been in Berlin 21 years, and he works as cook. Both German citizens, they were taking a month vacation in the country of their birth. They reassured me (our conversation was in German) that my fears of landing so late at night, an innocent American, were unwarranted—and that was true, though my taxi driver spoke neither a word of French nor English and couldn't find my hotel.

My visit is nine years after the end of the country's war. Most people say it was a 15 year war that began in 1975 and ended in 1990. But other observers date the end of the war to 1992, making it a 17 year war, following what people dub "Hariri's version" of the story. Rafik Hariri, last prime minister, self-made billionaire, and godfather of the Ta'if agreement that formally ended the fighting, would like the end of the war to coincide with the year he took over leadership of the country. He is an interesting figure and symbol here: of money, international stature, commerce, and now of "opposition." There is a current debate, a struggle, about strategies of remembering and forgetting focused around the terms of "anti-corruption" and "memorialization." A general amnesty was part of the agreement to end the war—hence no accountability for war crimes. Only one of the leaders of violence sits in jail, and for a crime he committed after the war. An anti-corruption campaign has turned into a witch-hunt against Hariri's friends.

My first impression was of the ostentation of those traveling—all those gold rings and chains even though only two people sat in the business class of the plane. Later visiting the beach (or Corniche here), which is full of all social groups from about 6pm to 9pm and then 2–4am, except perhaps the refugees, I noticed the same flaunting of wealth. Even saw two middle-aged women "jogging," trying to trim down (they say they ate out of nervousness during the war), who took their maids with them. One was Filipino, and she had on a body-tight jogging suit (how uncomfortable in all that sweat, it is humid), the other was a black girl, Sri Lankan, and she was made to wear a petite apron over her jogging shorts! My second impression was of the Syrian presence.

Assad's photo everywhere, soldiers with automatic rifles appear in strange places, but now that things are under control, they only appear and set up controls here and there. Assad did end the war, but now they all pay for that service: his importation of Syrian workers who take away jobs from lower-class Lebanese, and he and his friends take their cut on all deals in Lebanon.

On my second day I went to the Sabra and Shatila camp, site of the 1982 massacre. No markers of the slaughter. Another space entirely—am I still in Lebanon? Densely packed with people, stalls selling cheap versions of everything, including a lot of electronic equipment probably stolen from apartments in the Green Line. Garbage everywhere stinking in places, a goat sitting on top of one heap of rubble, buildings reduced to this mound by Israeli bombs. What else could such places, non-homes, breed except a new generation of resentment and terror? Those Lebanese I have met and in the media, are united in refusing to give all of these refugees citizenship. Most of the camp residents are Palestinians, but some Syrians, some Bedouins, some gypsies. Why would they ever want to accept this dump where they now exist as a substitute for a home? And that home, for the Palestinians, is now the green oasis of Israel. The South Lebanese Army in Israeli occupied territories is suffering large numbers of desertions, falling apart as Israel withdraws, and the soldiers (Christian and Amal Shiites) are going on trial.

My thoughts on departing from violence initially found no hearing here, as most people still did not dare believe such a departure is possible. There is a massive recession going on, cafes and restaurants normally full are empty, or nearly empty. Even with all this massive rebuilding of the center, new government buildings and private restoration everywhere, and without a war, people are withholding investment and enjoyment of what they have. But within ten days of my arrival, the Israelis bombed, and that incited people to recover memories of the war—to think of a before and an after.

On the night of the bombing, a friend called at 2:30 am. He thought I'd be freaking out. I had walked around town for half an hour, at about 8:30, everything very dark but cars still busy on the main roads. I went to bed around 11 but kept hearing these big bangs which reverberated and shook the building. Like fireworks in a mini-earthquake except extraordinarily loud. Israel was bombing south Beirut, the area of the Palestinian Hezbollah camps, in waves of about 20 minutes, each time setting off a car alarm that had been going off every night anyway, so I just sort of ignored it all, until the telephone rang. Did I sleep? Some, as best as I could, disturbed by the thuds, and then car siren, which played in three alternating registers of "alarm." Somehow I expected this and wasn't really surprised.

All summer long, due to the bombing, lights and electricity have been out for minutes at a time all day long, sometimes twice in the hour, then for whole hours; in some parts of the city, entire evenings. TV cable, because it is hooked to the electricity, also goes out all the time, especially as one of the films on a movie channel nears the end. Candles or darkness. This reminds people of the war. During the war after 8:00pm the streets were empty, now they are a quarter full. Men sitting around, just sitting and looking, next to the gas stations and the little stores.

The comments the day after the bombing: destroys tourism, all those Lebanese planning on returning will not. Someone's aunt is vacationing in Egypt for four days, left her two American daughters in Beirut; her husband, back in the States, is hysterical. How irresponsible of her. At Lebanese American University students seem unperturbed, but faculty were very caught up in this attack and felt unable to teach. Another friend said, "After this, I woke up thinking yes, let there be war. I'll never agree to peace with Israel, they'll never accept peace with their neighbors." Some faculty did not come in at all to teach. Those I talked to would have preferred not to. Syria provokes ambivalence because they stand up to Israel, the only force along with Hezbollah that does this. A general sense of castration after such a raid. Who will pay for the damages?

I am staying in the Hamra district of West Beirut, the most mixed section of the city, ugly but urban. Much of East Beirut, the Christian part, was not much damaged by the war, but it is considerably run-down, though still evocative of its former status, especially its ties with Frenchness, the architecture, the use of public space. East Beirut is out-of-center, a place to visit, with the most trendy restaurants, bars, cafes, but marginal and stale during the day. The old city center is on the green line, *ligne de démarcation* (French), the line of tension (Arabic), fully destroyed but being rebuilt in the latest style. Banks will soon open their new headquarters there. Rubble still everywhere. Remarkable skeletons of elegant buildings on corners; excluding the hollow shell of the former Holiday Inn, which is still standing, abandoned, empty, just nothing—but it is being renovated. The new seat of parliament, the majestic Serail, in part financed by Hariri's own wealth before his defeat in the last election, a few other wonderfully reconstructed buildings in the old center, but mostly new architecture but elegant, innovative, also the use of pleasant colors, light yellows and browns, burgundy, pastels.

Walking the streets is literally "the streets," since sidewalks often disappear, used as parking spaces or simply more driving space. And total "Mad Max" feeling when driving on the road. As pedestrian one feels approached by cars all the time; though they may be careful, they come very close, and they drive very fast. Main streets go on for miles with no crosswalks, even no exit or entrance ramps. Red lights are usually meaningless, no one pays attention. Fathers and daughters or sons often cross the main streets hand-in-hand, as often do adult men (mostly Syrians, I am told; Lebanese know the stigma of homosexuality, though this is a class thing), and they don't run or hurry, and they come awfully close to getting sideswiped, sometimes by the very cars I am riding in. I find myself holding my breath, waiting to get out.

It is a time of great skepticism about the future, and the present, despite the surface building boom. The recent bombing reinforced this pessimism; it probably doesn't take much. It reinforced the fear people mention it to me all the time. In this respect, they oddly name it "fear," and it has a concrete referent—war, bombs, harm—but the "it" is perhaps not fear but the traumatic loss about which they do not want to speak and cannot possibly recuperate. "It" is about the past, which has not yet been experienced because it is traumatic.

The new constitution has a provision, setting up a committee at the highest level of government, to eliminate sectarianism. Still dormant though. People here use the word, not tribal leaders but spiritual leaders, clans, confessional leaders. They still have much power, and are the true sources of identification, or so I am told. But I think clans, large families, are the only strong, enduring units of identification, strengthened during the war.

What does "public" mean in a place where "the social" has been destroyed? On the surface, the most damage has been to the sociality of public space. At times I think people here are still shell-shocked, damaged of hearing and sight from having lived through a long intermittent and arbitrary siege, which ended not by exhaustion or agreement but only with Syrian-imposed silence. They seem not to acknowledge the possibility of a shared public on the street. Perhaps it is only in cars, constantly passing each other that any public exists. Or perhaps it is only in the confined space of the "service taxis" where quick conversation with the others follows, a public is immediately created by the customers and the driver, a simulation of the home.

In this beautiful Mediterranean climate, with a long and graceful ocean-front, and with this openness to the West and East, trees and shrubbery and flowers should be *growing* everywhere, on all the apartment balconies and along the store fronts. But there are relatively few trees, no tree-lined boulevards, hardly any flowers on balconies. A few flower shops here and there, but not many customers, and even the flower shop owners lack the art of display that delights the eye in places like Paris or Amsterdam or Istanbul. I am told that this "neglect" may be a product of the war, but people attribute every blight to the war. Even fruit and vegetables are hardly "displayed" in front of shops, but just set out in their original, dilapidated-looking cardboard boxes; one box of watermelons, one of cherries, next radishes, then onions, then potatoes randomly thrown together, caked with some dirt as if just picked. Shop interiors are crammed with all essential goods—baking and cooking goods, teas, spices, mineral water, wines, hard drinks, candles, soaps, detergents, deodorants, a few cheeses and things kept cold, in no particular order. But there is no sense of symmetry or pattern in display, no seduction or enticement to buy.

I have been taking some Arabic lessons, but nothing systematic yet, just enough to get by. Having some difficulty carrying through with interviews with members of the militias, but that is perhaps expecting too much this time around. I have some contacts to pursue when I return. My circle of acquaintances here resembles a clan, of about 5 people, all between the ages of 24–26. They go to the few chic bars in the evening. Where are the people my age? Living in diaspora, or at home with their kids if they are married, which most are, or inexpensive restaurants with their best friends/family. People say this reduction of circles of acquaintances also is a result of the war. Perhaps changes in hospitality are due to lack of trust. The mass of poor women stay home at night; of poor men get a sandwich in a snack bar, or sit in front of their construction sites or homes until late in the evening when it cools off and they can go to sleep.

The cell phone is revolutionizing some behavior here, especially friendships and sex, as it is perhaps everywhere. It enables a private space to be developed by youth whose calls and goings-on no longer are mediated by their parents. One niece of a friend asked for her graduation not a car but a cell phone. Then they can arrange their schedules without their parents knowing, enabling some private connections unmediated by their parents or siblings. This is a key to creating privatized spaces within the family that enable some "autonomy." This autonomy is then turned into another kind of dependence as people give their number to their friends and call them at least twice a day. I've sat in a restaurant several times with people who had a phone on each ear.

The phone of my friends is ringing at least twice an hour while I am with them, and then at least 1/4 of that hour is spent on the phone, not with me or the public. They desire to be reachable everywhere, in other words connected to a select group of peers which replaces their parents.

The war, though articulated in terms of ethnosects, which were in turn strengthened in various public ways, flattened the difference between people with cultural capital and those with economic. Its greater impact was perhaps in terms of class realignment. In many cases, it reduced the "culture bearers" to lower middle class standards and created an entirely new class of nouveau riche. I am told that about 70% of the Lebanese are of a large middle-class (educated, with their own apartments, air conditioning in their homes), about 30% are excluded.

My own interests in understanding, in disclosure, can only be a disturbance, also in the case of these youths I hang out with, since they force a reflexion that is anathema to any scene that I know of here. The new youths' class position must ultimately bespeak an insecurity, perhaps the insecurities of the postwar-new money, new status, youth status. A secure status enabled the hippies in the '60s to rebel against their parents, to seek out the new, the outrageous, the blasphemous. But here I sense a clinging to money as paradigm-for-life, as providing the means for comfort, stability, status, as opposed to the use of money as tool to experiment, to change anything. Money is the universal equivalent. Cultural capital is largely defeated, and the older social networks of the ethnosects obtain whatever power they still have from the governmental policy of distribution on their basis. From political guarantees of their representation, and control of schools and marriage (no civil marriage here). Hariri represented this new victory of money, though many people resent that, hence they voted against him, but they still must submit to it. He will probably have a rebirth.

The Christians are the big losers in this war, or so they constantly tell me, which they were already losing demographically and in terms of political influence from abroad (as the European powers, especially France, lost their ability to inspire their own peoples to support Lebanese Christians through empire). Territorial displacement, a fate which all confessions and ethnosects share, effected through war, trade, barter, and theft, appears to be largely permanent. The war had its own measure of adventure, and a lot of people became wealthy off of the war, made it into a profitable game. But it also terrorized more civilians, was more unpredictable and arbitrary in its violence, and was longer and more confusing than most civil wars. Some of its violence was intrasect, intra-familial, hence making reconciliation more difficult. It was not fought around an ideology that one could favor or oppose. The randomness of its victimization created, then, in the postwar generation in Beirut, a basic insecurity. Petty crimes have risen here also, not murder and prostitution, but robbery, car theft, disrespect for public ordinances (cf. traffic violations, tax evasion).

This first postwar generation remains, by contrast with those in Berlin, and in both Sermanles, insecure, unadventurous, mercenary. They are extremely dependent on their parents, for money, a career, and love, and show no signs of rebelling. They are adopting the West, too, as had many of their parents (not true in the German case)—music, clothes, and a certain performance of heterosexuality propagated by Hollywood—but they are unpoliticized (as are most post-89 youth in the West), and hence show little interest in democracy—Western political form. They embrace capitalism, which was already well-developed here, not of the industrial sort, but in terms of global trade, commerce, and banking. But this new globalization leaves so many individuals unprotected, sensing a downward mobility.

Nonetheless, the Western look of the place is misleading, for most women and men work within a specifically Lebanese economy of desire. The Barbie doll look is part of the deal, that women look good in public; otherwise men and other women will make derogatory comments. But it is the "normal" look, hence not one that arouses men here. If it aroused men, as it would in the U.S., aroused them to chase after these women, to show a desirous gaze, then women "wouldn't like it," I am told. That is, the sexual desire of European and American men is not wanted by Lebanese women. They would find it out of place. Though they may dress in the image that men have of the woman, specifically a haute culture image that presupposes an opposition between feminine and masculine, they want only the social approval, of looking right, of being in place, and not the sexual desire of these men. If women look right-beautiful, with long hair, well-manicured nails, lipstick, miniskirt, breasts protruding, they will be able to find a husband, who secures for them a place in the society. Some young women have told me stories of rejecting their adolescent boyfriends/loves to marry a man better situated. That place, in the middle—upper-middle class, is to be taken care of, with the children taken care of. It is not to make it on one's own, it is not autonomy. To fight for a place outside the care systems of the family networks requires an extremely courageous or "crazy" woman. I have met only one, and she expressed her caution to me about how far she might go.

In Lebanon, I am told and it is my observation, that most women do not want more of everything, as they do in Germany; they want the security of marriage with a man, without which they risk being socially marginal, even outcasts. They display this insecurity with a stoicism, a nonplus attitude that works as an armor to ward off alternative desires. Sexual desire, being primarily non-discursively articulated, is direct between men. Women are not needed for its articulation. But they are needed by men to legitimate the status hierarchies—hence the bouncer who controls that men do not come into the clubs alone with other men, but with women in their clans. Eventually all of the men who can afford it get married; thereafter they are free to seek out prostitutes in Jounieh (male or female), or to have affairs with men on the side. Or if they can afford it but don't want to marry, they leave the country. Much employment, at least for men in their most productive years, (30–50) is in the other gulf states, like Kuwait, where men live fairly segregated from women and have sexual access only to each other, or prostitutes, while their wives frequently stay in Lebanon.

One of the novelties I have encountered is how to answer the question, "Who am I?" It is always posed as a question about marital status. Most men here do not wear wedding rings, perhaps because it is so taken-for-granted among men over 35. I've taken notes of every time the question was posed. The question is usually the first one posed to me. Hence a friend said, it's like an American, "How ya doing?" But it is much more than that; at some point I'll write something about my experience with it.

I hope your summer has gone well. After the two months here, I think I understand better some of the motivations behind your work on conflict resolution.

Have you ever presented it here, to academics here? That might provoke a very interesting and productive reaction.

I hope your summer has gone well, allowing you to recover some from all of the losses you suffered through the first part of the year.

Sincerely,

John Borneman
Professor of Anthropology
Princeton University

September 13, 1999
Dr. Karl Kroeber

Department of English and Comparative Literature
Columbia University

Dear Dr. Kroeber:

Your letter of September 7, 1999 was passed on to me by our Chair Paul Rabinow. It was a good letter, which made me feel the needlessness of your having to write it. At the time the departmental colleagues were drafting the statement I edited it, cutting it down to a brief paragraph or two, leaving out the unnecessary condemnations and promises, and at the same time including a statement about present day Native Americans. Most of what I suggested was left out, and I along with about 4 or 5 of my colleagues never signed the statement that went out as if it were departmental. I too was disturbed by the ignorance of history and the paternalistic tone of the piece.

As to the question of professorial staff researching and teaching about Native American cultures, the story is more complicated. After the older faculty retired, Bill Simmons took over the ethnography of Native Americans and began work with native groups in NE California. We then hired Kent Lightfoot to cover NA archaeology. Simmons left for Brown. In the meantime Ethnic Studies and NA Studies in particular moved into what used to be an anthropology slot, giving the administration a reason not to support anthropology requests in these and related fields.

Our department has not even been able to recoup any biological anthropology positions at all. En fin, I thank you for your letter and for its bluntness. I have great respect for your father's work (still ahead of his time), knew and appreciated your mother and her writing, and had the good fortune to read and hear your sister last year. Enclosed is a recent publication for your interest. Sincerely yours.

Laura Nader
Professor of Anthropology

September 17, 1999
Dr. David Price

Saint Martin's College

Dear David:

I received your letter of August 5 only after I returned from Connecticut and about the time school opened. Sorry for the delay in response to a matter that surely concerns you very much.

Certainly I can understand your dilemmas in trying to decide what to do after two reject/revise letters. On the other hand, I myself am stubborn enough to want to know where the process will end, and so usually pursue it if invited, and you have been invited. The letters all together are supportive and some of the comments useful. You can use them and make your paper better. What I would draw the line at is being told to go out and get interviews—not a proper request. Would they tell Stocking to do that? However, there are some things you can do beyond some of the very good suggestions.

For example, I myself would retitle it "The CIA, the AAA and the Comprehensive Roster of 1952: A Social Drama," or drop the social drama. I only suggest something like that to link your work to conceptual analyses in anthropology (eg. Turner). Then I would write an introduction in which I would say something about the work being done in the history of anthropology and point

FIGURE 5. A photograph taken on a Zapotec farm while visiting my student Robert Gonzalez in the field. Photograph provided by author.

out that it has been apolitical—if it has been, quote Stocking, Wold, and whoever you want. Then mention the paucity of work on the Cold War in the social sciences generally and in anthropology in particular naming some works. Then describe what follows as a modest addition to a poorly known period.

Then give them the social drama, and for the reviewers include some more social context if you are able to, and send it back to Sussman saying that you thought the critiques both good and bad were useful—they saw a need to tell the story—quote the good things they say, and give lip to the suggestions contextualize etc., and note that this work stands without a requirement to interview people which is another project that you might indeed undertake after it is published and there is reaction. Also mention what one of the reviewers notes that this should be published in the AA for reasons—they mention and not in *The Nation* or *The News Letter*.

Hope this is useful. Do it. If they should not take it a third time (unlikely) send to a sociology journal or a history of anthropology journal (critique of anthropology) first before you go to *The Nation*.

All the best,

Laura Nader
Professor of Anthropology

A TWENTY-FIRST-CENTURY WORLD

The letters from the twenty-first century do not come in clusters as they did in the 1980s with the letters from scientists in response to my Mitre Corporation talk, although they cover a scattered number of familiar issues such as mindsets in science, arguments over ADR mediation, and the need to regulate family law mediators.

Especially interesting was a short letter from an eighty-five-year-old Californian farmer, George Woegell, on the male proclivity to go to war. I later learned that Woegell was a pacifist who refused to fight in the Korean War and had gone to jail rather than do so. More letters came on war and violence—not surprising given the United States' prolonged wars in Afghanistan and Iraq, the continued conflict in Israel and Palestine, jihadism, terrorism, anthropology and militarism, silencing, and the role of politics and its problems in a globalized world in search of "modernity." Letters regularly appeared in my mailbox, especially after Berkeley faculty, myself included, appeared in a symposium on television just before we went to Iraq in 2003. More recent letters still range widely from legal change policies to revenge (especially during the search for Osama bin Laden), higher education and student debt, ways in which an understanding of control can lead to creative solutions in the workplace and everyday life, silencing, the starving of funds for libraries, and the amount of money that is being allocated for college sports. Letters from Zambia, other letters recognizing controlling processes as alive and well, academic taboos, and reverse policies in China and the United States keep me in tune with my various publics.

The first brief letter in this chapter comes from Beatrice Whiting, who became my thesis adviser at Harvard after Clyde Kluckhohn passed away in 1960. Beatrice and her husband, John Whiting, were primarily known for their cross-cultural work on child rearing, a project that included numerous field workers across the globe. My own work on the Comparative Village Law Project was fashioned after the Whitings' approach and, like their study, based on a positivist, laboratory-style science model. With passing years and critical thinking, I opted for a wider angle. My 1996 book on *Naked Science* veered away from a rigid laboratory science model and included publication of several letters I had received from scientists.[1] Bea Whiting's second letter in 2000 was a positive comment on the ADR model of which I was a critic. We disagreed.

The next four letters were written by me. One was in response to *Foreign Affairs'* ridiculous pitch for "the need for nuclear power."[2] The others went back to issues of ADR family mediation, the absence of concerns with corporate power, and university bureaucracies regarding retirement practices.

The same decade brought correspondence on pedagogy and censorship in the review process, including David Price's difficulties getting the *AAA* Journal to publish his findings on the relationship between the CIA and anthropologists. Price was also completing a book on American anthropology and McCarthyism. And there were more letters from lawyers on ADR, the "Barriers" article, and "Controlling Processes," including one by the investigative reporter Jonathan Rowe. My correspondence with then President Lawrence Summers of Harvard on silencing dissent on Israeli policies by conflating them with anti-Semitism was based on letters, as well as silencing tactics mentioned by Professor Chalmers Johnson regarding the Gulf War. The question of Israel appears in my exchange with US President Jimmy Carter and in a long letter from the Afghani anthropologist Jamil Hanifi, who drew a comparison between the United States and the Mongol Empire and discussed his perception of the anthropologist Ashraf Ghani—now president of Afghanistan.

Letters from my colleague Elizabeth Colson moved my thinking from US trends to Africa and the role of international capital in the reemergence of chieftaincy. Colson was an inveterate letter writer. The last letter I received from her was the week before she passed away at the age of ninety-nine—mind as clear and penetrating as ever, still interested in the here and now and always up to date on what was going on. When Elizabeth Colson died, she was given the burial of a tribal chief in Zambia. Then more letters came from lawyers seeking my advice on a Zapotec murder case, and this zigzag of topics continues throughout the twenty-first century. My letter to Harvard Law School Dean Martha Minow and Dean Robert Post of Yale Law School were in response to the extrajudicial assassination of Osama bin Laden by US forces, referred to as "justice achieved" by both President Barack Obama (a constitutional lawyer trained at Harvard) and Secretary of State Hillary Clinton (trained at Yale Law School), suggesting that the schools that taught them should emphasize continuing education of their alumni; *due process* is a key element in arriving at "justice."

There are a number of letters I sent to Chancellor Birgeneau about ever increasing money for sports while decreasing priorities for education, and to Chancellor Nicholas Dirks as well as Janet Napolitano about priorities and hikes in tuition.

Two other letters deserve note here. First, the work of the Belgian anthropologist Rik Pinxten on social and cultural biases in math education, and second, Noam Chomsky's response to my article "Three Jihads."[3] Although Chomsky's comments were short and sweet, they were indispensable for furthering my understanding of the history of "Jewish Jihadism." The letter from a former student about my course on Controlling Processes alleged abuses in experiments by UC Berkeley's Psychology Department. Her letter was forwarded to the dean of social sciences and the chair of the Psychology Department for remediation of such practices, if needed. A final letter from a lawyer/anthropologist compares what's happening in China as it relates to the United States.

I must also note that the twenty-first century brought me letters sent not only through the postal service but also by email. Times and technology have indeed changed since I received my invitation to join the Anthropology Department at Berkeley by means of a telegram sent to me while I was in the field in Mexico in 1960.

February 14, 2000

Dear Laura,

It feels right to pick up communication with you on Valentine's Day. However, as I read your letter and articles I realize we have drifted apart and it will be difficult to know where to begin. Science to me is an inferential process, the results of the inferential reasoning are part of the content of the knowledge of a group of humans who share a culture. The process involves inferences from observations and experiences, the inferences made possible by the assumption that all humans are created with the power to reason about causality. This assumption is basic to all my thinking. Reasoning about causality is a big assumption but is basic. This power to infer causality is essential for survival. Changes in inferences result from observing with a different pair of glasses, and/or having new experiences with results not expected from inferences based on other experiences. I think this is essentially Malinowski.

In order to talk to other anthropologists I need to know whether they share the basic assumption and whether they accept my definition of science as defined as a way of thinking—inference based on observation and experience. I found in talking with far out post-modern anthropologists that they did not believe that all humans believed in causality. It should be noted that the inferences may include magical or religious beliefs, but they must have evidence based on reported observations and experiences. Thus the content of science depends on what is perceived, recognized and bound to change with changes in the environment.

As I read this it sounds like [gobbledygook]. Maybe you can figure out what I am trying to say. I have not figured out just what the universal cognitive abilities are, but as Gardner has speculated, there are many kinds of abilities that are enhanced by certain environments and perhaps genes which influence inferences based on observations and experience.

In cross-cultural research, one puts on glasses with different lenses and they reveal new variables that had not been counted in former inferences. To me this is the excitement of cross-cultural work. Computers and computer managers know how to increase the number of variables that can be used in inferences. Equally exciting can be the creativity of a researcher who is an iconoclast and likes to turn objects upside down to see their shape from a different angle. That was the fun and sometimes exasperation of working as a member of John's group. John did encourage dissidents and take their projects seriously.

As for problem solving in groups put together by the National Science Foundation and other august institutions, they remind me of the fiasco of the early days of the Institute of Human Relations when great minds from various disciplines were invited as members of the staff whose goal was the integration of biology, psychiatry, sociology and anthropology. The big wigs sat around a table, made elegant speeches to each other based on their research, and then went back to their offices. There was little integration taking place. The excitement came when the goal was specified in concrete terms and the young participants were required to learn what was in their colleagues' heads. It took years of concentrated evening seminars and cooperative research projects to make progress in integrating theories of developmental psychology, sociology and anthropology.

Laboratories are places where the new technological apparatus needed for experiments and the collection and analysis of data can be performed, but the group that inhabits the laboratories would vary as their specific goals are reached or given up as poor projects. There should be new personnel and new leaders every five to ten years. John said 10 years was pushing the limit.

My wish is that anthropologists would define their goals. Obviously there are many if one looks at the list of splinter organizations. We need the goals and the assumptions clarified.

For example why do we want thick ethnographies? What will they be used for? There are all kinds of areas where one can increase the thickness of descriptions. Does one expect the data to be used cross-culturally? If so, will someone else's thick descriptions cover the same topics? Or is it a beautiful description of a new typology of categorizing experience, etc., etc.? What does Geertz believe is universally human?

So my plea is for the clear presentation of goals and basic assumptions. Scientific knowledge is always open to verification when new data is included in the sum of what shapes it.

So after trying for forty or more years, I think we have finally influenced developmental psychologists. It took a long time because the psychologist looked at different things than the anthropologist. They were blinded by their beliefs and values, say the anthropologist. The anthropologists' observational techniques and their basis for inference were faulty, said the developmental psychologists. Progress only came when those with training in both disciplines worked on the same data in the same or similar environments.

So I can only discuss science in context. What is the domain of the knowledge it generates? Maybe grassroots groups are better able than big groups at looking to our survival because they fractionate the problem and redefine their goals as they perceive the interrelation of the new observations they make.

Hope you are well. Sorry I am not a help in thinking of a title. Plea for defining goals, assumptions, and policy while working from grassroots consensus—small, clearly defined steps.
Love,

Beatrice B. Whiting
West Tisbury, MA

February 23, 2000

Dear Laura,

In my recent attempt to get back to writing, I have been reviewing again my work with the Paiute and thinking about my impression of their system of dispute settlement. This gets me back to our early interchanges and your long work on comparative legal systems. Suddenly I know what I wanted you to say to the AAA. Anthropologists can help policy makers who seek to solve the problem of youth shoot-outs, gang aggressive behavior, and suicides. I have been impressed that a variable that has come to light and should be pursued is the social isolation of the young criminals, their sense that they cannot belong to the dominant group. The school communities, if in fact they exist as entities, do not get involved in the resolution of the isolation of some of their young members.

"Support groups" of various types are being started and are thriving. *The Vineyard Gazette* publishes a long list of their meetings weekly. Suddenly the "Island" is becoming publicly aware of the needs of human beings.

Mediation is now becoming popular as a form of conflict resolution. Ordinary citizens are being trained in the mediation process. However, I must admit that you are the first person who has alerted me to the myth that power is not involved in the outcomes of mediation. You are probably aware that mediation is now taught beginning in the early grades of school. I am curious to know how the process works and how teachers manipulate it.

Maybe you should talk about how anthropologists can help the citizens that are trying to create communities whose members learned to work with each other—how to help the new grassroots movements and how to beware of the hidden use of power in mediation. Are there published cases of so-called "mediation" that can be studied to view the role of power in the outcome of mediation?

What can the community do to bring loners back into the community? What lessons can be learned from indigenous systems of conflict resolution? Weren't these the things we thought about and talked about in the societies? If it is like the child development researchers, they are only beginning to understand some of the basic findings of anthropologists.

I think it is time to advise, not to berate. Anthropologists should be able to contribute their knowledge to advice about establishing communities and monitoring the mediation process to keep it truly democratic. There are young people who want to help in grassroots movements. There are young millionaires who want to contribute to society. How can anthropologists help them make use of their money?

I am rambling on, partly stimulated by a young friend who is working in the Native American community here, young wanting to get delinquents back into the fold, and teachers wondering how to best teach mediation, still unaware of its potential pitfalls. There is an appalling gap between the haves and have-nots. Houses built by the new rich are being built with 27 rooms, often similar in spirit to Gates' house. The youngs' desire for money is whetted by observation of the behavior of the new millionaires. The "Island" is trying to cling to some of its old values. You remind me of your passionate plea for some relevance. Maybe some concrete examples of what can be learned from indigenous cultures would be inspiring, or examples of anthropologists who have been successful in helping start real community participations and help solve youth problems.

Anthropologists are helping child developers to tidy up their thinking, see new variables. The mental health people want to learn but few really understand the daily life of their communities. Many teachers are far from understanding the problems they face. More anthropologists should be working with these groups. You must have trained many of them.

Maybe the young in the AAA should know of this positive aspect of your career. Maybe you need to catch the young AAAs up on where you started and where you are now. In a sense it would review your entire career and suggest areas where anthropologists have contributed to problem solving in modern life.

Females are noted for their haranguing—prosocial dominance. The message delivered in this material style does not go over well with large numbers of people. It is too reminiscent of MOTHERS. Use a different style.
Love,

Beatrice Whiting
West Tisbury, MA

FIGURE 6.   Beatrice Whiting, my thesis director at Harvard University. Photograph from author's collection.

February 22, 2000

Editor/Letters to the Editor
Foreign Affairs

To the Editor:

"The Need for Nuclear Power" by Richard Rhodes and Denis Beller (in the same issue with an [essay] on oil glut) should have been titled "The *Desire* For Nuclear Power." The piece is a classic example of assertive rhetoric, as in "the world needs more energy," and hubris: "two billion people lack access to energy," implying that everyone wants electricity and all it implies without being asked. The article is also hyped by quotes about how much energy will be consumed in the next 60 years without humility or any reference to the numerous wrong projections about energy needs in the past.

Furthermore, quotes about how much nuclear power costs do not seem to include life-cycle cost: from the uranium mines, to ongoing contamination, or the decommissioning of the nuclear plants. And there is precious little said about nuclear waste from Asia for example. On the other hand, in their section on the decline and fall of renewables, which does not include conservation/efficiency, is devoid of any hard data to the point of sounding propagandistic. According to them, we "pour concrete for fields of windmills as if we don't pour concrete for reactors that do not require large space."

In sum, it is appalling that such a piece could have been submitted for publication especially since there are good people capable of more credible argument. The National Academy of Sciences published a number of volumes as part of their CONAES (Committee on Nuclear and Alternative Energy Systems) long-term study. It might be useful to look back in order to go forward. One thing we learned in the CONAES work is how easy it was to cook up figures, as well as the degree that tunnel vision influenced specialist analysis.

The authors tell us that "Nuclear power is environmentally safe, practical, and affordable." Tell that to David Freeman who revolutionized energy production in Sacramento, California with solar collectors in the middle of a dead nuclear plant Rancho Seco. Or tell that to the people of the American West whose land and water has been irreparably contaminated, and whose cancer rate exceeds the national average. Or tell that to Pacific Islanders who after the devastation of nuclear testing are being encouraged to take nuclear waste onto their atolls as a win/win solution. *Foreign Affairs* has done better on the issue of energy.
Sincerely,

Laura Nader
Professor of Anthropology

March 22, 2000
Adam Schiff

Chair of the California Senate Judiciary Committee
Sacramento, CA

Dear Senator Schiff,

Re: SB 2124. I would like to express my strong support for SB 2124 (Figueroa). The bill would prohibit family law mediators from making recommendations about child custody or visitation to the court. I have been studying the mediation movement since Alternative Dispute Resolution was made respectable by the work and advocacy of former Chief Justice of the U.S. Supreme Court Warren Burger in the 1970s. Indeed, I was in attendance at his famous St. Paul meeting in 1976 and followed matters very closely since then, in-and-out of family mediation cases. In 1992, I published a piece in *Family and Conciliation Courts Review*, "From Legal Process to Mind Processing."

Basically, my findings are that mediation abridges freedom, especially when mandatory, because it is often outside-the-law, eliminates choice of procedure, removes equal protection before an adversary law, and is generally hidden from view. There is no one regulating the education and practice of mediation, and there are too many mind games operating outside the purview of anyone—not a democratic practice. The best piece on this process still is Trina Grille's *Yale Law Journal* 1991 article. We have jumped from the frying pan into the fire. Judges rely too heavily on mediator recommendations because it is easier, but that does not mean it is good for parties concerned. The plain truth is that we have not enough data on how mediators operate because of confidentiality clauses, however it is clear that they do not contextualize beyond the parents and children. Custody is too important to be left to such a narrow specialty and one that is practiced in an unseen manner.

I hope the above articulations are useful if brief. If there is anything further I may provide please contact me. I will be away from March 23 to April 1.

Thank you for your attention.
Sincerely yours,

Laura Nader
Professor of Anthropology

April 17, 2000
Arjun Appadurai

Professor of Anthropology
University of Chicago

Dear Prof. Appadurai:

Every time I begin a piece authored by you I think I must write you, but I usually don't. This time I move myself to the typewriter. I am puzzled by your work for at least two reasons and perhaps you might help by responding to what I cannot find in the written materials.

First, I am surprised that someone of your particular background buys into the gloss of modernity. For me modernity is a Euro-American thing, as are the technologies that are used to spread the word. It is to my mind a continuation of colonialism. My second concern relates to the front-stage you give to the nation-state and the back stage to the multi-national corporations who are either responsible for much of what you describe, or at least are in cahoots with nations to accomplish what you describe, leaving agency to one side for a moment. Just as anthropologists working in Africa ignored the colonizers, so too today those anthropologists who do not see corporate conquests are centerpiece are making the same ideological turns.

Having said all this, I return to your self-ascribed position as bringing in the concrete with bewilderment. "Globalization" today is corporate America. This does not mean that one should not consider improvisation or imagination. I only call to your attention how odd it sounds to speak about the demise of the state without recognizing the issue that one CEO referred to when he titled his book *When Corporations Rule the World*, by means of "cinema, video, restaurants, spectator sports, and tourism, to name just a few." And by the way, what evidence do you have, apart from the lives of elites, that locality has "lost its ontological moorings?"

Perhaps the above can be the start of dialogue. I hope so. With all good wishes.
Sincerely yours,

Laura Nader
Professor of Anthropology

May 11, 2000
James Shapiro

Professor of English
Columbia University

Dear Prof. Shapiro,

I read with interest your piece in *The Chronicle of Higher Education*. There is much truth in what you say. There is also need for a fuller picture so that your words are not misused or misunderstood, especially by administrations in this world of corporatized universities.

For example, in Anthropology at Berkeley, every time a professor retires the FTE goes to someone, say in Biology. Thus, there is no replacement in Anthropology necessarily accompanying a retirement. We have been reduced from 36 to 24.

This university encouraged early retirement by bribing older faculty to leave. The older faculty contain the memory of the university which the new world order would just as soon see removed. We used to be classed as faculty, now as employees; we used to have an active Academic Senate, now it is barely operative. On the question of women and minorities, the figures are shocking since the Regental actions a number of women or minorities that are being "replaced" with retirement is next to nil or worse. And even worse perhaps the pitting of the younger generation against the older generation has made intergenerational exchange between established scholars almost impossible.

En fin, I guess that where we would disagree is where the problem lies. You say with old colleagues (which may be a problem), but I would argue that we put all this in the context of entrenched administrations of the world order type.

If we should argue on your premise I could give example over example where younger colleagues are negating funding, publication, etc., for older and sometimes very deserving senior colleagues. Perhaps the situation is different in English and Comparative Literature.

Thank you for your attention.

Sincerely yours,

Laura Nader
Professor of Anthropology

May 30, 2000

Dear Professor Nader:

This paper is dedicated to you. Thank you for making me think, for forcing to look beyond my comfortable, privileged position to see and question what operates beyond my everyday experience and perception. For showing me that my privileged, comfortable position is an incredibly powerful place from which to stand up and fight for things I believe in, to challenge others, and to keep challenging myself.

When I transferred to Berkeley two years ago, I found myself in a place that was much more different than I had expected. I had always been told that I should go to Berkeley, that I would fit in. People from all over would tell me: "you little social activist, liberal, I'm gonna make the world a better place girl . . . you'd fit right in at Berkeley." And then I got here and realized that a lot had changed. I found myself lost amongst a lot of students who had been raised to be doctor's and engineers and lawyers, people who thought that the system was great because if they went along with it, they could get a Mercedes and the right stock options (what more could you want?). I felt totally alone and out of place, I thought I might be fighting losing battles, I began to wonder what I came here for.

And then I showed up in your class. I discovered how to challenge my own and other people's ideas, to look beyond the easy answers, the common perception. I saw that an academic, intellectual leader (and woman) could stand up and challenge the systems and the structures that they so usually support. I heard you tell it like it is, and god love it, you weren't some old foggy white guy who separated the academy from the ideal world. I kept telling everyone "this lady is awesome!" Every college kid in the world should have to take her class! And while we're at it, let's send all the lawyers and politicians and CEO's. Let's send my mom! She'd finally understand me (and she might even think that I'll be able to get a job)!

You and your classes have helped me to realize why I came here. I needed to learn how to bridge my desire to help people, to challenge injustices and ignorance with my academic and intellectual capabilities. I realized that someone fighting from inside the system had a powerful, influential voice and presence.

One day in your Anthropology of Law class you said that more children had died in Iraq than in Hiroshima. Being your average American I found this idea ludicrous. Not being your average citizen (I am after all a college student at an amazing research facility), I decided to look into this claim. And that is where this paper began.

I have spent that past six months being consumed by this issue, fighting my way into a graduate class so I could have to opportunity to produce this paper. I have spent too many long days and nights in Doe library, emailing epidemiologists, leafing through magazines and newsreels, writing letters to the State Department in protest. The more information I discovered, the more missing information I realized needed to be uncovered. I began to understand that this issue was not isolated to Iraq, or America, or CNN. Instead, I realized that I needed to look at the Cold War, censorship, and the arms trade. How the U.N., the academy, and the media function. This is just the beginning. . .

And when I ran into a Dean of Public Health who announced that no matter what the evidence showed, it was still up to that lazy Iraqi government to take care of their own people, I was infuriated, but I thought of you. When epidemiologists and a U.N. representative told me that genocide could not be claimed because birth rates were increasing along with child death rates (genocide can only be declared if you "successfully" demolish the population and keep it from reproducing—ahhh Geneva law and epidemiology, where would we be without you), I shuddered and again, I thought of you. When I ran into health reports and U.N. statements that made me break down and cry, I had to remember that no battle is easy, and that there are other people fighting out there and not giving up. I had to keep reminding myself that if I can get through to one person, to inspire one person to action, just like you had done for me, then it would all be worth it, and someone would carry on the battle for me when I was gone. In times of deep sadness and pessimism, your optimism, your strength and the incredible impact you've had on so many lives kept me pushing forward.

As I go into the "real" world and leave the academy behind for a while, I thank you. For everything you've taught me, and for everything that you've made me figure out on my own. I promise you that when you aren't teaching these classes any more, I will be teaching them in some form, somewhere. The whole time, with thoughts of you in my mind and my heart, and with Big Brother shaking in his boots.

Thank you for opening my third eye. My vision will never be the same. Peace, love, and many thanks,

Kate Wilusz
Berkeley, CA

June 14, 2000

Dear Professor Nader,

Enclosed is a badly jumbled review recently published in *Science and Society*. This is NOT the review I wanted to publish, but rather the politically correct review the editors would print. My original review was deemed "too mean spirited" and I came up with this exceedingly polite review. Like you, I thought it important to critique the *New Press* and its editor. Unfortunately, the people at *Science and Society* do not send proofs of book reviews to authors; hence, I was unable to correct the errors in the review. This is very disheartening as any credibility I had was in my estimation completely lost because of the errors.

My work on Leslie White continues. It seems endless but I am hoping to finally finish this fall. I am also working with David Price on a couple pieces related to the Cold War and various anthropologists.

I was wondering if you are doing any follow up work you have published on the Cold War. If so, I would truly appreciate copies of your work. I do not have access to a good academic library and find getting scholarly publications difficult.

Best wishes,

William J. Peace
Katonah, New York

June 28, 2000

Dear Laura,

Thanks very much for your manuscript. It arrived while I was in Spain, hence the delayed response. I enjoyed reading it and am astonished at the behavior of Altamira. Like universities, publishers seem to think they should make what they consider to be business decisions without regard to intellectual content. It is an old story, though very well told in Sheila Slaughter and Larry Leslie's book *Academic Capitalism*.

Anyway, I profited from reading your commentaries on the papers and getting a sense of similarities between the world of workplace and community development I am working in and environmental work.

The most telling remark in your paper to me is about the muffled, held-back quality of the writing. I don't think it is any accident that the more strident voices of the 50s were silenced by the combined legacy of McCarthy (who I think won the battle for censorship of the academy by creating an environment of self-censorship) and by the corporate indebtedness of universities now. When an enormous portion of the budget of universities comes from the private sector and from courting federal and state politicians who are also courting the private sector, why do we expect that critical social science voices should not be muffled?

Constructivism, positionality, and all the "post-isms" seem to me to leave us in a position of criticizing the very possibility of having an ethical position firm enough to stand for in public. Of course, the loss of courage has gone with a loss of respect for anthropology, sociology, and political science. I must say, it seems deserved in many cases, and I don't see many rushing to change the scene.

Sorry. You caught me on a pessimistic day. I am moving offices this week to go to take over the Institute for European Studies here. I simply find the intellectual life in the Department of Anthropology too constraining for my own intellectual and moral health.

I am enclosing a recent chapter that Morten Levin and I did on action research and universities for the *Denzin and Lincoln Handbook of Qualitative Inquiry*. It is mainly a kind of program piece and lays out the turf that Morten and I are working over now in the slow process of producing a book about these issues.

Best wishes,

Davydd J. Greenwood
Professor of Anthropology
Cornell University

August 7, 2000

Dear Laura,

I have been meaning to write you for the past week but have been side-tracked as my brother and his family have been visiting from the Netherlands, and we have been in and out of town these last ten days.

First, thank you for contacting Louise Lamphere concerning the CIA paper. About 10 days ago she called me, talked to me about the paper, and had me mail her a packet containing all the peer review comments, and all three drafts of the paper. After reading those she contacted Sussman and urged him to reconsider his decision regarding the paper, telling him that she considered this to be important news for the members of the Association. Sussman told her he would try and get another set of readers to read the paper and he would reevaluate the situation once hearing from them. I do not expect him to decide to publish it as the comments thus far have given him plenty of opportunity to do so if he wanted to. Lamphere on the other hand does seem committed to getting the full paper into print in some publication of the AAA. She's discussed several alternate strategies that she is willing to pursue if Sussman declines to publish it.

Louise has decided that the best approach is to let Sussman continue to ponder his position, but to make some of findings of the paper public by printing a short excerpt from the paper in the Oct. *Anthropology News*, and using the AAA business meeting in San Francisco to present the paper, and then have a panel discuss the historical and ethical issues involved in the events described in the paper. I am not thrilled with the prospect of publishing a short CIA piece in the *Anthropology News* as the severe length restrictions create more opportunities to be misunderstood than understood. Louise's thinking is that it will draw people to the special session at the business meeting where they can get more details. Her plan for the business meeting is to deal with the

AAA's business (voting on whatever needs voting on, etc.) in a half hour and using the remaining half to address issues related to the paper. I think she has an interest in revisiting the PPR's current lack of explicit prohibitions against covert research, as well as opening the door for a wider consideration of numerous dormant, unfinished political questions. Her idea is to have a panel that would be more right-wing than left, perhaps some past members of the ethics board, and let much of the discourse emerge from the floor. With a full awareness of the Association's proclivity to attack the messenger more than the message. I'm willing to do this as I think addressing these issues now could prevent some bad situations in the brave new world that Bush or Gore have in store for us. I asked her to consider inviting you to be on the panel as you've worked on the Cold War, as well as relevant ethical issues, but I don't know if she will ask you as her comment to me was that there might be other individuals to bring into this issue.

The thing that I like least about all of this is the timing. The smart thing for me to do would be to finish the book on McCarthyism and American anthropology and then delve into a book on anthropology and intelligence agencies. I've just completed a rough draft of this book and had the feeling that I would be able to tell a story where we the anthropologists were the victims before mucking things up with a more sordid tale involving anthropologists collaborating with the CIA and Pentagon.

I will keep you posted as this situation develops. Thanks for your help. Best Regards,

David Price
Professor of Anthropology
Saint Martin's College

October 10, 2000

Dear Laura (if I may presume),

Thank you for your response to my little piece in the *AAA Newsletter* and, especially, for the paper on the "Phantom Factor." And apologies for taking such a long time. I read the paper with great interest and it brought back vivid memories of what I call our fighting days (as if they were over). It seems that there will be some heat at the upcoming AAA meetings. My fear is that it will again be only about righteousness. If there was evil in the Neel-Chagnon work it is not for us anthropologists to carry that evil and redeem ourselves. What we must carry is what Chagnon got away with intellectually all these years (and that has been revealed some time ago; favorite reference is the paper by

Leslie Sponsel, "Yanomami: An Arena of Conflict and Aggression in the Amazon (a totally misleading title). *Aggressive Behavior* 24 (1998): 97–122.

By the way, I am an unmitigated "epistemological radical" (to cite you) and I wish we would find an occasion to discuss why I think this is the only option aside from righteousness. Perhaps at the coming AAA meetings.
Best regards,

Johannes Fabian
Professor of Anthropology
University of Amsterdam

October 17, 2000

Dear Laura,

On the phone a few weeks ago you asked me to put a positive spin on my Cold War work, and to pass on general, positive contributions made by anthropology during the past century. For the general contributions I'm sure my list is no different than what you've already compiled: the critique of IQ, critique of the concept of race, we've learned quite a lot about the influence of a society's infrastructure on its structure and super-structure, advances in our understanding of human evolution and the peopling of the New World, we've learned how to study power structures at home and abroad, etc.

As to a positive spin derived from my Cold War work: I'm close to finishing my book on American anthropology and McCarthyism, so I now have 600 pages of manuscript based on archival documents and FBI files that indicate again and again the simple truth: activism matters. Though it has its obvious risks, anthropologist activists have served us all well, with a tradition stretching back from the work of James Mooney to the present. To some degree I'd argue that the extent to which the FBI has monitored our work is a testament of the effectiveness of our commitment to fighting for social justice (one negative proof of this postulate is that Socialist anthropologists who were not activists—such as Leslie White—were not actively pursued by the FBI as their lack of activism indicated a lack of threat to the status quo).

Those anthropologists who were persecuted by HUAC [House Un-American Activities Committee] and McCarthyism came under fire primarily because they used their research to challenge the biases of a cultural system based on a hierarchy of race, gender, and economic inequality. In many instances anthropologists were attacked more for their stance on racial equality than they were for holding Marxist position. For example, Joseph McCarthy and Roy Cohn attacked Gene Weltfish (as well as the then deceased Ruth

Benedict) primarily for her work on race. There was a wonderful exchange between McCarthy and Weltfish where McCarthy accused Weltfish of falsifying IQ data indicating that Southern Whites had lower IQs than Northern Blacks. Weltfish completely disarmed McCarthy by pointing out that she and Benedict had simply relied on the Army's own data in this study—at which point McCarthy and Cohn began badgering her by asking a series of questions that most civil libertarians would not bother answering under protection of the Fifth Amendment.

Hope this helps. I look forward to hearing your talk this next month.
Best,

David Price
Professor of Anthropology
Saint Martin's College

September 4, 2001

Dear Professor Nader:

Thank you for your letter and the enclosed articles. You make your point very articulately. I believe the primary points you made against ADR are:

1. You proposed it is a form of social control
2. You believe it attempts to supplant justice with harmony
3. You suggest it favors the more powerful and, I assume, disfavors the less powerful
4. You state it avoids concerns with fault thus frustrating people because they cannot "blame" someone

Allow me a moment to address each of these points then make a few which may give you something to consider in your evaluation of ADR—especially mediation.

Whether ADR is a form of social control is a political question. I suspect one could argue it is more than types of dispute resolution. However, such a characterization places a heavy mantle on processes that seem to resolve disputes which should not be in court. Justice should be reserved for the issues for which the court system can best address such as discrimination, criminal actions, and state actions. I have a difficult time finding the need for judicial intervention in issues such as traffic accidents, slip and falls, and a plethora of other legal claims flooding the court system.

Many legal claims are factually dependent. The involved parties are not interested in Locke, Plato, the Constitution, or Thomas Paine. They want their property fixed and life to be the way it was before the problem arose. The court system and all it entails frustrates this "want." Furthermore, the court system becomes more of a problem than a solution what with the additional cost, time, fees, and uncertainty.

In family law matters, the participants (and their lawyers) quickly learn how to use the legal system to vex the other party. The parties and their attorneys use the legal system and its "justice" to use the children as toys in a game of retribution for committed sins. ADR provides means wherein the parties can both solve their dispute and move toward a healing.

Granted, ADR is often done in private, unpublished, and with little accountability. This *could* lead to instances of impropriety. On the other hand, the judicial system is not above chicanery either. Recently, a judge was sanctioned because as he was hearing a man's criminal case, the judge was concurrently having sex with the accused's wife. The point is both systems can be abused.

I took a case to the highest court of military review. The prosecutor/victim completely recanted her accusation several years after the court martial. She recanted on her own. When I was advised, I contacted her and asked if I could take her video statement. When I took the statement I told her she could be prosecuted for perjury/and she could go to jail. Nevertheless, she recanted. We attempted to get the conviction overturned. The military legal system chose to look at finality as more important than justice. The case worked its way up the appellate system. Finally, the Court of Appeals for the Armed Forces chose to make no decision, thus forcing the matter to the Supreme Court. My client could not afford further appeals so he is adjudged for a crime he did not commit by default. I suspect Barry Scheck's "Operation Innocence" is also casting great doubt on the judicial system.

I see ADR as just another choice of resolving "conflicts." It may be better than some conflict resolution methods, worse than others, and about the same as many others. But, in my opinion, to say it is a means of social control gives it more importance than perhaps it deserves. To say ADR supplants justice with harmony is a harsh judgment. First, what is justice? If my neighbor's wife is raped, I want to see the full legal system prosecute the perpetrator. Spare no expense and let the law do what it should to both punish this criminal and send a message to others. That would be one version of justice. If the animal rapes my wife, justice may come from the end of a .45 ACP. Fast, summary, and complete.

Some would say my executing the criminal is wrong and abridges his liberty. Others would say a bullet is too kind. Often times, justice is defined by a subjective standard. Now let's get back to justice and a disputed car accident.

Why does society need to give a courtroom and all the attendant costs to two parties who disagree what color the light was before impact? In such a situation there will always be three stories: the plaintiff's version, the defendant's version, and the truth—the judge's or jury's version. Why shouldn't we let these disputants negotiate a settlement between themselves thus leaving society out of their self-imposed problem? What does society get from their dispute in the legal system? Nothing but cost and inconvenience.

In regard to your point that ADR favors the more powerful, I am not sure the premise stands under scrutiny. Of course, we can find instances where bigger and stronger parties negotiated with less powerful parties. However, that does not prove anything more than a big party negotiated with a smaller party. Look at the number of instances where a smaller party, say Vietnam, forced a larger party to the negotiation table, then really got the benefit of the bargain. We saw it again when Iran negotiated over the hostages. In each of these situations one could study the negotiation dynamics to find reasons why some things were done and others were not. However, one can not say one party or the other was at a disadvantage *because* of a ADR process.

In the everyday forum, insurance companies use the legal system to abuse claimants. Look at the "Legislative Findings" on Martha Escutia's bills, both in the Assembly and the Senate. The insurers know most individuals can not afford the legal system and they use the transaction cost factor in the same way a gambler uses the "table stakes" rule. If it were not for ADR, in its multiple facets, many claimants would never get a recovery or the recovery would be so small it would not cover the actual expenses. In such circumstances, ADR is the only thing which give a modicum of hope to the less powerful.

Finally, I am not sure why we should be concerned with assessing fault. In a marital dispute, when one spouse hits the other or one is unfaithful, the acting out is inappropriate but can we say the victim is without responsibility for the marital breakdown? Usually, the answer is no. Therefore, our society made divorce "no fault" because people played so many games to assess fault. We substantially got past this thorny thicket. Why do we want to go back? How is it productive? Perhaps ADR is helpful because it does stress personal responsibility, both for the problem and the solution.

Finally, the lack of accountability by the professions practicing ADR is an area of concern to the parties, the court, and the profession. SPDR [Society of Professionals in Dispute Resolution], SCMA [Southern California Mediation Association], CPR [International Institute for Conflict Prevention & Resolution], and a host of other professional organizations are all working to create meaningful standards of ethics, performance, training, education, and accountability. The power of a mediation is its promise of confidentiality (see California's Supreme Court decision in *Foxgate*). This is also its point of criticism. I believe the way this is handled is by the increasing professionalism in the field. As mediators and arbitrators become more and more skilled the marketplace will weed out the poor ones or they will not even get into the field because of more stringent licensing requirements.

It is fair to say there are some subjects wherein the courtroom is the appropriate forum. The issue may be so universal or may require uniformity of application. Perhaps the case may involve an issue with such far reaching ramifications that the higher court wants to send a message to society at large. In these instances, a trial with full exposure may be just the appropriate dispute resolution method. However, ADR may be an appropriate adjunct in many heretofore legal situations, including criminal cases. I see the time coming when the accused is tried in a court then, prior to formal sentencing by the court, the criminal, the victim, and the State may be involved in a mediation to determine the proper disposition. Shouldn't the victim have a say in the resolution of a crime against him/her?

I hope I have given you an opportunity to look at ADR from a different perspective. I sincerely look forward to your comments.
Yours very truly,

Michael B. Rainey
Michael B. Rainey & Associates
Woodland Hills, CA

October 6, 2001

Dear Laura Nader,

I was very moved by your letter. My book seemed to have vanished with hardly a trace across the Atlantic, and it was a great fillip to me to know that colleagues as distinguished and informed as you and Elizabeth Colson were reading it and finding something in it too. One of my anxieties when writing it was that the natives might find the ethnography faulty, or tone deaf, and I am also reassured that you do not seem to feel that I was writing about a different country entirely! (I have spent two and a half years altogether in the U.S.A.: 4 months teaching at Santa Barbara in 1969, a year at the Center in Stanford in 1980–1, and a year at the Princeton Center in 1994–5; but I have not really had a chance to get to know American campus society.)

Your comment that I could have written more about a different trajectory in American anthropology is well taken however, and I should perhaps have emphasized more strongly that I was writing about one thread in a complex disciplinary history. Perhaps there is also a problem about audience. In retrospect, I think that the book was clearly addressed in the first place to European anthropologists. (I enclose a recent interview I gave, largely about the book, for the journal of the European Association of Social Anthropologists that will make this clear). This may create a certain distance for American readers. It is hard to know, and that of course is a common issue for ethnographers writing about a literate society but for another audience.

Thank you also for the papers you sent me. As you suggested, I found the paper on the phantom factor particularly interesting, and it raises a number of issues that I should have gone into more myself, though perhaps as you hint, it would not be easy to find out some of the things that went on in those desperate days. (Though that is an experience which may become very relevant again now). It is a very complicated story, even if one limits oneself to the micro-history of the Parsonians at Harvard. For example, according to one recent biographical essay I read, Parsons was on an FBI list of suspect characters, and enquiries were made about him at Harvard. The transition from OSS to CIA was also a complex one, and for a man like Kluckhohn there may have come a moment when what had seemed at first a continuity of service, came to seem uncomfortably different. The equivalent history in the U.K. is very murky, and has not been studied at all, in contrast to the role of anthropology in colonial affairs. Did you know for instance, that Meyer Fortes was a senior figure in MIS during the war? Both Leach and Evans-Pritchard served in what would now be called special forces units, raising native troops behind enemy lines. It would be interesting to know who, if any, retained links with the security forces into the 1950s. In France, there are other histories just beginning to be told, including the history of resistance and collaboration in French anthropology during the war, and the fascinating history of French anthropology and Algeria, culminating in a way, with the rebellion of Jacques Soustelle, a distinguished anthropologist and war-time Gaullist, whom de Gaulle sent to Algeria as governor, and who defected to the pieds noirs and spent nearly a decade as a fugitive.

I am coming to the AAA meetings next month, and if you are there, and have an hour or two free, it would be very nice to be able to talk, and perhaps even share a meal.

Yours sincerely,

Adam Kuper
London, United Kingdom

October 31, 2001

Dear Dr. Nader,

I was pleased to see your article "Harmony Coerced is Freedom Denied" in *The Chronicle of Higher Education* because it saved me the trouble of looking up your address. I had your guest comment "Barriers to Thinking New About Energy" in *Physics Today* from 1981 on my desk and was planning to write to you. I got it when a physics student in my geology class tossed it on my lab table and said, "Read this!" I think it was in response to some gripe I had made about nuclear power. I thought the *Physics Today* article was insightful then, but I think your points are even more important today. This is in contrast to most of what was written in 1981.

I have been to many university bookstores where reprints of Garrett Hardin's essay "The tragedy of the commons" were piled up several feet high. They were required reading for various courses. The essay has been reprinted in books, and the American Association for the Advancement of Science kept it as an offprint for decades (and still does I hope). I think your essay is in the same class. I am going to try to convince the editors of *Physics Today* to bring it out as an offprint.

The essay is all the more important because of the success of *Hubhert's Peak* by Kenneth S. Deffeyes. It's already pretty high on Amazon.com, and I wouldn't be surprised if it makes the top ten. I think he is correct in predicting that in a few years world oil production will start to decline while demand continues to increase, just as the United States' oil production began to decline in 1970, as predicted by M. King Hubbert in 1956. However, Deffeyes is Mr. Macho when it comes to solutions, and these are not well thought out. He deals with solar power by jumping to the generation of electricity at centralized solar plants in the Nevada desert, instead of little solar heat collectors on the roofs or south sides of our almost nine million homes. He urges us to "get over our nuclear phobia." He doesn't talk about vegetarians but dismisses organic farming. Solar power isn't effective "at the moment. . . " Even his jokes are dirty, but having worked with drillers, I already heard most of them.

I wanted you to be aware of what I am doing. If the folks from *Physics Today* don't want to reprint it, perhaps there is some other way to get it out again. Sincerely,

Winston Crausaz
Professor of Geology
Elyria, OH

April 21, 2002

Dear Laura,

Many thanks for the letter and photocopy. As always, my effort is to pursue my subject in a fashion that allows for the most effective theoretical ordering of the facts. To throw matters such as American or other governmental bombing into the same category as, say the bombing of a pizza parlor full of civilians by nongovernmental Palestinians, is to destroy the possibility of a scientific theory of terrorism.

What is now common is theories of terrorism as a moralistic label rather than a analytical term. The case mentioned in *The New York Times* letter appears to be terrorism; however, not the type of behavior I am trying to understand.

I might also mention that what you call my "optimism" about the future of terrorism is merely an extrapolation from the present trend toward increasing social closeness at the global level, based on theory I cite at that point.

Incidentally, I've gotten a huge amount of feedback about the little terrorism piece. A lot of people seem to think the subject benefits from an approach that is less ideological than one normally encounters.

I look forward to reading your piece that you gave me at Hopkins.

Best,

Donald Black
Professor of Sociology
University of Virginia

May 28, 2002
Lisa Marsh Ryerson

President of Wells College
Aurora, NY

Dear President Ryerson,

I have meant to write you about the "Master Plan" (so-called) vision for Wells College with the intention of calling your attention to the misplacedness of it all. I am glad to see that there are alums who agree with what I see as misplaced energies. Wells is about education first and foremost, not about decorating—although the two could be compatible. Furthermore, the demolition mentality does not mix well with nostalgia and/or wonderful memories we all have of the music building for example. As for the Long Library, I know that it was not built with energy efficiency in mind, but there is retrofit and insulation. In other words, I am at a loss to see how the Board of Trustees can go along with such a plan while still asking alums for their "generosity."

I am in the midst of getting my grades in as my class is having its 50th reunion. Once again, I am not able to be there. I hope all is well with you and yours. Thank you for your attention.

Sincerely yours,

Laura Nader

June 27, 2002

Dear Laura,

I really like the concept of "controlling processes"—such a fertile way of looking at a culture and the dominant influences in it.

The material helped crystalize the question I posed to you originally. It concerns language itself as a controlling process. I don't mean just in the Orwellian sense of using words in a perverse and manipulative way. I mean the *nature* of a given language, whether certain ways of looking at the world are built into different languages, with the result that those who use those languages are stuck in that worldview or perhaps liberated from another worldview.

What prompted my interest in this was the realization that the myopia and circularity of conventional economic thinking is built into the language in which this thinking, or rather pseudo-thinking, is couched. Once you've defined anything, produced *anything* as a "good," then production itself must always be good. Try talking about bad "goods"—the language resists.

By the same token, define wealth as the result of monetary accumulation of any kind (*any*) then wealth must be always and forever good. When there is no concept of "illth" in John Ruskin's wonderful term, no possibility of accumulation that arises from or works ill, then you are stuck conceptually on a kind of velodrome bicycle with no neutral gear and no brakes. It can go in one direction only; and it must keep going until a crash or else the rider drops of exhaustion.

One could take just about the entire vocabulary of economics, term by term, and find a similar implicit coding. The language becomes a controlling process—controlling of thought which is the most fundamental kind.

This has raised a number of questions in my mind. Is the worldview implicit in the Anglo-American version of economics built into the language somehow? Was the language itself especially conducive to this way of thinking; and as English overspreads the globe, does this thinking tend to follow—quite, apart from the aggressive propagandizing of the market? Do other languages tend towards a different way of looking at the economic realm? (Is this part of the gap between Islam and the West for example)?

So that's the question, as I've been able to formulate it to date. I'd welcome any insights; and I'll plan a trip into the city over the next few weeks so we can get together.

Thanks again.

Best,

Jonathan Rowe
Tomales Bay Institute
Point Reyes Station, CA

August 24, 2002
Christopher Killheffer

New Haven, CT

Dear Mr. Killheffer,

My brother Ralph Nader shared with me a copy of the letter you wrote him in July after attending the New Haven rally. We both appreciated your thoughtful comments and had little to disagree with. What you say about powerlessness, about self-righteousness, and silliness are there all right. Unfortunately, all such are present in the university, but even worse is the indifference, which I see all around me. But when Ralph speaks, or when I teach there is no illusion that the concept of citizen is well-enough developed so that we might get the kind of behavior you speak of. Especially at these public rallies and especially in a democratic society, as no one knew better than Thomas Jefferson: mob behavior will color things. But like Jefferson, I would rather have that than the goose-step which we also have much of.

About sometime in the early 1980s I began to seriously think about how to deprogram non-thinking students to the left and the right—that is to teach critical thinking. I invented a course called "Controlling Processes" in which I sought to teach, students how to recognize knee-jerk positions, how to recognize the controls in their own lives. I ask them to find a controlling process in their lives and to write about how it works. For many, it changes their lives—they find they have a brain beyond regurgitating. For some the papers turn into honors theses. For me it may be turning anthropology or combining it with civics. Whatever, it seems to work, but I can't control what they do with their newly found knowledge.

As for preaching to the converted, yes there is some of that. But people also attend the rallies who are downright antagonistic to what Ralph has to say who come away with changed minds.

At any rate, letters like yours are appreciated—at least you're not indifferent. Thanks.
Sincerely,

Laura Nader
Professor of Anthropology
University of California, Berkeley

September 2, 2002

Dear Laura,

Thanks for sending on the letter you penned to Cathy Lutz and Anna Simons. I found your comments to be dead-on. As you know, dealing with the press is always a less than satisfying venture, but this instance was worse than usual; perhaps in part because most of NPR's staff goes on vacation during August and the place seems to be run by interns, but mostly because they live by that Tweedle Dee and Tweedle Dumber "every-argument-has-two-sides" garbage that Cockburn critiqued so well in his *Corruptions of Empire*. I'm just glad to live somewhere with a strong Pacifica presence, I wouldn't bother with the radio if it weren't for Democracy Now and such.

My understanding of how the story came to be is as follows: about a month ago they did a story where they interviewed two former FBI agents who are now members of Congress. I didn't hear the story as it aired but later found it and listened to it on the web. These congressmen said that if we're going to get on the war on terrorism, then we need people who speak Urdu, Basque, Farsi, Aymara, etc., (not the exact languages cited, but you get the picture). Apparently, some NPR listener wrote in and said that this sounded like the sort of thing anthropologists do, but that some anthropologists were resisting and opposing such work and sent on a copy of some of the critiques I've had in *Anthropology Today*.

I had some email exchanges and then odd phone calls with this twenty-year-old NPR intern, who really wanted to talk with CIA employed anthropologists, and was hell-bent on doing a "balanced" piece. I grew increasingly frustrated with him because my position was that the garbage these FBI/Congressmen had been spewing unchallenged on the air was unbalanced, and that a story presenting why anthropologists might oppose this war, or not contribute their skills to it, would be a small step towards correcting their imbalance. He told me that would go against their editorial policy. I think he started thinking that I was a lone "loony" (rather than a loony in good company...) after I lost my patience with him when a half hour into a conversation he asked for the 3rd time why would it be wrong for anthropologists to work for the CIA, obviously not understanding what I'd been saying about the problems of secrecy, nevermind having no historical conception of the CIA's history. When he started asking for names of others on both sides I named you, Cathy Lutz, Felix Moos, Anna Simons (who I don't know, but I am a discussant on a panel she's on at the AAA meetings this year on anthropology & warfare), and Carolyn Fluehr-Lobban.

I was glad to be done with them, but then they called and said they'd interviewed Lutz and Simons but they had no context for the piece, and then asked if I would do an interview on the history of anthropology and warfare. They had to work so hard to remove the political context of my interview that they spliced together different paragraphs in the same sentence. But all-in-all, I think the points that needed to be raised were raised by Cathy, who tells me they radically edited-back what she'd said.

One thing that I'm sure didn't come through in the transcript of the broadcast is the tone of the piece. The tone was clear, and as these things go that's very important. A few years ago, I moved my mother in-law into my neighborhood after she had a series of strokes. She is not fully functioning mentally, but she called me after the story aired and clearly hadn't understood the details of the argument, but she said "That woman from the military sounded like she was lying, she was too aggressive, interrupted, and sounded like she had something to hide." Bingo.

I am almost finished with the McCarthyism book's revisions (having cut almost 200 manuscripts pages, and carefully reworked the writing). I finished a long piece on American anthropology and the CIA for *Anthropology Today*, and listed you as a reader, though they seem to be wed to doing everything via email as they have such short deadlines.
Regards,

Dr. David Price
Professor of Anthropology
St. Martin's College

October 7, 2002
President Lawrence H. Summers

Harvard University
Cambridge, Massachusetts

Dear President Summers:

Your chilling position on dissent continues to disturb particularly because it falls right in with the Sharonites who would welcome the conflation of criticisms of Sharon-type policies with antagonism towards the Jewish people. As was noted in the *Chronicle of Higher Education*, it is possible to be against Israeli policies without being anti-Jewish or anti-Israel. I remind you of the famous 1948 letter to *The New York Times* (enclosed) in which Hannah Arendt, Albert Einstein, and other Jewish intellectuals made the same observations about Begin's policies.

Beyond the issue of Israeli policies today is the more general question of university policies regarding dissent. Are we to do McCarthy's job without a McCarthy? Slowly and over the past 15–20 years, I have noticed an antagonism toward debate in the country and in the academy, I teach about such matters. (Enclosed "Harmony Coerced is Freedom Denied" *Chronicle of Higher Education*). Note that in the last election Gore and Bush could not even get themselves to debate in the debates—extraordinary for a country that is exporting the idea of democracy worldwide. At this time, especially with all the talk of wars on terrorism and Iraq, it is unbecoming for a president of a great university to do anything that would chill debate, the scarcity of which is most obvious in our U.S. Congress.

When I was in graduate school at Harvard we believed that speaking up began at Harvard—that was where the trends were set. Given this flap on divestiture and Israel, following on the Cornell West debacle, it looks to some like you are leading Harvard in the opposite direction. "Unfortunate" would be an understatement if this be so.
Sincerely yours,

Laura Nader
Professor of Anthropology

November 4, 2002

Dear Professor Nader:

Thank you for your letter regarding my remarks at Morning Prayers. I spoke in the context of developments that I find troubling in the broad world and on the Harvard campus.

I certainly did not intend to imply that anyone who disagrees with Israeli policy is anti-Semitic. Having reread my address, I do not believe that is what I said. Indeed, I was explicit in saying: "There is much in Israel's foreign and defense policy that can be, and should be vigorously challenged."

My reference to "serious and thoughtful people advocating and taking actions that are anti-Semitic in their effect if not their intent" makes clear that in my judgment, certain actions that have been proposed or taken are anti-Semitic in their effect, without speaking to any individual's personal motivation.

A key point in my remarks was the idea that the University is singling out Israel for opprobrium would be extraordinary and inappropriate. Such singling out seems to me to be highly problematic, even if many disagree strongly with current Israeli policy.

Sincerely,

Lawrence H. Summers
Harvard University
Cambridge, MA

March 8, 2003

Dear Professor Nader:

What a pleasant invitation. I'd love to come to Berkeley and talk to the students about the current crisis and *Blowback,* but I am going to have to pass for now. I am writing the last chapter of my new book, *The Sorrows of Empire: How the Americans Lost Their Country,* to a deadline and I simply cannot put it aside. Also, at 71 I am not too frisky, partly thanks to rheumatoid arthritis. My goddaughter, a Brazilian woman who is an international flight attendant for Continental Airlines (she's actually laid-off because of 9/11 and is living in Shanghai studying Chinese), tells me that I have absolutely no business being in an airport these days. I think she's probably right. So I don't go much further than Los Angeles, where I can drive. I hope you understand, but I do not trust myself with Ashcroft's monkeys and the general paranoia surrounding civil aviation in the U.S. It's better to stay here and write. Perhaps next year if my publisher forces a "book trip" on me, Sheila and I will drive to the Bay Area for some bookstore appearances, and at that point I would love to speak to one of your (always) large classes.

Let me turn to your article, which I enjoyed very much. Your being visited by the Likudniks for assigning Peteet's *Gender in Crisis* is truly outrageous. It is why I am pleased to be out of academic life. You are quite right that young scholars cannot stand up to this pressure. That is one reason I wrote *Blowback.* I hoped in part to provide cover and space for a few young political scientists to say some things they want to say without having it come back to haunt them. As my former students said to me: you are invulnerable; if you won't take a stand, how can you even suggest that we should.

I also liked your list of the causes of the overall silence concerning the first Gulf War, particularly number 2: militarism. It is the subject of my new book but is close to taboo in our society. If you do not mind, I will send you some recent writing and journalism that you might find of interest. If you would send me your email address, I'll also send you a new preface to *Blowback* that the publisher is binding into new printings.

It might interest your students. It is entitled "The Blowback of September 11." Again, I appreciated your letter very much.
With Best Regards,

Dr. Chalmers Johnson
Japan Policy Research Institute

July 9, 2003
Pat Harrison

Editor—*Radcliffe Quarterly*
Cambridge, MA

Dear Pat Harrison:

I continue to read the *Quarterly* recalling the connection I had with the *Quarterly* when Aida Press was editor. The recent issue had two pieces featured about important subjects. "Promising Discoveries in Brain Research," was well done and informative. "Lethal School Violence" was paltry by contrast to what we know about the subject and the anxiety the subject generates in our country especially among young parents. To say that our best bet at prevention is to "coax kids who hear rumors to report them," grossly underestimates the possibilities for change in schools themselves. I suggest you might want to look into Alice Waters' *Edible Schoolyard* in Berkeley. Some 25 years ago, I studied school violence at Martin Luther King Jr. High and recommended structural changes that were not picked-up. Now Alice Waters is revolutionizing education at the same school through food. There is a lack of imagination in this country!
With all good wishes,

Laura Nader
Professor of Anthropology

August 14, 2003
Greg Starrett

Professor of Anthropology
University of North Carolina, Charlotte

Dear Greg Starrett,

Thank you for the revised copy of your paper. I enjoyed reading this elaborated version. The one comment I still have has to do with the "implicit comparison." It has increasingly been the problem that most anthropologists do not anticipate when they write about a subject—that is that the reader will make the implicit comparison. Thus, if one writes about abused women in India where no mention is made of the problem of abused women elsewhere (as in the US), the reader might think "those people" abuse their women absolving themselves and orientalizing the other.

In the case of your paper, what is the functional equivalent to suicide bombing on the other side in Israel? Learning from research such as yours such that we see it only part of the story. I often have the sense that the Sharonites of the world think they are fighting the Nazis. That is, they have displaced their aggression against the Germans by playing it out on the Palestinians. The other issue has to do with Muslim subjectiveness as if they were isolated or isolatable. I think that the work on the subject, eg. Mahmood, is as I have told her, ahistorical and decontextualized. Don't make the same mistake.

As I said at the AAA meeting, one job of the anthropologist is to break the academic taboos that get in the way of understanding. Your analysis is sophisticated but shrinks in importance because of the limited framing.

With all good wishes to you, and my appreciation for your having forwarded your interesting paper.
Sincerely yours,

Laura Nader
Professor of Anthropology

April 5, 2004
Hon. Jimmy Carter

The Carter Center
Atlanta, GA

Dear Jimmy Carter:

Some days ago, I read about your advice to my brother Ralph Nader. Somehow, the words you read did not fit as coming from you who are socially conscious.

In my work, I specialize in conflict resolution and mind colonization. Presently I am witnessing a bizarre spectacle, one in need of explanation: how can I explain why a Democrat at a unity gathering would yet again not go after the incumbent president who has a transparent record of misleading the Congress and the country, who has misspent tax money, who is destroying the Bill of Rights, but Ralph Nader? After all, 250,000 Democrats voted for Bush in Florida in 2000.

Our family grew up in Connecticut when we could register Independent and still vote for our candidate of choice. Then the Democratic Party was the workingman's party, the social justice party, but many New Deal ideas had come not primarily from party loyalists, but from independent progressive movements from the turn of the century, from the Midwest, from southern regions, some of them religious in inspiration. Today the Midwest and the South are increasingly voting Republican, voting against their own interests. That is a fact in desperate need of attention by the Democrats, at least those who do not have locked-down minds.

Even before 2002, Nader talked with Democrats in Congress and elsewhere on issues of strategy. Americans of like minds should be coming together to do something about defeating George W. Bush. Fear doesn't win elections and there is a shortage of ideas. It was in the early 70s that John Kenneth Galbraith, wrote a piece for *Harpers Magazine* titled "Who Needs the Democrats?"—warning of problems internal to the party. That was 30 years before Nader became a favored explanation of Democratic failure. Can you make a difference on these points with your fellow Democrats?
Sincerely,

Laura Nader
Professor of Anthropology
University of California, Berkeley

July 10, 2004
Celeste Robb-Nicholson, M.D.

Harvard Medical School
Boston, MA

Dear Dr. Robb-Nicholson:

Having been a guinea pig in an experiment on hormone therapy conducted by Dr. Somers Sturgis while I was a graduate student at Radcliffe College, I was particularly interested in the piece on "Hormone Therapy's Unanswered Questions." I used to think it would be different if women were in charge—I no longer think so.

The unanswered questions for me are: what do the experimenters do about their subjects? In my case the several high doses of premarin, progesterone, etc., resulted in breast cancer. Dr. Sturgis did not keep his data beyond 5 years when I asked him about the other 19 women in the "study." What the reader wants to know in the case of your newsletter is what happened to the trial participants when there was 40% increased stroke risk in estrogen takers? Whose responsibility? Was the trial worth the risk to those generous participants in scientific experiments?

The crass ending to the article in question was "more questions, more research." How about "more questions, more responsibility?"

Thank you for your attention.

Sincerely yours

Laura Nader
Professor of Anthropology

August 24, 2005

Dear Laura,

Your letter mailed in July arrived two days ago. Sorry to hear that the air-conditioned conference and plane and hotels and all have given you a month of back injury. I hope you had some good warm weather and the back responded by settling down comfortably. Otherwise, the time in the east with grandchildren who like libraries sounds delightful. I'm glad you had Tarek to help cope with Norman's house as well as Jose. Concern about this must all add to the tension that is anything but good for your back.

Monday I mailed off to you via airmail, the signed sheet on Jessica's dissertation. I did not send it express mail since the date for submission was already past by the time I received the form. As I said, usually I expected to read the revised draft before signing, especially when the earlier draft required as much revision as this one did, but in the circumstances, I accepted your judgement that the dissertation was ready. In her e-mail, Jessica said that you had told her I should just sign without reading again. Sorry that the form was so late in reaching me, but I had warned everyone that I was not in constant touch with any form of communication.

In fact, I was at a conference in Lusaka sponsored by the University of Leiden dealing with Zambian history. Disappointingly, few Zambian Scholars took part, though I could not find out why. They may have found at the last moment that they couldn't do the promised paper, but also some who might have come just to listen and discuss didn't show. There was a conflict with the beginning of a new term and a threatened strike by administrative staff at the university. But there were people from Netherlands, Germany, Finland, England, U.S.A., South Africa, as well as local Europeans and a few Zambians. And some interesting papers. James Ferguson was there and much cited. Some of us who have known Zambia a very long time found intriguing how the younger people read particular periods of Zambian history: it is very easy to misinterpret when you don't know the larger context. And while some of them had done intensive work on a particular time and place, it is difficult to clue in when so much of what is happening is taken for granted at the time as background information and so remains implicit. And it is so very easy to project back in time what one sees oneself at a later date as important and therefore thinks this must have been inevitable, whereas at the time there were any number of different outcomes that might have been possible.

After the conference, I brought back with me an old friend whom I first knew as a little girl in Nampeyo back in the 1940s. She went on to become the wife of a major politician and diplomat who has lived in Washington, Peking, Paris, and London, but remains very much a village woman at heart. We went to Mujika and Nampeyo, where I worked in the 1940s, where she has kin, and found a warm welcome everywhere. But other than that she was bored, for she is used to being active with her hands, in her garden or in her house. I have also had a visit from a chap whose parents were here in the 1940s, and whom I met as a baby. He is married to a lovely Belgian woman and they live in Belgium. We went hunting for the house where his parents lived on the Monze Agricultural station and then drove down to Chipepo Harbour on Kariba Lake over what is now only a bad road—it was dreadful when I went down two years ago. So now that I have a car of my own, I shall try to go to Sinafala and find out what has been happening there.

The car is a short-wheel base land cruiser, manual, diesel (and of course as soon as I got it there was a diesel shortage in Zambia), which Rabson (driver/gardener) declares is a fine vehicle despite the fact that we had to take it back immediately because a light kept coming on when it should not have done so. That has been corrected. Therefore, we should be able to reach Sinafala and Siameja and Musulumba, which I want to do before the heat really sets in. The Valley can be pretty dreadful in the heat. So that means several trips to the Valley within the next few weeks. Meanwhile, this week I am spending two days at the celebration of the centenary of the founding of Chikuni mission back in 1905 by the Jesuits. The Bishop of Monze has given me a special invitation and intimated that I shall sit among the notables. This means I must dig out a skirt and I am not looking forward to it. Fortunately I have one.

Problems here? Zambian plumbing seems to have a talent for getting out of whack. There is a water shortage on the farm, which means that most days now we have water only part of the day. Books are expensive, and to find even a reasonably mediocre bookstore one has to go to Lusaka. We still can't do e-mail from the farm. But on the whole things are going well. Judith Justice took a lot of pictures of house and garden and farm while she was here, and so you may have some idea of the surroundings.

Term must have started. Always a busy time. I hope that people return geared towards amiability, and interested in getting on with things. May your back cooperate.

I look forward to some walks along Bay and Tilden. I have not been walking much here. My exercise comes mainly from climbing in and out of cars which require a big step up.

Love,

Elizabeth Colson
Professor of Anthropology
Monze, Zambia

September 29, 2005
Dr. Vartan Gregorian

President
Carnegie Corporation of New York

Dear Vartan,

It was with pleasure that I read headlines in *Anthropology News* in September—"Carnegie Encourages Anthropological Research on Islam, and the Modern World." A closer look however, causes me to write you of my concerns.

First, I noted that the three Carnegie Scholars were all white males and American. Ok, I am not hung-up on that per se, but as Karen Hughes is finding out, the foremost area of disagreement about Islam and the West is that of the women's place. I then took an even closer look at Lawrence Rosen's stated purpose in relation to his work on four Moroccan men and couldn't help feeling that Orientalism was alive and well, as is also indicated by his work on Islamic law ala Weber. Then I looked even closer at the fine print and realized that it was not an open competition: "individuals must be nominated by an invited nominator (pre-selected by Carnegie) in order to be considered." For me this was the most discouraging observation.

From my vantage point at Berkeley, the supposed site of free-speech—open and free dialogue is closing down in this country. Only people like you can make a difference. Please do.

With all my best wishes, always.

Sincerely yours,

Laura Nader
Professor of Anthropology
University of California, Berkeley

June 24, 2006
Leland Y. Yee, Ph.D.

California State Assembly
Sacramento, CA

Dear Assemblyman Yee:

As a faculty member at UC Berkeley and as a citizen of this state I write to express my strong support for your bill AB 775, to amend Section 92020 et seq. of the Education Code regarding Open Meeting Law for the University of California. It is my understanding that the language you propose will extend the open meeting requirements to cover not only "the Board of Regents of the University of California and its standing and special committees or subcommittees," but in addition "advisory groups that include as members one or more regents and that have continuing subject matter jurisdiction or regularly scheduled meetings." Such a move is long overdue.

I have taught at Berkeley for over forty years and while I have experienced Regents both responsible and irresponsible, overall the Board of Regents of the University of California may be amongst the most unregulated university board of regents in the country. Secretive practices of the Regents seem only to have increased, as documented by my colleague Charles Schwartz, in spite of established principles in California open meetings law, and in co. with "other" public agencies in California. We need more accountability and transparency and possibly an Independent Inspector General if we are to have a public informed of what decisions are being made and by whom. Needless to say, I also support your amendment to Section 92032(b) (7) concerning open session consideration of executive compensation.

Thank you for your contributions to open government.

Sincerely,

Laura Nader
Professor of Anthropology

July 31, 2006

Dear Laura:

Thank you for giving me the opportunity to meet you personally. Over the years, I have admired what I have read from your pen, including and especially your views on the state of American anthropology, the comparative analysis of the domination of women, and the structure and behavior of the ruling machinery of the United States during the Cold War. In fact, some of my inspiration to write about the Cold War framework of North American anthropology of Afghanistan comes from your writings.

I have had a previous glance at some of the items in the package of writings you gave me. A second reading was enriching. In your graduation talk, the invitation to compare the Mongol Empire with its American version is quite instructive and I hope you will develop it for publication. Please allow me to comment on a specific point in this paper.

The popular and elite cultures of the Middle East (and I can speak confidently for the Iranian Plateau) view the Chengizid Mongol Imperial Era and experience with a degree of pride and satisfaction in spite of the violence and destruction associated with it. Chengiz, Helagu, Timurlane, and their successors are folk-heroes, albeit bloody and cruel ones. The Mongol-looking Hazara of the central highland of Afghanistan view themselves as descendants of Mongol armies. The Hazara owe their minority status to Shi'a Islam rather than to their Mongol descent. Of course, all Turkic people (Uzbek, Turkoman, Kirghiz, etc.) are considered connected to Mongols and Chengiz Khan. If an Afghan referred to the American occupiers as Mongol or Chengizid, they will be elevating them and equating them with the Hazaras and the Turkic people, especially of Central Asia, something they would not mean to do.

Afghans (including the Pashtun dominated Taleban) do (and will) not equate Americans with Mongols. The popular Afghan appellations for Americans and things American are *kafer* (infidel, impious, heathen, unbeliever, etc.), *wahshi* (wild, undomesticated), *sharabi* (drunkard, alcohol consumer, defiled), *khuk* (pig-like in color and skin, dirty), and *benamus* (without honor connected to their women). On a somewhat related issue: the Afghan intellectual elite of the 1930s portrayed Hitler as an anti-English, anti-colonial hero. These intellectuals thought very highly of Germans and the Third Reich. D-Day was a sad day in Afghanistan. Afghans were sold on the thesis that they were "Aryans" with special cultural and biological ties to Germans. Afghanistan is equated with "Aryana," land of the Aryans. This view continues to be a major element in individual and collective self-definitions among Afghans. Much of what modern Afghanistan is, and how it is understood by Afghans themselves, is constructed with elements derived from the country's colonial experience and encounters with European domination.

I enjoyed reading the paper on "Promise or Plunder?" and wish to comment on the section dealing with law in Afghanistan. I had read Barfield's article in the 2002 CJIL [*Chicago Journal of International Law*]. What he says applies to the current scene: a scene in which center and periphery are disconnected and pieces of the periphery have necessarily become fragmented and autonomous. In his earlier writings (like other Afghan specialists), Barfield wrote approvingly of the disintegration of the country inflicted by American sponsored mujahedin terrorists. In the 1980s, Barfield viewed Afghanistan as rampant with tribal and ethnic conflicts but a place where the soft state held its pieces together. And he was right because there was a fairly stable system of shari'a courts extending to sub-district levels run by the Ministry of Justice and buttressed by the Ministries of Interior and Defense. Barfield correctly characterizes the Afghan scene of those days as a highly developed local system of law and justice within very underdeveloped state structures. But, he neglects to explicitly tell his readers that the current scene is the direct result of the 1992 American-sponsored destruction of the Afghan center—the machinery that held together the highly developed local system.

In the early days of the American occupation, Barfield was quoted in the media as saying that there was no ethnic conflict in Afghanistan! In his 2005 *Current History* (vol. 104) piece he applauds the "elections" in Afghanistan and declares the Karzai government "legitimate!" He says nothing of the fairly stable judiciary throughout Afghanistan before the American rulers set out to avenge Vietnam on the turf of the fragile Afghan state. But I must be fair. Barfield is the most level-headed and most professional of North American anthropologists specializing in Afghanistan. On the destruction of Afghanistan by the United States, please see 2004 AN note enclosed herewith. Enclosed also is the *Iranian Studies* issue in which Barfield takes his usual Weberian look at Afghanistan. My article on hegemony through the Loya Jerga in this issue might also interest you.

I am surprised by your assessment of David Edwards's piece in AQ [*Anthropological Quarterly*] 75(1): 166. Edwards was a rabid supporter of the mujahedin terrorists. He accompanied them in their terrorist forays into Afghanistan. His dissertation and two books on Afghanistan are based on what these terrorists told him and translated for him from local languages at his base in Peshawar, Pakistan. His use of the "last stand" metaphor in the AQ article is consistent with the overall cowboy approach to Afghanistan by American anthropologists. I see nothing eloquent in his 2002 AQ piece. The article is a patchwork of his journalistic writings. I enclose my review of his latest book in the AA and the exchange with one of his admirers.

Virtually all US educated anthropologists specializing in Afghanistan, those who wrote their doctoral dissertations about Afghanistan, have heated anti-communist passions. These passions are transparent in what they have circulated as anthropological writings. And every one of them (except Ashraf Ghani) has published political commentary condemning the revolutionary government of Afghanistan, promoting Islam, and the American sponsored mujahedin terrorists in the aftermath of the 1978 overthrow of the Afghan monarchy. However, Ghani is unique in that he has openly participated in the construction of the American imperial presence in Afghanistan and the Kabul puppet government from which he has now been estranged.

I am fascinated by how Ashraf Ghani has become so popular in some corners of North American anthropology, mostly among some friends and admirers of the late Eric Wolf, and coddled as their Europeanized exotic "Afghan." A major reason for Ghani's popularity is that he has rarely faced an informed and critical academic audience, especially in matters dealing with the ethnology of Afghanistan and the general Middle East. His printed chapters are totally ignored by anthropological specialists of the Middle East, Central, and South Asia.

There is virtually nothing anthropological in Ghani's writings. The labels political science and journalism are more fitting. His 1982 Ph.D. thesis is a mysterious document—essentially a series of unusually long quotations mostly from European historians and colonial writers of Afghanistan. The document is, for all practical purposes, a duplication of his 1977 MA thesis in political science at the American University of Beirut which is now available on OCLC. Until the early 1990s, the MA thesis was sealed and non-circulating. However, there is nothing new about Afghanistan in either document. He has a knack for distorting important aspects of Afghan history and ethnography. For examples, please see my 2004 AN note and the Loya Jerga paper.

Ghani has repeatedly referred to his "fieldwork" in Afghanistan both in his writings and public speeches. But I have never seen anything in his work that is based on ethnographic specificity. Ghani, working together with his classmate Zalmay Khaiilzad, was directly involved in organizing the non-military aspects of the American occupation of Afghanistan, fully expecting to be appointed by the neocolonialists to the top job in Afghanistan. He is among those neo-liberal "native anthropologists," virtually all trained in the United States, who favor radical change—modernization and Europeanization of others. And he did this for more than ten years at the World Bank. During his tenure as minister of finance in the government of Kabul he wrote journalistic pieces in which he solicited Western capital investment in Afghanistan. Recently he has made the naive and silly observation that: the biggest enemy of democracy in Afghanistan is "a flower"—meaning poppies! Like other agents of the American imperial presence in Afghanistan, Ghani regularly reminds citizens of Afghanistan of their "inferiority" and "backwardness"—that if they want to become real human beings they should become European like himself. He and his younger brother, Hashmat, are closely associated with a number of NGOs to the thousands of which Afghanistan has been privatized.

Ghani is a remarkably impressive conversationalist but his good intellect is overshadowed by impatience (especially with Afghans) and bad temper. Reports have circulated in the Afghan local and diaspora media about his arrogance, violent temper tantrums in public, and instability. Not surprisingly, he seems to get along well only with a few European journalists (and a prominent American political scientist "specializing" in Afghanistan) with whom he has co-authored a number of market driven papers. His inability to get along especially with Afghan intellectuals, technocrats, and the former mujahedin terrorists (now in key positions of the government he helped create), along with his zealous pro-European attitude has marginalized him to the Kabul University post where he is both isolated and not very much liked. He is ill at ease with spontaneous scholarly and professional conversation in the languages of the culture of Afghanistan.

I am not sure about Ghani's prospects for the UNSG [United Nations Secretary-General] post. If he makes it, like you I would say, "it could be worse!" And we will all wish him success and stable mental and physical health. But unlike you, I believe the American occupation and administration of Afghanistan which Ghani actively facilitated (and continues to promote) was the worst thing that could happen to that country. The country has been forced to live under the flimsy roof of a neoliberal phony democracy, good only for drug-running, profiteering by NGOs, and a staging area for Central Asian markets and labor pools. The roof is held up only by a few hastily raised sticks that are doomed to crumble sooner than later. I believe Ghani, down deep in his soul, knows this. As an anthropologist, I understand this and move on sighing in disgust. The ethical and moral bankruptcy of Ghani's zealous participation in neoliberal realism does not surprise me. My anthropological understanding of supersonic capitalist expansion is inspired by Eric Wolf's refrain that Ghani's imperial master is solely interested in "techniques over purpose, the how of political relations over their whys and wherefores . . . what matters is the world as given . . . not how 'we' got there, but that 'we' are 'there'" (Southern Anthropological Society Proceedings, no. 3, 1969, p. 3). It would be quite timely to field a panel at the 2007 AAA meetings on an anthropological framing of the consequences of the convergence of neoliberalism, American high-speed capitalism, and Zionist fascism in the state structure of the United States for Afghanistan, Iran, Iraq, Lebanon, and Palestine. The June 2006 issue of *Current Anthropology* has an interesting article on a specific aspect of this proposition. You could provide the theoretical framework for the panel, I will speak about Afghanistan. There are plenty of authors for the other countries.

Have you read the recent paper on Israeli lobby by the political scientists Stephen Walt (Harvard) and John Mearsheimer (Chicago)? I could email it to your department and they can print it for you.

I would appreciate information about your upcoming publication by the World Bank.

Best wishes.

Dr. Jamil Hanifi
Okemos, MI

January 25, 2007
Hon. Jimmy Carter

The Carter Center
Atlanta, GA.

Dear Jimmy Carter:

Thank you for writing your book. *Palestine, Peace Not Apartheid* is about the obvious. It is also about a subset that is taboo for forthright discussion in the United States. I have been teaching the Anthropology of the Middle East at Berkeley since 1960—any discussion of even the absence of discussion of the Palestine/Israeli question brings on the sort of reaction you know well. I have had Israeli consuls speak to my class, Palestinians and myself lecture on the question from the anthropological viewpoint—it doesn't matter, there is only one side up for discussion and this is a university campus.

So thank you again. You may be interested to know that a New York based photographer visited Bethlehem during the Christmas season to document the plight of Christians there, so few are left—an exhibit that all thinking Americans should see when and if it opens here. And to questions about the word apartheid, one need only look at a roadmap.

All good wishes,

Laura Nader
Professor of Anthropology

January 30, 2007

To Professor Nader:

Thank you. I hope you'll never be intimidated.
Best Wishes,

Jimmy Carter
Atlanta, GA

June 6, 2007

Dear Laura,

May you be having a beautiful summer with lots of good fruit, warm weather, and some rest from the eternal grind. But enough going on to keep you interested.

I see that Wolfowitz finally resigned. *The Economist* seems to think the man who is replacing him will be better, but only if he decides he serves a public other than Bush. Valerie Estes was pleased when *The New York Times* backed

FIGURE 7. President Carter and I had previously met when he was an invited speaker at the University of California, Berkeley in 2000. Photograph from author's collection.

the appointment of Ashraf, but I never thought there would be the ghost of a chance that he would be appointed. Nor am I sure that he would have been happy in the post. It is a pleasure to escape from all the political posturing that is going on. I see a paper perhaps twice a week, which is more interested in Zambia than in the USA but is giving rather a lot of coverage now to South America and the building of the coalition against the U.S. I buy *The Economist* if I go to Lusaka which is about once a month.

So what do I do with myself? Not much. The first week was largely devoted to sleep—the trip out was not easy, especially since Heathrow as usual failed to supply a wheelchair. Then I have been trying to get my laptop to connect with the internet from here, and so far although five people have tried to set it up (two of them professionals), I am still having to go to an internet cafe and use one of its machines. When I arrived, Emily Frank was still here, she finished her dissertation at Indiana based on work here about a year ago and was back trying to extend her dissertation work. Lisa Cliggett arrived last week and is in Zambia for about 6 weeks all told. A young Zambian woman who has lived in England for 19 years (has a BA and also an MBA and now works for the U.S. Embassy in London having previously worked for Barclays Bank and Ford) stopped by to talk with me about her dissertation on how NGOs are effecting the status of Tonga women in an area to the south of here. She is coming back before she leaves sometime in July. She is doing degree at Westminster University in London. An American student from Hopkins is coming by next week. I have also been waiting for copies of my book on Tonga religion to reach the country. Supplies for here were sent by sea and have at least reached Durbin according to the last information the publisher has been able to get. So I still have the pleasure of giving that to some people here. And I have started reading the edited volume "The Manchester School" on which I agreed to write a comment for in *Current Anthropology*. I rather think I may argue that a Manchester School is a figment of the desire to have in-groups rather than any coherent intellectual focus that distinguished people from what others were doing. A lot of what is said to be distinctive, seems to me to have been rather common themes in the social sciences of the time. But I may change my mind as I progress.

And sometime this month I shall visit research assistants in Gwembe and that may stir me to some new writing.

Best wishes,

Elizabeth Colson
Professor of Anthropology
Monze, Zambia

April 5, 2008

Dear Dr. Nader,

The profound impact you had on my life began the first day I walked into your Law and Anthropology class at UC Berkeley in 1973 (or maybe it was 1974?). I couldn't believe how lucky I was to be in a classroom taught by someone with a perspective similar to my own uneducated sense of how things really are—versus what they are purported to be.

Galvanized by your insight through lectures and suggested reading (I read everything ever mentioned in your class, in addition to the reading list) I earned an A+ as a final grade in your class, and on the postcard announcing my final grade, you wrote "Thank you!"

I began to study law, thinking I could use the insights you sparked to make a change. Life intervened, and after graduating from law school and barely beginning law practice, my second child was born with life-threatening medical disabilities called VATER Assoc., a very rare group of congenital anomalies.

I became her advocate, and gradually as mothers, teachers, nurses, doctors, bureaucrats, and administrators around me saw the kind of advocacy I provided for my child, I was asked to "help" another mother, and another, and another. I provided all counsel on a pro bono basis because I couldn't bring myself to charge other mothers, who like me, were nearly destitute because of their children's overwhelming medical costs. In 1998, I declared bankruptcy, became a single mother, and literally relied on the kindness of my friends and family for sustenance.

I am writing to you for two reasons. First, to thank you for your inspiration. I hated school before your course—thinking seemed to be something that was discouraged in other classes demanding memorization and regurgitation. Because of your ability to appreciate my mind's products, I gained a confidence that carries me through to this day. I have passed along your gift to my own students. The second reason I am writing is that I believe I would best function in our society as a community lawyer/applied anthropologist in the field of medical anthropology.

Specifically, I am very interested in addressing the causes of violence in our society. I believe these causes are due to an inadequate amount of skin contact by infants with their mothers. I think the psychoanalytic view of infant rage caused by not "sufficiency" is a cause of later violence. The issue of breastfeeding v. bottle-feeding is my particular concern. I would like to spend the rest of my life working to increase the number of mothers who breastfeed, and increase the length of time that each infant is breastfed.

I understand that there may be a Ph.D. program in applied medical anthropology. Do you have any suggestions which would provide me with the tools

I need to investigate and address breastfeeding in America as a lawyer/community advocate/applied anthropologist? I do think that a degree in the subject would help my credibility, particularly since all of my education occurred before the advent of computers and the internet. I graduated in 1976, earning a B.A. from Cal's then-undergraduate School of Journalism, with a minor in Anthropology. I then attended U.C. Hastings College of Law, working more than 60hrs a week while attending my first two years of classes. My resume is included for your review.

Again, and again, and again—thank you so very much for influencing me. It was an unparalleled joy to be your student. And 34 years (or so) later, I am still affected by you and your description of that little village in Oaxaca, and the alcade's task to maintain balance.

All the best, always,

Nan Waldman
Santa Monica, CA

August 8, 2008

Dear Laura,

You haven't heard from me because technology stands in the way. My old computer would not work resenting being left idle for six months in heat. Judith bought me out a new computer, which comes with the most recent Microsoft system installed. Everyone agrees that it is a disaster and it is. It swallows work. And it would not work with my old printer. So I have a new printer. And still things do not go well and I get discouraged.

Otherwise, things go well enough. In June there was the Tonga Workshop organized by Lisa Cliggett from the University of Kentucky, and Ginny Bond a medical anthropologist who lives in Zambia. Lots of discussion. A few good papers. Others contained useful ideas or information. Lots of ideas for good research projects occurred to me, but I have no idea if anyone will ever pick up on them. One would be a good study of one of the small towns on the railway line, by an economic historian or an economic geographer. It's clear that a lot is happening, as they are expanding rapidly and I have no idea where the capital is coming from or who is investing in what or who they are. Then, nobody today seems to know what makes a legal marriage—my namesake who is a judge in the high court agrees with me that this is an important issue. And the role of international capital in the resurgence of chieftaincy and in generating hostilities between chieftaincies is fascinating. On the whole, I enjoyed it. But Bonnie Keller and Ute Luig both legged off coming on the grounds of recent illness. After that, some house guests of various nation-alities. In between, I have managed to get to one Gwembe village to see a research assistant and to one Plateau village just to see old friends. And been doing some reading. I found Carolyn Nordstrom's new book *Global Outlaws* fascinating—written with zest but I did wish that sometimes she would settle for one adjective instead of feeling the more the merrier. She traces the flow of goods, money, and people through illegal channels, working from roadside markets in Angola through long-distance lorry traffic, ports, and shipping, and gets the views of drivers, roustabouts, embassy people, police, port offi-cials, corporation officials, etc., etc.

And now I am just starting Anna Tsing's book *Friction* which puts together the interplay between international capital, national political order, local people, environmental activists and much else by considering the dev-astation of the Kelamantan rainforests. Younger people are doing some very exciting work. And they demonstrate the importance of what is happening elsewhere in the world. Despite the belief of George Bush and Paul Rabi-now that the only game in town is right here and nothing else needs to be considered.

Outside anthropology I've also just finished a magnificent book by Doris Goodwin, *Team of Rivals: The Political Genius of Abraham Lincoln*. It examines the strategies that led to Lincoln's election and how he then coped with his cabinet and the issues that faced him. Inspiring. It is very long but I found it difficult to put down.

I hope the summer has been a good and productive one. And that Rania's baby has arrived and is as fine a baby as Sebastian.
My best,

Elizabeth Colson
Professor of Anthropology
Monze, Zambia

January 19, 2009

Dear Dr. Nader:

I was referred to you by Caspar Rivera-Salgado of UCLA. I am currently representing a man from Taniche, Oaxaca. Taniche is located in El Districto de Ejulta de Crespo en Region Valles Centrales. From what I understand, Taniche is located in central Oaxaca.

I am currently representing my client on a murder case. My client allegedly killed his cousin because his cousin was having an affair with my client's wife.

My client's wife admitted to the affair and there was rumor that their second child belonged to the cousin.

This affair became common knowledge in the Oaxacan community here in Chino. My client stated that his cousin, "Me puso los cuernos," (metaphorically) placed horns on his head and as a result he felt shunned, ridiculed, and unworthy of being a man. My client claims that the entire community looked down at him because he failed as man by not being able to hang on to his woman, which impacted him psychologically and caused him to act in the manner that he did.

My client confronted his cousin about this affair and agreed to engage in a "Reto a la muerte," which we understand this to mean a "Duel to the Death." They had one encounter and they were separated by family.

The second encounter resulted in the death of the cousin. Here in Chino, a good portion of the Hispanic population is from Taniche. Most of these people live and work together. From what I understand, they seldom socialize or go outside of their group.

My client and his family claim they are descendants of Zapotecs but they do not speak the language. Their customs appear to be markedly different from the general population of Mexico.

We have been unable to find any literature or studies done on this metaphor "Me puso los cuernos," "Reto a la muerte" or its psychological or sociological impact. Could you please direct us to some literature, studies or articles that have addressed or discussed these subjects? Do you know of any studies on how Oaxacan men deal with issues of infidelity among their culture?

If you have any opinions on this subject matter from your perspective, I would certainly appreciate them. We certainly appreciate any guidance you can offer us and we thank you in advance for your professional courtesy and cooperation in this matter.

Yours very truly,

Eduardo M. Madrid
Madrid Law Firm
Chino, CA

June 29, 2009
Dr. Mark G. Yudof

University of California President
Oakland, CA

Dear President Yudof:

Thank you for eliciting response from faculty and staff in regards to the current UC budget. Since you are new to UC, I begin my response with a brief review of legislative history. Comments that follow flow from that history. First, the promise. The Organic Act of the University of California (1868), Sec. 31,14:

> "Any resident of California of the age of fourteen years or upwards of approved moral character shall have the right to enter himself in the University as a student at large and receive tuition in any branch or branches of instruction . . . For the time being, an admission fee and rates of tuition such as the Board of Regents shall deem expedient may be required of each pupil; and as soon as the income of the University shall permit, admission and tuition shall be free to all residents of the state. . . "

The goal was never achieved. In fact, fees were raised, and a tax was instituted for residents of the state to help pay for the operation. The original philosophy that the University, as a public institution should be accessible and within the financial means of every resident regardless of economic class and status has withered. The third president of the University, Daniel Coit Gilman, best articulated the original philosophy:

"This is the University of California. It is not the University of Berlin, or of New Haven which we are to copy . . . It is the University of the State . . . It is not the foundation of an ecclesiastical body or of the private individuals. It is 'of the people and for the people,' . . . It opens the door to superior education to all without regard to price."

Other and much poorer countries than the U.S. went on to achieve the goal of free higher education, leaving the U.S. behind. More recently, the California legislature passed an amendment: "Regents will be able persons broadly reflective of the economic, cultural, and social diversity of the state . . . 1974 amendment to Art IX, Sec. 9."

Politically selected Regents have not husbanded the University. Most have been negligent in their budgetary responsibilities, unaccountable on policy questions, deaf to students, staff, and faculty concerns, and disdainful of the very people who make a university great.

In a non-profit educational system there is no ethical place for comparisons with profit-making corporations and U.S. CEO pay that astonishes even CEOs in other countries. Like any entrenched bureaucracy, the U.C. administration has a vested interest in expanding its domain (see attached), and the regents have refused to undertake an investigation of millions of dollars wasted annually in overblown administration. (I am told that in Quebec less than 10% by law is allowed for administration). The University administration has grown out of proportion to its purpose. Legitimacy is in question when the president's salary exceeds non-profit status and the football coach's salary far exceeds the president's!

Intercollegiate sports? No word of cuts? A new sports center, fixing the stadium? If it is true that this is what most alums want, then faculty have done a poor job in educating. Everybody should read Sperber's book *Beer and Circus* on how inter-collegiate sports destroys undergraduate education.

In the context of the above and more, the options you present do not make sense. U.C. has a lot of loyal workers who are here because we are non-profit. The U.C. system in the past has been dubbed the worst university employer in the state. When you assumed office the morale was already at a very low level, and I say this from the vantage of a professor who has been at U.C. for nearly half a century. We need ethical judgment in the leadership, not *fail accompli*. We also need public debate. The Academic Senate has failed. Professor Schwartz's findings have been dismissed but never debated. What crisis? An ethical crisis not a budgetary one. Continuing the same path will lead to further deterioration of UC, in spite of boasting. Take direction from President Gilman or more recently from Chancellor Tien who donated part of his excessive salary for student scholarships.

Sincerely yours,

Laura Nader
Professor of Anthropology

June 30, 2009

Thank you for taking the time to write and share your thoughts on the furlough/salary reduction plan options the University is considering implementing. I hope you will understand that because of the tremendous volume of mail I have reviewed on this subject, I am sending the same response to all.

Please know that we welcome your views and concerns. I want to assure you that your comments rebelling were reviewed by my staff and we will take them into consideration as we move through the planning process.

Our faculty and staff are an essential part of what makes this institution so great, and I very much appreciate your dedicated efforts not only in good years, but most especially in these very difficult times.

With best wishes, I am. . .

Sincerely yours,

Mark G. Yudof
President—University of California
Oakland, CA

July 10, 2009

Dear Laura Nader,

Many thanks for your kind comments on my paper and for forwarding copies of two recent papers. You ask what my plans are in regard to publishing the paper? In the short term, I will publish a short version together with four papers by individuals who attended the conference last April in an issue of a new British journal called *The Journal of Legal Anthropology*. The issue will focus on how immigration law works comparatively, three papers are on the U.K. and two focus on the U.S. Hopefully it will be out in late 2010.

I also hope to publish a somewhat extended version; probably in a U.S. legal journal, perhaps you might have some suggestions as to which journals might be most appropriate. The individual whose case I follow in the paper is still imprisoned and his case is not concluded partly because his appeal is not fully exhausted but also because the British Government can renew the control order every 12 months without giving new reasons. His legal team have not allowed me to speak with him about the case for fear of undermining his defense; though as the paper argues it is impossible to defend a person held in such conditions. I am also seeking his permission to interview one of his legal team for further information about his hearing last July. I lack key information on the role of the government appointed "Special Advocate." It needs to be slightly updated in terms of the broader political and legal environment (but this material I already possess).

It may be of interest to you that the academic that you quote in your paper "What the Rest Think of the West," Issa Shivji, is an old acquaintance. My first teaching job was at the University of Dar es Salaam. Issa is what I call an unreconstructed Marxist whose politics date from the late sixties; his heart and soul are in the right place as he has done important legal work in Tanzania, but he finds it impossible to engage with "liberal" arguments and analyses. He is among a minority of aging left-wing scholars in Tanzania.
Yours,

John Campbell
University of London
School of Oriental and African Studies

July 30, 2009

Dear Laura,

You might enjoy the enclosed articles, particularly the part about restorative justice and its anthropological aspects. Judge Greenberg told me he liked your book and is still thinking about doing a review. I asked him to get in touch with you.

I'm out trapped by Washington—hundreds of billions of evildoers, virtually nothing for consumers. It is the greatest shift of wealth from the middle and working classes to the wealthy that we've ever seen.
Warmest regards,

George Brunn
Ret. Judge
Berkeley, CA

October 8, 2009

Dear Professor Nader:

I am writing in response to your handwritten note of September 21, which was attached to a letter you sent in June. I want you to know that I did indeed respond to your letter. Your assistant noted in her e-mail forwarding your letter, "If you choose to reply to her by email, please do so to this email address" so my response acknowledging your letter was sent to her on June 30.

I do appreciate having your thoughts, but I will not debate each of your points about the decisions my colleagues and I are taking in these very difficult economic times. You may be interested in the enclosed piece I wrote that recently appeared the *Chronicle of Higher Education*. I think you will find it addresses many of the issues raised in your letter. Let me just add that I believe in public higher education. I have spent my entire professional career working for public universities. The University of California is a treasured public asset and I see my role as trying to preserve its excellence and accessibility in the face of unprecedented budget cuts.

As public support through the State dwindles, the University needs to debate the alternatives. We will not give up on the goal of obtaining adequate State support; however, we cannot ignore the trend over the last twenty years of continuous State disinvestment in the University. We are not, should not, and never will be a private university, but we need to examine all viable revenue options, many of which are already used in public higher education in other states and other nations. As I mention in the *Chronicle* article, it would be easy to allow U.C. to slide into mediocrity, but that is unacceptable, and I assure you it will not happen on my watch. Difficult decisions and choices need to be made to avoid that fate.

As you know, I am not the one who chooses the Regents. I believe the Regents take their responsibilities seriously and are hard-working, engaged, and competent individuals who care very much about the future of the University. The faculty, staff, students, campuses, the Office of the President, and the Regents need to work together to address the major challenges we face. We need to come up with creative solutions to the funding dilemma that can garner the support of Californians and their elected officials. To that end, the U.C. Commission on the Future that Regent Russ Gould and I are co-chairing will be a venue to discuss and debate these tough issues and to seek new and innovative approaches such as some of those you refer to in your attachment.

I urge you to join with us in this effort to improve U.C. Constructive ideas are always welcome. Destructive attempts to place blame on U.C. leadership for the impact on the University that are due to State budget cuts and a general economic crisis do not further our common goal of preserving U.C.'s excellence as a public university.

With best wishes, I am...

Sincerely yours,
Mark G. Yudof
University of California President
Oakland, CA

December 23, 2009

Dear Professor Nader,

I heard you speak on the radio during the recent demonstrations at U.C. Berkeley against the orchestrated assault on affordable public education in California. In the past, I have taught at both the secondary and university levels in the United States and France, but presently I am teaching in a continuation school for the Los Angeles Unified School District, where I am given the students who have either been thrown out of regular high schools or are on juvenile parole.

It is my belief that virtually every problem this country presently faces is a symptom of the underlying disease, which is the premeditated failure to adequately educate our citizenry in this putative democracy. In my more paranoid moments, I think this is done to avoid the confrontation of the same type of misguided governmental policy that existed during the Vietnam War era.

In any case, I am tired of waiting for somebody else to fix public education, so I have built perdaily.com (Public Education Reform), which I foresee as a virtual commons where those who share my concerns can come to learn, share what they know, and network cross platform with the vast majority of people in this country that share our beliefs. I have discussed what I built on my own dime with Craig Newmar, who built Craigslist, and he thinks that sites like this have the same potential for the 21st century in redressing the balance of power as Guttenberg's Bible had for the middle of the 15th century.

It is clear that corporate owned media, whether it is radio, television, or papers like the *Los Angeles Times,* have their own agenda. Short of Amy Goodman's Democracy Now, the vast majority of Americans are kept ignorant and apathetic—this is something that I find especially pernicious among my fellow teachers, who should be the most optimistic people in our society.

My daughter just graduated from Berkeley Phi Beta Kappa in Spanish and Portuguese and moved to Rome, Italy (where my wife is from) because she did not like where she sees this country going with an education system that more and more is reflecting the class society that our ancestors left Europe to avoid—ironically, education in France and Italy is free. As for Silvio Berlusconi and Co., she'll have to figure that one out for herself.

Please check out our website perdaily.com We have only been up for several weeks and have much broader ambitions than file site presently reflects, but I think some of the articles that we have already published will give you an idea as to where we are coming from. It would be an honor to have your substance and insights (and those of your community) illuminate and give direction to our little project of fixing public education in this country. At the very least, I would be very interested in any input you might have as to how we can better achieve our goal.

Best Regards,

Leonard Goodman Isenburg
Los Angeles Unified School District

April 16, 2010
Michael Lerner

President of Commonwealth
Bolinas, CA

Dear Michael,

I received your letter dated April 14 today and was most touched by the compassionate tone and content. At the same time, I was concerned that active citizenship was left out. If we do not expect from our government we will get nothing but money that goes to wars and paying off the thieves who have stolen from organizations like Commonwealth. FDR said, "Make me do it." Obama quoted him, and I think we should push President Obama to do the right thing: not wars in Afghanistan, not clemency to those who order torture and do it, and not bailouts to the thieves. I cannot help but recall your father's programs that I listened to as a youngster. We need that sort of thing today more than ever. I am still teaching a course on Controlling Processes—our people are drugged with "Leave No Child Behind" education and need to add advocacy to helping. How about pushing President Obama on single-payer, especially since the insurance companies are pushing on him 24/7?

I have great admiration for all the work you have done. Maybe it's time for all of us to shift gears.

With all the best wishes,

Laura Nader

May 18, 2010

To Whom It May Concern,

There is a difference between knowing about something and knowing something. Dissecting the phrase "knowing about something," we can see that it is comprised of three parts: the most significant is the qualifying word "about" that determines the relationship between "knowing" and "something" (absent in the phrase "knowing something"). "About" has several meanings, but I would like to draw attention to what it means in relation to space— "about" means approximately or roughly. To say, "I'm about a mile away," implies that more travel and navigation will be required in order to reach a destination.

At Berkeley, and in academia at large there are a lot of people who "know about things." Most classes are structured in order for students to display a distanced knowledge of things, that is to say a relationship to the knowledge that is destined and mediated by texts, facts, and lectures. This gets students and academics "about" to "knowledge" while never actually arriving at knowing. "Knowing about something" is a wonderful tool for forming a common understanding for intellectuals, for flirting with intelligent women at parties, and for earning degrees, however it is terrible for finding happiness, baking bread, or writing a passing paper in Controlling Processes.

What is difficult about "knowing something" however, is knowing that you know it. My late entrance into academia was plagued by the fear that I was short of knowing things because to my knowledge, I did not know "about" things. Universities are built on the principle that they hold the roadmap to get you to "about," and I was eager to prove that I could hold the course long enough to get there. I did ok. After all, I made it to Berkeley.

I took Controlling Processes because it is a course of some reputation, and I was thrilled to find out that the syllabus was filled with the kinds of things I "knew about." I had read all the major authors; I had written ten-page research papers before. I began my research early, writing a paper that I felt I had come to Berkeley to write. These would have been appropriate steps to take had the intention of Controlling Processes been to give students knowledge "about" controlling processes, however this is not the intention of the course.

Instrumental to my experience in the course was the reading group that I organized to make the 300 plus pages of reading a week manageable. The seven of us divided the readings up with two persons per reading, outlined, summarized and met every Monday night to discuss, debate, gossip, and vent. Because there was a certain amount of intellectual respect for the group, it was impossible for me to not give my all to the readings and to my interpretations and reflections on them. I had to internalize the readings in order to deliver what I thought were the most important parts of my assigned work, and thus had to mediate my experience through my own words for them to understand.

In essence I had to know the readings, not just know "about" them. I cannot express how important this group was to my experience in the course.

As the semester was running out, I had almost finished my paper. I was seven pages and fifteen sources in, and the conclusion was comfortably in sight. I felt that I had shown that I knew a lot about the things I was writing about.

That is, until the last lecture Professor Nader made it expressly clear that this wasn't intended to be a research paper, or rather that it was a research paper, however the research was intended to have been comprised of things we knew, not things we knew "about." She also asked the class a question that she had given to us repeatedly throughout the semester, one that we had learned to expect on the final, "imagine a world without advertising." It then occurred to me, she wanted us to imagine a world where our scars were our footnotes, our calluses and crow's-feet our bibliography. She wanted us to imagine a knowledge without qualifying.

She wanted us to write a paper in which academia was just as interested in what we know, as it is in what we know about. As though the only source I needed was what I had spent 26 years living—my life. So I took the paper on as though my life were a text that I had been assigned to read and present to my study group. I noted the controlling processes and mediated them, internalized them through self-examination. I thought critically about authorship and themes and started writing my paper again, coming to dramatically different conclusions. Thus the paper is inarguably the most thoroughly researched, yet unbearably personal work I have ever produced.

This is how one arrives at knowledge.

Thank you,

Blake Kasemeier
Student in Controlling Processes
Berkeley, CA

May 31, 2011
Martha Minow

Dean
Harvard Law School

Dear Martha Minow:

One of Harvard's distinguished alums and now President of our country recently announced that the revenge killing ("targeted assassination") of Osama bin Laden was "justice." Whatever happened to the Rule of Law? Perhaps the Harvard Law School should consider revising the curriculum.
Best wishes,

Laura Nader
Professor of Anthropology

May 31, 2011
Robert C. Post

Dean
Yale Law School

Dear Robert Post:

One of Yale Law School's distinguished alums and now Secretary of State of our country recently announced that the revenge killing ("targeted assassination") of Osama bin Laden was "justice." Whatever happened to the Rule of Law? Perhaps the Yale Law School should consider revising the curriculum.
Best wishes,

Laura Nader
Professor of Anthropology

On June 13, 2011, Martha Minnow wrote that continuing education of law school graduates would be a good thing.

June 14, 2011

Laura,

Do you remember me from Berkeley? Thanks for your letter of May 31. I assume that you know as well as I do that no dean can or should control the opinion or actions of their alumni, faculty . . . I hope you are doing well. Every time I see Berkeley mentioned in connection to the budget crises it pains me. Sincerely,

Robert Post
Dean of Yale Law School

August 8, 2011

Dear Laura,

May nice things be happening in your family that might offset some of the wrath and humiliation associated with the country. Goodness, what a mess! I get little news but that much has managed to penetrate here, probably because Thea is paid in U.S. dollars by the grant that finances her work on the rollout of ARVs [antiretrovirals].

Politics exist here too. A presidential election is set for September and campaigning is in high gear. Fortunately, I need pay no attention nor decide which of the candidates is worse. Instead, I continue to sit on my verandah and watch for birds or read for a bit. We had an earthquake that shook the house and my chair—it was over 5 on the scale. It has been cold, meaning that a nighttime fire has been pleasant. I have had houseguests—Nancy Williams en route to Bay Area for her younger sister's 80 birthday, Kate deLuna (a linguistic historian from Rice), Alan Haworth (a psychiatrist long settled in Zambia whom I first met down in Gwembe Valley in 1966) my namesake and her mother and two daughters. Now I am awaiting arrival of a Thai economist working on Gwembe and an American doctor who teaches at Boston University Medical School who will be working on a project involving training local midwives. That kind of thing is something Judith Justice wrote about in Nepal in the 1980s when it was then a current preoccupation of the development community. How things come around again. Judith was also due to come when she had a workshop in Ethiopia but her flight got cancelled and her schedule was so tight we decided she should not try to make the trip. And here visiting Thea for a month are Emily Frank (medical anthropologist with a Ph.D. from Indiana), her geographer husband who teaches in Montreal, and their two children. Emily and John first came out here with Lisa Cliggett and have worked on the Plateau on things like HIV/AIDS, inheritance, land usage, etc.

I've been to Gwembe three times—twice to Lusitu in the northeast of the Valley, and once to Mweemba in the southeast where I collected diaries from the two men still keeping records for me. Some interesting new things emerging, but I am in no mood to try to write about them. Let the younger people do so—though of course they may not be interested. Of course, life here is a barrage of requests for help—two daughters of Chepa, the headman who welcomed me in 1946, want me to build them a house; various youngsters are desperate to get money for school fees before the new term starts and some also need money for school clothes; others need money for medical expenses, or funerals, or to organize camp meetings, or to cover the school's assessment for a contribution to the district fund, or for a new soccer ball for the local team. Yes, I know—I do ask myself what they would do if I were not here. But in some cases I remember how much people helped me when I was doing fieldwork and I think again.

The shipment by sea finally arrived. I am now awaiting delivery of some ordered bookcases but the promised date is retreating into the past and nothing happens. We suspect that they may not have started on the work. You will recognize the craftsman syndrome. Other than that? Yesterday there were monkeys in the garden—a large troop. The day before an eagle alit in a tree overhanging my wall. I hear from the Woman Geographer's headquarters that Marilynn Salvador's membership has been approved but they are waiting to hear from her of her acceptance. I hope she meets their deadline for acceptance.

And you must be gearing up for the new school year. May the students be good, colleagues at least sometimes reasonable, and other work going well. My Best,

Elizabeth Colson
Professor of Anthropology
Monze, Zambia

January 9, 2012
Dr. Robert J. Birgeneau

Chancellor
University of California, Berkeley

Dear Chancellor Birgeneau:

Sometimes the people at the top of an organization are disconnected with what is going on in their organization. While I approve of your "Project Excellence," I wonder if the connection has been made with the core values of a great academic institution. I enclose two examples. The first is the desperate straits our libraries are in—a situation totally unbecoming a great public institution. The second is an article by Dave Zirin on intercollegiate sports, which may not affect Berkeley's administration of academic resources, but which I believe should if we want to be leading the way to more reasonable support for intercollegiate sports on this campus.

With best wishes for a happy new year.
Sincerely yours,

Laura Nader
Professor of Anthropology

January 30, 2012

Dear Laura,

This is a belated response to your note of Jan. 9. Thank you for the memos on both libraries and intercollegiate athletics.

First, I agree with you completely about the importance of a well-functioning library system with robust collections and as extensive opening hours as possible. Unfortunately, the libraries have budgets, which are as constrained as those of every other unit on campus, and frankly I simply do not know why particular decisions were made at the micro-level. One of the reasons for my appreciation of long opening hours is that when I was an undergraduate my family was so impoverished that I could not afford to buy textbooks so I had to use those on the library shelves. Hence, the fewer hours that the libraries were open the less time that I could study.

I understand that the specific issue with the Anthropology Library has been resolved, at least for now. You and I simply disagree on the value of intercollegiate athletics. Of course, I decry the distorted salaries in certain sports and the unethical behavior that occurs on some campuses. However, compared with both the University of Toronto and MIT, our student spirit is much higher here at Berkeley; there is no doubt that our outstanding intercollegiate sports play an important role in that. You need only go to a volleyball, soccer, basketball, or football game to witness that for yourself.

In the past year, my wife and I attended the end of year banquets for both volleyball and football. These were extraordinary uplifting events. As you may know, our women volleyball players are an impressive group; they are excellent athletes by national and international standards and they rank among our top undergraduates academically. At the football banquet each graduating senior gave a 3 minute speech; in all likelihood few or none of these students will continue on with a career in professional football. About 80% were African

American. Close to half of the graduating seniors began their speeches with a religious invocation. Then every single one of them expressed his gratitude that he was able to attend and graduate from this wonderful university and that this would hold him in good stead for the rest of his life. I was extremely proud of the players, their coaches, and our university.

Finally, I should add that I have a familial prejudice. My youngest daughter was a star athlete in college (she even played against Berkeley). Her college athletic experience transformed her from being an indifferent student to a student who won academic awards. The discipline she learned from playing intercollegiate athletics serves her well to this day enabling her to raise four daughters and run her own business. I am sure that this holds for most, if not all, of our athletes here at Berkeley.

With warm regards.
Sincerely yours,

Robert Birgeneau
Chancellor
University of California, Berkeley

February 1, 2012
Robert J. Birgeneau

Chancellor
University of California, Berkeley

Dear Chancellor Birgeneau,

Thank you for your most thoughtful letter of January 30 and your personal thoughts on intercollegiate athletics. In fact, we do not disagree. My children and grandchildren all played serious sports in school and beyond. We also agree on distorted salaries are a part. What the revolutionists called for was a "live within your means" philosophy for intercollegiate which means no subsidies. That is where my efforts have been.
Sincerely yours,

Laura Nader
Professor of Anthropology

March 11, 2012

Dear Dr. Nader,

Thank you for shedding light on the origins of political dysfunction. Nine out of ten people in prison are male, and yet we continue to send this violent cohort of our gender to the United Nations to seek peace—it ain't gonna happen!

Eighty percent of our government is made up of male lawyers. Most lawyers go to the mat for the corporation that pays them. Citizens United makes this bad for the voter.

Thank you for seeking reasons for this in our genes. Chimps and Bonobos are ninety-eight percent of what we are genetically. Chimps are patriarchal, violent, and combative knuckle draggers. Bonobos are matriarchal, peaceful, more upright, and promiscuous. Women are bonobos and men are chimps. How do you like my theory?

In the news men wave flags, march and carry guns, clubs, and torches. Women and children are seen as tired, wounded, hungry and fearful refugees. I met a woman from England who lost her twenty-three year old son in Iraq. She said "war is against mothers and children!"

Thank you for having such a wise brother.
Sincerely,

George Woegell
85 years a farmer
Sacramento, CA

March 13, 2012

Dear Laura,

I have heard from Irving and from Katie that the Symposium was a huge success with an interesting program, good speakers, and a plus both for anthropology and for you who have done so much to try to make anthropology responsible. They also spoke of the warmth of appreciation shown by former students and your fellow faculty. I am glad so many of the students were able to be there. You were someone who really cared about their development and their life after university. My regrets are great that I could not be there and hear what was said and judge for myself if it was appreciative enough. We worked together with so many students, I probably had a better chance than most to know your dedication and how much you stimulated them to think outside the box. Of course, I would also have loved to hear Ashraf who has really had a chance to judge whether anthropology can make a difference. He certainly tried.

But instead of being in Berkeley to do you honor, I have been here. The rains have been slow and erratic which probably means a poor harvest over much of Southern Province, but Lake Kariba is the highest I have ever seen it, which also means that people who counted on cultivating fields along the shore were unable to plant. On the other hand, I have been surprised at how pleasant the rainy season is here—I hadn't spent those months in Zambia since the 1980s at the latest. Mostly cool and since the rain comes in short showers for the most part, one can get on with things. Recently a Thai economist has visited for a few days so we could get on with the editing of a workshop—on resilience in drought prone regions—held last August. He now lives and works in Japan and in our off hours he also talked of conditions there and in Thailand. I had not realized that sea level rises were already affecting Thailand. He said that a portion of Bangkok on a lagoon off the sea was already under water.

Among my reading is a book which I think might interest both you and Tarek, written by Karen Engle who is a lawyer teaching in Texas. She has done a good deal of work with indigenous organizations in Columbia and perhaps elsewhere in Latin America. The book is entitled *The Elusive Promise of Indigenous Development: Rights, Culture, and Strategy*, and discusses what has happened when people have tried to protect themselves and their areas by claiming that they are unique because of ethnicity, or culture, or prior occupation of the land. I can recommend it. I've also read *Field Notes*, in which biologists, geologists, archaeologists, and anthropologists write about the importance of keeping written field notes, what should go in, how to organize, how they learned from others and their own mistakes, etc. Anya sent me the last and said she has been using it in her seminar on writing ethnographies. If I were teaching, I would probably insist that graduate students must read it. The most recent issue of *Anthropology Today* would also interest you—it has an editorial by Jonathan Benthall on mediation and an article by David Price on HRAF [Human Relations Area Files] and its connections with military research as well as a number of other items, including one on anthropologists and street theatre as protest which I would dearly love to have your opinion on.

Gisele Bousquet was here over Christmas when we spent two days at a game lodge on the Chobe River in northern Botswana. I had camped there back in 1992 when there was only such lodge on the river and one could camp anywhere and game roamed undeterred by gazing tourists. Now there are dozens of lodges on both sides of the river and I began to think that soon there would be no space for game because of all the space needed by the people who come to see game. Wherever we went, there were other game buggies or boats full of people looking and photographing the same animals we were looking at.

I've sent my gardener off to do a gardening course which will give him some kind of certificate that will help him get a better job if he wishes to leave here. My cook is soon signing up for a catering course. And my driver-mechanic now has his own car which he is having used as a taxi while he moonlights as a mechanic repairing cars and tractors for people off the farm. They know they are free to leave at any time as far as I am concerned and that I am investing in their future not my own. At the moment the Zambian economy is booming given all the foreign investment that is taking place despite the determination of Zambian bureaucrats to make things difficult for the foreign investor to get the appropriate papers. Chinese are becoming more and more visible. A few months ago, a shop opened in Monze selling cloth and used clothing at prices undercutting the market women. The latter marched on the town council office in protest and were told that Zambia was a free country. Since then we have seen a Chinese selling "talk-time" from a kiosk on the main street in Monze and another selling buns. So it is not only high level investors who are arriving. The world indeed is in flux.

My nephew Bob and his wife are coming out for two weeks late in May. I wish I could look forward to a visit from you and Claire. But I know that you will be preoccupied this summer with the new grandchild. My congratulations to Tarek and Robin.

And now, my very best to you.
With warm affection,

Elizabeth Colson
Monze, Zambia

October 3, 2012

Dear Laura,

Your letter with the enclosures came long since. And now summer is over and you have had another birthday and are well into the new school year. I hope there was plenty of time during the summer to get acquainted with the new granddaughter and to have visits from the older ones of such a nature that you enjoyed them and still had a rest. I have been wondering if Robin has found a way to stay in graduate school or if she has decided to take some time out to be with the baby.

I found "Rethinking Salvation Mentality and Counterterrorism" very insightful. I have been thinking about this as the U.S. seems to get ever more involved with Africa in its determination to ignore historical realities for the myth that the U.S.A., and by extension the West, is good and anything that challenges it is bad, and if violence is invoked then this is terrorism—interesting that we should continue to think of the U.S.A. as the model for how people ought to live given the idiocy of our current politics and the increasing immiseration and dumbing down of the population.

Early in September, I attended a workshop in Lusaka on the postcolonial history of Zambia. Michael Burraway gave the keynote speech. He did his MA here at the University of Zambia back when it was a good university, with Jaap Van Velson as one of his mentors. He also went to prison for a few days when he took part in a student protest which I think was aimed at the Zambian government's support for the Savimbi faction in Angola which associated with the U.S.A. and South Africa. This was the first time Burraway has been back here since the 1970s and he was thoroughly ebullient as a result, although he must have been shocked by the current state of the University of Zambia. I know the UC system is now a mess—had lunch while in Lusaka with a chap working on folklore who is usually at UCSD, and he was commenting on how difficult things there were now. But UNZA is much worse. Burraway had various things to say about the Manchester School whose approaches were rubbed into him by Van Velson. He held it to task for failing to make explicit its theoretical foundations. It has occurred to me that this may have been because in those days people trained in England all read the same books and knew where everyone else was coming from. There was no need to constantly identify oneself to one's colleagues, and given that they were also trying to write for those interested in an area or a subject who might not be anthropologists they could avoid jargon. With the growth of the profession, people are constantly trying to signal who they are by genealogical references to ensure they are recognized as belonging.

I finished David Graeber's *Debt*. A great book and I see it has been on a best-seller list in Britain. There were points I would take issue with, having seen something of the difficulties associated with barter when you really did seek a buyer who had what you wanted and was willing to take what you had. But it is a book that helps one think and see things in a new light. I have also read George Stocking's *Looking Into My Own Black Box*. I almost felt some sympathy for Mina Caulfield, I've read a very good ethnography on medical training in a teaching hospital in Malawi and what happens to the formation of doctors when you train with technology you will never have available to you and know that your success will depend on your ability to learn how to diagnose by looking at, smelling, and touching the patient and your ingenuity in improvising from whatever is available to handle the situation. Judith Justice is coming out for part of the Christmas holiday and I have managed to book us into a game lodge on the Chobe River in northern Botswana, just over the border (Zambezi River) from Zambia. I also hope to book us in a tourist camp at the southeast end of Kariba Lake for a night or two. Thea and I spent a weekend there at the end of August where we found ourselves being gazed at by bush buck who were either very bored or making a study of human beings. All in all, Judith will have very little time here at the farm but she has been here before. It would be good if you and Claire could make that promised visit. Lenore Ralston says she may come in June and bring a friend from her Bryn Mawr days.

Various Zambians have come for a couple of days to read in my library. I won't let any of the material on Zambia leave the house. As a result, I do have a chance to get to know some of the young people doing research and to listen to their views on the contemporary world. Interesting and informative. But a lot of my time is spent sitting on the verandah, watching for birds and reading when the spirit moves me.

I was saddened to hear that the Foster house is up for sale. It is closely linked with the good times of the department in my memory as George and Mickie did so much to try to have occasions to bring people together.

I am too late to say Happy Birthday. Who knows when I will marshal thoughts to write again. So Happy Christmas. I do think of you and hope all goes reasonably smoothly. You must be getting ready for the AAA meetings.

My best to Tarek and Robin, Katie Milton, and anyone else.

My very best to you,

Elizabeth Colson
Professor of Anthropology
Monze, Zambia

January 30, 2013
Letter to the Editor

The New Yorker
NOT THEIR BUSINESS:

I was appreciative of Jeffrey Toobin's thoughtful comment on "The People's Choice," and I'm struck by his last line. . . "the voters and the President they elect will decide whether abortion rights survive for the next four decades" (January 28, 2013). When my mother in her late nineties was watching television debates over abortion she asked me to explain the issues. When I finished she sat straight up in her chair and in her strong voice said, "It's not their business." My-mother was born in Lebanon, a part of the world where politicians did not get into personal issues. The idea that a Congressman would publically opine on when a woman's rape is really a rape would have been more than anathema to her. Not their business is more radical than *Roe v. Wade*.

Laura Nader
Professor of Anthropology
University of California, Berkeley

July 4, 2013

Dear Laura,

How are you doing? It's been a while since we wrote each other. I take the time this quiet evening to send you a letter.

We are doing fine. I must say more, the children are doing great: Simon is very good at school (ten years now and almost leaving primary school with fine results); the twins are four years old and very vivid. We are expecting another baby, not planned but very welcome. Imagine me after all these years of academia as a full-fledged father of four! I love it, and Ellen certainly does as much.

That is the big news, I guess. The little news is that since I have officially retired, I have no time anymore. Between the kids and my wife, I have been engaged in several projects: science-as-art on "the source," which opens tomorrow and will last the whole summer (exhibit of 20 artists, several scientists, books, etc., great fun). But also, a transition project I have been working on with some colleagues and friends. Then the academic work which keeps me busy for the next year or so: writing an English language book of high standard (for a HPJ on math education and culture). My former work on Navajo space, but now generalized to encompass the dropout problem in the math classes at primary level—that and to take a serious political stand on the place of math education in the emancipation process. I sent you a text on that previously "multimathemacy" as a project. Suppose we broaden the preschool knowledge that is allowed and recognized in the math classes, and then look at the dropout rates. Mathematicians either embrace the idea with great enthusiasm, or abhor of it. That is a positive outcome, I think.

If I manage to have people reconsider the social and cultural biases and presupposition in the so-called "neutral" math education, I will have done a good job. The bonus for some circles might be the so-called crises within math education (tremendous dropout rates and threats of a lack of mathematically sophisticated researchers for our economy) might be that dropout groups will be recruited again. If the contracts are decent, then that is a bonus on all sides. The general point that I will try to make is that diversity in math teaching (and in other, "softer" domains of course) is a good thing, and a democratic right. I am working on that book now, and it is progressing slowly.

Meanwhile, the Vienna University Dept. of Anthropology has asked me to be a visiting professor next year, and I will try out that math stuff on them. We will see what it comes to. This may postpone my visit to the U.S.A. for a while, but it is scheduled in my little family: the twins keep asking "when are we going to see the Indians? (since they have some paraphernalia by them in their rooms).

Laura, oh I miss your warm and critical presence. Let us hug through this letter. Very best to you and keep in touch.

Love,

Rik Pinxten
Ellen, Lisa, Simon and Anna (and the next one around New Year)
Ghent, Belgium

July 15, 2013
Dr. Nicholas Dirks,

Chancellor
University of California, Berkeley

Dear Chancellor Dirks,

In my note of November 19, 2012, I congratulated you as incoming chancellor, noting that my email would be followed by a letter. Before too much time passes, I write that letter. I have been teaching at Berkeley since 1960 and have seen much come and go. What follows are a few thoughts.

In all the talk about new administrative hires, the subject of educational mission seems not to be seen. There needs to be dialogues with faculty to discuss the educational mission of the university.

A good choice for Provost would help. One suggestion is Eng. Professor Alice Agogino. Prof. Agogino knows that education is the business of academics and it would be good if the Provost as well as the Chancellor supported this idea in practice, whoever is selected. Confusing operation excellency with efficiency diminishes the university's ability to grow in academic excellence. Bain cost the university needlessly. We have unused campus talent that might put academics first.

Fix the plumbing. We build new buildings and let the rest deteriorate. Implement efficiency standards. Solarize. It would be a good model for the labs where federal monies for alternatives are not used in practice either at the labs or on campus.

When students object to policies peacefully speak to the students directly as Chancellor Tien used to do. Calling in the police is worse than counter-productive.

It has been a habit for many of your predecessors to brag. Bragging is a strategy of weak leadership, making constituents self-satisfied when they might be challenged to improve.

Be nice to the governor. He really is interested in ideas, not celebrities. Many of us look forward to substantive conversation. Good luck as you embark on the challenge to turn Berkeley's educational mission around. Where we can help please don't hesitate to ask.

Warmest Wishes,

Laura Nader
Professor of Anthropology

February 3, 2014

Dear Laura,

I have had good intentions of writing a real letter but am defeated by technology and the continued automatic updating of my word processing program. They've now "improved" it to the point that I can no longer do many things that used to be simple—such as setting margins. Capital letters appear where none are wanted, so do line breaks, and much else makes writing offline a nightmare. So I have reverted to an e-mail.

Good to get your family news. I did get an e-mail from Tarek about some soap his organization is selling. It sounded good but before I could send in an order I got another e-mail saying stock was already exhausted.

It must be popular which suggests it is also very good indeed. I hope Adnan is enjoying Columbia and the feeling that he is learning a lot and enjoying doing something useful while doing so. It must be a contrast with fishing off the coast of Alaska. He probably likes the contrast. I have wondered if Samya made it to Norway and what she made of it. Some months ago, I read a review of *The Thistle and the Drone*. It sounded good and I ordered it. It arrived before Christmas but I haven't gotten into it yet. First, I had to think through and write a review for a local social science journal of a book on the economic and political context within which Kariba Dam was built. It was done by a young German historian who worked in various archives, read a lot of the published material, and even interviewed a few of the surviving Italian and African workers who actually constructed the dam. It's a good history and I learned a fair amount from it. My only real quarrel with it lies in her attachment to current expectations of how up-and-coming historians ought to frame their analyses, using the jargon of her time. This will inevitably out-mode it as fashions change. But it did make me think about the old fashionable "modernization theory'" and the inevitability of the "trickle-down effect," and the way social theories become outmoded along with their vocabulary while the justifications offered by those in power remain pretty much the same. They are still building dams and still assuring people that the dam will ensure economic growth that even if they suffer some immediate ill-effects, [. . .] those who will suffer the brunt of the scheme can expect to benefit eventually. It is ironic that most of those displaced by dams and other projects in the last 50 years have received less compensation and fared less well than the Gwembe people back in the late 1950s when they were under the British colonial system and could use it to make demands. Independent governments are much freer to disregard their citizens.

I've also read *Inside African Anthropology: Monica Wilson and Her Interpreters*, edited by Andrew and Leslie Bank which arrived early in December as a gift from the editors. They chose to ask their authors, including themselves, to use the theme of the importance of interpreters and other field assistants, which they say anthropologists once failed to acknowledge in the subsequent ethnographies. This is a theme popularized, I think, by George Marcus or someone of his ilk and now apparently accepted doctrine. It did set me thinking about all the various people who have worked with me and what they contributed. Most were good assistants but only one understood what we were about and kept suggesting avenues to explore and how we ought to be sure to interview different kinds of people so we got different viewpoints. The rest more or less did what I asked them to do though they often eased my access to people or occasions. I made a mistake of sending some comments, especially on how women like Wilson were viewed by their male colleagues in the 1940s and 1950s, to one of the editors who has now asked me to read and comment on chapters of the book he is now writing on various South African women anthropologists—Hoernie, Wilson, Kuper, Heilman, and Krige.

Coming from this celebration of the role of the interpreter; to Riles's recent article in the *American Anthropologist* gave me a particular slant on the way she showed connections between a number of different trends that I had noted but thought about separately: the loss of faith in experts, the new emphasis on the importance of collaboration and those involved in research as interpreters and assistants, the attempts being made to computerize more and more records including field notes with the hope that machines will come up with connections unnoticed by humans and more likely to stand up. I thought it a great article.

And that reminds me, do you know if the three items I submitted to the *Kroeber Society Journal* back in 2010 before leaving Berkeley were ever published? I have asked and received no answer.

I'm well. Birding is not as good as it is during the dry season. Things happen that keep me interested.

And books and journals still arrive although correspondence and such things seem to have a hard time moving through the postal system. Something Judith Justice mailed December 10 has still not arrived.

This letter has become much too long, but I do yearn for intellectual discussion. May all be well with you and yours and the Energy course pleasing to you.

My best,

Elizabeth Colson
Monze, Zambia

May 3, 2014

Dear Laura,

That must have been an interesting conference, working out what lies behind the attempts to make legal language very explicit with all meanings pinned down.

You ask about *The Thistle and the Drone*. A confession. I have been trying to read it for over a month and just can't do it. I read the first chapter or so and was turned off by his insistence that segmentary lineage systems provided the basic political order for everyone everywhere in the past. Where did he learn his anthropology? I know it's a good book. The reviews said so. You say so. I trust your and the collective judgements. But I still look at the book and go off and find something else to read first. I suppose part of it is because I have already made up my mind that the use of drones for military or spying purposes is both a crime and a mistake since it can only enrage anyone subject to such atrocious behavior. But then, the U.S. wars in Afghanistan and Iraq were miserable decisions. What is surprising is that the U.S. government doesn't seem to have learned anything from all the tragedy released on the world by its policies. So I may be able to read the book someday, but right now I boggle at the thought.

What is going on here? Cold season about to start. Around here, the rains were bad and the harvest is poor. Some of the people in nearby villages are already complaining of hunger, and this is the time of year when they should be eating well from the new crop. Nevertheless, friends are bringing me sweet potatoes, squash, pumpkins, ground nuts. Over Easter, Thea, who owns the farm, and I along with another woman went to a game camp on the Upper Kafue River for a few days. Great comfort in camp.

Misery on game drives from tsetse fly that seem to find me particularly succulent. Restful just to sit and look at the river flowing past in flood. After that my Zambian namesake's mother came to spend a few days with me. I've known her since 1946 when she was a nine year old girl at Chona. Last Saturday, she and I went to the 100th birthday party of a man we had known when he was a court messenger at Chona back in the 1940s. His granddaughter is now working for me as a cook. And what I'm reading? A manuscript for someone in Cape Town who is writing a book on South African women anthropologists who taught and did fieldwork in South Africa beginning in the 1920s, 1930s, and for some years later: Winnifred Hoernle, Monica Wilson, Audrey Richards, Ellen Heilman, Hilda Kuper, and Eileen Krige. Three of them I knew fairly well and I had met at least two of the others. The man writing the book has already co-edited a volume of essays honoring Monica Wilson which came out about a year ago. Just for fun, I've also read a book you may have come across: *Lost Enlightenment*, about the scholars who wrote between about 300BC and 1400 AD in the region now occupied by Kazakhstan, the other Turkish speaking states of inner Asia, Afghanistan, Iran, etc.—fascinating.

A former student of Louise Fortman has just e-mailed me that she is retiring at the end of this term. I somehow think of her as much too young for retirement, but she may have something she wants to do or perhaps she is fed up with Berkeley as it is now. I haven't heard from her for some months and I don't remember her mentioning retirement. I have also just gotten the letter from the American Academy on Leslie Berlowitz. Earlier I had seen somewhere that she had resigned but hadn't realized that this was due to a major scandal. I knew her slightly and thought of her as a good administrator rather than a scholar or scientist and so had been somewhat surprised when she became president of the Academy. The whole thing must have been a major blow to the Academy's reputation since there had been no proper research into her credentials when she was elected to the Academy or when she was appointed as president. On the other hand, it should be a good lesson on the fallibility of intellectuals and so a corrective to spiritual pride.

You must be glad to see the end of term, given the big class and all the rest of the things you are doing. I hope all is well with the family. Give my greetings to Katie and tell her that I do plan to e-mail her one of these days.
My best,

Elizabeth Colson
Monze, Zambia

August 28, 2014

Dear Laura,

Greetings from Beirut. Many thanks for your two books *Naked Science* and *Culture and Dignity*. All well received of course, and I look forward to reading them. I hope that you received a copy of my book. I would very much like to read your reactions. As I start reading yours, I see more and more the different approaches we pursue. I look forward to the day when we can spend a day together reflecting on our differences.

Since I received your envelope, I tried to call you almost every day. Tried to do it early in the evening, but unsuccessfully. Please confirm your home telephone number by sending me an email.

The crumbling of the Arab countries is very distressing. There are numerous battles on the ground. Interestingly people are optimistic about the outcome. I find that I am not as optimistic as the rest of my friends. The most interesting development is that the desperate unequal fight between the Arabs and their enemies is in science and technology. Until recently, one noticed little explicit interest in closing this enormous gap. During the past ten years, there is a modest attention to this dimension. Alas, not enough but the dynamics of the process may change. Very best and many thanks,

A. B. Zahlan
Professor of Physics
Beirut, Lebanon

November 17, 2014
Janet Napolitano

President of the University of California

Dear President Napolitano:

When you were appointed president, I told Governor Brown that I was disappointed. He said, "Give her a chance." Tomorrow at the Regents meeting you will have your chance. "It's not about meeting with six guns outside the Long Branch Saloon." It's about arms over the shoulders of the young. Poorer countries than ours have free tuition because they are investing in the future of their country. Do the right thing!
Sincerely yours,

Laura Nader
Professor of Anthropology

December 18, 2014

Dear Professor Nader:

I am sorry that you were upset by the form response you received regarding the recent tuition proposal. I understand your concern, but the simple fact is that the proposal generated a flood of emails and letters from concerned faculty, legislators, parents, staff, students, alumni, and the general public. Timely, individual responses were impossible given the volume and the small staff we have to handle such correspondence. It was clear, before and after The Regents' meeting, that there was a great deal of misinformation about the proposal. We felt it imperative to provide as quickly as possible an acknowledgement of the messages, and more importantly, accurate information about the plan. Hence, the form response that included the assurance that we are reading and paying attention to the views being expressed.

Please know that no disrespect to you, your faculty colleagues, or indeed to any of our correspondents was ever intended by the use of a form response. Yours very truly,

Janet Napolitano
President—University of California
Oakland, CA

April 15, 2015
Rush Holt Jr.

Chief Executive Officer
American Association for the Advancement of Science (AAAS)

Dear Dr. Holt,

Thank you for your letter. I feel it my duty once again express my concern (even amazement) that scientists and science executives are so unconscious about why "the public appreciation of science has slipped." It's assumed that the public is ignorant, that science priorities are always best. I dedicated my book *Naked Science* to the generosity of the American taxpayer because such generosity is never recognized except as never enough.

I recommend that the AAAS conduct an investigation of public opinions—wide ranging—not simply bragging. Maybe techno-twits ala Silicon Valley are not a top-priority. Maybe we speak about innovation because there is so little real innovation. In my book *The Energy Reader*, I write, as do other scientists, about real innovation given the state of the earth.

Please acknowledge receipt of this letter. Thank you for your concerns.
Sincerely,

Laura Nader
Professor of Anthropology

April 20, 2015

Dear Laura,

It takes me a very long time these days to do the things I plan to do, such as answering your e-mail. Obviously, I am never going to write you that letter for regular mail—my printer right now is on the blink. But I do write you often in my head. And wonder if the new grandchild has arrived, and if Tarek and Robin like the house, and if your back has decided to shape up and stop paining, and how the term has gone, and what new challenges the university and department face.

Of course, I am saddened by the death of Jim Anderson but glad that the long ordeal is over for him, Emmi, and the daughters. He was a good friend over all the years I lived in El Cerrito, even the last several when he was already worried and upset by not being able to remember things. Somehow, Alzheimer's seems the great indignity. George suffered from Parkinson's but his mind kept going.

He would be pleased, I think, at the article in the February issue of *Current Anthropology*, "Revisiting the Image of Limited Good: On Sustainability, Thermodynamics, and the Illusion of Creating Wealth." He still has an impact including outside anthropology, but then so do you. Reading journal articles and ethnographies, I quite often see your work cited but this usually it is the old article on "Studying Up." I was therefore glad to see that the later work is also now having a wide impact, as witness Doughty's article in the December issue of the *American Anthropologist*, where she draws on your work on "coercive harmony" and cites other studies that have been influenced by it. More power to you.

I'm glad I was in the department when both of you were there. I would have loved to have had a phone call from you and Katie Milton but the phone system must have defeated you. It often defeats me. For the last six weeks I have been unable to make a phone call, though for the first month or so I was still receiving some incoming calls. But for the last ten days I have had no incoming calls. The telephone company continues to bill me for full service. We also continue to have power outages making e-mail impossible now and then. On the other hand, my Palestinian friend from Monze who has been trapped in Gaza for the last three months—he was able to get in to visit kin but now the Israelis won't let him out even though he has an Irish passport—has phoned his wife that never again will he complain about ZESCO (our power company) and its service after experiencing the uncertain and scant supply of electricity in Gaza. In about two weeks, four guests are arriving: two from Canada, one from Britain, one from Greece. All anthropologists whom I met through the Refugee Studies Centre in Oxford. One of them is Barbara Harrell-Bond who founded the Centre. One is Doreen Indra who was an undergraduate student at Berkeley and took your courses. I have borrowed a houseboat to take them floating on Kariba Lake for several days and am sending them off with Rabson, my driver, to Livingstone to see the Victoria Falls, and will take them to a village or two and hope they think the trip worth it. Barbara, of course, will find it agonizing not to be fully engaged every moment of the day and night in providing legal services for some unfortunate refugee who is the victim of the international determination to bracket refugees out as illegal migrants.

By the time they get here, the rains should have stopped. Last year they ended in February. This year they began late, fell scantily, stopped in March for long enough to let the crops wilt, then began again with determination just when the crop was almost ready for harvesting when it needs to dry out. But, even if the crop is ruined, we still haven't had enough rain to restore the water table, well down after two dry years.

But you too have shortages. I hear that California has instituted water rationing, everyone being told to cut usage by 25%, and that trees and shrubs are dying. Reminds me of 1973 when people began to brag about how dirty they, their cars, and their houses all were.

I will not speak of the political situation in the U.S.A. or here. You must be completely depressed by it all as I am. What is most depressing is the idiocy of most of those involved. I have no television, do not listen to the radio, buy a Zambian newspaper only several times a week, and sometimes bless the fact that only one out of three issues of *The Economist* arrives and then usually three weeks to a month late. Otherwise, life is reasonably good for me. I hope it is the same for you. My very best,

Elizabeth Colson
Monze, Zambia

July 7, 2015

Dearest Laura,

Yes, we are doing very fine. Our eldest son, Simon (the one who strolled around in the theatre at the time) just finished his first year of High School.

I speak English to him most of the time. He also plays the sax and sports a lot. The twin girls are six now and start with Primary School in September. Twins defeat math: when the two get going together they should be counted as three, at the very least. Adorable girls. And then there is Titus, the small emperor. He is 18 months now and starting to move around quickly, on the verge of walking as well. So we have a lot on our hands and are very happy with them.

Intellectual things: I did read the piece in AN over a month ago, and liked it a lot. You are right of course. The one-sidedness, decreed by those temporarily in power, is horrendous and makes it possible to wage war on the others whenever things are a bit more complicated. With the way Greece is maltreated now, I really hope the corporations do not push for a big war again. Greece is a symbol (and first in line) for the whole south of Europe, including France to some extent. Of course, the reaction which is finally shaping up in Spain, Portugal, Greece and Italy is very interesting, but let's be cautious. I do speak (and write) a lot in public about the responsibilities of social scientists and damn-conservative philosophers about such things. I wrote two books over the past three years about this for a "lay public": "Little revolutions" and "Beautiful protest," both analyzing neoliberalism and the alternatives in new Commons which are emerging. Some economists (not many though) start saying similar things: Rifkin, Stiglitz, Piketty of course. So there is good hope.

Apart from these engagements, I have finally managed to finish my academic book on math teaching and culture. I worked on it for five years, going back for thirty years in fact. It looks at what children have as pre-school knowledge, and how math education should take this into account and start from there. This is opposite of OECD [Organisation for Economic Co-operation and Development] and such, but will help with the dropout and backlash in life chances, I guess (and project), when thought through. Here also, a small group of math people are interested in this perspective (combining anthropology and a bit of philosophy, in which I think I am at home) with elementary math. It is called "Multimathemacy: Anthropology and Math Education." I thought it pretty exotic as a book, but I do not trust my judgment anymore in these matters. So I presented the MS to Springer, NY which is THE publisher in math education. A fortnight later, I had a contract with them. It will probably be out within a year. In a "noble" sense this is political as well, and I hope the discussion will get going. It was difficult to write since the culture of mathematicians and that of anthropologists are eons apart, as you know from your work on energy.

It is not very clear from your letter what the scope of your next book will be. If you think I can do a decent job reviewing it for AN or another channel, please let me know and indicate it to the publisher. You know, I am still Fellow of the Royal Anthropological Institute of the UK. Good for them, right?

Dear Laura, let me know when you are in the neighborhood. I will do the same when I land somewhere with my gang of four. Meanwhile, a nice and warm hug to you.
With love,

Rik Pinxten, Ellen and the kids
Ghent, Belgium

September 18, 2015

Dear Laura,

The book sounds great but I knew it would be. You've been working on it for a long time as new material turned up and you thought about each one and how they all added up. Congratulations. You must now be deep into the new term. An article in the last *Atlantic* on the need to safeguard tender student psyches makes me thankful I stopped teaching before people became so fragile. It sounds worse than ever. The article pinpoints protective parents reacting to increasing awareness of potential physical risks, but I think probably the decision that children must be made to feel good about themselves, no matter how badly they did in school or how badly they behaved has a lot to do with their inability to accept criticism or disturbing material at college level. I wonder how you are faring under this kind of censorship. Interesting that this should have happened while at the same time political invective is getting nastier and nastier.

I hope the rains in southern California move north and you get a good drenching. Here the hot season is upon us and the rains still distant. Water in the reservoirs is so low that our hydroelectric dams, including Kariba, are unable to generate much power. We now have power outages of about 8 hours a day, from 5 am to 2 pm, and are told it will get worse. It already is worse in Lusaka. So I have gone solar for lights, refrigeration, and (I hope) eventually the internet.

Cooking is a bit of a problem but we cope. And we hope the water in the borehole holds out. Not perhaps an ideal time to have guests but I am still looking forward to a three-day visit in early October by Elizabeth Ogbu, a flourishing architect with a growing international reputation. She will stop here after having climbed Mt. Kilimanjaro with an old school friend.

Tarek's son must now be at the point where he is laughing at life, beginning to recognize people, and steadily getting more interesting. Given the state of the world, it is probably a good age to be.

I hear the fall SWG [Society for Women Geographers] meeting was interesting—I always found it the most interesting of the year given the different interests of the members. You must be glad to have Katie back and in fine fettle.

My best to you,

Elizabeth Colson
Monze, Zambia

October 30, 2015
Abdel al-Jubeir

Royal Embassy of Saudi Arabia
Washington, D.C.

Ambassador Abdel al-Jubeir:

As a professor at this distinguished university, I have responsibilities to teach students about the Middle East, especially the Arab Middle East. I have published two recent books about the area: *Culture and Dignity* (2013), and most recently *What the Rest Think of the West: Since 600AD* (2015). My question is this: how do I explain to students the recent militarism of your country against other Arabs? How do I explain to them that Yemen is now popularly referred to as Saudi Arabia's Gaza, placing Saudi Arabia in the same moral or immoral camp of what the Israelis do in Gaza and elsewhere in Palestine? My home education included deep respect for Arab civilization, especially as my parents had migrated from Lebanon.

Please advise.

Sincerely yours,

Laura Nader
Professor of Anthropology

February 1, 2016
Nicholas Dirks

Chancellor
University of California, Berkeley

Dear Nick:

First, I wish you and yours a good New Year for 2016 although the clouds at the national level are not encouraging.

But secondly, I want to convey some additions to the check-list that I sent you when you first took office. Many of us recognize that the job of Chancellor is not an easy one, in part because, in your case, you inherited problems from the previous chancellor for which he has not apparently had to take responsibility—putting the campus into unnecessary debt for example. So...

1. May the New Year bring decisions on the following:
2. Dump the Richmond campus idea—we do not need it or the headaches ranging from environmental clean-up to more debt.
3. Put maximum attention to dealing with the main Berkeley campus, one that needs attention. There is too much adhockery.
4. Begin the process of reducing, administration wherever possible—too many meetings with too little result.
5. Increase academic needs—increase faculty hires at all levels, and support for Academics First.
6. Bring the money for football slowly into line with the ahead of his time philosophy of former Chancellor Tien.
7. Advise on reorganization need not come from corporations that do not have a clue about education at the higher levels. The staff find the constant changes in technology a pain and "can't wait to retire" is a common refrain.

For what it's worth, a view from the bottom, a private view. When you have done your best for the campus, we will welcome you to our faculty.
Warmest Wishes,

Laura Nader
Professor of Anthropology

March 22, 2016
Elizabeth Colson

Monze, Zambia

Dear Elizabeth,

I hope this letter finds you well and enjoying the books, the monkeys, and whatever else distracts from this crazy world. Thank you for your letter to Katie and me—something is better than depending on the mail service. Here it is Spring vacation and I am trying to clean up and at least fill the basket everyday—but I keep finding interesting tidbits of the past half century at Berkeley.

In addition, I have been reading history. A rather amazing book *The Human Smell* by a novelist and non-fiction writer named Baker . . . covering everybody's actions, including our own, that led up to WWII . . . material I had never known about since during war it is always black and white. Best argument for pacifism I have ever read. Another interesting book by two French historians on the so-called Anthropocene over the past 2–300 years was also eye-opening. That one has just been translated from the French.

On another front, my book *Culture and Dignity* has been translated into Arabic and is getting good circulation. *What the Rest Think* . . . is doing very well as well, whatever that means . . . was number one best-seller at the meetings for UC Press. I wrote an article "What is Anthropology?" for an online text for community colleges that was well received, and am gearing up on a few other projects including one on letters to and from LN . . . the range of letters in this office is just too tempting and a press is interested.

On the family front: Samya, who had a paper accepted for Denver and then applied to a global health program in Denmark, finds herself in Tanzania; Adnaan is teaching at the American school in Fez, and Tor is visiting him enroute to Germany. He applies to college next year. Rania is doing fine, has a project going. Tarek is still with Caura and raising money, while starting a business with 2 others in Peru with palm fruit. Robin is still working on a thesis on migration. Their youngest is 7 months . . . Claire and Ralph more of the same work on democracy . . . Ralph opened the first law museum in the world probably in Winsted, the American Museum of Tort Law . . . beautiful exhibits with help from the Smithsonian etc., and more given the crazies running for office. Bernie Sanders seems to be the only sane one, and under no circumstances would I ever vote for the Clinton machine. At any rate Sanders is doing us a favor. . .

So that is about all I have energy for Elizabeth. I should take time to rest since it is "vacation" . . . at least I still walk every day, and go to the Chinese care on Sat. The Chair has resigned so we need to choose another . . . but no need to go there. Take our love from Berkeley . . . we still enjoy all the beautiful gifts you left for us.
Warmest Wishes,

Laura

May 26, 2016

Dear Laura,

Am leaving the country, won't be back to my office (where letters get printed) so this will come unsigned.

Glad you liked the discussion with Amy and thanks very much for sending the articles. Do you have electronic versions? If not, I'll get them scanned. I had read Ahmed's book (and have had some correspondence with him), and very much

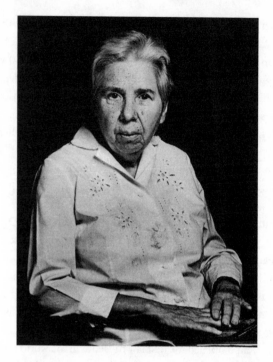

FIGURE 8. Elizabeth Colson, my dear friend and colleague. Photograph from author's collection; photograph taken by G. Paul Bishop.

share your opinion. The jihad article is very insightful. I had never thought of the points, but they are quite convincing and pertinent. Brown's comparison doesn't make much sense. Rabbinic texts should be compared with Muslim philosophy, the Koranic texts with the Bible, which is the most genocidal text in the literary canon. As for the crazed Rabbis, it goes way back, and it's not just military rabbis. Also the chief Rabbis. And it's a deep tradition. If you've never seen it, you might want to check Israel Shahak's *Jewish History, Jewish Religion.*
Sincerely,

Noam Chomsky
Professor of Linguistics
Massachusetts Institute of Technology

March 14, 2017

Dear Dr. Nader,

Thank you so much! I hope that finding Robert Merton's letter did not prove any hardship for you, and I greatly appreciate your willingness to send me a copy of his letter.

Actually, no one "told" me about RKM's letter to you. I found two mentions of it in a folder titled "Cognitive Conduits" housed in the Merton archives at Columbia. The folder contains various working notes for a possible paper RKM was considering writing on the matter. On one note page, dated July 19, 1986 (or in his Sartonian style, 8607.19) and titled "Cognitive Conduits & Elucidations," RKM lists a set of instances drawn from "personal experience & sustained observation": the Thomas Theorem, "trained incapacity," and Whitehead Epigraph. Following trained incapacity he writes "draw on letter to Laura Nader."

A second working-note, "On Notion of 'Cognitive Conduits,'" referred me to a letter RKM sent to Piotr Sztompka on Easter Sunday, 1984. Here, in a 15-page letter in which RKM comments on Sztompka's proposed outline of the intellectual profile of RKM he intended to write, and did publish in 1986, RKM spends a full page on the concept of cognitive conduits, this time when referring to Veblen, writing in parenthesis "This rather more fully described in a letter to Laura Nader," (herewith enclosed). I now see, having just taken Sztompka's book off of my shelf, that RKM's letter to you, dated December 24, 1978, is listed as one of the letters quoted with permission—although a quick look in the index under "trained incapacity" shows four mentions, none of which mentions the letter.

There must be a third reference to this letter—how else would I know about the bibliography of misattributions of Veblen's concept of trained incapacity to RKM, but it escapes me for the moment . . . Since you note that this is "quite a story," I thought that I would share one of mine (really just a gloss on the project) in the hope that you might want to share yours at your leisure.

As I mentioned, I was a student of RKM and Harriet Zuckerman's research assistant back in the late 1970s and early 1980s. During that time, I had access to some of their unpublished works and always intended, when I would be able to make a concerted effort, to write an intellectual biography of Merton.

So intermittently over the past few years, I have been inching my way toward this goal. For example, a number of years ago I transcribed an entire semester of RKM's lectures (he allowed me to tape the entire set of lectures which transcribed, runs to 300+ pages), and two years ago I spent 2 weeks at the archives back at Columbia, coming back with roughly a thousand pages of his lecture notes, works-in-progress, correspondence, etc. (this due, of course, to the wonderful technology of an iPhone which allowed me to simply snap a picture of each page).

This past month (I'm happily on sabbatical this semester) I have been looking at RKM's lectures on Marx from the 1950s–1970s and examining how he analyzed Marx's (often tacit) sociological theory, noting its "genius" in some instances, noting its limitations in others, and identifying "gaps" that need further attention and explication.

In addition, I have also gone back over RKM's publications and (of course) find that aspects of Marx's sociological (not political) ideas have been selectively and fruitfully extended and then partially incorporated into RKM's evolving theoretical work from the start—dating back to RKM's dissertation on science and technology in England and his landmark papers on unanticipated consequences, social structure, and anomie in the 1930s. In fact, by publishing an early paper in the journal *Science and Society*, thought by the government to be an avowedly Marxist journal, RKM came to the attention of the FBI and was "investigated" a number of times (an interesting story, too).

RKM, you probably know, was often lumped together with his former mentor, Talcott Parsons and mischaracterized as a "consensus" theorist. On rare occasions, he confronted his critics in public, but he mostly "bit the bullet," preferring to forego public polemics. He was of course, very much a structural and conflict theorist and took great pains to show how structurally patterned disjunctions, contradictions, and conflicts are built-in to the very fabric of most, if not all, highly differentiated societies. It really couldn't be any other way; he doggedly specified and located these potentials for conflict within prevailing social structures. (Would this be antithetical to "harmony ideology?").

So one of my intentions is to indicate important overlaps between RKM the so-called "consensus theorist," and the decidedly conflict theorist and highlight what is surely an under-appreciated pattern of intellectual growth: the selective and partial incorporation of ideas.

RKM, of course, never disavowed the selective affinity he had with Marx. In fact, in a very rare and hard to find published interview—so hard to find that I will quote the relevant passages for you. RKM says:

> "Remember the period of history we are dealing with. Know the crucial decade obviously for me with regard to sociology was the latter part of the 20s through the 1930s. You can imagine that in the Great Depression, though it obviously had a differential impact on the already poor, that a sense of differential access, as I was to turn to opportunity, was so intensified that. . . [it] couldn't help but be a learning [experience]."

RKM also states that he was "improbably introduced to Marx" by the corner shoemaker.

"I used to bring the shoes to him and sit and talk to him by the hour . . . and when I say that I was five, it may have been six, four, or seven . . . but it wasn't he was indoctrinating me here . . . but I was learning about Marx in my very, very youth by word of mouth from him. I suppose that what really was maintained was more of an attitude than a great understanding. So that when I did start to read Marx in my teens, particularly in the 30s, I was not 'never a Marxist.'"

Other tidbits: "I was a student of Marx. I would like to think a critical student of Marx. . . " "So it is not my being a Marxist but being Marx oriented." And more to the point, in a letter written in 1943 to his one-time-student and then colleague/combatant-at-a-distance Al Gouldner, RKM writes, "I think it misleading to claim that Marxism provides either a valid or an invalid approach to problems in this field. I have long since abandoned the struggle to determine what 'Marxism' is or is not. Instead, I have taken all that I find good in Marxian thought, and that is a considerable amount, and neglected conceptions which do not seem to me to meet tests of validity."

BTW: It was a comment by Gouldner that came to mind while reading RKM's Marx lecture notes that put me on the path of my second goal for this piece of research—to more fully explore RKM's notion of a cognitive conduit. In his *The Coming Crisis of Western Sociology*, an important and influential book in the discipline, Gouldner writes that in the 1940s RKM "was always much more Marxist than his silences on that question may seem" and that he "sought to make peace between Marxism and Functionalism precisely by emphasizing their affinities, and thus make it easier for Marxist students to become *Functionalist* professors" (italics added). RKM, of course, was quick to respond, "here, Gouldner surely does me too much honor. I had neither the far-seeing intent nor the wit and powers thus to transmogrify my students."

For RKM, Marx was there to be appreciated but not to be blindly followed. Seeing precisely which of Marx's ideas found their way into RKM's lectures, how they were placed in a broader cognitive and theoretical context, and how they resonated with RKM's thinking, has been quite a lot of fun as well as incredibly enlightening. And I've only just scratched the surface. . .

So once more, I really appreciate your offer to send me a copy of the letter RKM sent to you about Veblen since it will have some bearing on my discussion of "cognitive conduits." I hazard the guess that it would be easiest to send it as an attachment to my email address, but if snail mail suits you better, would you please post it to my home address—since I am on sabbatical and working mostly in my study at home.

P.S. Is the paper in the *Yale Law Journal* that you mentioned, "Disputing Without the Force of Law" or am I missing it? It's the only one I found under your name in that journal.

Best wishes and kindest regards,

Dr. Larry Stern
Professor of Sociology
Collin College

June 9, 2017

Dear Dr. Nader,

I was an anthropology major for a time when I was at CAL from 1994–98. Attending the recent conference at the Alumni House made me want to tell you what an impact you made on my education at CAL. You were easily one of my favorite and most memorable professors. I particularly was impacted by your "Controlling Processes of Industrial Societies" so much so that I strongly recommended that course to my bright and socially conscious niece, who is now a junior at CAL studying Political Economies and who hopes to later study Public Interest Law. I was so disappointed to find that the course is no longer offered.

I believe the course made me a stronger critical thinker and opened my eyes to unconscious dynamics of power and control that are too often taken for granted in our daily lives. I wrote a paper in that class on the dynamics of power in a psychology lab, where I was working at that time as a research assistant. It helped me understand the subtle ways that power and control played itself out and how difficult it made true informed consent in a study on emotions and culture that included showing research subjects potentially traumatic material (dated surgical footage of a leg bone being cut open, a young girl being raped, etc.), while being literally strapped to a chair with sensors and being told not to avert their eyes from the screen.

If you ask what I learned in other classes I took, or the subject of other papers I wrote 20 years ago, there is little that stands out as clearly or feels as relevant to my life and understanding of society as this class and this paper. The process of writing the paper was very validating and it allowed me to process and articulate what caused the gnawing sense of unease I felt about my experience and what I was subjecting people to in that lab.

Later, while completing my master's degree in counseling, I learned about the abuse of communities of color at the hands of researchers, and how ethical practices, such as informed consent, were established to prevent such atrocities as the Tuskegee Study. But the process of writing this paper showed me how even with such practices in place, unconscious institutional power dynamics can still serve to control and intimidate people into compliance.

I have also come to see this dynamic in the medical field, and am especially aware of it in the arena of childbirth, as my sister who is a homebirth midwife has sensitized me to the way in which power has been removed from women giving birth in the institutional, medical professional-centered and litigation-averse setting of hospitals which treats birth primarily as an illness needing to be controlled, rather than a natural process that sometimes needs intervention. The female body cannot be trusted, instead it needs to be proactively interfered with, immobilized, numbed and subdued by a cascade of interventions that makes the next intervention more likely and by a patriarchal medical institution that knows best.

Wanting to focus more on contemporary societies at Cal, I ended up creating a major in the Interdisciplinary Field Studies Department called "Authoritarian and Totalitarian Government and Society." Interestingly enough, in my career the understanding of dynamics of power became a strong theme. I ended up managing a domestic violence shelter-based program serving Asian immigrants for 10 years. In our community advocacy work, we were acutely aware of dynamics of control in our clients' personal lives that ranged from physical and emotional abuse, intimidation and threats by their partners, to less obvious dynamics of racism and sexism from patriarchal institutions. These dynamics led to further re-victimization from the community, legal system, law enforcement, and religious institutions that belittled and retraumatized victims, minimized abuse, and was more invested in protecting father's rights than preventing further victimization.

Currently, I am a Mental Health Services Act program manager at the City and County of San Francisco's Department of Public Health/Behavioral Health Services, overseeing "innovation" programs funded to improve the public mental health system. While studying for my master's degree in theology, as well as my second masters in counseling psychology, I was sorely disappointed to find that my education in each of those programs lacked the kind of social analysis, "sociological imagination," and cultural self-awareness that I was taught at Cal through my social science courses, especially at the Anthropology department in particular and in your course. I feel so fortunate to have received the education I did and I thank you for your part in that, for the impact you have on your students, and the strength of your passion for critical thought, uncovering social dynamics of power, and the importance of educating students about relevant and contemporary issues.

Please share this email with the relevant person(s) in your department. It is my sincere hope that this course can be offered again so that other students, like my niece, can benefit as greatly as I did.
Best regards,

Teresa Yu
Former Student

April 30, 2018

Dear Laura,

I'm writing on my last day here in Hong Kong as visiting professor at HKU. I don't think I ever properly thanked you for your Anthropology of Law reader, which I got great inspiration from. It also allowed me to read some of your latest articles—good stuff, including the very good piece on justice vs injustice as organizing by words, and the different effects they produce.

Teaching anthropology of law in HK has been extremely rich. The "rule of law," its contestation by the Chinese government, and the strength or capacity of the judiciary to resist this pressure from the mainland are everywhere. It is clearer than ever that the so-called rule of law (which should be called "the ability to call the rich and powerful to accounts") is just as strong as societal support of it. This societal support is being slowly eaten away by the Chinese Communist Party's infiltration of all of the main business, industry and financial power centers.

It's a complete mirror image of the way government in the U.S. has been infiltrated by corporate interests, except that Chinese see what's happening and have seen for months & years, whereas US citizens are just waking up now. And it may be too late!

It's a glum time and the only way to feel less powerless is to read, write and go back to Ithaca to flip our local congressman's seat to a progressive—which is where I'm going next.

Let's talk!
Love,

Ellen Hertz
Hong Kong University
Hong Kong, China

April 9, 2019

Dear Laura,

I want to follow our meeting of last Friday, April 5 with this note. First, thank you very much for coming to Kroeber Hall and being game enough to spend time with me while so deeply grieving for Samya in that horrid Boeing 737 Max 8 crash. I was and am overwhelmed with sadness for you, for her, for your family. There are no words . . . no consolation. I am so very sorry, was not aware of your family's loss, and would never have wanted you to come in while grieving just to visit with me. But you did, thank you for joining me— and here we are.

I wanted to communicate some of the results from your life's work in anthropology, your specific teachings, and your pervasive influence on count- less people you will probably never meet.

When I took your Anthropology and the Law course, I think it was 1975 or 1976, I was in my junior year in the last undergraduate class of the UC Berkeley School of Journalism. I had already taken Dr. Dundes' Folklore class, and was thinking about applying to law school at Hastings College of the Law. I wrote the best paper I have written in my life as my final exam in your class. You gave me an A+ and thanked me for it. I wish I still had it. I would include it here, as Exhibit A.

In class, you described a Zapotec culture in the mountains in Oaxaca, and its system for conflict resolution. I loved being in Oaxaca. I was comfortable in their culture, having lived there at the impressionable age of 14, and spoke Spanish fluently. Coming to your lectures was like coming home.

Critical to the history I am recounting in this note is that in your class, because of your many insights, I understood that a face-to-face culture requir- ing restorative justice as a means to achieve social harmony is a way to make the world better, and not merely for the parties to a conflict. I realized that zero-sum-gain conflict solutions only made the world "a little bit colder" to quote John Lennon. The federal, state, and local/administrative legal processes and law were inadequate to meet the needs of people in conflict, because there were no restorative acts which would return harmony to those involved in the dispute. An anonymous society isn't welcoming, or one in which I wanted to live. I decided I would make a difference and you helped me.

Fast forward a few years. As the mother of a child with disabilities, I was working hard in administrative law settings and in special education meet- ings with my daughter's public schools to get her an education worthy of her cognitive abilities. Other parents of students with disabilities saw the many educational benefits I was "winning" for my child, and asked me to help them at their Individualized Education Program (IEP) meetings. I did it pro bono for decades.

I learned with experience fueled by your anthropological insight how to create an IEP team using the conflict resolution tools you taught: assuring a process and tailoring solutions to create an environment where face-to-face relationships can flourish. A school is after all, a small village. Everyone knows, sees, and understands that what happens to one happens to all. I found ways to encourage everyone to "win," by solving problems outside the prescribed win/lose box.

Your work and mine melded again when I was asked to teach a course in education law to students at Loyola Law School while also working as a staff attorney in the Education Advocacy Program at Disability Rights Legal Center (DRLC). I then taught an Education Law & Clinic course to grad students who were future principals, administrators and teachers at Loyola-Marymount Graduate School of Education. Students came with me to IEP meetings and actively participated in creating just solutions, with the consent of parents and school administrators on IEP teams. We created a cohesive team, with team spirit, which carried our students forward and made collaborators out of institutional adversaries.

Next, teaching education law and clinical workshops to grad students and social workers at Westside Children's Center and then at Drew Child Development Corporation in Los Angeles, caused underserved students across South LA to have knowledgeable and capable education advocates for the first time in most of their lives. I taught IEP workshops and writing seminars for UCLA medical students and their medical professors. The students enrolled in CHAT, which was UCLA Medical School's Community Health Advocacy Training program; the CHAT program included nursing grad students, dentistry students, and more. The CHAT participants embarked on education advocacy in the way they knew how, and worked as a team with underserved preschools and child services agencies. With me and public health nurse Lawren Miller Askew, RN, MSN, PHN, they implemented the first "child find" protocol in South Los Angeles. Children with disabilities were "found" and their needs were met.

I say all this not to brag, but to demonstrate that every single student of mine/ours was trained and infused with a desire to create a sustainable and harmonious process which would inure to benefit someone else. Because of this one concept you taught to me, that face-to-face conflict resolution requires restorative justice (rather than zero sum gain results), I/we put into practice in real life and in real time the processes which created value for many thousands of lives, and which continue to do so.

Let me give you an example of restorative justice in action: a boy with an IEP attending a public (charter) school lacked saccadic eye movement due to ocular and neurological anomalies at birth. He couldn't read and was 14 years old. No IEP in the past had ever provided anything to help him read. He dreamed of reading and was very motivated, but could not move his eyes to the next letter in order to read a word. He loved listening to stories, though, and remembered everything he was told. His mother would read text out loud to him every night for hours, trying as best she could to keep him on par cognitively with his classmates.

The IEP team was unsophisticated and lacked an ability to solve problems as evidenced by his history of their failure to teach him. They were at first defensive because of their failures and assumed I was there to build a case against them. I started the meeting looking at them glaring at me as the only lawyer in the room. I told them we were a team with special knowledge of this student and that every team member was equal, and had something to contribute. They were amazed by this team approach from a lawyer, and after I was done speaking about teamwork, asked me to write an IEP with them to help solve the puzzle: how to teach and test someone who would "never be able to read."

I asked them to question their assumptions. What would enable someone without saccadic eye movement to read? We discovered there was one place, 40 or so miles away, which might be able to teach him to read. In the meantime, we all agreed that he could orally answer all test questions, and that all tests would be read aloud to him in a quiet and private place, and that he would be furnished with tech solutions like DragonSpeak, Books on Tape, and recorded textbooks from The Braille Institute (this occurred at the dawn of the ubiquity of the internet, so all resources now extant were not then available). I could keyboard as quickly as they could speak. We ended up with a lengthy document, which provided for a unique IER with an education plan that had never before been implemented by LAUSD.

Most importantly, the student felt welcomed by the school because he felt they "didn't hate him" and sincerely wanted to help him and were no longer wasting his and his parents' time. He, his mother, and his father could walk through the halls at school and be greeted with smiles and feelings of community. The administrators were no longer afraid of litigation and they tried to actually help—and they did! They voluntarily and on their dime sent him to a special private school so he could learn to read with special instruction. Today he is a college graduate, and he can read.

They say it takes a village to raise a child, but if that village is fragmented by factionalism caused by threat of losing value due to the results of zero-sum gain conflict resolution (litigation), the village will ignore its children, as my student was ignored for so many years until we removed the threat of litigation from the equation. And most of my students were in the same boat. I'll say "my students" as shorthand: their parents asked me to help them improve their child's education.

The team approach to problem solving in special education conflicts creates a face-to-face opportunity as a form of restorative justice: what works best for this particular student? Let's find out, together! This team approach destroys conflict and in so doing, creates partnerships, which can and do, design the most desirable outcomes.

I've been contacted by many members of many an IEP team, and by members of that particular IEP team, all of whom wanted me to know that creating a feeling of team membership changed the IEP processes in which they were members, ever since. Multiply that by all the grad students in-serviced with the restorative justice model for civil rights equality in access to education, and you can see there is an armada of new thinkers making changes that count.

The theoretical ivory tower that people deride actually has real impact outside the classroom. Sometimes we need a perspective that only time can provide, as here where the impacts of your theory can take 20–40 years to make themselves known.

You set the ripples moving through the pond by throwing the stone. I'm so very glad to know you, and value the many gifts you have given to me and this world. Saying "thank you") seems so inadequate, but it is all I have after years working pro bono. Thank you. Thank you. Thank you.
With deep gratitude, I remain your faithful student,

Nan Waldman
Connected.

Epilogue

This book is not only about my life with letter writers. Rather, it is also about what has been happening in our country over the past sixty years as the Ivory Tower slowly erodes. The university is now viewed as being more intimately linked with the outside world. Thus this collection of letters deserves some concluding comments indicating what value, and for whom, such a small archive enlightens.

My career in anthropology began with an interest in law, first among the Zapotec peoples of the Sierra Juarez in Mexico. As a byproduct, I necessarily interacted with American missionaries from the Summer Institute of Linguistics. In the early 1960s, language was important for my understanding of kinship and court users in a bilingual town and for any sophisticated understanding of the style of court proceedings, which I later dubbed "harmony ideology." Thus letters to and from missionaries were critical not only for improving my understanding but also in arranging for transport.

As the years passed, my interest in Zapotec law expanded to a comparative interest in dispute resolution movements worldwide after the demise of colonialism and the founding of new states. At the same time, we began to see a movement in the United States to address the failings of the civil justice system, which was seen erroneously as "too litigious." The push to change the civil justice system in the United States is referred to as Alternative Dispute Resolution (ADR), actually, from my point of view, a political movement against the social justice movements of the 1960s. The few letters selected indicate much of the pro and con arguments in favor and against the movement—debates which are found in a large segment of my letter files.

Along with the ADR movement, a serendipitous interest in science and academic freedom in our national laboratories brought together many members of the faculty at UC Berkeley. I had been invited to speak at Los Alamos Laboratory on "Barriers to Thinking New about Energy," and this sparked a number of letters from scientists, some ousted or soon-to-be ousted (fired), and spurred my anthropological curiosity about what I called *Naked Science*. I use some of these letter contents in my article "Magic, Science, and Religion Revisited." To quote my friend Paul Feyerabend, "What's so great about science anyways?"—a question that is always relevant to scientific research.

The invitation to serve as the only anthropologist on the National Academy of Sciences' study of nuclear and alternative energy systems (CONAES) led me to write "Energy Choices in a Democratic Society." The work raised many questions not found elsewhere because as one of the letters in this volume noted: "it was political." Perhaps because our work was controversial, I was invited to speak at the Mitre Corporation in the DC area. The talk was published in *Physics Today*, then republished in *ChemTech* and *The Industrial Physicist*, all of which generated more than a hundred letters expanding on my remarks about "Barriers to Thinking New about Energy." By this point, twenty-five years after starting at Berkeley, there was a clear fork in the road—incoming letters related to law and ADR, and those related to science and specifically questions of energy.

My letters to people in high places were mainly outgoing—in part advocacy for women's rights in the workplace related to maternity leave, equal pay, and respect. I also sent letters pushing people in high places to do the right thing, whether it be in regard to student debt and high tuition, academic freedom in the university, or better priorities in university spending—especially related to the football program—while in addition highlighting hypocrisies in the criminal (in)justice system. As my range of advocacy expanded, so did the response in letters. The issue of fluoridation was one example of the increased range, including support of a biologist who was being demonized for siding with the antifluoridation movement.

As my research and teaching began to incorporate ideas about controlling processes, it became clear that attention to silencing techniques needed to be addressed. The move to the right in the United States centered on the issue of government regulation. We had passed through Washington's successful and consumer-friendly environmental regulation of cars, as well as clean air and water and more. Now came the backlash. Although I was invited to present at a conference on regulation, my co-authored paper "A Wide Angle on Regulation," which posited that government regulation was not the only kind of regulation, was not accepted for publication in the resulting volume. The reasons for not accepting our paper were flimsy, so I decided to send the piece out for review to a wide variety of professors. Their responses (included in this volume) at the time left the editor of the regulation volume with no reason not to publish.

As stated earlier, the criminal justice system in our country is a mess, as policymakers are increasingly noting, but those in the criminal justice system and our prisons were already well aware of the problems. So too were young activists willing to give their time to improve conditions of incarceration. Thus the letters from death row, another from a prison inmate, another from a critic of prisons, and more. Why were they writing to an anthropologist? I make a concerted effort to leave the Ivory Tower regularly. The documentaries, the newspaper articles, and hundreds of talks to nonacademic audiences filtered into a varied population, including the Department of Justice and the White House.

Meanwhile foreign policy issues brought anthropologists into the public arena once again after a long quiescent period following the Vietnam War. These included the National Security State, the Palestinian-Israeli conundrum, Islam and Sharia law, terrorism, and undeclared wars. After 9/11, the war in Afghanistan was central, and letters came in from Afghans residing in this country. Letters also came from the government and proxies requesting information about Middle Eastern countries or about former students who had worked in the Empty Quarter of Saudi Arabia, for example. Once again, the issue of anthropological involvement with the US military came in letters either of concern or wanting information.

The few letters filtering in from undergraduates who had taken my course on controlling processes once again raise the question of whether our pedagogy equips students to challenge authority—something that we desperately need in this "Brave New World" of the United States. The few included reminded me that even though letters may now be coming to me via email, they are still being sent. That is good news for a world that is both increasingly connected and disconnected.

Acknowledgments

First, my thanks to the letter writers in my life. They both taught me a lot and enriched my research. Two undergraduates inspired me with their enthusiasm. Having "never seen letters"—Kade Percy and William Goodanetz helped select letters of general interest and for over a year did the necessary detective work on getting permissions to publish. William Goodanetz was absolutely indispensable in scanning letters, typing drafts of the manuscript chapters, and generally helping out when help was needed. For thoughts on publishing I thank Barbara Rose Johnston, an enthusiast for a "cross-over book" that includes audiences beyond academic disciplines. Tarek Milleron's assistance was indispensable as always. Roberto Gonzalez's comments on the manuscript were helpful, and as always I am thankful to my family, who understood the importance of letters, for being my best colleagues.

Thanks also to the Abigail Reynolds Hodgen Publication Funds at Berkeley for indispensable assistance, and to my colleague Paul Rabinow for suggesting Cornell University Press. Mary Kate Murphy, a production editor there, provided a keen eye on the many pieces. Jim Lance, my editor at Cornell, could not have been more supportive during the review process. He better than any editor I had spoken with understood the value of this collection, a collection that reflects sixty years of an American history usually not seen by the public.

LETTERS IN ORDER OF APPEARANCE

Chapter 1

Fr: E. R. Leach (4/23/1961, comments/advice on kinship work)

To: Lee Loevinger (12/28/1961, response to idea that it would be more difficult to study own court system)

Fr: G. E. von Grunebaum (1/24/1962, Comp. Village Law in Middle East and Mexico)

To: G. E. von Grunebaum (2/10/1962, fieldwork in Lebanon)

Fr: G. E. von Grunebaum (2/26/1962, thanks for response/rundown of Lebanon work)

Fr: Sherwood L. Washburn (4/11/1962, comments on Anthropology 125 and pedagogy)

Fr: Claude Good (10/19/1962, mission work in Mexico, comments on Trique language)

Fr: Paul Bohannon (12/19/1962, comments on Hymes's "cognitive system" and Goodenough's paper on "Residence")

Fr: James C. N. Paul (6/10/1963, establishment of Institute for Ethnological Legal Research in Ethiopia)

Fr: Claude Good (7/20/1963, comments/suggestions on manuscript from fieldwork in Mexico)

Fr: Walter S. Miller (1/27/1964, comments on flights in Mexico, flights into Yagallo)

To: Walter S. Miller (3/11/1964, Thanks, comments on Floyd Bishops flying)

Fr: Walter S. Miller (3/16/1964, comments on John Crawford, fieldwork, and filming in Mexico)

Fr: Zensuke Ishimura (3/31/1965, experiences at Columbia University, Mead's, Merton's, and Goode's classes)

Fr: Margaret Mead (4/16/1965, [lack of] academic appointments for women)

To: Clark Howell (5/14/1965, comments on the Department of Defense's attempt to recruit social scientists for intel research)

Fr: Stephen T. Boggs (9/14/1965, anthropologists and the military, Project Camelot)

Fr: Stephen T. Boggs (9/15/1965, AAA board discussion on militarism and anthropology)

Fr: Claude Good (11/11/1965, unique aspects of Trique "language of conflict")

Fr: Francis L. K. Hsu (11/30/1965, "Effect of Dominant Kinship Relations on Kin/Non-Kin Behavior," mending fences after possible antifemale intellectual comments)

Fr: Rob Burling (1/4/1966, comments on negative reviews, negative review by Charles Leslie)

Fr: Vilhelm Aubert (12/7/1966, Burg Wartenstein discussions, sociology of law)

Fr: Paul Bohannon (2/13/1967, remark on negative comments received from Gluckman)

Fr: Hortense Powdermaker (1/3/1968, discussion of current work on "black/white relations" and "black identity")

Fr: Richard Abel (1/24/1968, work on law in Kenya, relatedness to "Comparative Village Project")

Fr: William McGregor (4/2/1968, comments about Bennett's article on American Agrarian Society)

Fr: L. Lon Fuller (4/16/1968, comments on labor arbitration and "primitive" adjudication)

Fr: Rodger P. Davies (10/16/1968, regarding presentation on conflict resolution in Arab states and paper on "Communications")

Fr: Pyong Choon Hahm (12/28/1968, personal update, help with paper on religious and rural values of Korea)

Fr: Pyong Choon Hahm (2/27/1969, work on indigenization of Western law in Korea)

To: Albert Hirschman (4/30/1969, Ralph's comments on the court system as being a "voice institution"

Fr: Pyong Choon Hahm (5/12/1969, published work in Kroeber papers, *Politics of Melancholy*, Occidental formal logic)

To: Gordon Tullock (7/2/1969, discussion of "are criminals ill?," cost-benefit analysis of crime)

Fr: Richard Abel (9/16/1969, comments on published work—notions of "balance" and "equilibrium")

Chapter 2

To: Chancellor Roger Heyns (1/10/1970, maternity leave on campus)

Fr: Dell Hymes (1/21/1970, *Reinventing Anthropology*, comments on "ethnography of power")

Fr: Gene Anderson (2/20/1970, work for "Reinventing Anthropology," cultural ecology)

To: Dr. Robert E. Connick (3/16/1970, discussion about the D.E.C.)

Fr: Pyong Choon Hahm (11/8/1970, comments on "Style" paper, thoughts on conflict avoidance analysis)

Fr: James Omar Tull (9/15/1970, seeking advice for legal assistance, trouble obtaining adequate defense lawyers/representation, on death row)

To: Marc Swartz (10/12/1970, discussion of review for Law in Culture and Society)

Fr: Pyong Choon Hahm (10/12/1970, thoughts on American women and gender equality)

Fr: Marc Swartz (11/2/1970, reply to comments on *Law/Culture* review, discussion of Bohannon/Gluckman controversy)

To: Edward Thompson (10/6/1971, brief note on small claims in New York court system)

To: John Merryman (1/5/1972, reply to comments regarding lawyer participation in dispute resolution, anthropologists focusing too heavily on dispute resolution)

Fr: T. K. (3/24/1972, failures of U.S. legal system in regard to African-Americans)

Fr: Donald S. Miller (4/6/1972, discussion of difficulty with conveying importance of anthropology/archaeology to public/other actors)

Fr: Sol Tax (4/6/1972, comments on "Up the Anthropologist," geographical limitations of the article's assertions)

Fr: Stephen C. McCabe (4/18/1972, regarding comments on similarities between modern law and law in the time of Thomas Aquinas)

To: T. K. (5/17/1972, reply to previous comments, words of encouragement for overcoming adversity)

Fr: Melvin J. Lerner (6/7/1972, Waterloo conference on injustice)

Fr: Fred Eggan (6/22/1972, comments on "Up the Anthropologist," the lack of "anthropologists" contributing to *Reinventing Anthropology*)

Fr: Paul K. Bowmen (7/18/1972, thoughts on the fairness and flaws of justice system, incarcerated)

Fr: John C. Lynn (8/12/1972, the "sham of corrections")

Fr: Jessica Mitford (10/12/1972, comment on murder in primitive society, *Types of Crime, Cheaper than Chimps*)

Fr: Ryan Petty (11/15/1972, disrespect from professors at Texas Law, reply to "the goal of a profession should be to eliminate the need for it")

Fr: James F. Short (1/23/1973, role of social scientists in history of crime stats)

Fr: Alice Schlegel (4/6/1973, position of Zapotec women in divorce settlements, discussion of *Women and the Law*)

To: Sterling Wortman (10/25/1973, thoughts on foundation's assessment of the National Science Foundation, suggestion that NSF should study its own effect on US science)

Fr: M. Brewster Smith (6/26/1974, thoughts on antifluoridation, Groth letter)

Fr: Paul V. Lemkau 8/5/1974, thoughts on fluoridation, Groth letter)

Fr: John Gofman (10/15/1974, request to join Task Force Against Nuclear Pollution)

To: Chancellor Bowker (10/22/1974, refusal to serve on campus committees until maternity policy is adopted)

To: Robert Middlekauff (10/23/1974, Institute of Governmental Studies report on fluoridation)

Fr: Stephen H. Franke (2/3/1975, Near Eastern Studies PhD, anthropology, experience with Saudi military)

Fr: Joel F. Henning (2/4/1975, radioactive materials, Air Line Pilots Association)

Fr: Richard Tropp (7/9/1975, consultation on President Ford's "crime message," letter from Spradley)

To: Kenneth Keniston (8/16/1975, thoughts on white-collar crime, ensuring that corporations consider how they affect a worker's family)

Fr: James Q. Wilson (9/23/1975, thoughts on white collar crime, business fraud)

Fr: David Riesman (10/15/1975, comments on paper for *Journal of Social Issues*, thoughts on discussion of legal pluralism, conflict between local/national law, etc.)

Fr: David Riesman (10/24/1975, forwarded transcript of his talk at American Sociological Association meeting)

Fr: Phillip R. Lee (10/29/1975, Health and Policy Program efforts to combat inmate experimentation)

To: Phillip R. Lee (11/4/1975, comments on *Biomedical Experimentation on Prisoners*)

To: Charles White (11/5/1975, response to "Teacher Training Notes" and workshops)

Fr: Greg Alcalay (11/19/1975, experience with Peace Corps in the Marshall Islands)

Fr: Edward T. Hall (12/8/1975, insularity of anthropology, comments on the pervasive nature of Western technology)

Fr: Richard D. Jones (10/20/1976, fieldwork experience, Sapir's *Culture: Genuine and Spurious*, unreleased Energy Research and Development Administration report on US energy expansion)

To: Warren E. Burger (12/10/1976, decision on paid pregnancy leave)

To: James Brown (6/1/1977, response to previous letter, students in clinics and student experimentation)

Fr: Otis Dudley Duncan (6/1/1977, thoughts on the CONAES meeting and the CLOP [Consumption, Location and Occupational Patterns] report)

To: David Saxton (4/15/1978, response to argument for inadequacy of faculty salaries)

Fr: John McGuigan (5/2/1978, response to lecture in Dan Rose's class, thoughts on the futility of changing American mindsets)

To: Dr. John Raleigh (5/16/1978, thoughts on inadequate faculty pay, arguments against compensation tied to in-class time)

Fr: George Bush (6/20/1978, brief on the progress of the Future Conduct of American Foreign Policy and the conclusions of the Advisory Council)

Fr: Robert K. Merton (12/24/1978, response to inquiry on Veblen's "trained incapacity")

Fr: M. Kyle Aiken (2/23/1979, use of *To Make the Balance* for Minnesota State Supreme Court training)

Fr: Bertram Robert Cottine (11/13/1979, comments on presentation at Georgetown Law faculty seminar, discussion of adjudication process for occupational safety)

Chapter 3

Fr: William C. Jones (2/12/1980, work on Chinese law, effect of "societal model" on legal structure/system)

Fr: J. M. Pick (4/11/1980, response to CONAES contribution in *Nature*, the Earth Enterprise Project, faulty "expert" opinions/assessments of environmental impact, energy = finance)

Fr: Martin H. Krieger (2/25/1981, response to "Barriers" article)

Fr: George Wald (2/26/1981, response to "Barriers" article, changes in attitude of scientists since the beginning of the twentieth century)

Fr: Alan Sweedler (3/3/1981, response to "Barriers" article, comment on the irrationality of scientists on discussion of energy)

Fr: Albert A. Bartlett (3/3/1981, positive response to "Barriers" article, comments on "American religion of growth")

Fr: Edward V. Ashburn (3/5/1981, positive reply to "Barriers" article, comment on tendency for scientists to conform/blindly follow "authority")

Fr: Richard B. Firestone (3/11/1981, reply to "Barriers" article, bureaucratization of the "hard" sciences, shortcomings of technical curriculum)

Fr: Arno A. Penzias (3/16/1981, reply to "Barriers" article, comments on lack of independent intellect, diversity among the hard sciences)

Fr: Gordon L. Love (3/19/1981, reply to "Barriers," comment on "homo scienticus," discussion on dowsing, specialization, and the value of small scale scientific projects)

Fr: Theodore M. Edison (3/25/1981, positive response to comments in *Physics Today*)

Fr: Michael H. Horn (3/27/1981, positive response to "Barriers" article, heard it read on the radio)

Fr: John R. Neighbours (4/3/1981, reply to "Guest Comment" in *Physics Today*, mention of engineers and scientists being "macho")

To: Harold Davis (4/6/1981, letter to editor of *Physics Today*, discussion of responses to the article, reaffirmation of what should be strived for—thinking new)

Fr: Elliot Aronson (4/16/1981, committee meeting and visit from Department of Education representative, issues with the Reagan administration)

Fr: Asher Peres (4/28/1981, conflation of support for solar energy initiatives to ancient beliefs in "sun gods," dismissal of concerns over nuclear energy safety)

Fr: Claude Ginsburg (4/30/1981, positive response to "Barriers" article, comments on the issue of the "technocratic establishment")

To: Mark Gibson (5/7/1981, comments on the SERI/Solar/Conservation Study)

Fr: Seymour Melman (6/18/1981, inquiry about comments on the Public Broadcasting System, report on "Energy Choices in a Democratic Society")

Fr: Jack Down (7/26/1981, response to article "Complainer Beware," comments on experiences with the IRS, American Motors, Pathway Products, etc.)

To: Elizabeth Colson (10/22/1981, comments on Burton being wrong, anthropologists studying "common knowledge")

Fr: James H. Ray (11/25/1981, rebuttal to comments published in Oct. 1981 *Physics Today*, thoughts on energy regulation and public perception, nuclear safety v wind safety)

To: James H. Ray (1/6/1982, rebuttal to rebuttal, argument against conflation of dangers posed by windmills and nuclear energy)

Fr: Mary H. Hartford (1/25/1982, response to "Barriers" article, thoughts on 70–50 scenario, opposition to nuclear energy)

Fr: C. Arthur Compton (1/30/1982, response to presentation at MIT, reply to comments on physicists, differences between physicists and technicians, need to change methods/attitudes of scientists)

To: Roger Noll (2/8/1982, success of conference, inspiration to think/write about regulation, discussion of the anthropological perspective on regulation)

Fr: Harry Dickinson (4/23/1982, response to "Barriers to Thinking New about Energy," stereotypes and myths about engineers)

Fr: Rose Marie McFarland (6/23/1982, speech at Nuclear Chemistry Gordon Conference, discussion of reactions to speech, tendency for people to be offended by the critique of the culture within the hard sciences)

Fr: Thomas Larry Watts (11/22/1982, comments on *Little Injustices*, impediments to swift dispute resolution)

Fr: Louise McMillan (11/24/1982, comments on *Little Injustices*, experience working as legal counsel to elderly people, discussion of the difficulties they face)

Fr: John Makdisi (2/2/1983, critique of Weber's concept of Islamic law, discussion of dissertation project arguing against assertions of Islamic law being irrational)

Fr: James A. Gardner (2/23/1983, discussion of guest lecture for anthropology course, Marxist versus American ideas of law and change)

Fr: Colin M. Turnbull (5/19/1983, note on receiving negative comments from Derek Freeman)

Fr: Stewart Macaulay (6/14/1983, reply to comments on "Private Government," discussion of the value of "comparative law")

Fr: Ashraf Ghani (6/15/1983, comments on manuscript for "Regulatory Policy and the Social Sciences," discussion of Roger Noll's research agenda)

To: Stewart Macaulay (6/19/1983, comments on censorship, draft of regulation paper turned down by Noll, anecdote of argument with president of Academic Press)

Fr: Stewart Macaulay (6/24/1983, reply to "A Wide Angle on Regulation," issues with criticisms the piece received, failure of the reviewer and their lack of understanding of the subject matter)

Fr: Paul Bohannon (7/31/1983, comments to "Regulation" piece, suggestion to be more subtle in your presentation of the anthropological perspective)

Fr: Lawrence M. Friedman (8/9/1983, comments on "Regulation" piece, suggestion to consider Knoll's ideas for revision, surprise at negative response the piece received)

Fr: Kathleen Gough (11/12/1983, comments on meeting, idea that USA is primary aggressor in the Cold War, capitalist countries perpetuate war to maintain wealth, US investment in Third World is strictly for its own benefit)

Fr: O. F. Bizri (12/19/1983, response to "Barriers" article, brief mention of experiences that confirm article's assertions)

Fr: Christopher Dodd (2/9/1984, reply to issues with actions of Reagan administration, forced resignation of Peter Bell)

Fr: Clark Bullard (9/19/1984, use of "Barriers" article in engineering courses, combating "technocratic arrogance")

Fr: Cushman Haagensen (3/14/1985, personal update, comment on essay "Ideology as Covert Power")

Fr: Sheila Harty (5/22/1985, reply to comments made at Dispute Resolution Forum, experience as Corporate Initiatives Director for National Wildlife Foundation)

Fr: A. B. Zahlan (10/10/1985, reply to "Barriers," discussion of work in Sudan and Jordan—trying to look at agriculture through the eyes of the farmer)

To: Ira M. Heyman (10/15/1985, comments on Special Salary denial, review summary, and petition for reconsideration)

To: Ira M. Heyman (5/16/1986, further comments on Special Salary status and inequitable treatment and pay on the basis of gender)

To: Bruce Ames (7/2/1986, materials supporting downward trend in cancer rates in United States, comment on potential false perception of rising cancer rates)

Fr: Bruce Ames (7/24/1986, reply to cancer rates, some cases up—some down, notions of large general increase based on bad science)

To: Derek Freeman (7/29/1987, comment on *LA Times* review of his book on Mead and Samoa)

Fr: Elizabeth Colson (7/29/1987, experience in Zambia, Jonathan's arrival)

Fr: Elizabeth Colson (7/31/1987, mail troubles in Zambia, housekeeping)

Fr: Elizabeth Colson (8/13/1987, discussion of family topics, finding a house sitter, etc.)

Fr: Elizabeth Colson (8/25/1987, finding a good house sitter, trip to New Zealand)

Fr: George N. Sfeir (9/26/1987, work on legal reform in Saudi Arabia)

Fr: Robert Mann (10/5/1987, response to denial that United States is unusually litigious)

Fr: Ashraf Ghani (7/6/1988, Islam in Pakistan, occidentalists in Kabul, history of anthropology in region)

Fr: Neil Gold (10/17/1988, dispute settlement and negotiation)

To: Paul Feyerabend (12/30/1988, birthday letter)

Fr: Paul Feyerabend (12/31/1988, thanks for birthday dinner)

To: Bob Guccione (3/28/1989, response to "The Importance of Hugging" by Howard Bloom)

Fr: Dick Strohman (4/13/1989, crosstalk, tendency for scientists to toe the line)

Fr: Donald Black (6/9/1989, Windsor paper, why ideology of harmony)

Fr: Paul Bohannon (8/9/1989, book chapter on law and order, comments on religion and comparative studies)

Chapter 4

To: Margaret Singer (2/11/1990, macro forces impacting controlling processes)

To: David P. Gardner (2/21/1990, *Daily Cal* article, CALPIRG funding)

Fr: Paul Bohannon (3/22/1990, response to lecture on controlling processes, discussion of "anomie," US culture and society)

Fr: Gene Anderson (4/15/1990, science in America, postmodernism)

Fr: Paul Feyerabend (4/17/1990, resignation from Berkeley)

Fr: David P. Gardner (5/14/1990, CALPIRG, student fee collection)

To: Philip H. Abelson (6/20/1990, editorial on "America Bashing")

Fr: Mondher Kilani (7/27/1990, hierarchy/hegemony, Maghrebi immigrants in Europe, universalism versus relativism)

Fr: Tatsuya Fujii (5/25/1990, courses on controlling processes and comparative society, controlling processes in Japan)

To: Wayne Cornelius (7/24/1991, *Profmex Policy News*, response to pollution in Mexico due to poverty, effect of free trade on poor people in United States and Mexico)

Fr: Carol Gillam (8/27/1991, cultural information on workers from Oaxaca, need for information to build prosecuting case)

To: Rajesh Choudree (6/25/1992, mediation and Alternative Dispute Resolution among indigenous peoples)

Fr: M. Estellie Smith (8/10/1992, pro bono analysis of fishery management, public anthropology)

Fr: Donald S. Moir (10/30/1992, family law, mediation and policy issues in family law)

Fr: Robert A. Kagan (3/4/1993, critique of harmony ideology, formal adversarial litigation)

To: Mary Claire King (4/25/1993, issues with assertions about breast cancer, lack of acknowledgment of outside factors that affect its likelihood to occur)

Fr: Stewart Macaulay (6/17/1993, personal update, thoughts on ADR and "From Legal Process to Mind Processing")

Fr: James W. Zion (7/20/1993, effect on ADR articles on Navajo Nation courts

Fr: Patricia Vandervort (8/4/1993, letter on discrimination and wrongful termination for speaking out against sexual harassment/discrimination at University of Auckland)

Fr: Ota Shozo (9/21/1993, general thoughts on ADR, Japanese society, and comments on ADR in Japan)

Fr: Norman A. Larson (10/18/1993, comments on *San Francisco Chronicle* article, coercive harmony)

Fr: Donald R. Wells (4/6/1994, electing regents of UC Berkeley)

Fr: Edward J. Markey (8/30/1994, securities arbitration process, Civil Rights Protections Act of 1994)

Fr: Peter White (1/6/1995, project proposal/advice for documentary on the political economy of Chiapas)

Fr: Alejandro de Avila (3/3/1995, comments on government exploitation of indigenous land, Zapotec/Chinantec communities using satellite data to develop long-term plans, NGO presence in region, oil exploitation in region)

Fr: George McGovern (3/16/1995, comments on need for corrections to civil justice system, tort reform battle)

Fr: Eugene Crew (5/3/1995, comments on debate with Judge Renfrew, efforts of US corps to reduce access to courts, ADR)

To: David Hamburg (5/22/1995, double-sided nature of harmony/harmonizing)

Fr: Ann Sayonara (7/7/1995, discussion of the Badie v. Bank of America case, "Coercive Harmony")

Fr: Anthony Wallace (8/27/1995, note on Francis Hsu's *Psychological Anthropology*, paper on "Biological Factors and Cultural Factors in Mental Illness")

Fr: Gene Anderson (2/20/1996, comments on "Big Science," lack of empiricism in US science)

To: Richard C. Lewontin (4/5/1996, comments for piece on the Cold War's transformation of the academy, note that the information presented is totally decontextualized)

Fr: Richard C. Lewontin (4/15/1996, reply to comments, clarification, Cold War had negative impact on the academy but also had benefits, distributed piece was rough draft)

Fr: Sydney W. Mintz (5/4/1996, personal update, time in Hong Kong, research on piscophagy)

To: Richard C. Rueben (9/2/1996, response to "The Lawyer Turns Peacemaker," propaganda published in trade journals)

To: Richard Blumenthal (10/9/1996, concerns over future of Winsted Memorial Hospital, Berger's war against law)

To: Ira M. Heyman (10/27/1996, assertion that Heyman and co. failed to understand Molella's exhibit on "Science in American Life")

Fr: Sandy Davis (3/9/1997, comments on piece about Cold War anthropology, reaction to stated experiences at Harvard grad school, discussion of own fieldwork and rediscovery of the history of anthropology)

Fr: D. P. Agrawal (4/6/1997, comments on *Naked Science*, discussion of Muauni Jagars)

Fr: Arthur P. Molella (5/1/1997, discussion of "Science in American Life" exhibit, ACS decision to withdraw support)

Fr: Ben Anderson (5/7/1997, response to Price's work on Cold War anthropology, thoughts on Geertz, personal anecdotes of fieldwork experience in Indonesia)

Fr: Jonathan Marks (9/22/1997, comments on Cold War and anthropology, effect of the Cold War on physical anthropology and notions of race)

Fr: Alice B. Kehoe (11/26/1997, comments on the conservatism of American archaeology)

Fr: Davydd J. Greenwood (4/19/1998, draft commentary on theory and practice in anthropology, dismay at current status and approach of anthropology—lapdog status, tendency to wallow in self-pity, etc.)

Fr: Joan Leach (6/3/1998, thoughts on piece about the suggested alliance between popular media and academic press, UK initiatives to get the public to understand science)

Fr: George Marcus (9/7/1998, comments on essay about Cold War anthropology, notes on "Phantom Factor")

To: George Marcus (9/19/1998, reply to comments about the "Phantom Factor")

Fr: Kendall M. Thu (12/8/1998, comments on the use of legal and legislative pacification strategies to discourage conflict)

Fr: Kim Fortun (3/19/1999, justice "being traded for harmony," critique of momentum toward harmonization)

To: Linda S. Wilson (6/4/1999, comments on "historic agreement" between Radcliffe College and Harvard)

Fr: Rainer Brömer (6/9/1999, comments on "Orientalism, Occidentalism, and the Control of Women," inspiration for reflection on occidentalism)

Fr: David Price (8/5/1999, seeking advice, trouble getting paper published in the *Anthropologist*)

Fr: John Borneman (8/26/1999, personal update, discussion of experience in Lebanon)

To: Karl Kroeber (9/13/1999, department drafted statement, state of professional staff researching North American cultures)

To: David Price (9/17/1999, suggestions on how to improve his paper, advice for getting the piece published)

Chapter 5

Fr: Beatrice B. Whiting (2/14/2000, science as an inferential process, anthropological influence on the field of developmental psychology)

Fr: Beatrice B. Whiting (2/23/2000, introduction of mediation into primary school curriculum, ability to anthropologists to combat youth violence)

To: Editors of *Foreign Affairs* (2/22/2000, response to article published on the need for nuclear power)

To: Adam Schiff (3/22/2000, support for bill prohibiting family law mediators from making recommendations on child custody status)

To: Arjun Appadurai (4/17/2000, critique of author's seeming ambivalence to modernity and power of multinational corporations)

To: James Shapiro (5/11/2000, comments on university bureaucracy, issues with hiring and retirement processes, etc.)

Fr: Kate Wilusz (5/30/2000, comments on how Anthropology 157 changed her perspective)

Fr: William J. Peace (6/14/2000, note on published review troubles, work on Leslie White)

Fr: Davydd J. Greenwood (6/28/2000, loss of intellectual integrity among universities and publishers)

Fr: David Price (8/7/2000, issues with Sussmann, publishing piece on the relationship between the CIA and anthropologists in AAA journal)

Fr: Johannes Fabian (10/10/2000, note on the "Phantom Factor" and Napoleon Chagnon)

Fr: David Price (10/17/2000, reply to comments about putting positive spin on Cold War anthropology work, discussion of progress on *American Anthropology* and *McCarthyism*)

Fr: Michael B. Rainey (9/4/2001, reply to critique of ADR, argument in favor of ADR as presenting another choice)

Fr: Adam Kuper (10/6/2001, reply to comments received for book on American anthropology, note on "Phantom Factor")

Fr: Winston Crausaz (10/31/2001, rediscovery of "Barriers" article, comments on its relevance, suggestion of a reprint)

Fr: Donald Black (4/21/2002, effort to develop scientific theory/understanding of terrorism)

To: Lisa M. Ryerson (5/28/2002, comments on Wells College priorities, issues with poorly thought-out renovation plans)

Fr: Jonathan Rowe (6/27/2002, comment on controlling processes, attempt to see if different languages influence/construct different [fixed] worldviews)

To: Christopher Killheffer (8/24/2002, comments on self-righteousness and indifference within the university, lack of critical thinking in schools)

Fr: David Price (9/2/2002, comments on NPR piece on "Anthropology and the War on Terror," issues with reporter not understanding ethical issues of the militarism of anthropology)

To: Lawrence H. Summers (10/7/2002, comments on Israeli policies, issues with the conflation of policy opposition and anti-Semitism)

Fr: Lawrence H. Summers (11/4/2002, reply to previous comments, note on "inappropriate" nature of the university singling out Israel)

Fr: Chalmers Johnson (3/8/2003, comments on *Blowback*, invitation to guest lecture, militarism and the silence surrounding the Gulf War)

To: Pat Harrison (7/9/2003, comments on *Radcliffe Quarterly* publications, note on Waters's *Edible Schoolyard* and initiatives to positively change school structures)

To: Greg Starrett (8/14/2003, note on paper and tendency for readers to make "implicit comparisons")

To: Jimmy Carter (4/5/2004, note of work on conflict resolution and mind colonization, issues with the Democratic Party)

To: Celeste Robb-Nicholson (7/10/2004, note on student health experimentation)

Fr: Elizabeth Colson (8/24/2005, note on Patricia's dissertation, experiences in Zambia)

To: Vartan Gregorian (9/29/2005, comments on Carnegie anthropological research on Islam)

To: Leland Y. Yee (6/24/2006, support for bill regarding Open Meeting Law for UC)

Fr: M. Jamil Hanifi (7/31/2006, comments on comparison of United States with Mongol Empire, paper on "Promise or Plunder," Afghani perceptions of Americans, Ashraf Ghani)

To: Jimmy Carter (1/25/2007, comments/appreciation of *Palestine, Peace Not Apartheid*)

Fr: Jimmy Carter (1/30/2007, reply to comments on *Palestine, Peace Not Apartheid*)

Fr: Elizabeth Colson (6/6/2007, personal update, comments on Wolfovitz resignation, experience with grad students in Zambia)

Fr: Nan Waldman (4/5/2008, appreciation for Anthropology of Law class, inquiry about programs in applied medical anthropology)

Fr: Elizabeth Colson (8/8/2008, personal update, note on the role of international capital in resurgence of chieftaincy)

Fr: Eduardo M. Madrid (1/19/2009, seeking advice on legal case, inquiry about Zapotec customs in regard to dealing with infidelity)

To: Mark Yudof (6/29/2009, comments on UC budget, failures of politically selected regents)

Fr: Mark Yudof (6/30/2009, reply to comments on UC budget, and furlough/salary reduction plans)

Fr: John Campbell (7/10/2009, creation of a new journal—*The Journal of Legal Anthropology*, note on relation to Issa Shivji)

Fr: George Brunn (7/30/2009, note on enclosed articles about anthropological aspects of restorative justice, disparity of wealth in Washington)

Fr: Mark Yudof (10/8/2009, personal reply to comments received on UC budget, Regents, etc.)

Fr: Leonard Isenburg (12/23/2009, note on the failures to adequately educate our citizens, efforts to fix public education)

To: Michael Lerner (4/16/2010, note on the need to push Obama toward enacting progressive policy change)

Fr: Blake Kasemeier (5/18/2010, comments on the value of Controlling Processes course)

To: Martha Minnow (5/31/2011, comment on the justification of the extrajudicial killing of Osama bin Laden)

To: Robert Post (5/31/2011, comment on the justification of the extrajudicial killing of Osama bin Laden)

Fr: Robert Post (6/14/2011, reply to comments on assassination, inability to control alumni, note on Harold Koch)

Fr: Elizabeth Colson (8/8/2011, personal update, notes on Zambian election, and personal experiences)

To: Robert Birgeneau (1/9/2012, note on "Project Excellence" and the priorities of UC Berkeley administrators)

Fr: Robert Birgeneau (1/30/2012, response to comments, discussion of the importance of libraries, importance of priority for intercollegiate sports)

To: Robert Birgeneau (2/1/2012, reply to remark on intercollegiate athletics, appeal to unsubsidize them)

Fr: George Woegell (3/11/2012, note on US prison population, background of national legislators, violence, etc.)

Fr: Elizabeth Colson (3/13/2012, comments on success of anthropology symposium, personal update, note on Karen Engle's work with indigenous populations in Colombia and Tarek's new child)

Fr: Elizabeth Colson (10/3/2012, comments on "Rethinking Salvation Mentality and Counterterrorism," workshop on postcolonial history of Zambia, Graeber's *Debt*)

To: Editors of the *New Yorker* (1/30/2013, comment on abortion debate)

Fr: Rik Pinxten (7/4/2013, personal update, comments on retirement, work on social/cultural biases in math education)

To: Nicholas Dirks (7/15/2013, comment on the need for dialogue about educational mission between administration and faculty, suggestions on things that need to be done to improve the university)

Fr: Elizabeth Colson (2/3/2014, comments on *The Thistle and the Drone*, discourse on the role of interpreters in anthropological fieldwork, inquiry about status of work submitted to *Kroeber Society Journal*)

Fr: Elizabeth Colson (5/3/2014, personal update, thoughts on *The Thistle and the Drone*, comment on Leslie Berlowitz scandal)

Fr: A. B. Zahlan (8/28/2014, comment on *Naked Science* and *Culture and Dignity*, crumbling of Arab countries due to years of war/turmoil)

To: Janet Napolitano (11/17/2014, comment on Napolitano's upcoming meeting with the Regents, need for prioritization of affordable education)

Fr: Janet Napolitano (12/18/2014, response to comments on tuition proposal)

To: Rush Holt Jr. (4/15/2015, request for survey of public opinion on science)

Fr: Elizabeth Colson (4/20/2015, comments on the loss of Jim Anderson, issues with technology, hosting a group of anthropologists, political situation in United States and Zambia)

Fr: Rik Pinxten (7/7/2015, update on the family, comments on struggling countries in the European Union, completed work on math teaching and culture)

Fr: Elizabeth Colson (9/18/2015, comments on the fragility of students, troubles with electricity in Zambia)

To: Abdel al-Jubeir (10/30/2015, comments about the militarism of Saudi Arabia, war in Yemen)

To: Nicholas Dirks (2/1/2016, further suggestions for improvements to the university)

To: Elizabeth Colson (3/22/2016, comments on the Anthropocene, the translation of *Culture and Dignity* into Arabic, update on what the children/grandchildren are doing)

Fr: Noam Chomsky (5/26/2016, reply to comments on interview with Amy Goodman, need for comparisons between the Koran and the Bible—point out similarities between the two)

Fr: Larry Stern (3/14/2017, comments on Robert K. Merton letters and work on Merton biography)

Fr: Teresa Yu (6/9/2017, value of Controlling Processes course, course's effect on the development of critical thinking skills)

Fr: Ellen Hertz (4/30/2018, comments on teaching experience at Hong Kong University, the "rule of law," and the Communist Party of China's efforts to errode rights of citizens (comparable to corporations in the United States)

Fr: Nan Waldman (4/19/2019, condolences on loss, personal updates, comments about impact of life's work)

Notes

PREFACE

1. Margaret Mead, *To Cherish the Life of the World: The Selected Letters of Margaret Mead*, ed. Patricia Francis and John Caffrey (New York: Basic Books, 2006).

2. Victor Golla, ed., *The Sapir-Kroeber Correspondence: Letters between Edward Sapir and A. L. Kroeber, 1905–1925*. (Berkeley: University of California, Survey of California and Other Indian Languages, 1984).

3. Niko Besnier, *Literacy, Emotion, and Authority: Reading and Writing on a Polynesian Atoll* (Cambridge: Cambridge University Press, 1995).

4. Helena Wayne, ed., *The Story of a Marriage: The Letters of Bronislaw Malinowski and Elsie Masson*, vol. 1: *1916–20* (New York: Routledge, 2014).

5. Mark Goodale, *Letters to the Contrary: A Curated History of the UNESCO Human Rights Survey* (Stanford: Stanford University Press, 2018).

INTRODUCTION

1. Laura Nader, dir., *To Make the Balance* (University of California Extension Media Center, 1970).

2. Laura Nader, "Barriers to Thinking New about Energy," *Physics Today* 34 (1981): 9. Reprinted in *Chem Tech*, November 1981.

3. Terry Rockefeller, dir., *Little Injustices: Laura Nader Looks at the Law* (PBS, 1981).

4. David W. Brown, "The Public/Academic Disconnect," *Higher Education Exchange* (2015): 6–10.

5. Laura Nader, *No Access to Law: Alternatives to the American Judicial System* (New York: Academic Press, 1980); Rockefeller, *Little Injustices* (1981).

6. Laura Nader, ed., *What the Rest Think of the West: Since 600 AD* (Oakland: University of California Press, 2015).

7. Zeyneb Hanoum, *A Turkish Woman's European Impressions*, ed. Grace Ellison (Cambridge, UK: Cambridge University Press, 2012).

1. GETTING STARTED IN THE SIXTIES

1. Laura Nader, dir., *To Make the Balance* (University of California Extension Media Center, 1970).

2. Laura Nader, "The Trique of Oaxaca," in *Ethnology*, ed. Robert Wauchope and Evon Z. Vogt, vol. 7–8 of *Handbook of Middle American Indians* (Austin, TX: University of Texas Press, 1975), 400–416.

2. REINVENTING ANTHROPOLOGY IN THE SEVENTIES

1. Dell H. Hymes, ed., *Reinventing Anthropology* (New York: Pantheon Books, 1972).

2. Laura Nader, "Disputing without the Force of Law," *Yale Law Journal* 88, no. 5 (1979): 998–1021.

3. Edward T. Hall, *The Silent Language* (New York: Anchor Books, 1959).

4. Laura Nader, dir., *To Make the Balance* (University of California Extension Media Center, 1970).

5. Laura Nader. "Energy Choices in a Democratic Society," *NASA STI/Recon Technical Report* no. 81 (1980).

3. UNCOVERING ACADEMIC MINDSETS IN THE EIGHTIES

1. Laura Nader, "Barriers to Thinking New about Energy," *Physics Today* 34 (1981): 9.

2. Laura Nader, "Barriers to Thinking New about Energy," *Industrial Physicist* (August–September 2002): 27.

3. Laura Nader and Claire Nader, "A Wide Angle on Regulation: An Anthropological Analysis," *Regulatory Policy and the Social Sciences* (1981): 141–60.

4. Derek Freeman, *Margaret Mead and Samoa: The Making and Unmaking of an Anthropological Myth* (Canberra, ACT: Australian National University Press, 1983).

4. THE IVORY TOWER IS NO MORE IN THE NINETIES

1. Laura Nader, "Sidney W. Mintz Lecture for 1995: Controlling Processes Tracing the Dynamic Components of Power," *Current Anthropology* 38, no. 5 (1997): 711–38.

2. Laura Nader, "The Phantom Factor: Impact of the Cold War on Anthropology," in *The Cold War and the University: Toward an Intellectual History of the Postwar Years*, by Noam Chomsky et al. (New York: New Press, 1997), 107–46.

5. A TWENTY-FIRST-CENTURY WORLD

1. Laura Nader, *Naked Science: Anthropological Inquiry into Boundaries, Power, and Knowledge* (New York: Routledge, 1996).

2. Richard Rhodes and Denis Beller, "The Need for Nuclear Power," *Foreign Affairs* (January–February, 2000).

3. Laura Nader, "Three Jihads: Islamic, Christian, and Jewish," *Anthropology Today* 31, no. 2 (2015): 1–2.

Bibliography

Besnier, Niko. *Literacy, Emotion, and Authority: Reading and Writing on a Polynesian Atoll*. Studies in the Social and Cultural Foundations of Language. Cambridge: Cambridge University Press, 1995.

Brown, David W. "The Public/Academic Disconnect." *Higher Education Exchange* (2015): 6–10.

Freeman, Derek. *Margaret Mead and Samoa: The Making and Unmaking of an Anthropological Myth*. Canberra, ACT: Australian National University Press, 1983.

Golla, Victor, ed. *The Sapir-Kroeber Correspondence: Letters between Edward Sapir and A. L. Kroeber, 1905–1925*. Berkeley: University of California, Survey of California and Other Indian Languages, 1984.

Goodale, Mark. *Letters to the Contrary: A Curated History of the UNESCO Human Rights Survey*. Stanford: Stanford University Press, 2018.

Hall, Edward T. *The Silent Language*. New York: Anchor Books, 1959.

Hanoum, Zeyneb. *A Turkish Woman's European Impressions*. Edited by Grace Ellison. Cambridge: Cambridge University Press, 2012.

Hymes, Dell H., ed. *Reinventing Anthropology*. New York: Pantheon Books, 1972.

Mead, Margaret. *To Cherish the Life of the World: The Selected Letters of Margaret Mead*. Edited by Patricia Francis and John Caffrey. New York: Basic Books, 2006.

Nader, Laura. "Barriers to Thinking New about Energy." *Physics Today* 34, no. 2 (1981): 9. Reprinted in *Chem Tech*, November 1981.

Nader, Laura. "Barriers to Thinking New about Energy." *The Industrial Physicist* (August–September 2002): 27.

Nader, Laura. "Disputing without the Force of Law." *Yale Law Journal* 88, no. 5 (1979): 998–1021.

Nader, Laura. "Energy Choices in a Democratic Society." *NASA STI/Recon Technical Report*, no. 81 (1980).

Nader, Laura. *Naked Science: Anthropological Inquiry into Boundaries, Power, and Knowledge*. New York: Routledge, 1996.

Nader, Laura. *No Access to Law: Alternatives to the American Judicial System*. New York: Academic Press, 1980.

Nader, Laura. "The Phantom Factor: Impact of the Cold War on Anthropology." In *The Cold War and the University: Toward an Intellectual History of the Postwar Years*, by Noam Chomsky et al., 107–46. New York: New Press, 1997.

Nader, Laura. "Sidney W. Mintz Lecture for 1995: Controlling Processes Tracing the Dynamic Components of Power." *Current Anthropology* 38, no. 5 (1997): 711–38.

Nader, Laura, dir. *To Make the Balance*. University of California Extension Media Center, 1970.

Nader, Laura. "Three Jihads: Islamic, Christian, and Jewish." *Anthropology Today* 31, no. 2 (2015): 1–2.

Nader, Laura. "The Trique of Oaxaca." In *Ethnology*, edited by Robert Wauchope and Evon Z. Vogt, 400–416. Vol. 7–8 of *Handbook of Middle American Indians*. Austin: University of Texas Press, 1975.

Nader, Laura, ed. *What the Rest Think of the West: Since 600 AD*. Oakland: University of California Press, 2015.

Nader, Laura, and Claire Nader. "A Wide Angle on Regulation: An Anthropological Analysis." In *Regulatory Policy and the Social Sciences*, edited by Roger G. Noll, 141–60. Berkeley: University of California Press, 1985.

Rhodes, Richard, and Denis Beller. "The Need for Nuclear Power." *Foreign Affairs* (January–February 2000): 30–44.

Rockefeller, Terry, dir. *Little Injustices: Laura Nader Looks at the Law*. PBS, 1981.

Wayne, Helena, ed. *The Story of a Marriage: The Letters of Bronislaw Malinowski and Elsie Masson*. Vol. 1: *1916–20*. New York: Routledge, 2014.

Index